THE PAPAL STATE UNDER MARTIN V

THE PAPAL STATE
UNDER MARTIN V

*The administration and government
of the temporal power in the early
fifteenth century*

By

PETER PARTNER

PUBLISHED BY THE
BRITISH SCHOOL AT ROME, AT 1 LOWTHER
GARDENS, EXHIBITION ROAD, LONDON, S.W.7
1958

Printed in Great Britain by Richard Clay and Company, Ltd.
Bungay, Suffolk

PREFACE

It is not generally realised how large the temporal power bulked in the lives of the medieval Popes, how great a part it played in the daily business of papal administration, and how important it was in the shaping of papal policy. The Pope was both a spiritual and an earthly ruler. To be Christ's vicar is a great and glorious thing. To be the head of a state is also something which cannot fail to impress itself deeply upon the consciousness of any human being, no matter what priority he may accord to his spiritual duties. And, indeed, it would be wrong to set the spiritual duties of the Popes in necessary opposition to their temporal rule; the medieval Popes did not understand the matter thus, but merely saw the temporal power as one aspect (and an essential one) of the universal papal monarchy.

Modern historians, viewing the medieval Papacy across the events of 1860 and of the Protestant Reformation, have not all seen the matter in this light. The emergence of the Popes as 'Italian princes' is something which, with Creighton, they have tended to place in the fifteenth century, to understand as one of the symptoms of the decadence of the medieval Papacy, and to represent as one of the causes of the Reformation.

This is fundamentally to misunderstand the medieval Papacy. The temporal power emerged in the eighth century, and from that time onwards it was continuously one of the most important factors of papal policy. A right understanding of its history is essential if we are to apprehend the important place it occupied in papal aims and interests. And with the aid of a proper appreciation of the temporal power we can make some sense of the interminable squabbles of Popes and nobles which compose the history of medieval Rome.

The present work was originally written as a thesis for the degree of Doctor of Philosophy in the University of Oxford. Little has been changed in the body of the text, but I have added an introductory relation of the temporal power from the time of the Donations. I am well aware how inadequate this relation is, by reason of limited space to express it, of limited time to write it, and of the general intractability of the subject. But the theme of the temporal power is not often treated in English, and a brief account of this sort seemed necessary before entering on such a detailed work.

I have incurred many obligations during the six years that I have been engaged in these studies. My thanks are in the first place due to the Faculty of History,

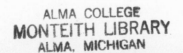

Archaeology and Letters of the British School at Rome, for undertaking to publish what follows. A subsidy was also accorded for the printing of the work by the Board of the Faculty of Modern History of Oxford University.

I am also indebted to the British School for the award of a scholarship tenable for a year in Italy. Another scholarship was awarded me by the British Council, and I am grateful also to the President and Fellows of Magdalen College, Oxford, for a grant to travel in central Italy.

In embarking on the difficult terrain of the Vatican Archives I often had recourse to the help of more experienced scholars. I would particularly thank Fr. Anselm Strittmatter, O.S.B., of St. Anselm's Priory, Washington, whose readily-extended courtesy is known to most English-speaking students who have frequented the Vatican Library in the past few years, and my friend and former colleague, Fr. Romualdus Dodd, O.P. I have received many kindnesses from the officials of the Italian libraries and archives mentioned in the text, but particularly from those of the Vatican Archives, and from that gentle and learned scholar, the late Monsignor Angelo Mercati.

For help at various stages in the preparation of the text I must express my particular gratitude to Dr. Walter Ullmann, to Professor Leo Butler, to Mr. Richard Bass, and to Mr. Alan Tyson. Professor J. McGrath Bottkol taught me how to read proof, though he does not have to bear responsibility for my errors.

I must acknowledge long-standing debts of gratitude for the kindness, encouragement and support accorded me by the Director of the British School at Rome, Mr. J. B. Ward Perkins, and for the kindness of Mrs. D. W. Brogan, who cheerfully bore the duties of editor.

Professor E. F. Jacob, my teacher and friend, has encouraged and directed my studies from their hesitant beginnings, and this work has benefited from his advice at every stage of its composition. I owe it principally to him that my historical studies have led me to some concrete result, however modest.

I must finally thank my mother and my wife for their constant forbearance, and for help which I could not have forgone.

Winchester College.
    29 *June* 1957.

CONTENTS

LIST OF ABBREVIATIONS

1. ARCHIVES

(a) *Vatican Archives.*

Arm.	Armarium.
Div. Cam.	Diversa Cameralia (in Arm. 29, see Fink, *Vatikanische Archiv*, 52).
IE	Introitus et Exitus.
Inst. Misc.	Instrumenta Miscellanea.
Reg. Vat.	Registra Vaticana.

(b) *Archivio di Stato, Rome.*

Arch. Cam.	Archivio Camerale.
Tes. Prov.	Tesorerie Provinciali.

2. PERIODICALS

AKKR	Archiv für katholisches Kirchenrecht.
AKöG	Archiv für Kunde oesterreichischer Geschichts-Quellen.
AMDR	Atti e memorie della R. Deputazione di Storia Patria per le provincie di Romagna.
AMSM	Atti e memorie della R. Deputazione di Storia Patria per le Marche.
ARAcLinc	Atti della R. Accademia dei Lincei.
ASI	Archivio Storico Italiano.
ASL	Archivio Storico Lombardo.
ASPN	Archivio Storico per le provincie Napoletane.
ASR	Archivio della R. Società Romana di Storia Patria.
BDA	Bullettino della R. Deputazione Abruzzese di Storia Patria.
BSU	Bolletino della R. Deputazione di Storia Patria per l'Umbria.
EHR	English Historical Review.
JEccH	Journal of Ecclesiastical History.
Mélanges	Mélanges d'Archéologie et d'Histoire de l'Ecole Française de Rome.
MIöG	Mittheilungen des Instituts für oesterreichische Geschichts-forschung.
QF	Quellen und Forschungen aus italienischen Archiven und Bibliotheken.
RQ	Römische Quartalschrift für christliche Altertumskunde und für Kirchengeschichte.

RSDI   Rivista di storia del Diritto italiano
ZSSRG   Zeitschrift der Savigny-Stiftung für Rechtsgeschichte.

3. ABBREVIATED TITLES OF OTHER WORKS

Commissioni Commissioni di Rinaldo degli Albizzi per il Comune di Firenze, ed.
             C. Guasti (Documenti di Storia Italiana, vols. 1–3).   1867–73.
Raynaldus   O. Raynaldi, Annales ecclesiastici post Baronium.   Lucca,
             1747–56.
Theiner   A. Theiner, Codex Diplomaticus Temporalis S. Sedis.   1861–2.

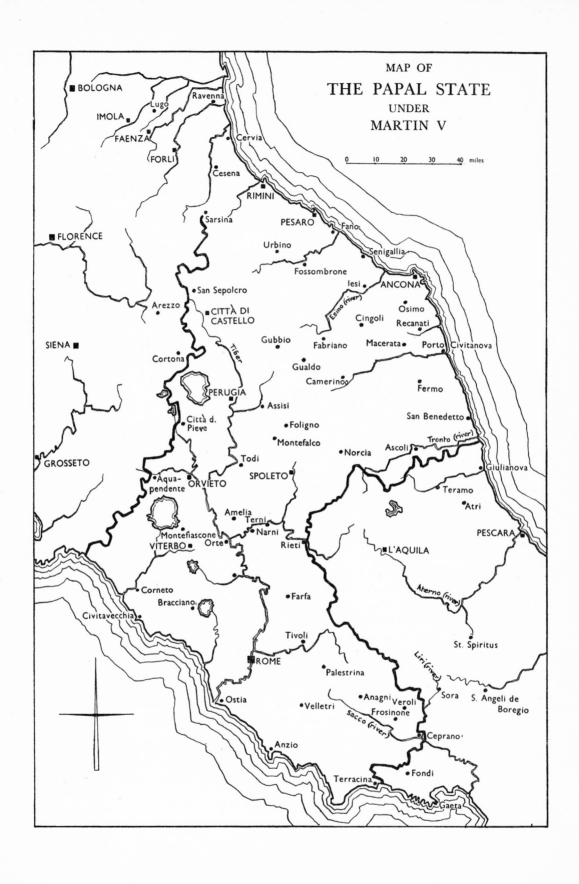

MAP OF
THE PAPAL STATE
UNDER
MARTIN V

0   10   20   30   40   miles

BOLOGNA
Lugo
Ravenna
IMOLA
FAENZA
FORLI
Cervia
Cesena
RIMINI
Sarsina
PESARO
Fano
FLORENCE
Urbino
Senigallia
Fossombrone
San Sepolcro
Iesi
ANCONA
Arezzo
CITTÀ DI
CASTELLO
Osimo
Cingoli
Recanati
Gubbio
Fabriano
Macerata
Porto Civitanova
Cortona
Gualdo
Camerino
Fermo
PERUGIA
Assisi
San Benedetto
Città d.
Pieve
Foligno
Tronto (river)
Montefalco
GROSSETO
Todi
Norcia
Ascoli
Giulianova
Aqua-
pendente
ORVIETO
SPOLETO
Teramo
Atri
Amelia
Terni
Narni
PESCARA
Montefiascone
Orte
Rieti
L'AQUILA
VITERBO
Aterno (river)
Corneto
Farfa
Bracciano
Civitavecchia
St. Spiritus
Tivoli
Liri (river)
ROME
Palestrina
Sora
S. Angeli de
Boregio
Ostia
Anagni
Veroli
Velletri
Frosinone
Sacco (river)
Ceprano
Anzio
Fondi
Terracina
Gaeta

Esino (river)
Tiber

ORIGINS AND DEVELOPMENT OF THE PAPAL STATE 753–1378

I

THE Papal State did not come into existence by accident, but as the result of deliberate and long-evolved policy, and at a time of critical change in the history of the Papacy. When in the eighth century the Popes threw off the Byzantine yoke and assumed the spiritual leadership of the Germanic peoples of the West, there was a sudden and immense expansion of papal claims. The extent of the advance in papalist theory can be seen in the forged Donation of Constantine. The most important practical success of the new papal policies was the creation of the Papal State.

The early history of the Papal State is obscure and controversial, and cannot be satisfactorily treated in a few paragraphs. The sources are incomplete, and have been variously interpreted, and the prejudice aroused on either side by the Roman Question has not assisted the historian who is anxious to obtain the truth. It is hardly necessary to warn the reader that many important questions are scarcely touched upon in the interpretation of events which follows, and that none are given the ample discussion which they deserve. But so important for the later history of the Papal State are the circumstances in which it arose—so important is the very obscurity of those circumstances—that I have thought it better to give a summary relation of the subject than none at all.

What came to be called the Papal State grew out of two earlier developments, the landed estates of the bishopric of Rome—the *patrimonium sancti Petri*—and the political leadership exercised by the Popes in Rome and central Italy.[1] Both these things have a long history, and were already important in the time of Leo the Great (440–461) and Gregory the Great (590–604). In the early eighth century they acquired a new and particular significance. The grip of Byzantium on her Italian possessions was at this time slack. The subject population was left more or less to look after itself, and in Rome, as in other cities, the power of the Imperial officials was supplanted by that of the Bishop. The administration of the Popes already supervised the administration of the City of Rome; judges and notaries of the City were attached to the papal palace, and the finances of the papal patrimony were inextricably entangled with the finances of the City. The *militia* of the Duchy of

---

[1] For the creation of the Papal State see in general : L. Duchesne, *Les premiers temps de l'état pontifical* (1904); E. Caspar, *Pippin und die Römische Kirche* (1914), and idem, *Geschichte des Papsttums*, ii (1933); J. Haller, *Die Quellen zur Geschichte der Entstehung des Kirchenstaates* (1907). and idem, *Das Papsttum*, i, ii (1950); W. Ullmann, *The growth of papal government in the Middle Ages* (1955), 44–142; J. Ficker, *Forschungen zur Reichs- und Rechtsgeschichte Italiens*, ii (1869), 328–58; Brackmann in *Realencyklopädie für protestantische Theologie und Kirche*, bd. xiv.

Rome, in addition to the *militia* recruited locally on the papal estates, was in the control of the Popes.   The Papacy had by this time lost the patrimonial possessions it once had in Illyria, Africa and Gaul, and was shortly to suffer further losses from the confiscation of its lands in Sicily and Southern Italy by the iconoclastic Emperor, Leo the Isaurian.   But it still retained very extensive estates in the rest of Byzantine Italy, that is, all over the Duchy of Rome, in the provinces of Ravenna and Emilia, in Pentapolis, and in parts of Tuscia.   These 'patrimonies' were administered by *defensores* for the Holy See.   The Popes were determined to keep these remaining lands, and to defend them against the aggression of Lombards or any others, and in this determination can be found the germ of subsequent events.

In the early eighth century it became apparent that Byzantium was unable further either to control or to protect the Papacy.   Pope Gregory II (715–731) was involved in a double struggle with the Byzantine Emperors, first over his refusal to pay certain taxes, and second over the iconoclastic decrees of Leo the Isaurian.   The result was a rebellion against Byzantine rule involving the greater part of Byzantine Italy.   The Duke of Rome was blinded by the people; the Exarch of Ravenna and the Duke of Naples were defeated and murdered.   The new Byzantine Exarch was accepted only through papal mediation, and Byzantine control over the Duchy of Rome became thenceforth little more than nominal.

Whether or not the letters to the Emperor in which Gregory II boasted of his spiritual and political power are genuine, the rebellion showed unequivocally the reality of papal leadership in Byzantine Italy, though a distinction must be made between the direct control which the Popes exercised in the Duchy of Rome, and the influence which stemmed from the prestige of the Roman See in other parts of Italy. Yet, being no longer protected by Byzantine arms, the Popes were bitterly afraid that they might fall under the heel of the expanding Lombard kingdom, and this fear accounts for papal reluctance to cut the last thin strands of allegiance which bound them to the Eastern Empire.

The Lombard peril nevertheless compelled the Popes to look elsewhere for protection.   Inevitably, their glance turned towards the newly converted Germanic nations, whom they hoped would redress the balance against Pavia and Constantinople.   The first hint of this new policy came in 739/40, when Gregory III's policy of playing off the Dukes of Spoleto against the Lombard kings failed.   Duke Trasemond was defeated, and King Liutprand seized the strong points of the Roman duchy, and laid siege to Rome.   Gregory III (731–741) thereon appealed to the Frankish Mayor of the Palace, Charles Martel, inviting him to rid the Papacy of the Lombards, and to receive some title of dignity over the Roman duchy.   Charles was already Liutprand's ally, and the appeal came to nothing.   But the precedent was of momentous importance; for the first time the Papacy had invoked the protection of Germanic Christendom.

Gregory's successor Zacharias (741–752) was forced to come to terms with the Lombards.   The terms of his agreement with Liutprand are important as indicating the status of the Papacy in the Duchy of Rome.   Liutprand 'restored' to the Pope,

without mention of the Imperial supremacy, a large number of patrimonial possessions in the Roman duchy, and also the cities of Amelia, Orte, Bomarzo and Bieda.
In these cities the Pope took the same rights as the Emperor had done, including the
ceremonial delivery of the keys. What title the Pope had to the cities was left
unstated, but the transaction implicitly recognised that the Pope was the ruler of the
territories of the *respublica Romanorum*, the political head of the Duchy of Rome.
The Popes had thus already crossed the line—at that period very ill-defined—which
distinguishes the landlord and estate-owner from the head of a state.

The effective temporal influence of the Popes did not stretch outside the Duchy,
although for a time the province of Ravenna itself came more or less under their protection; the Papacy several times intervened with the Lombards to dissuade them
from its conquest. But with the accession of Aistulf in 749 the Lombard attitude
hardened. Aistulf seized Ravenna from the Byzantine Exarch and claimed taxes
from the Duchy of Rome as a sign of his supremacy. This was followed by the
seizure of the papal city of Ceccano, on the southern frontier of the Roman duchy.
Rome could expect no help from the East, although the Byzantine ambassadors
continued to come and go. In 752 Stephen II (752–757) sent messengers to Pippin
to ask for his aid. On the receipt of a favourable reply, he asked for an escort to
enable the Pope to travel to the Kingdom of the Franks.

How far the Papal Court had a preconceived plan for the establishment of a
papal or a papal-dominated state when Pope Stephen II set off from Rome in 753,
the documents do not reveal. One is tempted to believe that the Donation of
Constantine, which was probably forged for the Papal Court at this period, was
manufactured partly in order to justify the claims which Stephen made at the
Frankish court. Even if this is not so, there is every likelihood that the Pope was
from the start of his journey prepared to claim for the Papacy and the *respublica
Romanorum*, those territories which 'had been gathered in the possession of one
lordship'—that is, the Italian territories which the Greek Emperor had until recently
held and had now lost.

But these wider claims were nevertheless secondary to the primary necessity of
obtaining guarantees for the protection of Rome from Lombard attack. It was of
Rome that the Pope talked in Pavia, when he travelled there with the Frankish and
Imperial envoys in November 753, and of Rome he first spoke to Pippin, when,
with the rest of his clergy, he knelt in sackcloth and ashes before the King at their
first meeting at Ponthion (January 754).

What kind of promise Pippin made at Ponthion can never with certainty be
known; it seems that he swore an oath to protect the Holy See and follow the
instructions of the Popes. The papal chronicler would have it believed that he swore
also to effect the 'restoration' of the places lost by the 'respublica Romanorum' and
the 'return' of the Exarchate of Ravenna. At Braisne and at Kiersy-sur-Oise
(*Carisiacum*) at Easter, the national assembly of the Franks met to give consent to
Pippin's guarantees, and to the Lombard war which they would entail. Against
some opposition, this consent was given. Further, Pippin at this time issued a

document in which he agreed to give the Pope not only the Exarchate of Ravenna, Spoleto and Benevento, but also the whole Lombard Kingdom south of a line drawn from the Gulf of Spezia to Parma, Reggio and Mantua, and further the island of Corsica. This document, now lost, was the fundamental title-deed of the later State of the Church, and constant reference was made to it by the later Popes, while its existence was not denied by the Emperors.

The protectorate which the Franks thus assumed over the Papacy was emphasised by the Pope's grant to Pippin and his sons (though it was never assumed by Pippin himself) of the title of 'patricius Romanorum'. 'Patricius' had been a title applied to the Exarch of Ravenna and the Duke of Rome, and it is significant that when the Frankish kings visited Rome they were received with the same honours as those formerly due to the Exarch. By terming him 'patricius' it was hoped to acquire the loyalty of the Frankish king for that *respublica Romanorum* to which the papal court cautiously referred as the subject of these wide territorial rights. In practice, the *respublica Romanorum* was led and represented by the Roman Church. It may have been felt in the Papal Court that, independently of the *respublica*, the Church had a claim based in some way on its situation as heir of the Roman Empire, but there was no document to justify the claim save the false donation of Constantine, and the ink was too fresh on this forgery (if, indeed, it was yet made) for it to be yet used as the title-deed of a new state.

The Pope's new state—still hardly sufficiently defined to claim the title of state—was long in assuming more than a modest size. The first Frankish campaign in Italy, although it led to an overwhelming Lombard defeat, did not result in more than the return of some of the strong points in the Roman duchy which the Lombards had seized. Then a second Lombard attack on Rome led to an appeal being made to Pippin, and to a second Frankish expedition (756). Another Lombard defeat followed, and after the peace the Abbot Fulrad of Saint Denis was deputed to supervise the handing over of the cities to the papal representatives. Fulrad then went to Rome, and deposited the keys of the cities, together with a copy of the text of Pippin's 'Donation', at the Confession of St. Peter. It was at this point that Pippin refused to return the re-conquered land to the Byzantines, alleging that he had fought out of love for St. Peter and for the remission of his sins, and that he would not take back from St. Peter what had already been offered to him.

The Pope was now in possession of the Roman duchy, and of the lands which stretched from Iesi and Senigallia in the south to the mouth of the Po in the north. Shortly afterwards, the support given by the Pope to the Lombard king Desiderius induced the latter to promise to 'restore' Faenza, Imola and Ferrara and some cities in Picenum such as Osimo, Ancona and Humana. But of these cities only Faenza and Ferrara were handed over; the remainder of the engagement was unfulfilled.

On whose military support did the new state depend? Ultimately, on that of the Franks. But immediately, on that of the Roman aristocracy. And from this period onwards the main features of the history of the City of Rome in the Middle Ages are determined. The two powers left supreme in Rome were the military aristocracy and the clergy. Conflict between them was inevitable, and although the clergy, being usually able to invoke overwhelming support from without, had the last card to play, the aristocracy could always unleash disorders by which the clergy were temporarily overwhelmed. These were the main lines in which Roman politics were destined to run until the time of the Renaissance, but in interpreting these struggles it is necessary to use a great deal of discretion. The Roman nobility and the Roman clergy were two bodies never sharply defined one from another, and conflicting groups usually commanded a following both of nobles and of clergy, although a particular group might have a predominantly aristocratic or a predominantly clerical character. It is never safe, even for the period of the Reform Papacy, to assume that the interests of nobility and clergy were absolutely opposite; they always to some degree coincided, and not only (as is generally recognised) was the aristocracy indebted to the Papacy for giving Rome a position of international importance, but also (as is less generally recognised) the Papacy was always indebted to the aristocracy for help in the administration of the temporal power, which it could not effectively conduct alone. Many periods of 'aristocratic domination' have been of much benefit to the organisation of the Papal State. And indeed, as Schramm has suggested, the territorial ambitions of the Roman nobility may lie behind the original temporal claims of Stephen II.

The first clash between clergy and nobility came after the death of Pope Paul I (757–767). The enmity between the *primicerius* Christopher and the Roman nobles resulted in the Lombards being called in, and in two barbarously conducted *coups d'état*, first that of Christopher against Pope Constantine II (767–769), whom he caused to be blinded and deposed, and secondly that of Afiarta and the Lombards against Christopher, who was overthrown and brutally murdered three years later. It is noticeable that in both cases the *coup d'état* was consolidated by the arms of a foreign power : in the first case by those of the Franks, whom Christopher called in as judges at the synod which deposed Constantine II, and in the case of Afiarta by those of the Lombards.

Hadrian I (772–795) lost no time in summoning Charles the Great to assist him against Lombard aggression. Charles duly appeared in Italy, and when he visited Rome in 774 he subscribed to a 'donation' on the same generous scale as that supposed to have been made by Pippin in 754. The Pope was granted the Duchy of Rome, the Exarchate of Ravenna and Pentapolis, Venetia and Istria, the Duchies of Benevento and Spoleto, and the whole Lombard kingdom south of a line from the Gulf of Spezia through Parma, Mantua and Padua. It has been convincingly suggested that, like the previous 'donation', this document was an agreement for a partition of the Lombard kingdom to be carried out at some unspecified time in the future : what was not assigned to the Pope would remain for the Franks. At the time that the document was executed Pavia still held out, and the Frankish king did not yet hold most of the territories referred to in his 'donation', which was therefore a provision against a future dismemberment of the Lombard state, and not a disposition of territories which were already in Frankish hands.

The Lombards were duly and finally conquered, but Charles had himself proclaimed King of the Lombards in the same year, 774, and showed no sign of wishing to dismember his new kingdom as he had promised. The Roman claims and the document by which he had agreed to support them were ignored. A part of the Lombard lands (Bologna, Ferrara and other parts of Emilia) was seized by the Archbishops of Ravenna, although these territories afterwards passed back under the jurisdiction of Rome. But these lands in Emilia were all that the Church at first gained from the fall of the Lombard kingdom, and when Charles paid his next visit to Rome in 781 Pope Hadrian, far from pressing his claims home, was compelled to give up his rights over the Duchies of Spoleto and Tuscany.

Charles' third visit to Rome in 787, to settle the affairs of the Duchy of Spoleto, was made the occasion for a further amicable extension of the bounds of the Papal State. The Pope was given an important tract of Lombard Tuscia, comprising the area which stretched north of Rome to Soana and Piombino, and north-east to Viterbo and Orvieto. The Duchy of Spoleto remained outside the Papal State, but its Duke, Arichis, was made to agree to cede the Pope certain places in the Roman Campagna and others along the road to Naples as far south as Capua. The southern donations, however, did not take effect.

Hadrian I had thus obtained possession of the greater part of the Italian lands claimed by the Church under the 'donation' of Pippin. The Papal State had reached, very approximately, the boundaries which it was to retain until 1860. The heart of the new state was the former Byzantine Duchy of Rome, which by the acquisition of the places in Tuscia was extended north as far as Piombino. In the centre of Italy the Duchy of Spoleto was still outside the Papal State, but the Pope controlled the rest of Umbria, including Perugia and Città di Castello. On the Adriatic coast, the Church held the coastal strip from Ancona to Ferrara and to Monselice north of the Po; inland in Emilia her possessions extended as far as Bologna. Little is known of how these territories were governed: in the Adriatic area the Archbishop of Ravenna seems to have usurped many of the former privileges of the Exarch, and it is probable that everywhere outside the former Duchy of Rome papal control tended to be indirect and fluctuating. Nevertheless, the vital steps had been taken and the bold programme of Stephen II made good. In less than a century the bishops of Rome had turned themselves from landed proprietors into territorial princes. Their title to their lands was badly defined: their political control was shadowy and dependent on Frankish protection. But a new state had been added to the map of Europe. Partly because of the vagueness of its antecedents, partly because of the later counter-claims of the Emperors, the Middle Ages were uncertain what was the political status of this new power. It could not be called a *regnum*; the usual titles afforded it were those of *terrae seu patrimonium ecclesiae*. The Donations speak of the papal lands as 'in iure principatu et ditione' of the Church; Otto I swore to defend the 'terra sancti Petri'. But although from its earliest years a protected, sometimes a puppet state, it is hard to deny that the Papal State was a political unit fully as coherent as many others. There was nothing extraordinary in an ecclesiastic being made into a temporal ruler; many medieval examples may be found. And although the Popes, perhaps more than most rulers, had difficulty in exercising their temporal supremacy, they had no doubts about its existence. On the other hand, they never fully succeeded in throwing off the links which, from its very inception, bound the Papal State to Pippin and Charlemagne and Charlemagne's successors in the Empire.

That the Pope was not fully master in his own house, and that he must always lean on the Franks, was once again demonstrated by the events leading up to the Imperial coronation of Charlemagne, on Christmas Day 800. Leo III (795–816) could not extinguish with his own forces the rebellion which broke out against him in Rome in April 799, and he was eventually forced to purge himself before the future Emperor of the accusations which the conspirators brought against him. The events of that fateful year lay heavily upon the Papacy for the rest of the Middle Ages; even the defeat of the Hohenstaufen did not finally throw off the Imperial protectorate.

II

The period between Charlemagne and the Gregorian reforms is distinguished in the Papal State by the persistence of Imperial interference and intervention, and by the gradual penetration of the territorial aristocracy into all the institutions of the Papal State.[1] The Emperors, both Carolingians and Ottonians, confirmed the territorial privileges of the Church in a series of documents, beginning with the privilege of Louis the Pious in 817. Lothar's *Constitutio Romana* of 824 provided for an oath of allegiance to be taken by all papal subjects to the Emperor, and laid down an arrangement by which the Emperor was given a permanent place in the higher justice of the Papal State. But even while the Carolingian power remained intact, Lothar's constitution was not followed, and with its collapse the Imperial rights fell into disuse, only to be revived by the Ottonian dynasty after the lapse of almost a century. Only Otto III, among the Emperors, wished to take the Imperial supremacy to a point which involved the virtual suppression of the Papal State; other Emperors were content with an indefinite protectorate, which they exercised now in one way and now in another, without any very strictly-defined principles.

Otto III, in the very extraordinary document by which he donated eight counties in Pentapolis to Silvester II (999–1003), challenged the fundamental title-deeds of the State of the Church and asserted their nullity. But even he was content that the

---

[1] See, besides the works quoted above, P. Fedele, 'Ricerche per la storia di Roma e del Papato nel secolo X', *ASR*, xxxiii–xxxiv (1910–11); K. Jordan, 'Das Eindringen des Lehnwesens in das Rechtsleben der römischen Kurie', *Archiv für Urkundenforschung*, xii (1932); W. Kölmel, *Rom und der Kirchenstaat im 10. und 11. Jahrhundert bis in die Anfänge der Reform* (1935); M. Uhlirz, 'Die Restitution des Exarchates Ravenna durch die Ottonen', *MIöG*, 1 (1936); P. Schramm, *Kaiser, Rom und Renovatio* (1929); O. Vehse, 'Die päpstliche Herrschaft in der Sabina', *QF*, xxi (1929/30). W. Sickel, 'Alberich II. und der Kirchenstaat', *MIöG*, xxiii (1902) and L. M. Hartmann, 'Grundherrschaft und Bureaukratie im Kirchenstaate vom 8. bis 10. Jahrhundert', *Vierteljahrschrift für Sozial- und Wirtschaftsgeschichte*, vii (1909) are both to be corrected in the light of later work on the subject.

Church should possess a certain *potestas legalis* in the territories attributed to it, while reserving to himself the *jus publicum* and *legitima potestas*.   And although they were unwilling to go to the full extent of the huge territories mentioned in the Donation of Otto I (just as Charlemagne had been unwilling to 'restore' all the lands mentioned in his own Donation) yet the Ottonians, not excluding Otto III, were instrumental in returning to the Church most of the Exarchate of Ravenna and part of the area later known as the March of Ancona.

What was permanent and all-pervasive in the constitution of the Papal State was the influence of the landed aristocracy.   More and more, the offices of the Papal State and of the Papal Court itself fell into the hands of a few powerful Roman families, a development which culminated in the so-called Pornocracy—as Baronius has it—of the Crescenzi, and in the despotic rule of Alberic II as *princeps et senator* over Rome and the whole Papal State (932–954), while the Popes were his relatives or nominees.   But often where Alberic II and the other Roman nobles who exploited the temporal power appear to have acted only in their own interests, they were in fact strengthening papal power.   The effective government of Sabina and Campania through papal Rectors dates from the time of Alberic, and papal government again in some degree benefited from the strong rule of the Counts of Tusculum in the early years of the eleventh century.   It would be paradoxical to assert that the aristocratic control of lands and offices was entirely beneficial to the Papal State; the Popes could not but in many ways lose by the process, particularly in the loss of their demesne lands, which melted away and were impoverished in the course of the tenth century.   They lacked the essential strong hand to create and control a true feudal monarchy, in which fiefs were distributed against real obligations of military service and loyalty.   But nevertheless, all that followed from the hegemony of the Crescenzi and the Counts of Tusculum was not pure loss, and the later reforms in the Papal State owe more than a little to the work of Alberic II and the Tusculan Benedict VIII (1012–1024).   The pendulum of papal nepotism had begun to swing in a manner which was to continue for many centuries; a nepotistic dynasty would strengthen the hand of the temporal power so long as their candidate was on the papal throne, but when he left it they would become a source of disorder and revolution.   By slow and crab-like movements the central authority pushed itself forwards, with its allies of one day becoming its enemies of the next.

At the accession of Leo IX (1049–1054) to the Papacy, the Church possessed a somewhat shadowy organisation to control its territories.[1]   The heart of the papal

---

[1] For what follows see Ficker, *Forschungen zur Reichs- und Rechtsgeschichte Italiens*, ii, 284 f.; Vehse's article quoted above and also his 'Benevent als Territorium des Kirchenstaates bis zum Beginn der Avignonesischen Epoche', *QF*, xii (1930/31); Jordan's article quoted above, and also his 'Zur päpstlichen Finanzgeschichte im 11. und 12. Jahrhundert', *QF*, xxv (1933/34); L. Halphen, *Etudes sur l'administration de Rome au Moyen Age* (1907); G. Falco, 'L'amministrazione papale nella Campagna e nella Marittima', *ASR*, xxxviii (1917) and idem, 'I comuni della Campagna e della Marittima nel Medio Evo', *ASR*, xlii, xlvii–xlix (1919 f.); A. Overmann, *Gräfin Mathilde von Tuscien* (1895); F. Schneider, 'Zur älteren päpstlichen Finanzgeschichte', *QF*, ix (1906); D. B. Zema, 'Economic reorganisation of the Roman See during the Gregorian Reform', in *Studi Gregoriani*, i (1947); P. Fabre, *Etude sur le liber censuum de l'Eglise Romaine* (1892); J. Haller, 'K. Heinrich VI. und die Römische Kirche', *MIöG*, xxxv (1914).

dominions continued to be the former Duchy of Rome with its northern gains in Lombard Tuscia. This is the area 'from Aquapendente to Ceprano' which was in the twelfth century thought of as the essential *patrimonium beati Petri*. The southern part of this 'patrimony', the province of Campania, was spasmodically ruled for the Popes by a *comes Campaniae*; the northern part appears to have been directly administered from Rome. To the east of the Tiber lay the province of Sabina, stretching to the lake of Fucino on the east and to Tivoli in the south. This was ruled by papal Rectors, who had to compete there with the powerful and aggressive abbey of Farfa. The rectorate, besides, was at this time in the hands of the Crescenzi family. East and north of Sabina, the Church seems to have exercised only the most occasional and tenuous hold over the lands which it claimed on the Adriatic coast and inland. The 'restoration' to the Church by the Ottonian Emperors of the Exarchate of Ravenna and the cities of Pentapolis seems to have taken effect only for a few years at the most; there is no sign that papal domination here was a reality in the eleventh century. Rimini is once or twice mentioned as having been granted by the Church to certain Counts, but it is beyond doubt that papal power on the other side of the Apennines was negligible.

It was the task of the Reform Papacy and its successors to oust the intruding nobility from their position in the Papal State, and to restore, reform and expand the temporal power. In spite of the protests of St. Peter Damiani, this policy was initiated by Leo IX and Hildebrand, and was carried through with dogged persistence by successive Popes for over a century, until the collapse of the plans of Henry VI enabled Innocent III at last to put the Papal State on a firm and relatively stable footing.

In the beginning the Reform Papacy was assisted in this, as in many other things, by the Empire. It was with the help of Henry III that Leo IX acquired the allegiance of Benevento in the south, and that Victor II (1055–1057) acquired for a short time the Duchy of Spoleto and the March of Fermo. But matters were decisively changed when the Papacy abandoned the role of buffer state between the Empire and the Norman princes, and assumed the guise of feudal lord of the whole of southern Italy. By the Treaty of Melfi (1059) Robert Guiscard received the title of Duke for his lands in Apulia and Calabria, and swore fealty to the Roman See, and his neighbour Richard of Capua probably followed suit. The Papacy thus at one stroke acquired the services of the best soldiers in Europe, and made St. Peter the overlord of the greater part of Italy. Nothing, of course, could guarantee that the Normans would not turn against their new overlord, and this in fact occurred. But this did not alter the fact that the temporal supremacy of the Papacy had made its greatest advance since the time of the first Donations. Nor were the indirect effects of the new connexion with the Normans any less important; papal power in the existing Papal State received a great access of strength from the diplomatic victory in the south.

This is not the place to chronicle the fluctuating success of the eleventh- and twelfth-century Popes in recovering and holding their patrimonies. Suffice that it

B

was a slow and painful process, in which the Popes continually appeared to slip back to their starting point.   A nucleus of the papal lands gradually acquired a small but effective governmental organisation directly controlled by the Papacy, and the anarchic tendencies of the territorial lords were gradually pushed back and subjected to certain basic feudal dues and duties; but in its earlier stages this effort appeared to be vain.   In spite of his pretensions to military power, Gregory VII (1073–1085) never achieved anything tangible in the government of the Papal State and he ended his life, as he had spent a good deal of it, on the run before enemy troops. Gregory's immediate successors had little better fortune, and Paschal II (1099–1118) had to carry out a bitter struggle, with the assistance of the family of Pierleoni, in order to preserve a certain temporal supremacy.   The tide seems to have turned with Calixtus II (1119–1124) and Honorius II (1124–1130).   With these Popes begins a long series of submissions by the barons of Lazio and the Roman Campagna, and the gradual acquisition by the Curia of many of the key castles and strong-points.   The highest level of security and stability in the Papal State was reached under Hadrian IV (1154–1159).   This was followed by a period of decline, occasioned by the growing success of Frederick I's energetic resumption of Imperial rights in Italy, and by the long and weakening schism under Alexander III (1159–1181). Frederick's policies were continued and expanded by his son Henry VI, whose death in 1197 is a dividing line in the history of the Papal State, as it is in many other fields of medieval history.   With him ended the last ready opportunity for the Emperors to turn their ambiguous protectorate over the Papal State into a real hegemony.   By the end of the pontificate of Innocent III (1198–1216) the papal lands exhibited all the characteristics of a firmly established state.

The area actually governed by the Popes achieved little expansion between 1059 and 1197, although the Popes never abandoned their claims to the wider territories mentioned in the Donations.   The papal dominions continued to be, essentially, the lands between Radicofani (north of Aquapendente) and Ceprano, with the addition of the province of Sabina and the city and district of Benevento.   In this limited area certain principles of government may be discerned.   First, it was the curial policy to buy or annex strongpoints and castles in order to secure military control of the provinces.   Second, the feudal principles were gradually brought into play to the advantage of the Popes; lands were granted against the feudal obligations of *ligium hominium et fidelitatem*, of *hostem, parlamentum, servitutem, placitum et bannum*.   Third, the expanding new institution of the commune was exploited by the Popes to their advantage; the communes were granted papal privileges and used as a counter-weight to baronial power.

Behind these policies stands the reorganisation of the Roman Curia itself.   The old and now feudalised office of *arcarius* and *sacellarius* of the *sacrum palatium Lateranense* at the end of the eleventh century disappear, and are replaced under Calixtus II and perhaps earlier by the new *camerarius domini papae*.   The *camerarius* is responsible for papal finances in general, and hence, inevitably, for much of the administration of the Papal State.   The major testimony of the interest of the

papal Chamber in the affairs of the Papal State is the great compilation carried out at the end of the twelfth century for the *camerarius* Cencius, known as the *Liber Censuum*. Here is collected a variegated mass of documents of various periods, dealing with both the demesne possessions of the Papacy and the Papal State proper.

Although laymen continued to be used in the government of the Papal State, clergy were increasingly appointed as Rectors during this period. The growing power of the College of Cardinals found an outlet here, and in the mid-twelfth century can be seen traces of the later practice of appointing Cardinals to act as Legates for the Pope in the papal provinces.

One important development cannot here be overlooked, the rise to power of the commune of Rome. So far as the sources reveal this was sudden and revolutionary, occurring in the revolution of 1143/4, which created the Roman Senators as the main officials of the new commune. The Popes usually made good their claim to appoint these Senators, but the commune remained, always present to act as the rallying point of local interests and a focal point of disaffection. Thus was revenged the old *respublica Romanorum* which the eighth-century Popes had exploited and disinherited. As late as Celestine III (1191–1198) the Senator Benedetto Carissimi (Carushomo) seized the provinces of Maritima and Sabina from the Church and ruled there in his own right.

The papal patrimony was in theory enriched in the early twelfth century by a new donation, that of the allodial lands of the Countess Matilda, who in 1102 bequeathed these possessions, which were scattered all over north and north-east Italy, to the Holy See. After her death in 1115, a conflict broke out between the Church and Empire over the possession of her lands, which lasted for over a century. The Popes never had the means of entering into possession of the lands they claimed, and the conflict went on the whole in favour of the Emperors, the decisive points of the struggle in the twelfth century being the grant of the Matildine lands in fee to the Emperor Lothar in 1133, and the failure of Alexander III to extract any promise from Frederick I about the restoration of these lands at the time of the peace of Venice (1177). But although the struggle went on far into the thirteenth century, in the event neither the Empire nor the Church gained permanent possession of the bulk of the Matildine lands, but the local interests, and principally the communes.

III

With the death of the Emperor Henry VI and the accession of Innocent III the final period of the medieval Papal State begins.[1] The great architect of its territories

---

[1] For what follows see the works of Vehse, Falco and Jordan quoted above, and Ficker, *Forschungen*, ii, 369–472. See also H. Tillmann, *Innocenz III.* (1954); idem, 'Die päpstliche Rekuperationen', *Historisches Jahrbuch*, li (1931); A. Luchaire, *Innocent III, Rome et l'Italie* (1904). J. Seeger, *Reorganisation des Kirchenstaates unter Innocenz III* (1937) was inaccessible to me. See further E. Jordan, *Les origines de la domination Angevine en Italie* (1909); W. Hagemann, 'Fabriano im Kampf zwischen Kaisertum und Papsttum bis 1272', *QF*, xxx, xxxii (1940, 1942); O. Vehse, 'Benevent und die Kurie unter Nicolaus IV', *QF*, xx (1928/9); G. Ermini, 'La libertà comunale nello stato della chiesa', *ASR*, xlix (1926) and second par l'L'amministrazione della giustizia', Rome, 1927; idem, 'Caratteri della

and constitution was Innocent III.   First of all, it was Innocent who made into a
reality the papal claims on the March of Ancona and the Duchy of Spoleto, supporting
them with concrete administrative action and with new privileges from the Emperors.
The papal claims on these areas were far from new; Alexander III had claimed a
part (though not the whole) of the March of Ancona from Frederick I, and certain
beginnings had been made in asserting papal rights in the March in the period
between the death of the Emperor Henry VI and that of Pope Celestine III.   But
it was Innocent who, in spite of formidable counter-action by Otto IV, made a
serious bid for papal supremacy in the Duchy and the March, and although he had
to confer the March of Ancona for a time as a fee upon Azzo d'Este, he must be
given credit for the addition of these two important provinces to the area effectively
governed by the Popes.   Thus under Innocent III the Papal State began to take
the shape it was to retain for the rest of the Middle Ages, from Radicofani in the north
to Ceprano in the south ; the town and district of Benevento as an enclave further
south ; the province of Sabina ; the Duchy of Spoleto, and the March of Ancona.
It is this area which is described in the important donations of Frederick II in 1213
and 1219, and which Honorius III (1216–1227) dominated with Frederick's help.
Only the area by this time known as Romagna was now lacking ; Innocent had laid
claim to this, but failed to enforce it.

For half a century after Honorius's death, from the break with Frederick II in
1227 until the Angevin victory at Benevento in 1266, the Popes and the Emperors
were engaged in a bitter struggle for supremacy in the papal lands.   The issue,
particularly in the more distant provinces from Rome, was fluctuating and uncertain ; the Italian cities changed their allegiance according to the exigencies of
the moment or the influence of the party in power there.   But the Popes were
tenacious in holding to their State and administering it directly through clerical
Rectors and Legates ; though they often lost ground, they were always in haste to
recover it.   The great Guelph victories of 1266–1268 finally grounded the stable
government of the Papal State.   The new Angevin power was centred in the south
and away from the Papal State, and the Hohenstaufen were finally broken.

The confused situation in Romagna was regulated to the advantage of the Popes
under Innocent V (1276) and Nicholas III (1277–1280).   The actual influence of the
Popes in the area between Ravenna and the March of Ancona—Romagna—had been
small ; the Imperial privileges spoke of an 'Exarchate of Ravenna', which was by
this time topographically obsolete.   The Church had exercised some influence over
Ferrara, and further west over Bologna, but this was practically all.   Now Nicholas
III obtained from King Rudolph the formal recognition of the Empire for the rule
of the Church in Romagna (1278).   Thus the last item on the expansionist pro-

sovranità temporale dei papi nei secoli XIII e XIV', ZSSRG, Kanonist. Abt., xxvii (1938); idem,
'I rettori provinciali dello Stato della Chiesa da Innocenzo III all'Albornoz', RSDI, iv (1931); S. Sugen-
heim, Geschichte der Entstehung und Ausbildung des Kirchenstaates (1854); P. Sella, 'Le costituzioni dello
Stato della Chiesa', ASI, 7th ser., viii (1927); C. Calisse, 'I prefetti di Vico', ASR, x (1887); D. Waley,
Mediaeval Orvieto (1952).

gramme of Innocent III had been gained, and the territories of the Church had assumed their more or less permanent shape.

The thirteenth century is the great period of administrative development in the Papal State. The whole skeleton of later papal government can be traced back to this period, beginning with the organisation of the Papal State into provinces each ruled by a Rector or Legate, as was arranged by Innocent III. To the early thirteenth century can be assigned the growth of a system of papal courts, and the beginnings of a body of legislation issued by the provincial Rectors; a little later the Rectors were regularly holding Parliaments to promulgate their decisions.

Much depended, for the future of the Papal State, on the relations of the Popes with the communes. It is impossible to speak of a consistently 'communal' or 'anti-communal' policy of the Popes, as some historians have tried to do; as usually happened between the central power and local interests, the Papacy would give 'privileges' which legitimated existing de facto rights (e.g. the election of the *podestà*), but would try to reserve the rights of the central power and exercise them when it could. Thus most of the major communes in the course of the thirteenth century gained the right to nominate their own *podestà*, and to administer their own justice. The period of maximum communal freedom seems to have been the middle of the century, the time of the introduction of the office of *capitano del popolo* in most of the cities of the Papal State, and of the Roman revolution of Brancaleone degli Andalò (1252). But when towards the end of the century the Church felt itself stronger than before, it would often challenge the exercise of *merum et mixtum imperium* by the commune, and even try to withdraw the privilege of nominating the *podestà*. At the same time the financial grip of the Church became far tighter than hitherto, through fines and such taxes as the *tallia militum*, and the exercise of the right of *preventio* or concurrent ordinary jurisdiction. The constitutions issued to the various provinces by Boniface VIII (1294–1303) grant extensive judicial privileges to the communes and condemn certain excesses and injustices of papal Rectors. They point to a state of affairs in which provincial administration was already highly organised and developed, and they also represent the furthest point to which the communal liberties received explicit recognition from the Church.

Boniface VIII did not grant these privileges from weakness, but as part of a policy of strength. Like all the great nepotistic Popes, he was solicitous for the interests of the temporal power, so far as they could be made to coincide with the interests of his family. And up to a point they could be made to coincide; the complex and sometimes sordid negotiations for the aggrandisement of the Caetani, first in the Aldobrandeschi lands in southern Tuscany, and then in the Roman and Neapolitan Campagna, did not prevent Boniface from bargaining and coercing the whole area of the Papal State into a condition of relative quiet and obedience. But the violence of Caetani cupidity had its reward in the violence of the reaction which followed Boniface's death; within two years the entire Papal State was in a condition of chaos.

The fourteenth century is the period in the history of the Papal State which has been most misunderstood by historians.   Until fairly recently it was assumed that the exile of the Popes in Avignon meant more or less the abandonment of their dominions in Italy, and was accompanied there by misgovernment and chaos, mitigated only by the action in the Papal State of the Spanish Legate Gil Albornoz (Legate from 1353 to 1357, 1358 to 1363).   This view has now been corrected by the recognition that their Italian lands were among the very first concerns of the Avignonese Popes, that they spent most of their revenues in warfare to maintain their position there, and that in spite of many setbacks the record of the Avignonese Popes in the State of the Church is one of steady administrative advance.[1]   In this scheme of things Albornoz takes his place as the most distinguished and able of a series of soldier-administrators sent by the Avignonese Popes to Italy.

The end of the thirteenth century and the succeeding period saw the decline of the free commune and the rise of the new institution of the *signoria*.   The Church was swift to react to these events, which on one hand provided her with new problems, but on the other gave her fresh opportunities.   The *signori* were far more difficult to control than the communes, and their appearance threatened and in some cases led to political chaos, of which the condition of the province of Romagna in the second and third decades of the fourteenth century is a gloomy example.   It was the achievement of Albornoz temporarily to have subdued the *signori* of Romagna and the March of Ancona.   But when a city which had been under the rule of a *signore* fell once again under the direct governance of the Church, the commune was not usually re-accorded all its ancient rights; the Church tended to step into the shoes of the late *signore*, overruling the constitution of the commune in the same way that he had done.   Thus at this period appears a new type of papal Vicar or Rector of the cities, who either inherits the power of a past *signore*, or even makes innovations of a similar type on his own account.

The communes lost ground rapidly during the whole century; one of the most important to lose its effective self-government to papal representatives was the commune of Rome, which was brought into papal leading-strings during the pontificate of Benedict XII (1334–1342).   The later explosion against papal rule under Cola di Rienzo in 1347 was short-lived, and did little or nothing to displace the *signoria* of the Church in Rome.

One of the main problems of this period was how to strike a satisfactory bargain with those *signori* or tyrants whom the Church was unable to eject from their usurped positions.   The system adopted was the grant of the city concerned to its tyrant as an 'apostolic vicariate', against considerable annual payment of *census*.   This indeed, was only to save the face and pocket of the Papacy as much as possible and to make the best of an essentially bad bargain.   In fact—as is related at length below—the *signori* fulfilled few of the obligations they undertook, and the only real solution was their extirpation.   Nothing could alter the fact that the very existence

---

[1] See particularly G. Mollat, *Les Papes d'Avignon* (9th edn., 1950), 137–295; K. H. Schäfer, *Deutsche Ritter und Edelknechte in Italien*, i (1911); A. Eitel, *Der Kirchenstaat unter Klemens V* (1907); F. Filippini, *Il cardinale Egidio Albornoz* (1933).   The voluminous periodical literature is listed by Mollat, in the work cited above, pp. 295–308.

of the tyrant or *signore* was inimical to good government. But since the Church did not possess the military force to deal with the tyrants in any other way, she must needs accept this compromise, which was extended all over the Papal State by Albornoz.

The formal machinery of administration continued to expand and to become more effective; most of the complex organisation of the *curia rectoris* was in being in the time of Albornoz. The number of communes which elected their own *podestà* diminished rapidly. And to Albornoz is due the codification of the many constitutions issued by former Rectors and Popes to the papal provinces, in the form of the *Constitutiones Aegidianae*, which became the mainstay of the public law of the State of the Church.

In spite of these great advances in government, the problem of disorder in the Papal State remained more or less unchanged. Local particularism was the rule, and the central government had to come to terms with it as best it could, not possessing the armed force or the revenues to use any tactics but gradual ones. Even though the free communes were in decline, they continued fiercely to impose their own influence and government over the surrounding district or *comitatus*, so that each city became more and more of a coherent governmental unit—and, in consequence, the more difficult to manage. The return of the Papacy to Italy under Urban V (1362–1370), and Gregory XI (1370–1378) did not improve the situation of the State of the Church; it was, on the contrary, marked in 1376 by a widespread and serious rebellion. In this and the following period the central government can act with a heavy hand on occasion, but when its glance is elsewhere every variety of local particularism comes out into the sun and flourishes. And with the restoration of another line of Italian Popes in 1378, to the problems of particularism was added the revived problem of papal nepotism, which brought back yet another body of local interests into the arena of papal politics.

In every medieval state the problem of local particularism and disorder was a chronic one. But the peculiar structure of a state ruled by priests, who often lived only a short time in office and were occupied by problems diverse from their temporal responsibilities—all this made government rather weaker in the Papal State than elsewhere. It was in the nature of the Papacy that the Popes could not devote their whole attention to temporal government. Their spiritual functions could be useful to their temporal ones—certainly the money derived from the spiritual power was—but also deleterious, as in the case of schism. Their temporal rule lacked the continuity of lay states, and was weakened by the complete overturn of the complex mechanism of patronage, at the end of every pontificate. Local interests, on the other hand, were deep rooted and continuous, and could be properly dealt with only when the Popes had their hands free and were unencumbered by attacks on their spiritual jurisdiction. The Great Schism which followed the double election of 1378 was thus bound to be deeply harmful to the government of the Papal State.

CHAPTER I

THE PAPAL STATE IN THE LATTER PART OF THE GREAT SCHISM

I. *The Aggression of Ladislas of Durazzo*

§ 1. THE Schism ended by being almost fatal to the Papal State. But such an issue was not apparent during the last years of Boniface IX, who, having made himself almost undisputed Pope in Italy, sat so firmly in the temporal power as to be universally feared—'Victoriosus fuit; multas civitates et iura Ecclesie aquisivit ac Rome dominium temporale libere primus obtinuit.' [1] He ruled in Rome more absolutely than any other Pope had done; he ordered that all officials in the Papal State be appointed by the Pope, an act of power which no previous Pope had even attempted. [2] Death served him well, by a timely disposal of his enemies no less than by a kind intervention against Boniface himself : Biordo dei Michelotti, the tyrant of Perugia, was murdered at an opportune moment in 1398; Gian Galeazzo Visconti died at the point when that formidable tyrant's hand was closing upon Umbria and Romagna; and the Pope himself died before Ladislas of Durazzo was fully ready to turn against the Church. But perhaps the subtle and resolute Tomacelli would have had more fortune against Ladislas than had his weaker successors. Boniface practised simony and nepotism as cynically as any Pope had ever done; under him the offices of the Curia began to become venal. But at least the temporal power was a main beneficiary from these defects; the Tomacelli brothers recovered great tracts of land for the Church, and much of the money which Boniface had by dubious means acquired was spent on the payment of soldiers. Boniface left the State of the Church as strong as it had been since Albornoz' time, perhaps stronger, and the Guelph faction had good cause to lament his death. [3]

The same instruments did not respond so well in the hands of Boniface's successor, and the less so because Ladislas of Durazzo turned all his dangerous talents towards the undermining of the State of the Church. Ladislas owed his throne to the Church, and in his earlier years appeared to be her grateful son. By 1402 this brilliant and ruthless prince had broken the dangerous part of the Angevin faction in the Kingdom of Sicily, and, having reorganised his state, was seeking paths for

[1] *Annales Forolivienses* (Muratori, *RRIISS*, xxii, pt. 2), 81 ; *Liber Pontificalis*, ed. Duchesne (1892), ii, 531, 'tota Italia eum timebat'. Cf. M. Jansen, *Papst Bonifatius IX. und seine Beziehungen zur deutschen Kirche*, 20, 24 ; E. Göller, 'Aus der Camera apostolica der Schismapäpste', *RQ*, xxxii (1924), 84.

[2] Theiner, iii, no. 69, p. 125.

[3] Mathaei de Griffonibus, *Memoriale historicum de rebus Bononiensium* (Muratori, *RRIISS*, xviii, pt. 2), 94, 'Nova valde lacrimosa fuerunt hic, quod dominus papa Bonifatius nonus, erat mortuus, de quo omnes boni cives Bononiae debuerunt valde tristari, quia fuit optimus pastor . . .' His rapacity has been excused (*Liber Pontificalis*, ii, 550–1) on the ground that the money was needed to combat tyrants. For a list of his donations to his relatives, A. Cutolo, *Re Ladislao d'Angiò-Durazzo*, ii, n. 45, p. 89.

foreign aggression. Boniface IX's attempt to divert him to the East by arranging his marriage with Mary of Lusignan, sister of Janus of Cyprus, was a short-lived palliative; the marriage was as barren of children as of political effect. In 1403 Boniface sacrificed his credit with Sigismond of Hungary to support Ladislas' Hungarian expedition. In the autumn of this year Ladislas returned empty-handed to Italy, which was from this time onwards the field of all his ambitions. Tension with Boniface grew, and in March 1404 the Pope gave an important *condotta* to Paolo Orsini, and began to raise money for defence.[1] As soon as Boniface died, and before the conclave had even elected a new Pope, Ladislas moved on Rome. He entered the city two days after the election of Cosimo Migliorati as Innocent VII, who thus began his pontificate with a Neapolitan army in Rome. Ladislas knew how to use the revolution of the Colonna and the hankering of the Romans for a popular government as excuses for a most profitable piece of mediation. He forced the Pope to accept a popular government in Rome, under a treaty which gave Ladislas rights of arbitration between commune and Pope. He also obtained a virtual protectorate over Ascoli Piceno, made the Pope appoint the Neapolitan Count of Troja as Rector in Campania and Maritima, and finally made him agree to the humiliating and indecent condition that he would not end the Schism until Ladislas' rights on the crown of Naples were generally accepted.[2]

The subjection of the Holy See to Naples was brusquely broken on 6 August 1405 by the murder of a group of Romans of the popular government by Ludovico Migliorati, nephew of the Pope.[3] In the confusion which followed, the Neapolitans and their adherents the Colonna failed to gain the upper hand. The Pope retired to Viterbo, but the Count of Troja's attack on the City failed, and Orsini support, together, perhaps, with Roman interest in keeping the Pope in Rome, brought back Innocent as the master of the City in March 1406. The main armed force which achieved this was that of Paolo Orsini, and from this time Orsini began to be, as Dietrich of Niem remarks, the real master of Rome.[4] The Pope could make war only by employing and favouring such powerful *condottieri* as Orsini. But only a Papacy which was politically healthy could control these *condottieri*, and as the Schism progressively weakened the Papacy, the Papal State fell further and further into the hands of such men as Orsini or Braccio of Montone.

---

[1] Cutolo, ii, n. 52, p. 138.

[2] Raynaldus, ad a. 1404, par. xiv. For events following the death of Boniface, see Gregorovius, *History of the City of Rome in the Middle Ages*, vi, pt. 2, 567 f.; Cutolo, i, 274 f. The treaty of Innocent VII with Rome in Theiner, iii, no. 71, p. 131. The grant of the right to nominate all officials in Ascoli, made at this time, is referred to in its revocation, Theiner, iii, no. 81, p. 145.

[3] Gregorovius, vi, pt. 2, 576; Cutolo, i, 295 f.; A. Pietro dello Schiavo, *Diarium Romanum* (Muratori, *RRIISS*, xxiv, pt. 5), 8–9; Sozomenus, *Chronicon Universale* (Muratori, *RRIISS*, xvi), 1184; Dietrich of Niem, *De Scismate* (ed. G. Erler, 1890), 191–2; Leonardo Bruni, *Rerum suo tempore gestarum Commentarius* (Muratori, *RRIISS*, xix, pt. 3), 434 f.; I. Giorgi, 'Relazione di Saba Giaffri Notajo di Trastevere', in *ASR*, v (1882); H. Finke, 'Eine Papstchronik des XV Jahrhunderts', *RQ*, iv (1890), 351–2; N. Valois, *La France et le Grand Schisme d'Occident*, iii, 407–8.

[4] *De Scismate*, 305; the remark is made at a rather later point in the narrative than this. Cf. Pietro dello Schiavo, *Diarium*, 28. Orsini possessed a considerable state; for his seizure of Toscanella see the *Cronica volgare di Anonimo fiorentino* (Muratori, *RRIISS*, xxvii, pt. 2), 369–60.

In August 1406 Ladislas made peace, receiving the whole province of Campania and Maritima in vicariate, in return for which he promised to pay Innocent 20,000 florins, a formidable bribe.[1]   On 6 November 1406 Innocent VII died, and the election of Gregory XII on 30 November marks a further stage in the disintegration of the Papal State.   The old Correr, ferociously greedy for himself and his family, seemingly indifferent to his spiritual as to his temporal duties, seems to have deliberately hastened the death of the temporal power rather than to have tried to save it.   The gaps in the documents make it difficult to get behind the damning picture drawn of him by the publicists and the fathers at Pisa, but he seems to have behaved with appalling cupidity and weakness.   That he was a party to the attack of the Colonna on Rome on 17 June 1407, as Niem suggests, is not supported by convincing evidence.[2]   Certainly he may claim some sympathy, in that his departure from Rome on 9 August 1407 to go to the conference with Benedict XIII at Savona, led, as he had feared, to the collapse of the temporal power, just as, at a far more favourable moment, the temporal power failed to survive the departure of John XXIII from Bologna for Constance in 1414.   But how far Gregory intended to care for the lands of the Church was shown in the astonishing bull which he addressed to the College of Cardinals at Viterbo on 29 August 1407, asking them to approve the donation of various lands of the Church to his brother and nephews, not under the form of a vicariate, but in fee to his relatives and their heirs.   The lands he intended to donate, Faenza, Forlì and Orvieto, were of such importance as to suggest that he already had neither hope nor intention of keeping the temporal power in being.[3]

In the March of Ancona the dismemberment of Gregory's state began even before he left Rome.   Ludovico Migliorati, Rector of the March for his uncle Innocent VII, and then for a short time for Gregory XII, had made himself tyrant of Fermo, and intended to carve for himself as large a state as he could hold.   He seized the rich and important town of Ascoli Piceno, which commands the entrance to the March from the Abruzzi, and was threatened by the new Rector, the Bishop of Montefeltro, allied with Braccio da Montone and a coalition of towns of the central March. Migliorati's natural protector was Ladislas, to whom by August 1407 he had trans-

---

[1] Reg. Vat. 335, fols. 204v–205 (16 August 1406). Leonardus etc., venerabilibus viris dominis Nicolao de Ursinis de Urbe, priori domus hospitalis sancti Johannis Ierorosolimitani de Venetiis Castellan' diocesis, ac eiusdem hospitalis magisterii locumtenenti, et Simoni de Novaria apostolice camere clerico, salutem in domino. Cum illustrissimus princeps dominus Ladizlaus Jerusalem et Sicilie rex pro necessitatibus apostolice camere et oneribus facilius supportandis ad requisicionem dicti domini nostri pape vigintimilia florenorum auri de camera liberaliter mutuare disponat. Nos de mandato domini nostri pape vive vocis oraculo nobis facto vobis recipiendi a dicto domino rege dictam florenorum summam, et conficiendum eam, recipisse nomine dicte camere, cum pactis condicionibus et clausulis oportunis tenore presentium concedimus facultatem. In quorum etc. Datum Rome etc., anno domini MCCCC sexto, indictione XIIII, die sextadecima mensis Augusti, pontificatus etc. anno secundo. The document originates with the Apostolic Chamberlain.

[2] Gregorovius, vi, pt. 2, 586 f.; Pietro dello Schiavo, 17; Niem, *De Scismate*, 233–4; L. Bruni, *Epistolae*, ii, 47; *Cron. di Anon. fior.*, 363. Valois, iii, 523, rejects Niem's story; Cutolo, ii, 151–2, accepts it, but without proffering fresh evidence.

[3] The bull is in Theiner, iii, no. 103, p. 168. Cf. Niem, *De Scismate*, 238 f. and *Nemus Unionis* (edn. of 1609), iv, cap. 1.

ferred Ascoli.   In return he at once received support from the troops of the Count
of Carrara and Martin of Faenza.[1]   Gregory in consequence instructed the Bishop of
Montefeltro to take the proper measures of defence, and ordered Ladislas to withdraw from Ascoli and Fermo, castigating the rebels who supported him.[2]   Ladislas
was deprived of his vicariate of Campania and Maritima.[3]   Thus, although Gregory
had used the threat of Ladislas as an excuse to ward off his departure from Rome
and his meeting with Benedict XIII,[4] he was, in the autumn of 1407, by no means
the *âme damnée* of the King which he afterwards became.

At the end of April 1408 Ladislas marched on Rome ; Paolo Orsini came immediately to terms with him and made no move to defend the City, and the King
entered Rome in an atmosphere of rejoicing.[5]   On 19 June Ladislas agreed to accept
the *signoria* of Perugia, and thus acquired as a vassal state the richest and most
strategically important city in Umbria.   To the manifest alarm of Florence, to
which he had in April given guarantees to the contrary,[6] Ladislas in the course of
the summer occupied all the lands of the Church in the Patrimony and Umbria, and
threatened Cortona, Arezzo and the approaches to Tuscany.

Gregory was in this period in a piteous position.   His Cardinals had abandoned
him in May, and by the time of the further desertions in September and October it
was evident that the action of Florence and France would lead to an independent
Council.   That he distrusted and feared Ladislas, and knew that the King was
anxious to have him entirely in his hand,[7] that Ladislas was patently indifferent to
the interests of the Church, and had from the beginning opposed every move toward
the meeting with Benedict XIII, could not alter the facts of the distribution of
power.   Ladislas was the only great ruler in Italy who would protect him, and he
must in the end become his creature.   There are indications that matters were
drifting in this direction as early as the spring of 1408, and that in that year, either
before or after the occupation of Rome in April, an agreement or series of agreements
was made by Gregory with Ladislas, which made over to the king the whole or the
greater part of the State of the Church.[8]   The details of these negotiations are

---

[1] See, for these events, P. Compagnoni, *La Reggia Picena* (Macerata, 1661), 281 f. ; *Cronache della
città di Fermo* (ed. de Minicis, 1870), 30 f. ; J. A. Campano, *Braccii Perusini Vita et Gesta* (Muratori,
RRIISS, xix, pt. 4), 29 f. ; F. A. Marcucci, *Saggio delle cose ascolane* (Teramo, 1766), 309 ; Francesco
Adami, *De Rebus in Civitate Firmane gestis*, 65 f. ; *Cron volg. di Anon. fior.*, 361–2, 366 ; Niem, *De Scis-
mate*, 231.   Earlier in 1407 Braccio had assisted Migliorati in the siege of Ascoli, but before the end of
June the Rector of the March had detached him and engaged him in the service of the Church.

[2] Reg. Vat. 336, fol. 118, 149v ; Theiner, iii, nos. 104, 105, p. 169 ; Raynaldus, ad a. 1407, par. xix.

[3] Raynaldus, loc. cit.

[4] Valois, iii, 531 ; Raynaldus, ad a. 1408, par. v, 'concurrentibus periculis et immutatis conditionibus
verisimiliter . . . ex traditione urbis per dilectos filios Romanos charissimo in Christo filio Ladislao regi
Siciliae illustri facta . . .' and par. x, 'emersis novis casibus, videlicet de occupatione urbis Romae
attentata per Petrum de Luna et suos sequaces ac traditione ejusdem Romanae urbis per Romanos facta
Regi Ladislao illustri.'   See also J. Vincke, *Schriftstücke zum Pisaner Konzil* (1942), 47–9, 85, 103.

[5] Gregorovius, vi, pt. 2, 595 ; Niem, *De Scismate*, 272–4 ; Pietro dello Schiavo, 27 f.

[6] J. Salviati, 'Cronica, o memorie', in *Delizie degli eruditi Toscani*, xviii, 290, 362 f.

[7] *Commissioni di Rinaldo degli Albizzi*, i, 161, 'comprendiamo che lo Re lo (*scil.*, Gregorio) vorebbe
nelle suo' forze.   Ecostui (Gregorio) non si fida di lui ma non glile vuol dire' (report of 30 June 1408).

[8] See endnote at foot of this chapter.

obscure, but there is no doubt that Gregory's independence of action was progressively sapped during the critical months preceding the Council of Pisa, and that by the end of the Council in August 1409 he had become Ladislas' merest puppet.

Ladislas exercised a virtually despotic power in the Papal State. In October 1409 he permitted Gregory, who had formerly assigned the tallage of the March of Ancona to him, to re-assign them to Ludovico Migliorati for the payment of his *condotta*.[1] In the Patrimony, Marco Correr acted as papal Rector only under Ladislas' protection.[2] In Campania and Maritima, in Orte, Rieti, Amelia, Ladislas appointed his own officials and ruled as *signore*.[3] In Perugia, which remained faithful to him until his death, Ladislas appointed a Viceroy, and although he conceded the city liberal powers of self-government in many matters, the city became for practical purposes a part of his kingdom.[4] The loyalty of the city was only increased by the constant depredations and threats of Braccio da Montone and the exiles.

§ 2.   From this point the only hope of the temporal power was in the Legate in Bologna, Baldassare Cossa. Cossa had from the beginning of his legation proved himself an administrator of energy and ability. He was largely responsible for the recovery of Bologna from the Visconti in 1403, and in October 1404 he succeeded in seizing Faenza from the Manfredi. Confirmed as Legate by Innocent VII, he carried out energetic war against the rebellious *condottieri* and tyrants of the Romagna. By 1408, when the rest of the Papal State was in dissolution, Cossa had made Romagna and the papal lands in Emilia into a strongly defended unit. Cossa showed equal energy in moving against Ladislas. In May 1408 he formed a league against the King with Florence,[5] who was well aware of the danger she stood in; the Legate at once supplied the city with 300 lances. Florence for the succeeding seven months moved unsteadily and unhappily, unwilling to make war on Naples, but justly frightened of the consequences if she failed to resist. Ladislas' understanding with Paolo Guinigi the *signore* of Lucca gave her additional cause for fear. But from January 1409, when Florence adhered to the Council of Pisa, war was inevitable. On 2 April 1409 Ladislas left Rome for Orvieto, and then for Siena, which narrowly escaped a formal siege. Continuing through Tuscany, he was met by a powerful force of mercenaries : Braccio da Montone, Pandolfo Malatesta of Pesaro, Bartolomeo Gonzaga, Francesco of Prato. He had one striking success, the capture of Cortona, but was halted near Arezzo in the early summer, and had to retire to the Abruzzi. The ablest captain in the Florentine league was Braccio, who in the districts of Spoleto and Todi commanded a very effective pocket of resistance, and who kept up

---

[1] Raynaldus, ad a. 1409, par. lxxxvii.

[2] L. Fumi, *Codice diplomatico della città di Orvieto*, 615–6; Niccola della Tuscia, *Cronache*, in *Cronache e Statuti della città di Viterbo* (ed. Ciampi), 48; L. Pinzi, *Storia di Viterbo*, iii, 494–5.

[3] Gregorovius, vi, pt. 2, 603 n.; A. Borgia, *Istoria della chiesa e città di Velletri*, 342.

[4] Pellini, *Dell'Historia di Perugia*, ii, 168–9; Cutolo, i, 312–13, ii, 156; 'Regesto e documenti di storia Perugina' in *ASI*, 1st ser., xvi, pt. 2 (1851), 571, letter of 23 April 1408.

[5] It was announced in Bologna on 6 June, *Corpus Chronicorum Bononiensium* (Muratori, *RRIISS*, xviii, pt. 1, vol. 2 of text, 526); cf. *Chron. volgare di Anon. fior.*, 374, and J. Salviati, *Cronica*, 300.

a fearsome harrying of the *contado* of Perugia.[1]   At the same time the Legate Cossa in the Romagna not only repulsed the forces of Alberigo da Barbiano, who had marched north against him with Neapolitan assistance, but with the help of the Este and Carlo Malatesta counter-attacked, and on 16 May had Cotignola and Barbiano, the last strongholds of the Counts of Cunio in Romagna.[2]   In the March of Ancona the peace ratified in Macerata on 7 February 1408 endured only a few months. Braccio returned there before the June of that year and attacked Cingoli.[3]   Migliorati in December 1408 abandoned Ladislas and adhered to the Council of Pisa, but left Ascoli in the King's hands.[4]

The success of the league against Ladislas probably reached its highest point with the Angevin intervention of the autumn and winter of 1409–1410.   Between September and November of 1409 the Angevin army cleared almost the whole of Umbria and the Patrimony of Ladislas' troops, save for the forces of Perugia and of the Prefect of Vico.   The army on the right bank of the Tiber at Rome succeeded on New Year's Day 1410 in forcing a way into the City and capturing it.   But the league was never a very healthy body; the Florentines bore their contribution most unwillingly, and were always on the lookout for a separate peace, and Louis of Anjou was an unequal commander, who seems to have seen war as a series of single battles without political or strategic connexion, which, once fought, left him only with the duty of celebrating his victories in church.   The main army had withdrawn from Rome in November for lack of money and supplies, and it was by treason within Rome, and not by generalship, that Malatesta and Orsini managed to take the city.[5]

The worst fortune which the league had was the revolt of Genoa against Boucicault in September 1409, and the subsequent alliance of the city with Ladislas. This led on the night of 16 May 1410 to the utter destruction of the Angevin relief fleet off Pisa by a Neapolitan and Genovese force, with the loss of great quantities of men, arms and treasure.   This fleet, raised with immense toil in France, was the last effort of the Angevins before they were overtaken by bankruptcy and civil war, and its defeat left Louis of Anjou little hope of victory in Italy.[6]   Florence sent him an embassy of condolence, while at the same time another of her embassies went to negotiate with Ladislas.   The league also experienced a number of checks in Romagna; in January 1410 Giorgio Ordelaffi occupied Forlimpopoli and narrowly missed in an attempt to occupy Forlì.[7]   In June Gian-Galeazzo Manfredi took Faenza, although two months later he agreed to hold it as a vicariate from the

[1] Campano, *Vita Braccii*, 40–2; Gregorovius, vi, pt. 2, 603 f.; *Cronaca Sanese* (Muratori, *RRIISS*, xv, pt. 6), 764; *Annales Estenses* (Muratori, *RRIISS*, xviii), 1083–4.

[2] *Corp. Chron. Bonon.*, 527, 531; Griffoni, 97; *Cronaca Bolognese di Piero di Mattiolo* (ed. C. Ricci, 1883), 204; C. Ghirardacci, *Della historia di Bologna*, ii, 578; *Annales Estenses*, 1083.   The unexpected death of Alberigo da Barbiano on 26 April made this victory easier.

[3] Campano, *Vita Braccii*, 33–4.

[4] *Cron. della città di Fermo*, 35–6; P. Compagnoni, *La Reggia Picena*, 284–5.

[5] For the campaign of 1409/10, see Gregorovius, vi, pt. 2, 608; Pietro dello Schiavo, 44–5; Valois, iv, 123–6; Niem, *De Scismate*, 323; Campano, *Vita Braccii*, 44.

[6] Valois, iv, 127–35.

[7] Hieronymus de Forlivio, *Chronicon* (Muratori, *RRIISS*, xix, pt. 5), 14; *Annales Forolivienses*, 83; *Corp. Chron. Bonon.*, 533–4; Matteo Griffoni, 97–8.

Pope.[1] In July Ladislas wrote jubilantly to the Palatine Count Ludwig, relating the sea victory, and holding out hopes of an imminent victory against Bologna of his troops under the Count of Urbino in Romagna.[2] But this victory did not in fact follow.   Florence, despite her wish for peace and the mediation of Venice, failed to reach acceptable terms with Ladislas, and when Cossa, the Legate of Romagna, was elected to the Papacy as John XXIII in May 1410, she despatched an embassy to offer to continue the war.[3]

In the March of Ancona the fortunes of the league were variable.   In January 1410 the Bishop of Luni and Sarzana, who had arrived in October 1409 as Rector for Alexander V, accepted the submission of Macerata and of Ludovico Migliorati to the Pope of the Council.[4] Later in the year Migliorati went over to Gregory XII, only to return once more to John XXIII's obedience in May 1411.[5] In Umbria the mercenaries Braccio, Paolo Orsini and Muzio Attendolo Sforza waged a war of attrition against Perugia, and forced the city into serious straits of finance and supply.[6] In Campania the Orsini had much success against the Neapolitan faction; in January 1410 the Savelli, in June the Conti, and in July the Colonna were reduced to obedience.[7]

But without a decisive victory for one side or the other these successes turned only to the advantage of the mercenaries and barons who obtained them.   Both John XXIII and Gregory XII made enormous assignments of tallage and *census* in their lands to pay mercenaries, so that few parts of their temporal income can have been even in theory due to be paid directly to the Church.[8] And the assignments of

---

[1] *Corp. Chron. Bonon.*, 534, 536; Matteo Griffoni, 98–9. Cf. Reg. Vat. 342, fol. 19, where the Pope orders Giovan Galeazzo Manfredi not to enter into alliances with any spiritual or temporal powers without his licence (1 August 1410).

[2] H. Finke, *Acta Concilii Constanciensis*, iv, no. 498, p. 639.

[3] Cutolo, i, 352–8.

[4] P. Compagnoni, *La Reggia Picena*, 285–6; *Cronache della città di Fermo*, 38; Niem, *De Scismate*, 231; Cutolo, ii, 185–6.

[5] Migliorati's *condotta* from Gregory XII in Reg. Vat. 335, fol. 184v (16 November 1410).   His appointment by John XXIII as Rector of the March, Reg. Vat. 341, fol. 27v (1 May 1411).

[6] Campano, *Vita Braccii*, 47 f.; Cutolo, i, 377; Pellini, *Dell'Historia di Perugia*, ii, 177 f.; A. Fabretti, *Documenti di Storia Perugina*, ii, 68, printing the text of an extraordinary taxation.

[7] Theiner, iii, no. 114, p. 176; Reg. Vat. 340, fol. 30; Reg. Vat. 342, fol. 100v, Francesco the Abbot of S. Martino al Cimino of Viterbo is commissioned to receive Giovanni and Nicola Colonna into obedience, and to rent them the possessions of certain monasteries.

[8] The tallage of whole provinces was assigned to Paolo Orsini for the payment of his *condotta*, e.g. Theiner, iii, no. 87, p. 151; ibid. nos. 100, 101, pp. 160, 165. On 25 September 1410 John XXIII assigned most of the temporal revenues outside Bologna and the March to Paolo Orsini, 'super satisfactione stipendii ac provisionis huiusmodi, omnes et singulos fructus redditus et proventus ac emolumenta quecunque ad nos et prefatam ecclesiam spectantes et pertinentes, ac pertinencia et spectancia apostolicamque cameram . . . ex urbe Romana, necnon provinciis Campanie, Maritime, Patrimonii Beati Petri in Tuscia, Sabine, Spoletan' ducatus, civitatum et terrarum specialis commissionis et Arnulphorum, tam debitos quam debendos, etiam ratione tallearum aut subsidiorum . . . usque ad integram satisfactionem stipendiorum et provisionum . . . damus concedimus et assignamus' (Reg. Vat. 342, fol. 48v). This assignment was made when the lands were barely out of the hands of Ladislas; when matters improved it was cancelled (Theiner, iii, no. 122, p. 183, and Reg. Vat. 342, fol. 244, which cancels assignments in Campania and Maritima, 8 May 1411). A year later, on 17 April 1412, Paolo Orsini was authorised by John XXIII to collect tallage in the Patrimony up to the sum of 12,207 florins (Reg. Vat. 344, fols. 5v, 46v). John XXIII also authorised Braccio da Montone, on 2 August 1412,

tallage were taken by the mercenaries as authority to collect from individual towns, and, where payment was refused, to use force. It was in this way that Braccio da Montone seized Iesi from the Church in March 1408, 'sotto colore de' taglie, che devia havere dalla Ecclesia.' [1]

The last Angevin victory was the quite unexpected one at Roccasecca on 19 May 1411. But Louis of Anjou was unwilling or unable to pursue the beaten Ladislas to his camp; leaving the enemy to re-form as they saw fit he returned to Rome, and embarked for Provence on 3 August.[2] This withdrawal had the most important consequences; Florence was unequal to protecting the Pope in Bologna on her own account, and, now that France was about to fall into a savage civil war, the only possible protector for John XXIII was Sigismond of Hungary. The death of Rupert von der Pfalz on 18 May 1410 had enabled John to recognise Sigismond as King-elect of the Romans,[3] and the swing toward Sigismond became more pronounced as the Pope's political position in Italy continued to weaken. In January 1411 Carlo Malatesta of Rimini, who a year before had been willing to negotiate with John XXIII over possible solutions of the Schism, was known to be entering the service of Ladislas.[4] In April he was devastating the countryside round Bologna, and assisting the insurrectionary movements against John XXIII in the Romagna.[5] On 11 May 1411 Bologna itself revolted, and declared for a popular government; the papal governor was seized and expelled, 'lui tremando più che foglia a vento'; the papal castle, after holding out for a few weeks, submitted and was destroyed.[6]

The defection of Florence, and her separate peace with Ladislas at the price of his

---

to collect 20,000 florins from the *census*, *affitti* and *decime* of the March of Ancona (Reg. Vat. 344, fol. 142v). The largest assignments of this kind were probably those of the peace of San Felice.

The Gregorian observance made similar assignments, e.g. Carlo Malatesta, as Governor of Romagna, was authorised to impose a tallage of 20,000 florins to pay his own *condotta* (Cutolo, ii, 198). Gregory also assigned the tallage of the March, first to Ladislas and then to Migliorati (Raynaldus, ad a. 1409, par. lxxxvii). When Migliorati returned to the Pisan obedience in May 1411 John XXIII made him Rector of the March for his lifetime, and made over to him the entire revenues of the province, in settlement of his *condotta* of 500 lances and 100 foot (Reg. Vat. 341, fols. 27v, 33).

[1] Fragmentary chronicle printed by A. Fabretti, *Note e Documenti* to *Le biografie dei capitani venturieri dell'Umbria* (1842), 88. The passage quoted is also in G. Baldassini, *Memorie istoriche dell'antichissima e regia città di Jesi* (1764), 119. It was, of course, the practice of Braccio and other mercenaries to use the claims of reprisals for tallage unpaid, as an excuse for every sort of brigandage.

[2] Gregorovius, vi, pt. 2, 616–7; Valois, iv, 138–40; Pietro dello Schiavo, 67–9.

[3] E. Goeller, *König Sigismunds Kirchenpolitik* (1902), 76. In May 1410 Sigismond's ambassadors were with John XXIII in Italy.

[4] Finke, *Acta*, i, 5, and no. 2, p. 24. Malatesta conferred with Cossa about the Schism when the latter was Cardinal Legate, on 25 September 1405. The conference included the Venetians, the Este, and other *signori* of the Romagna (*Corp. Chron. Bonon.*, 528–9). For negotiations after Cossa's election to the Papacy, Martène and Durand, *Thesaurus novorum anecdotorum*, vii, 1171 f., and Finke, *Acta*, i, 4–5.

[5] Finke, *Acta*, i, 6; he assures Bologna that his warlike acts are directed against the Pope and not against the city, 16 April.

[6] *Corp. Chron. Bonon.*, 537–8; Matteo Griffoni, 98–9; Piero di Mattiolo, 228–9, 233. Malatesta continued to attack Bologna after the revolution (Piero di Mattiolo, 235–6, Finke, *Acta*, i, no. 3, p. 24–5) and was not reconciled to the new government until 30 May, when he was paid 30,000 lib. bonon. to accept peace (*Corpus Chron. Bonon.*, 539; Hieronymous de Forlivio, 19).

cession of Cortona, had already occurred at the beginning of 1411.[1] During the following year the Florentines used all their diplomatic resources to obtain a reconciliation between Ladislas and the Pope, hoping to save enough of the Papal State to preserve it as a barrier between Ladislas and Tuscany. But they had little success; John XXIII not only continued to support Louis of Anjou, but on 9 September 1411 excommunicated and deposed Ladislas.[2] In November 1411 the papal envoy Bertoldo Orsini was in Venice, attempting to mediate in the war between Sigismond and the Republic which had followed the Venetian purchase of Zara from Ladislas in 1409, and also trying to secure Venetian approval for the expedition of Sigismond to Italy.[3] Carlo Malatesta received submissions to Gregory XII from towns in the March of Ancona.[4] The Prefect of Vico organised a formidable rebellion in the Patrimony, where the rule of John XXIII was said to be in collapse.[5]

In Umbria, however, the rule of John XXIII was far from collapse.[6] In January 1412 John sent the Cardinal de Challant to win over the Count of Montefeltro, and on 27 May 1412 the Count signed a treaty with the Pope, deserted his former employer Ladislas, and agreed to accept a papal *condotta* for 400 lances and 200 foot.[7] In return he was made various territorial concessions, and it was promised that he would not be required to make war on his ally Carlo Malatesta. Sigismond also wrote to Montefeltro urging him to submit to John XXIII, but, characteristically, his letters do not appear to have arrived in Italy until the *condotta* was already signed.[8]

Perhaps intimidated by the loss of this important mercenary, Ladislas now showed himself willing to make peace. On 17 June 1412 peace was signed at San Felice; the King agreed to perform a *volte face*, and repudiated Gregory in favour of his rival, while in turn the Pope abandoned both the Angevins and Sigismond, promising not to invite the latter into Italy to be crowned.[9] The territorial gains of Ladislas were considerable, but not, perhaps, considering his military advantages, more than he could have expected. They were Perugia, Terracina, Ceprano, Ascoli, Benevento and San Felice, all in various forms of vicariate. But Dietrich of Niem

---

[1] *Capitoli del Comune di Firenze*, ii (1893), 145 f.

[2] Cutolo, i, 377–8; Reg. Vat. 341, fols. 117, 135.

[3] Goeller, *König Sigismunds Kirchenpolitik*, 93 f.; Finke, *Acta*, i, no. 23, p. 98; Otto Schiff, *König Sigismunds italienische Politik bis zur Romfahrt* (1909), 5, 12–13; H. Heere, 'Die Beziehungen König Sigmunds zu Italien, vom Herbst 1412 bis zu Herbst 1414', *QF*, iv (1901), 2.

[4] P. Compagnoni, *La Reggia Picena*, 288–9; cf. Cutolo, ii, 198.

[5] Valois, iv, 143–4, quoting a Venetian report.

[6] Terni submitted to Cardinal Oddo Colonna in May 1411 (Reg. Vat. 343, fol. 31), and the important *signore* Ugolini Trinci of Foligno was reconciled to the Holy See in July 1411 (Reg. Vat. 341, fol. 182).

[7] Theiner, iii, no. 128, p. 187, and Cod. Vat. Barb. lat. 2668, fol. 46. The actual *condotta*, dated 23 July 1412, is in Barb. lat. 2668, fol. 40. The treaty was guaranteed on behalf of the Pope by the College of Cardinals, Theiner, iii, no. 130, p. 198.

[8] Sigismond's letters to the Count of Montefeltro and John XXIII were carried by John Usk, Bishop of the Five Churches in Hungary, and are printed by Finke, *Acta*, i, nos. 25–6, pp. 101–2, with the conjectural date 'vor Mai'. As Usk did not arrive at the papal court until August, when John XXIII wrote to the Count of Montefeltro to announce his arrival (Theiner, iii, no. 131, p. 199), August, rather than May, seems a more probable terminal date for Sigismond's letters.

[9] The peace is printed by P. Fedele, *ASPN*, xxx (1905). Ladislas' proclamation of his defection from Gregory XII is in Raynaldus, ad a., par. ii.

may be right in saying that Ladislas was corrupted by money to make this peace.[1] To the King himself, under the form of a *condotta* for 1,500 men, the Pope promised to pay 68,000 florins a year out of various named forms of income. For the *condotta* of Sforza John promised to pay 120,000 florins, and to give Todi, Frosinone, Torrice, Montefiascone and Città Castellana to a Florentine commission as security for their payment.

How far John XXIII can ever have intended to carry out these immense payments is not clear. That he did not in fact pay much more than the initial deposits is made probable by the claims for 200,000 florins which Ladislas was making through Florence in March 1413.[2] Perhaps the most cogent reason for non-payment was that many of the revenues assigned as payment existed only on paper; in times as turbulent as these the tallage of the March of Ancona and elsewhere was almost impossible to collect. Relations between the Pope and Naples never seem to have taken on any real cordiality, and Sigismond writes early in 1413 urging that the new quarrel between the Pope and Ladislas be settled.[3] The grounds of the break were probably financial: on Ladislas' side, the default of payments due under the treaty, and the imposition of a tariff barrier against Neapolitan wine coming into Rome, and on John's side, dissatisfaction with his share of spiritual revenues and nominations to benefices in the newly acquired Neapolitan obedience.[4] No doubt Ladislas was also perturbed by the success of the peace negotiations between Venice and Sigismond, which went on in Dalmatia from November 1412, with the assistance of the papal envoys, the Legate Branda and Bertoldo Orsini.[5] Nor can the proclamation in Rome on 11 March 1413 of an impending Council have increased Ladislas' confidence in the Pope, revealing as it did the increasing influence of Sigismond.[6]

After the peace of San Felice John XXIII continued with the pacification of the Papal States. On 14 August 1412 the popular government of Bologna was turned out by a revolution, instigated in great part by the lawyer, Jacopo Isolani. He then engineered the return of the city to the obedience of the Church, which followed on 26 September.[7] Malatesta's troops were driven from the important strongpoint of S. Giovanni in Persiceto, and in the winter and spring of 1412/1413 a long row of imprisonments and executions were ordered in Romagna for conspiracy with him.[8] In Campania and Maritima papal authority was re-asserted,[9] in the March the

---

[1] *De vita et factis Constanciensibus Johannis Papae XXIII*, in von der Hardt, *Rerum concilii oecumenici Constanciensis*, ii, pt. 15, 367–8.

[2] Heere, 23. The initial deposits were in fact paid. On 18 February 1413 Giovanni dei Medici and Ylarione dei Bardi were given a quittance for 35,000 florins paid by them to Ladislas on John XXIII's behalf (Reg. Vat. 341, fol. 301).

[3] Finke, *Acta*, i, no. 28, pp. 103–5.

[4] See Dietrich of Niem, *Vita Johannis*, in Von der Hardt, ii, 374–6.

[5] Heere, 10–14; Goeller, 95.

[6] Raynaldus, ad a., par. xvi. The break must have been after mid-December 1412, as on 6 and 12 December Ladislas' representatives swore allegiance to the Pope on behalf of the king for the new vicariates and the kingdom of Sicily (Barb. lat., 2668, fols. 97v, 100v).

[7] *Corp. Chron. Bonon.*, 537–42; Matteo Griffoni, 100; Piero di Mattiolo, 242, 244.

[8] *Corp. Chron. Bonon.*, 544–6; Matteo Griffoni, 101; Piero di Mattiolo, 251.

[9] The absolution of Torrice in Theiner, iii, no. 135, p. 203; a privilege for Velletri, ibid. no. 133, p. 202.

C

machinery of administration was re-imposed after Ludovico Migliorati had returned to the Pisan obedience in July 1412.[1] In the Patrimony the eternally rebellious Giovanni di Vico, the Prefect of Rome, came to terms with the Pope on 21 January 1413.[2]

What seemed to be the last agony of the Papal State began early in 1413. At the end of February Paolo Orsini was sent to the March with a strong force to support his brother, who arrived in March 1413 as Cardinal Legate. But Orsini, by an error which was to cost John XXIII Rome, allowed himself in May to be boxed up in Rocca Contrata by Muzio Attendolo Sforza. Sforza was joined by Malatesta of Cesena and the Count of Carrara, and this imprisonment of his main force meant that when Ladislas, at the end of May, moved against Rome, the Pope's people there were unable to offer more than a token resistance.[3] There was again a total collapse of papal rule in the Patrimony and Umbria, where only Todi, Orvieto and Spoleto remained as effective centres of resistance, and Ladislas' troops penetrated as far as the boundaries of Siena, while the Vicar-General in the Patrimony, Cardinal Oddo Colonna, the future Martin V, fled hurriedly from Viterbo at the same moment that the Pope was leaving Rome.[4] John XXIII sought a precarious refuge in the suburbs of Florence; the city was too cautious to admit him, and his requests for an alliance were at first ineffective. But in July he managed to rally Florence to the point of guaranteeing the payment of the *condotta* of the Count of Montefeltro, whom the Pope engaged in that month.[5] Montefeltro prepared for war,[6] and Braccio relieved Paolo Orsini in Rocca Contrata; the latter pair resumed the war in Umbria until the end of the year, when Orsini deserted to Ladislas. In the March, Macerata found itself without a protector, and submitted for a time to Rodolfo Varano of Camerino as

[1] Compagnoni, 290. His *condotta* for 200 lances in papal service dated 14 September 1412 is in Cod. Vat. Barb. lat. 2668, fol. 49. Recanati was pardoned for rebellion on 1 September 1412, and Antonio, Prior of the Hospital of St. John of Jerusalem in Rome, was at this time appointed as *reformator* in the March (Theiner, iii, no. 132, p. 199). Norcia, on the borders of Spoleto and the March, submitted in November 1412 (Reg. Vat. 344, fol. 223 v).

[2] He is pardoned for rebellion and granted the vicariate of Orcla, Barb. lat. 2668, fol. 103v. Todi submitted in December 1412, Reg. Vat. 341, fol. 260.

[3] Gregorovius, vi, pt. 2, 627 f. For Paolo Orsini's failure in the March see P. Compagnoni, *La Reggia Picena*, 292–4; Campano, *Vita Braccii*, 67–8 and n.; Antonio Minuti, *Vita di Muzio Attendolo Sforza*, ed. G. B. Lambertenghi, in *Miscellanea di storia italiana edita per cura della Regia Deputazione di Storia Patria*, vii (Turin, 1869), 169; *Cronache della città di Fermo*, 39–40.

[4] R. Valentini, 'Braccio da Montone e il Comune di Orvieto', *BSU*, xxv (1922), 79. Cardinal Oddo Colonna was the Vicar-General, and not the Rector of the Patrimony. The latter position was held by John XXIII's brother, Michele Cossa, who was appointed *reformator* in the Patrimony in January 1412 (Reg. Vat. 343, fol. 206), and is thereafter variously addressed as Rector (Reg. Vat. 344, fol. 179v) or Governor (ibid. fol. 264). Oddo Colonna had been appointed Vicar-General in Perugia (which was in fact of the obedience of Ladislas), Todi, Orvieto and the rest of Umbria, in February 1411 (Reg. Vat. 341, fol. 55). After the flight of John XXIII from Rome in 1413 he seems to have been appointed Legate in Rome and the Patrimony (Reg. Vat. 345, fol. 180v, 12 June 1413).

[5] Florentine caution is fully illustrated in the instruction to their envoys dated 16 June (Finke, *Acta*, i, 171 n.) and the formal alliance which the Pope asked Montefeltro to conclude with Florence and Siena (Theiner, iii, no. 140, p. 206, 19 June 1413) does not appear to have been reached. The eventual compromise seems to have been that the Count become *raccomandato* to Florence (*Capitoli del Comune di Firenze*, i [1866], p. 545, 14 July 1413) and that Florence guarantee the payment of his salary. His *condotta* dated 7 July 1413, is in Theiner, iii, no. 142, p. 206.

[6] Cf. A. Pellegrini, 'Gubbio sotto i Conti e Duchi di Urbino', *BSU*, xi (1905), 173–4.

signore; Ludovico Migliorati achieved yet another *volte face*, and accepted a *condotta* from Ladislas in January 1414.[1]

Beside this display of armed force, Sigismond's action on behalf of John XXIII seems mere threats and diplomatic *pourparlers*. After the failure of Pippo degli Scholari at Motta in August 1412, when the Venetian captain, Carlo Malatesta, defeated him sharply, and a second failure in the March of Treviso in January 1413, Sigismond was willing to make a temporary peace with Venice, and to concede her the lands in Dalmatia as an imperial vicariate. The peace negotiations in Trieste ended in the signature of a five years truce, made at Aquileja on 25 March 1413 and confirmed in Venice on 4 April.[2] At this point it seemed that the war in Italy would be not only against Ladislas, but also against Filippo Maria Visconti, who, having been refused the concession of the Duchy, had swung round to Ladislas, and had also formed an alliance with Carlo Malatesta, Genoa, and the Este of Ferrara (although the Pope and the Florentines managed to detach the Este from this league by 26 September 1413).[3] Sigismond in the summer of 1413 left Feltre for Germany, to raise money and troops for the approaching war.[4] But he achieved little; Bertoldo Orsini was despatched to Italy with some military aid, but the main forces which Sigismond was trying to obtain in Austria, Switzerland and Germany (besides the fleet which he hoped to borrow from Henry V of England) never appeared in Italy.[5]

In October 1413 Filippo Maria Visconti, evidently intimidated by the preparations against him, submitted to Sigismond as an imperial vicar, and agreed to support him against 'rebels', by whom was intended their common enemy, Pandolfo Malatesta of Brescia. Visconti took the oath of obedience to Sigismond between the hands of Cardinal Zabarella in November 1413.[6] At the conferences at Lodi, where the Pope and the Emperor arrived at the end of November, there is no doubt that resistance to Ladislas was discussed, as well as the forthcoming Council. The meeting was in the nature of an Italian conference: Florence, Genoa, Venice and probably other states were represented there, and if Buonamente Aliprando is to be believed, there was discussion of a league between Florence, Genoa, Sigismond, Venice and the Pope.[7] Certainly such a proposal would fit well with the instructions given to the Florentine envoys on 14 October 1413.[8] But evidently the project broke down, and soon after the congress Sigismond's Italian policy disintegrated.

---

[1] Compagnoni, 294 f.; *Cronache della città di Fermo*, 41.

[2] Schiff, 20, 25, 29–31; Heere, 16, 18; Goeller, 95; F. Cusin, *Il confine orientale d'Italia*, i, 293.

[3] Tonini, *Storia civile e sacra Riminese*, v, 46. Cf. R. Archivio di Stato in Lucca, *Regesti*, iii, pt. 2, no. 23, p. 5.

[4] Schiff, 38–42; Heere, 24–9.

[5] Finke, *Acta*, i, no. 29, p. 105, and no. 30, p. 106. The troops assembled on the borders of Milanese territory, Schiff, 42. John XXIII later made an independent appeal to England, Raynaldus, ad a. 1414, par. v.

[6] Finke, *Forschungen und Quellen zur Geschichte des Konstanzer Konzils* (1889), no. 8, p. 311; Schiff, 42 f.; Finke, *Acta*, i, no. 47, p. 246.

[7] In *Cronica* (Muratori, *Antiquitates Italicae Medii Aevi*, v), 1239. See also Schiff, 50–52; Heere, 29 f.; Finke, *Acta*, i, 178–9 and no. 49, p. 248.

[8] Finke, *Acta*, i, 178.

In March 1414 Milan and Venice concluded an alliance directed against him,[1] and in April Visconti reached an agreement with Ladislas which probably provided for a Milanese attack on Bologna.[2]

Thus Sigismond had effected neither the defence of John XXIII, nor the assertion of his imperial rights against Venice and Milan. When Cardinal Zabarella met Sigismond at Pontestura in the spring of 1414, no military aid on a large scale had yet been found against Ladislas. Florence, although well aware of her own danger, was in despair at the failure to form an effective alliance against the King, and at the harm which Neapolitan sanctions were working on her commerce. The renewed activity of Ladislas' army, which had led to the despatch of Zabarella to ask for aid,[3] caused a clerical panic in Bologna when Ladislas advanced into Umbria in May 1414. Cardinals and curialists sent their goods out of the city, and the alarmed Sigismond wrote to ask for denial of the rumours that the Pope was preparing to fly to Ferrara.[4] On 5 May 1414 Orvieto, despairing of reinforcements from either John XXIII or Florence, capitulated to Ladislas.[5] At this point only Spoleto, Todi, Trevi and Foligno continued to hold out in Umbria for the Pope. In the south of the March of Ancona his cause was lost; in Romagna he had to face the constant threat of a Malatesta attack on Bologna, although the Alidosi of Imola remained in his pay.[6] On 6 March 1414 Ladislas was reported as sending a fleet against Pisa, and a full scale attack against Tuscany seemed imminent.[7]

On 22 June 1414 Florence, although profoundly divided as to her right course between John and Ladislas, signed peace with the King.[8] Room was left in the peace for the Pope, and Bologna was reserved to him, but little else. In the peace between Florence and Ladislas the temporal power of the Papacy is treated as dead. Rome, the provinces of Campania and Maritima and of the Patrimony of St. Peter in Tuscia, Terni, Colle Scipione, Amelia, Orvieto, Perugia, Ascoli Piceno, are all referred to as though the property of Ladislas. It was hard even to save Bologna from him; the Florentines claimed to John XXIII, while they were urging him to accept the peace, 'che per salvare Bologna abbiamo consentite dell'altre cose a noi non grate'.[9] The Pope refused to accept the peace as long as Ladislas detained the temporalities of the Church. But the Papal State seemed doomed.

It was now, with the conquest of Bologna, of Tuscany, perhaps of Italy in sight,

---

[1] Schiff, 52–3; Heere, 37–8.

[2] Schiff, 53; Romano, 'Contributi alla storia della ricostituzione del Ducato Milanese sotto F. M. Visconti', ASL, 3rd ser., vi (1896), 280–1.

[3] Heere, 40.

[4] Finke, Acta, i, no. 54, p. 255; cf. Niem, Vita Johannis, in Von der Hardt, ii, 385–8.

[5] Valentini, in BSU, xxv (1922), 106–7.

[6] He gave the rose to Alidosi in early 1414, Corp. Chron. Bonon., 548; Matteo Griffoni, 102.

[7] Finke, Acta, iv, no. 455, p. 443.

[8] Commissioni, i, 238; Finke, Acta, i, 181; Heere, 45; Schiff, 56; Buoninsegni, Storie della città di Firenze (1637), 7. The peace is printed by Cutolo, ii, 218 f., but the text he gives is rather indifferent, e.g. 'interapuensis' for 'interapnensis' or 'interamnensis', 255.

[9] Finke, Acta, i, no. 55, p. 256, instructions to envoys to John XXIII, dated 7 July 1414, and no. 56, p. 258, where in August it is reported to the Aragonese that John still refuses to come to terms with Ladislas. Cf. Heere, 45–6 n.

that Ladislas was overtaken by his last illness. On 15 July he was dying, and at the beginning of August he died in Naples. The scene was immediately and drastically changed. In Rome and all over Umbria and the Patrimony there was a revolt against Neapolitan rule. John XXIII saw that here at the last moment was an opportunity to escape from the clutches of Sigismond and the conciliar party, and immediately attempted to form a league with Florence and Venice, so that the ultramontanes should not enter Italy—a league which would have meant the avoidance of the Council in its agreed form and place.[1] Sigismond, it was known, would try to use his hold over the Pope in order to make an expedition into Italy to be crowned, and the assertion of Imperial rights in Venezia and Lombardy which was likely to accompany such an expedition was extremely distasteful to the Italian powers, particularly to Venice.

To the Cardinals John XXIII protested that rather than go to the Council he wished first to return to Rome and recover the State of the Church.[2] Dietrich of Niem admits that such a return would have enabled John to recover the provinces and govern them 'cum maximo eius emolumento'.[3] But the Cardinals demanded that he act personally at the Council, and through Legates in the temporalities. Compelled to accept their advice, John set about appointing Legates and mercenaries for the defence and recovery of the Papal State. On 9 September 1414 he appointed Cardinal Jacopo Isolani as Legate in spirituals and temporals in Rome, Campania and Maritima, the Patrimony, Perugia and the rest of the lands of the Church in Italy.[4] Tartaglia di Lavello was on 16 September appointed vicar in Toscanella and other towns in the dioceses of Sutri, Castro and Bagnorea.[5] Ludovico Migliorati was confirmed as Rector of the March of Ancona, and sums of money were in this connexion assigned to him on 10 October from clergy in the diocese of Verona.[6] On 1 October 1414, the day on which John left Bologna for Constance, Antonio Casini, Bishop of Siena, was named Governor of Bologna and the Romagna.[7] Marino Tomacelli had his rights as Rector of the Duchy of Spoleto reserved in the bull of Isolani's legation.[8] To provide for the defence of the Papal State, Braccio, Tartaglia, and, presumably, Migliorati were given *condotte* by the Pope; Braccio had been called to Bologna by John in August, and, whether or not, as the report went, John had it at first in mind to have him murdered, in the event he left him in a strong position.[9] Braccio went on on behalf of the Church to harry Forlì and

---

[1] Finke, *Acta*, i, 183, and no. 57, p. 261.
[2] Fillastre's diary, in Finke, *Acta*, ii, 15. Cf. Raynaldus, ad a., par. v.   [3] Finke, *Acta*, iv, 596-7.
[4] The bull is printed in C. Petracchi, *Vita di M. Iacopo Isolani*, in *Miscellanei di varia letteratura*, (Lucca, 1762), i, 176.
[5] Finke, *Acta*, iii, 35 n. He claimed the title of Rector in September 1414, Valentini, *BSU*, xxv (1922), 120. Cf. Leonii, 'Giovanni XXIII ed il comune di Todi', *ASI*, 4th ser., iv (1879), 193, and Levi, in *ASR*, iii (1880), 417, where Isolani is shown as recognising him as Rector in September 1416.
[6] Finke, *Acta*, iii, 35 n.   [7] Finke, *Acta*, i, 258 n.
[8] Cf. C. Bandini, *La Rocca di Spoleto* (1934), 79. The chronicle of Zampolini (in *Documenti Storici Inediti*, ed. A. Sansi, i, 1879) calls him 'castellanu e signiore . . . per la chiesia de Roma' (p. 142). John XXIII had appointed him Rector of the Duchy of Spoleto on 1 July 1410 (Reg. Vat. 342, fol. 233).
[9] Campano, *Vita Braccii*, 74, says he was called 'ne vacuam praesidio provinciam relinqueret'. But he goes on to discuss the report that John intended to capture or kill him on his arrival at Bologna.

Ravenna, and then Fano, Rimini and Pesaro, which were still holding for Gregory XII under the Malatesta.[1]

But as John XXIII well knew, only the forceful and personal intervention of the Pope himself could have pieced together the Papal State from the chaos in which it lay in the autumn of 1414. The decentralised machinery of Legate and Rectors which he set up before leaving Italy left all the armed force in the hands of independent and self-seeking *condottieri*, and could only deliver the temporal power into the hands of local interests—principally into the hands of Braccio da Montone and Muzio Attendolo Sforza, who, after Ladislas' death, were the two most powerful military leaders in central Italy. John XXIII had been no contemptible or pusillanimous ruler of the temporal power, and in this even Dietrich of Niem was compelled to recognise his virtues.[2] Both Niem and the fathers at Constance accused him of overloading the Papal State with taxes, and especially Rome and Bologna.[3] But it is doubtful if his rule was particularly onerous, considering the turbulence of the times. Cardinal Zabarella commented on the Bolognese complaints of his misrule, that they probably had more profit than they sustained loss from his sojourn there.[4] That John put down conspiracy ruthlessly is evident; the list of prisoners released from his castles after the rebellion in Bologna in 1416 is a long one. But firmness is in a temporal ruler no vice; when compared with the disastrous weakness of Gregory XII, the claim made for the Council of Pisa and its Popes, that it restored the temporal power of the Church, seems by no means absurd.[5] But now that John had to leave Isolani in Rome, without financial resources, without real diplomatic or military support, the temporal power was in effect sacrificed to the Council.

II. *The Temporal Power and the Council*

§ 1. The career of Braccio da Montone, one of the Perugians exiled by the faction of the Raspanti, began to acquire political importance from 1407, the date of his accepting the *signoria* of Rocca Contrata, after he had relieved the town from a siege by Ludovico Migliorati.[6] When Migliorati was declared a rebel by Gregory XII in the summer of 1407, Braccio was enrolled as a mercenary of the Church, and given the title of *reformator Marchie*.[7] In this period he established a sphere of influence

---

[1] Campano, 76; Hieronymous de Forlivio, 24–5; L. Cobelli, *Cronache Forlivesi*, 164.

[2] *Vita Johannis*, in Von der Hardt, ii, 353–4.   [3] Finke, *Acta*, iii, 184–93, and iv, 762 f.

[4] Finke, *Acta*, iv, 818. 'Et quantum ad temporalia credit, quod respectu terrarum ecclesie, que sunt in Italia, recuperandum ad manus ecclesie fuerit magis utilis quam dampnosus, et quod pauci potuissent hoc facere, quod ipse (scil., Johannes) faciebat'. Dietrich of Niem, although he admits 'de temporalibus vero, si d. papa illa bene vel male dispenset, parum nobis curandum est', nevertheless accuses him of pocketing the revenues of the temporal power for himself and his family (Finke, *Acta*, iv, 632). But see the Bolognese chronicler on his expulsion from Rome in 1413, 'et questo fu per la mala signoria ch'egli faceva' (*Corpus*, 547).

[5] Cardinal de Challant's speech before Sigismond, 13 October 1413, in Bzovius, *Annales Ecclesiastici*, xv, 344–5, 'unitas diu desiderata Ecclesiae restituta est, Roma, Patrimonium Beati Petri et tota fere temporalibus Ecclesiae de manibus potentissimorum hostium vi erepta'.

[6] Campano, *Vita Braccii*, 25–6, 'Haec prima iacta fundamenta futurae magnitudinis, primum tam magni imperii domicilium'.

[7] Campano, *Vita Braccii*, 29 and n.

in the March which went as far north as Fano.[1] Having accepted the *condotta* of Ladislas for a few months at the beginning of 1408, he conceived the suspicion that the King intended to betray him, and returned to his depredations against the towns of the March.[2] From this time until long after the beginning of his conflict with Martin V, all his actions were in the rôle of mercenary and paladin of the Church. He took part in the expedition of Alexander V against Rome, and then from the spring of 1410 was engaged with his Perugian exiles in a war against the *contado* of Perugia, which went on until the peace of San Felice in 1412.[3] The peace stipulated the return to Perugia of the castles which Braccio and the exiles had conquered in the Perugian *contado*, and to obtain this the Pope had to pay Braccio a compensation of 30,000 florins.[4] Braccio then returned to Bologna and was employed against the Malatesta and other supporters of Gregory XII and Ladislas.[5] In 1413 he relieved Orsini at Rocca Contrata, and then returned to Umbria. But only after the deposition of John XXIII at Constance in 1415 were the real foundations laid for his power as a territorial prince.[6]

Jacopo Isolani entered Rome on 19 October 1414, a month after Sforza had failed, through the resistance of the Romans under Piero Matuzzo, to seize the City for Giovanna II.[7] The Legate had already, on his way to Rome, received the submissions of Città di Castello, Montefiascone, Bagnorea, and 'maggior parte delle terre di Campagna'.[8] On 19 November he secured a truce from the Neapolitan forces north of Rome, under Sforza and the Count of Troja, but he failed to reach a truce with the Neapolitans in Castel Sant' Angelo, Marino and Ostia.[9] In the south, Sezze submitted on 20 November, but Terracina continued to hold out for Giovanna.[10] On 24 November he announced that the Savelli and Francesco Orsini, who at that time held Todi, had submitted.[11] In the Patrimony Tartaglia took Corneto for the Church and sacked it; the city was granted an amnesty by Isolani on 1 January 1415.[12] Viterbo submitted on 24 January,[13] and an equally important gain was that

---

[1] Campano, *Vita Braccii*, 30. [2] Ibid. 38–9.

[3] Ibid. 47 f. The *condotte* granted by John XXIII and Louis of Anjou to Braccio on 29 February 1411 and 30 July 1412 are to be found in Cod. Vat. Barb. lat. 2668, fols. 43, 60v.

[4] See Valentini's note in Campano, *Vita Braccii*, 65, and Barb. lat. 2668, fol. 142, where is the agreement for the return of the castles by Braccio to the Pope, dated 12 January 1413. The Pope agrees to pay him 30,000 florins, but much of this money was already owed him for arrears of his *condotta* (see fol. 43 of the same MS.). Some of the payments of this debt to Braccio are recorded in *ASI*, 4th ser., xiii (1884), 182.

[5] Campano, 66.

[6] Braccio's possessions in July 1414 are listed in the agreement by which he became *raccomandato* to Florence in that month. They were Montone, Pietramellina, Terricella, Colazone, Fratta, Titignano and Pruove (*Capitoli del Comune di Firenze*, i, 551).

[7] Pietro dello Schiavo, 92, 95; A. Minuti, *Vita di M. A. Sforza*, 176. [8] *Commissioni*, i, 265.

[9] G. Levi, 'Nuovi documenti sulla legazione del Cardinale Isolani in Roma', *ASR*, iii (1880), doc. 2, p. 411. Isolani asked Florence to help arrange a truce with the garrisons of Ostia, Castel Sant' Angelo, and Marino, *Commissioni*, i, 275.

[10] For Sezze, *Documenti dal Archivio Caetani, Regesta Chartarum*, ed. G. Caetani, iii, 241.

[11] *Commissioni*, i, 275.

[12] Printed by Levi, *ASR*, iii (1880), doc. 3, p. 412. Cf. L. Dasti, *Notizie storiche archeologiche di Tarquinia e Corneto* (1878), 234.

[13] Theiner, iii, no. 144, p. 212.

of Orvieto in March 1415, although the latter submission was occasioned more by the anxiety of the ruling party, the Melcorini, to strengthen their position, than from any inherent strength of Isolani.[1] In April 1415 Isolani granted an amnesty to Orte, a town on the Tiber of some strategic importance.[2]

Thus by the time of John XXIII's deposition from the Papacy on 29 May 1415 only a part of the lands of the Church had been recovered, and that part not very securely. Isolani's hold on the Roman District and the Patrimony was most unsure; the Neapolitans held their positions in Marino, Terracina, Castel Sant' Angelo and Ostia, the Prefect of Vico still held Civitavecchia against the Church. North of Orvieto, Sforza's forces held a large group of possessions stretching from the north of the Patrimony into Tuscany. Round the lake of Bolsena Tartaglia had his own sphere of influence, and another group of towns on the borders of Umbria was held for Braccio da Montone. Perugia was ruled still by a Neapolitan governor, and Assisi by the Count of Montefeltro; communication with Bologna was thus most difficult. Paolo Orsini, after his captivity in Naples a power in decline, but still a source of disorder, ruled in Narni and Amelia, and his brother Francesco in Todi. Tomacelli was still in Spoleto for the Church. In the March of Ancona there had been scarcely an attempt to stem the chaos. Migliorati, the nominal Rector, ruled no further than the borders of his own state, which he was hard put to defend from the Malatesta. Ascoli Piceno had been granted by Ladislas in 1413 to the Count of Carrara, who on the King's death ruled unchecked there, and added himself to the number of the tyrants of the March. The influence of the Malatesta, still the protectors of Gregory XII, went as far south as Recanati, where Gregory took up residence. Macerata, the Varano of Camerino and Ancona placed themselves in the obedience of Gregory. In Bologna, beyond the row of tyrants on the Via Emilia— the Ordelaffi, Manfredi, Alidosi—the Bishop of Siena ruled with an unsteady hand, fearing aggression from his professed friends no less than from his enemies.

On 2 August 1415 the Venetians refused the Bishop of Siena a loan of 15,000 ducats; evidently at his wits' end to pay the *condotta* of Braccio, he had asked for the loan in order that the city might continue in the obedience of John XXIII.[3] He was obliged to give Braccio, in pledge for the arrears owing him, Castel S. Pietro, Medicina, Castel Bolognese and Pieve del Cento.[4] Later in the month Venice refused the Bishop her aid in securing an alliance for him with the Este. Braccio was at this time harrying Cesena and the rest of the Malatesta lands,[5] but already he was meditating aggression in Umbria; Isolani had appointed Braccio's henchman

[1] The terms sought by Orvieto are printed by Monaldeschi della Cervara, *Commentari historici* (1584), 126–8. Cf. Fumi, *Codice diplomatico*, 665–7, and Valentini, in *BSU*, xxv (1922), 127–9.

[2] Printed by Petracchi, *Vita di M. Isolani*, 191 (dated 19 April 1415) and also by Justi Fontanini, *de Antiquitatibus Hortae* (Rome, 1723), 455.

[3] H. Finke, *Forschungen und Quellen*, no. 20, p. 317. Braccio's *condotta*, dated 29 January 1415, and operative for the year beginning 1 April 1415, is in Cod. Vat. Barb. lat. 2668 A, fol. 186e. It is for 500 lances and 200 foot, at an annual cost to the Church of 96,200 florins. The document is the original one, still bearing the imprint of the seals.

[4] Finke, *Forschungen und Quellen*, no. 21, p. 318.

[5] Hieronymus de Forlivio, 25; Campano, *Vita Braccii*, 68.

Giacomo degli Archipreti lieutenant in Orvieto on 13 June, and at the same time the ambassadors of the city were at Braccio's camp.[1] Isolani was on 25 July 1415 reappointed as Legate for the Council,[2] but conditions in Rome grew worse; a letter of 5 September reports further attacks from the Neapolitan garrison at Sant' Angelo, and a skirmish at Ponte Milvio,[3] there were executions for conspiracy with the Neapolitans, and trouble was to be expected from Pietro Stefaneschi, the Cardinal of Sant' Angelo, who having entered the city on 16 June 1415 became a centre of intrigue on behalf of Naples and Benedict XIII.[4] Tartaglia had seized Castro for himself,[5] and on 5 October 1415 a letter from Isolani was read to the Council in Constance, complaining that Rome and the Patrimony were in a disorder which could not be remedied until money was sent to engage troops.[6] On 28 November 1415 Paolo Orsini entered Rome with a small force and remained there until 12 December on behalf of the Neapolitans. He sacked the Cardinal's palace and carried out extensive brigandage, without being strong enough to remain there and set up a permanent regime; the incident shows the helplessness of Isolani.[7]

§ 2. On 4 July 1415 Carlo Malatesta tendered at Constance Gregory XII's abdication from the Papacy. He pressed on the Council the necessity of sending an embassy to Italy,[8] and on 17 August 1415 two embassies or commissions were appointed. One consisted of Bartolomeo della Capra the Archbishop of Milan and John Usk the Bishop of Pècs or 'of the Five Churches' in Hungary; the other of Antonio di Rieti the Archbishop of Ragusa, the Bishop of S. Flour, Nicolò Giussoni the Abbot of S. Maria at Florence, and the Englishman John Stokes.[9] The Archbishop of Milan and John Usk were sent through the centre and south, to Todi, Viterbo, Corneto, and, perhaps, Rome and Naples, and the second embassy to the Legate Correr and the March of Ancona.[10] One of the embassies, presumably that led by the Archbishop of Milan, was at the beginning of October in Florence.[11] A

---

[1] Valentini, *BSU*, xxv (1922), 134, 136.

[2] Petracchi, *Vita di M. I. Isolani*, prints the bull.

[3] Niem, *Vita Johannis*, 418–9.

[4] Pietro dello Schiavo, 97–100.

[5] Petracchi, loc. cit., the Council complains of the occupation to Isolani.

[6] Petrus de Pulka, in *AKöG*, xv (1856), 34, 'quod nisi in brevi notabili quantitate pecuniae succurreretur, quin satisfieret armigeris, nequaquam posset in subjectione ecclesiae conservari'.

[7] Pietro dello Schiavo, 102; Niem, *Vita Johannis*, 435–8; Gregorovius, vi, pt. 2, 653; Finke, *Acta*, iv, no. 517, p. 667.

[8] Finke, *Acta*, iii, no. 157, p. 352. [9] Von der Hardt, iv, 493.

[10] The despatch of Usk and the Archbishop of Milan was announced by letters of 21 August to Todi. Leonii, 'Giovanni XXIII ed il commune di Todi', *ASI*, 4th ser, iv (1879), prints the bull, rendering John Usk the 'prepositus Rumque ecclesie'—a rum go, indeed! Letters were also addressed to Viterbo (Theiner, iii, no. 146, p. 215) and Corneto (idem, *I due concilii generali* (1861), 40–1). The despatch of the mission was also announced to Lucca, L. Fumi and G. Lazzareschi, *Carteggio di Paolo Guinigi* (1925), no. 1140, p. 391. The conciliar bull appointing the Archbishop of Ragusa and his fellow commissioners to go to the Legate of the March is printed in Colucci, *Antichità Picene*, xxix, *Codice diplomatico della terra di Santa Vittoria*, no. 125, p. 228.

[11] K. Dieterle, 'Die Stellung Neapels und die grossen italienischen Kommunen zum Konstanzer Konzil', *RQ*, xxix (1915), 12*, 67*. There is no specific evidence that they reached either Rome or Naples, although the despatch of a Neapolitan embassy to Constance in January 1416 suggests that a conciliar embassy may first have been in Naples. Cf. Finke, *Acta*, iv, no. 280, p. 17.

conciliar embassy, which I take to be still the same one, was in Siena on 16 October 1415,[1] further I have been unable to trace its progress, until the Archbishop of Milan and Usk appear at Recanati, from whence they presumably rejoined the Archbishop of Ragusa, on 10 February 1416;[2] the Archbishop of Milan returned to Constance at the beginning of April 1416 and related the progress of the Embassy.[3]

The path of the Archbishop of Ragusa and his fellow commissioners is easier to trace. They were destined to the erstwhile Gregory XII, now appointed by the Council as Legate in the March of Ancona.[4] On 10 September 1415 they were in Venice, where they asked the Senate to ratify the decisions of the Council.[5] They went to Bologna, reached Forlì on 23 September,[6] and went on to Gubbio on 30 October.[7] On 25 December 1415 their arrival was announced to Macerata by Carlo Malatesta, from Rimini,[8] and during December Rodolfo Varano of Camerino, Ludovico Migliorati and Antonio Nofrii of Sanseverino all announced their submission to the commissioners.[9] At the beginning of January they were in Recanati, with the Legate Angelo Correr and the emissaries of the lords of Fermo and Camerino.[10] On 29 January 1416, from Recanati, they asked Macerata to send ambassadors there.[11]

On 9 January 1416 the envoys of Carlo Malatesta on one side and the Varani, Migliorati and Ancona on the other had been in Constance before the Council to lay complaints and counter-complaints of aggression sustained after the entry of the ambassadors of the Council into the March,[12] an appeal which hardly suggests that the conciliar embassy was finding success or acceptance in its work of pacification. The Council delivered an eirenic reply and promised to hear the case as a formal process of law : after this no more is heard of it. But there is no doubt that in spite of his zeal for the union of the Church, Carlo Malatesta had few friends at Constance. The influence of Sigismond at Constance was notorious in Italy and could not fail to affect the instructions of the Council's ambassadors, who are indeed three times

---

[1] *Cronaca Sanese*, 783.

[2] Compagnoni, *La Reggia Picena*, 300. The Archbishop of Ragusa and his party were also at Ancona, two days before, C. Lilii, *Dell'Historia di Camerino*, ii, 145–8. The Archbishop of Milan had probably been at Fermo in the March as early as 14 December 1415, *Cronache della città di Fermo*, 44 ('Mediolanensis' should probably be read here for 'Mutinensis').

[3] Finke, *Acta*, iv, 17.

[4] Mansi, *Sacr. conciliorum nova et amplissima collectio* (Venice, 1784), xxvii, 777.

[5] Finke, *Acta*, iii, no. 129, p. 282; M. Sanudo, *Vite de' Duchi di Venezia* (Muratori, *RRIISS*, xxii) 897.

[6] Hieronymous de Forlivio, 25–6.

[7] *Cronaca di Ser Guerriero di Gubbio* (Muratori, *RRIISS*, xxi, pt. 4), 39, but without an exact date. The 'Ristretto di fatti d'Italia e specialmente d'Urbino dal 1404 al 1444', ed. Bacini, in *Zibaldone* (i, Florence, 1889), is more explicit. 'Li ambasciatori del Concilio et de lo Imperatore venero ad Ugubio al nostro Signore cum honorevole ambasciata, et li ambasciadori furono lo arcivescovo de Ragusia, lo vescovo di Santa Fiora, lo abbate di Fiorenza et messer Docto' (p. 51, under the date 30 October 1415). This MS., said to be in the Archivio di Stato at Florence, appears to be one of the sources for the version printed by Mazzatinti of the *Cronaca di Ser Guerriero*.

[8] Compagnoni, 298; Macerata, Archivio Priorale, Riformanze, vol. 11, fol. 36v.

[9] Macerata, Riformanze, vol. 11, fol. 37v.

[10] J. Hollerbach, 'Die gregorianische Partei, Sigismund und das Konstanzer Konzil', *RQ*, xxiv (1910), 129; L. Tonini, *Storia civile e sacra Riminese*, v, 62.

[11] Macerata, Riformanze, vol. 11, fol. 22v.   [12] Von der Hardt, iv, 560–1.

referred to as ambassadors of the Council and the Emperor.[1]   So feared and resented was the hegemony of Sigismond in the Council that Venice virtually boycotted Constance until after the election of Martin V, and Florentine policy toward the Council was scarcely more friendly.[2]   Sigismond and Venice were still at odds in Dalmatia, and the truce of 1413 had already been violated.   As the successful leader of the Venetian army in the war of 1413, Carlo Malatesta could hardly expect a great deal of benevolence from Sigismond,[3] and it seems possible that this, no less than Malatesta's past rôle as the protector of Gregory XII, must have influenced the Archbishop of Ragusa and his fellow commissioners, when they not merely took the part of the Varano and Migliorati against Malatesta, but carried their partisanship to the point of war.   It would be hard to tell from their conduct that John XXIII had been deposed; they seem to have continued all the feuds and alliances which Cossa had left in the March.

On 8 February the commissioners were in Ancona, where they confirmed in the name of the Council the vicariate of Rodolfo Varano, absolving him for offences against the Church and forgiving him his arrears of *census*.[4]   On 13 February they moved to Fermo,[5] and here they found themselves in a storm centre.   Carlo Malatesta at this time still held his gains from Ludovico Migliorati in the war of 1414–15; one of these was S. Elpidio sul Mare, which on 26 February rebelled, declaring for Migliorati and the Church.[6]   War immediately broke out all over the March, and the Archbiship of Ragusa entered into a league with Migliorati, Rodolfo Varano and Ancona,[7] against Malatesta and the Legate.   It is also probable that the embassy or

---

[1] *Cronaca Sanese*, 783; *Cronaca di Ser Guerriero di Gubbio*, 39; *Cronache della città di Fermo*, 44. The Imperialist colour of the embassy is shown particularly by the inclusion of the Archbishop of Milan and Johannes Usk. The former, Bartolomeo della Capra, was Visconti's envoy to Sigismond in the negotiations of 1418, Romano, *ASL*, 3rd ser., vii (1897), 114, and in 1421 he is referred to by the Pope as 'consiliarius et orator' of the Emperor, Fink, 'Politische Korrespondenz', *QF*, xxvi (1935/6), no. 3. Johannes Rudolfi de Adel, from Usk (the German Aussig, now Usti nad Labem in Czechoslovakia) is not to be confused with Johannes Kirchen de Usk, Sigismond's Vice-Chancellor, but he also was in the Emperor's service. He was given a benefice in 1411 'non obstante statutis dicte ecclesie . . . quia diversis s. Rom. imperii negociis in servitio Sigismondi in Rom. regem electi et Hungarie regis impeditus fuit' (Fink, *Repertorium Germanicum*, iii, 1935, p. 251). He was Sigismond's envoy to the Roman curia in 1412, Theiner, iii, no. 131, p. 199, and *Repertorium Germanicum*, loc. cit. Nicolò Giussoni, the Abbot of S. Maria in Florence, was Sigismond's envoy to Florence in 1417, Finke, *Acta*, iv, 438 n.

[2] Finke, *Acta*, iv, no. 461, p. 452, no. 462, p. 453, no. 475, p. 478, and, especially, 438–9, where he shows the absolute refusal of Venice to send an embassy to Constance. In Florence it was said to be necessary for the Italians to all unite against the Emperor (ibid.). Cf. iv, no. 517, p. 668, 'lo dit enperador voldria fer les coses a sa bella guisa, co que no plauria james ha Ytalians'. Further, *AKöG*, xv, (1856), 56, 'dicitur etiam, quod aliquae communitates Italiae forte in odium regis si possent acciperent eundem Petrum de Luna'.

[3] Finke, *Acta*, iii, 326 f., Malatesta appeals to Venice for aid against Braccio; it was through Venetian intervention that Braccio eventually liberated Carlo Malatesta, ibid. iii, 308 n.

[4] Printed by Lilii, *Dell'Historia di Camerino*, ii, 45, and, far more fully, by Octavo Turchi, *De Ecclesiae Camerinensis Pontificibus* (Rome, 1762), cxlix. The Roman, Cincius Pauli, later a secretary of Martin V, was on the staff of the Archbishop of Ragusa in 1415–16, and he tells a scurrilous story about the conduct of the Archbishop during his stay in Ancona, L. Berthalot, 'Cincius Romanus und seine Briefe', *QF*, xxi (1929/30), 225–6.

[5] Macerata, Riformanze, vol. 11, fol. 29.   [6] *Cronache della città di Fermo*, 44.

[7] Ibid., and Compagnoni, 300, where the league gives a guarantee of protection to Macerata, dated 7 March; cf. Riformanze, vol. 11, fol. 39v.

perhaps the Council itself issued some document purporting to inhibit Correr's functions as Legate.[1] In April Malatesta made an unsuccessful attack on Ancona, and was repulsed by the troops of the league.[2]

While the conciliar embassy was thus implicated in the affairs of the March, events were succeeding in Umbria and Romagna of the greatest importance for the future of the ecclesiastical power. On 5 January 1416 Bologna rose against its Governor the Bishop Antonio Casini, and set up a popular rule. On 10 January Braccio appeared below the walls of the city, and demanded his price for his acquiescence in the revolution. He obtained a sum variously estimated between 80,000 and 180,000 ducats (the lower figure appears the more likely), and agreed to return to the city the castles which he held in pledge from Antonio Casini the Governor.[3] Although in form the agreement with Braccio preserved the obedience of the city to the Church, the expulsion of Casini was not reversed, and under the nominal governorship of its Bishop the city enjoyed virtual liberty.

Braccio now turned to the formation of a new state in Umbria. On 15 March 1416 his troops occupied Orvieto.[4] At the beginning of April he left Bolognese soil, and after harrying Imola left for Umbria to carry out the most important and critical of his enterprises, the siege of his native city Perugia. The moment was favourable; not only did the internal divisions and palace intrigues of the early years of Giovanna II of Naples forbid any move to protect the city which was still, though only formally, held for her, but Muzio Attendolo Sforza, Braccio's greatest rival in Italy and the possessor of many lands in Umbria and Tuscany, lay in the prison where he had been thrown by Giovanna's consort the Count of March. Perugia engaged for her defence the two most important *condottieri* of central Italy, Carlo Malatesta and Paolo Orsini, and a campaign ensued which ended in the disastrous defeat and capture of Malatesta on 12 July 1416, and in the immediate fall of Perugia.[5] This most important victory determined the distribution of power in central Italy for the succeeding eight years. Braccio became absolute *signore* of

---

[1] Mansi, *Sacr. conciliorum nova et amplissima collectio*, xxvii, 1053–8, a decree of 31 March 1417, ordering the inhabitants of the March of Ancona to regard Correr as their rightful Legate, disregarding any decrees to the contrary. Cf. Finke, *Acta*, iv, no. 517, p. 667, a Spanish report of 11 December 1415, saying that the Council has revoked Correr's legation, because of his complete dependence on the Malatesta.

[2] *Cronache della città di Fermo*, 45, with the date 5 April. In October 1414 Malatesta had made a full scale assault on Ancona, *Croniche Anconitane di M. Lazzaro de'Bernabei* (ed. Ciavarini, in *Collezione di documenti storici antichi delle città e terre marchigine*, i, 1870), 149 f. Ibid. 158, a song in *volgare*, 'io dico al Malatesta, Che in dispregio del sacro Conseglo Ne fa la guerra et chiamane in periglo'.

[3] *Corp. Chron. Bonon.*, 552–3; Piero di Mattiolo, 270, 273–4; Niem, *Vita Johannis*, 435–8, erroneously dated 1415; Campano, *Vita Braccii*, 78–9; Minuti, *Vita di M. A. Sforza*, 190; Buoninsegni, *Storie della città di Firenze*, 10; Bonincontri, *Annales*, 111, placing the sum at 60,000 ducats. Ghirardacci, ii, 606, summarises the agreement under the date 12 March 1416, but this date is hard to accept, especially as the agreement was known at Constance on 1 February (Niem, loc. cit.). The difference in the figures of the money paid probably arises from Braccio's demanding money on three counts, for his future *condotta* (which Ghirardacci puts at 30,000 ducats), past arrears, and for the restoration of the castles. Cf. Zaoli, *Libertas Bononie e papa Martino V* (1916), 13–14, 26–7.

[4] Valentini, *BSU*, xxv (1922), 143. The formal offer of the city to Braccio was not made until 9 June 1416, Fumi, *Codice diplomatico*, 667.

[5] Campano, *Vita Braccii*, 93–103; Buoninsegni, 11; Orsini did not fight at the battle of 12 July.

Perugia,[1] and as the ruler of such a powerful state he immediately set about the subjugation of the greater part of Umbria. Paolo Orsini, his one remaining enemy in Umbria, was on 5 August murdered at Colfiorito on the confines of the March.[2] His lands, Narni, San Gemini and Amelia, were shared between Braccio and Tartaglia. Spello and Todi had already fallen, the latter in June, and Rieti submitted in the same summer.[3]

While Braccio expropriated the greater part of the papal lands, the Council and its embassy accepted his protestations that he did so as a soldier of the Church. In June 1416 the Council is reported as having despatched a *condotta* to Braccio and Tartaglia, to combat a reported aggression of Paolo Orsini against Viterbo.[4] In August 1416 Braccio moved to the March, where the head of the Conciliar embassy, the Archbishop of Ragusa, in conformity with his previous policy admitted Braccio into the league against the Malatesta, and gave him a *condotta*.[5] In the same month the Archbishop entered Macerata to take up residence there under the joint guarantee of Braccio and Migliorati.[6] The Archbishop, completely isolated and helpless, ruled there as Governor for the Church, and continued there and in Fermo as late as May 1417.[7] On 17 August 1416 Braccio in the presence of the Archbishop, Migliorati and various notables of the March, acted as arbitrator between the Varano of Camerino and Antonio Nofrii of San Severino, in a quarrel about the possession of lands.[8] The war against the Malatesta was continued; the army of the league claimed to have subdued all the countryside first as far north as the Esino, and then by 17 September as far as Fano.[9] In September Braccio returned to Umbria, where

---

[1] Zampolini, *Annali di Spoleto*, 144, 'senza fare capitoli'. Cf. Campano, 109, Valentini's note, and Pellini, ii, 225–6.

[2] Campano, 114; Buoninsegni, 11; Sozomenus, 7; Zampolini, 145; Pietro dello Schiavo, 103. Cf. Valentini, *BSU*, xxvi (1923), 4.

[3] Campano, 114–5.

[4] Finke, *Acta*, iv, no. 293, p. 37; cf. Theiner, iii, nos. 150, 151, p. 218. Not everyone was as blind as the fathers at Constance; the despatch sent by an Aragonese embassy on 11 December 1415 predicts that Braccio will move first against Bologna and then against Rome (*Acta*, iv, no. 517, p. 669). Isolani in September 1416 gave Tartaglia a further *condotta*, *ASR*, iii (1880), 417.

[5] Macerata, Riformanze, 11, fol. 75. The tallage formerly assigned to Paolo Orsini is now to be paid by Macerata to Braccio, ibid. fol. 80v. Cf. Compagnoni, 301.

[6] Compagnoni, 301, prints the agreement, with date 16 August 1416; it is also in the Riformanze of Macerata, vol. 11, fol. 77, with the date 21 August.

[7] Macerata, Riformanze, vol. 11, passim. He refers to Macerata as 'civitas noster', fol. 127, and the town refers to him as 'dominus noster', fol. 156v. His rule was by no means despotic, and the Riformanze record a series of refusals by the town to appear before his court. He described himself as 'Antonius dey gratia Archiepiscopus Ragusinus in nonnullis Italie partibus et speciale in provincia Marchie Anconitane sacri concilii commissarius etc.', Riformanze, vol. 11, fol. 163v. The town continued to name its own *podestà*, ibid. fol. 121. The Archbishop also, in April 1417, stayed in Fermo (Macerata, Riformanze, vol. 11, fol. 149v). His treasurer, the Florentine Nanni de Pergolattis, was still the same treasurer appointed by John XXIII for the March of Ancona on 1 February 1413 (Reg. Vat. 341, fol. 284), and he called himself 'pro sancta Romana ecclesia et sede apostolica provincie Marchie Anconitane thesaurarius generalis' (Div. Cam. 4, fols. 26–29v). He attempted to make the towns of the March pay the sums they owed Cardinal Orsini for the expenses of his legation in 1414, but without effect (ibid.).

[8] Lilii, *Dell'Historia di Camerino*, ii, 152–3, prints part of the act. Cf. *Cronache della città di Fermo*, 46.

[9] *Cronache della città di Fermo*, 46; Valentini, *BSU*, xxvi (1923), 169.

he took Sassoferrato and Gualdo Nucerino, and the confederates in the March obtained the submission of Recanati early in October.[1]

At the end of the year both Florence and Venice were pressing the combatants to make peace, and demanding the liberation of Carlo Malatesta; the Venetians and the Count of Montefeltro joined in the negotiations at Florence, and peace was reached at the beginning of February 1417.[2] Malatesta was released against the payment of a huge ransom, and both Correr and the Archbishop of Ragusa were included in the peace.

The Council of Constance was pushed into the arms of such doubtful allies as Braccio and Migliorati largely by fear of Benedict XIII's intrigues in Italy. Nor were their fears unfounded. In January 1415 Dominicus Ram, Bishop of Huesca, Benedict's ambassador to Naples in the matter of the marriage proposed between the Infante of Aragon and Giovanna II, was told to find out whether Isolani would be willing to betray Rome. He was also to tell Giovanni di Vico the Prefect of Rome and the Breton garrison of Soriano that if the Neapolitan marriage were effected Benedict would be brought to Rome.[3] In the spring of 1415 preparations were made to assemble a fleet to take Benedict to Sicily,[4] and only Giovanna's rejection of the Aragonese offer and her marriage to the Count of March put an end to this plan. But intrigue continued. In October 1415 Lello Capocci was executed in Rome for a plot involving Benedict XIII and the Count of March, and in the same month Isolani wrote to the Council that Benedict was preparing to descend on Rome.[5] But when Paolo Orsini took Rome in November 1415, at the orders of the Count of March, Benedict XIII was not in fact called in; a likely explanation is given by an Aragonese correspondent, who suggested that the Count of March intended to hold Rome, so that whatever Pope prevailed, could be forced to confirm him in the Kingdom of Sicily.[6] Following this the ambassadors of the Council were reported to have signed an agreement with the Count of March and the Romans, under which the former expressed his submission to the Council. But both these ambassadors and those sent to Italy by Ferdinand of Aragon referred to the intrigues of Benedict XIII, the Prior of S. Maximin, and the Count of March.[7] In May 1416 Benedict and the Count both applied to Venice for naval help to bring Benedict to Italy; the aid was refused and the attempt reported to the Aragonese.[8] Early in June the Council wrote to Alfonso of Aragon, asking him to prevent this threatened Neapolitan fleet from sailing.[9] But in sum the progress of Benedict in Italy up to this date was

[1] *Cronache della città di Fermo*, 46.

[2] Campano, 116–8; *Cronaca di Ser Guerriero di Gubbio*, 39; Macerata, Riformanze, 11, fol. 131v, where is Braccio's letter, dated Rocca Contrata, 24 February 1417, announcing the peace, and calling for its ratification. Cf. Valentini, *BSU*, xxvi (1923), no. 28, p. 170.

[3] Finke, *Acta*, iii, 368 f., and no. 164, pp. 405–7.

[4] Finke, *Acta*, iii, nos. 165–6, pp. 408–12.

[5] Pietro dello Schiavo, 97, 100. Isolani's letter is quoted above.

[6] Finke, *Acta*, iv, no. 517, p. 667.

[7] Finke, *Acta*, iv, no. 280, p. 17; ii, 294–7. The Aragonese embassy, under the Bishop of Malta, was despatched in February 1416, and returned in May, having visited Genoa, Lucca, Florence, Bologna, Ferrara and Venice, but having failed to reach Rome (*Acta*, iii, 390; ii, 294).

[8] Finke, *Acta*, iii, no. 175, p. 423, and iv, no. 293, p. 37.   [9] Finke, *Acta*, iv, no. 291, p. 35.

small. The occupation of Rome by Paolo Orsini, which was probably intended as a foothold for a Neapolitan invasion in strength, had no permanent result. The officials he appointed there were removed after his murder in August 1416, and 'reformers' appointed to strengthen the government—whether with or without the approval of Isolani, it is impossible to say.[1]

It was inevitable that after the capture of Perugia Braccio should fall to the temptation to march on Rome. In mid-June 1417 he wrote from his camp at Narni asking Isolani to send ambassadors. When the Cardinal's emissary Jacomo del Bene arrived in his camp, Braccio declared his allegiance to Isolani, but advanced to within three leagues of Rome. He was there visited by Stefaneschi the Cardinal of Sant' Angelo, and three days later he demanded the *signoria* of Rome. With bread in the City for only two days, Isolani was forced to come to terms. Braccio was granted the title of 'Defensor Sancte Romane Ecclesie ac protector reipublice Romanorum'. His demand to appoint the Senator was refused, but he was promised that the office would be held by someone acceptable to him. He was granted one or two gates of the City, and Isolani willingly allowed him to take over the finances and offices of the City—'perchè sono tute povertà'. Finally Isolani promised to accept only a Pope who was generally accepted in Italy.[2] Braccio thereupon entered Rome, and Isolani took refuge in Sant' Angelo.[3] But the occupation was a short one. Sforza, resentful of the lands he had lost in the Sienese *contado* through Braccio's influence,[4] and bitterly jealous of his power, had been freed from prison in November 1416. On the news of Braccio's success he marched north, crossed the Tiber near Ostia instead of attacking from the south, and arrived so rapidly at the gates that Braccio, taken by surprise, was hard put to extricate himself from the City before Sforza's arrival. Braccio withdrew to Umbria; he was in Narni on 24 August. Tartaglia retired to Toscanella and the other ally Berardo Varano to Camerino. Sforza released and reinstated Isolani; with the fall of the Count of March in September 1416 the Neapolitan connection with Benedict XIII had ceased.[5] Isolani, thinking perhaps of the long list of medieval emperors and their short-lived occupations of Rome, had written on 1 July 'Legiera cosa è ad acquistare oma, ma mantenerla è assai difficile', and he had been proved right.

---

[1] The new officials are called 'gubernatores' by Pietro dello Schiavo, 104, but 'reformatores' in the letter of a Roman citizen to the Cardinals at Constance (Finke, *Acta*, iv, no. 377, p. 205), and 'refurmatori' in the treaty with Tartaglia, printed in *ASR*, iii (1880), 418.

[2] See L. Fumi, *Braccio a Roma* (1877), and doc. 25 below. The letter to Nicola Uzzano is also in Fumi's *Codice diplomatico della città di Orvieto*, 673–4. Braccio claimed to the Orvietani that Isolani and the Romans called him to Rome ('me vocaverunt', *Braccio a Roma*, 21), and Pietro dello Schiavo says (p. 109) that he came 'de mandato et voluntate' of the Legate. But I cannot, as do Levi (*ASR*, iii, 1880, p. 408) and Valentini (*BSU*, xxvi, 1923, p. 24 n.) allow that Isolani can have wished Braccio to enter Rome or asked him to do so. The reference may be to an agreement made with Isolani emissary, Jacomo del Bene,—an agreement made under threat of force. Doc. 25 below confirms that Braccio was not 'called' to Rome, but this is, of course, the papal version of the story.

[3] Fumi, *Braccio a Roma*; P. Pagliucchi, *I Castellani di S. Angelo* (1906), 72–3; Pietro dello Schiavo, 109; Infessura, 21; doc. 25 below. [4] Cf. Valentini, *BSU*, xxvi (1923), 22 n.

[5] Fumi, op. cit.; Campano, *Vita Braccii*, 120 f.; Minuti, *Vita di M. A. Sforza*, 197–209; Infessura, 21–2; Pietro dello Schiavo, 111. Cf. N. F. Faraglia, *Storia della Regina Giovanna II d'Angiò* (1904), 67 f.; 98 f.

That Braccio had been in touch with the agents of Benedict XIII is certain; Isolani claimed that Cardinal Stefaneschi's nephew had revealed a plot involving Tartaglia, the Savelli, Jacopo Colonna and other Roman notables. Benedict was said to have agreed to pay Giovanni di Vico 12,000 florins for the surrender of Civitavecchia, and 20,000 to Stefaneschi for the surrender of Rome.[1] Stefaneschi probably tried to interest Braccio in some such design when he visited his camp outside Rome. On 3 August 1417, while Braccio was still in Rome, his chancellor was in Venice proposing to the Senate an understanding with Benedict XIII. But he also proposed an alternative which the Pope in Peñiscola would not have found so attractive; that was, to have an 'acceptable' Pope elected in Rome.[2] The effect and extent of the collusion between Braccio and Benedict XIII were thus not very great; Braccio merely profited from the struggle with the anti-Pope, just as he had profited from the struggle with Angelo Correr and the Malatesta.

Sforza went on to rout Piccinino, and to pursue Tartaglia on his way to his base at Toscanella. Braccio retired to winter quarters at Perugia, and thus matters stood when on 11 November 1417 Oddo Colonna was elected Pope at Constance. Braccio had been repulsed but not defeated and he, and not Sforza or Isolani, remained the most powerful ruler in central Italy. The timely death of Ladislas in 1414 had at the last moment saved the Papal State from extinction. But only a strong ruler and a strong army could re-weld the scattered pieces of the papal dominions into something approaching a state, and the Council of Constance delayed the appearance of such a ruler for four dangerous years. Cardinal Isolani had no material resources and no real authority; he could only bluff. The conciliar 'commissioners' had shown themselves pitifully impotent. Weak and helpless, the Patrimony of Peter awaited its deliverer.

Did Gregory XII Sell the Papal State to Ladislas of Durazzo?

Mandell Creighton, *History of the Papacy from the Great Schism to the Sack of Rome*, i (1899), 213, 217, acquits Gregory XII from the commonly proffered charge of collaboration with Ladislas. But the evidence in the other sense is very persuasive. At the Council of Pisa the articles of 23 May accuse him of certain alienations of the lands of the Church: 'Gregorius alienavit multa bona ecclesiae Romanae . . . necnon terras notabiles, ut Romam, Perusium, Beneventum, et alias in Marchia, et alibi existentes, ac provincias Campaniae et Maritimae pro certa pecuniarum summa ad ditandum fratrem et nepotes suos.' (Raynaldus, ad a. 1409, par. lix.) The later articles of 1 June specifically name Ladislas as benefiting by the alienation, 'Acta Concilii Pisani', published by J. Vincke in *RQ*, xlvi (1938), 261–4. In the evidence to this article, Matteo de Strata (cf. Von Hofmann, *Forschungen zur Geschichte der kurialen Behörden*, ii, 107) is said to have written the bull of

---

[1] Fumi, *Braccio a Roma*, 35 f.; C. Calisse, *Storia di Civitavecchia* (1936), 177–9; Pietro dello Schiavo, 112. That Jacopo Colonna was in some way involved is confirmed by Sforza's expedition against him as a rebel against the Church (dello Schiavo, loc. cit.), and by the sentence passed against him by Isolani, which Martin V lifted in December 1418 (Reg. Vat. 352, fol. 225, printed by Petrini, *Memorie Prenestine* (1795), doc. 41, p. 438).

[2] Finke, *Acta*, iii, no. 176, p. 426.

alienation.   Poncello Orsini is said by the same source to have been sent to Lucca by the Romans to plead with Gregory not to execute the act of alienation, and he gives evidence that Gregory had insisted on making it, probably in return for a payment of twenty thousand florins.   This would fix the date of the alienation between January 1408, when Gregory XII went to Lucca, and April 1408, the date of Ladislas' occupation of Rome. Some colour is given to Poncello Orsini's story by the extraordinary letter, to which he refers, in which the Romans on 9 August 1407 asked Benedict XIII for armed help against Ladislas, since no aid was forthcoming from Gregory XII (published by Ehrle, in his edition of Martin de Alpartil, *Chronica Actitatorum temporibus domini Benedicti XIII*, app. no. 12, p. 544).   In the same evidence given at Pisa, Cardinal Antonio Caetani claimed to have been present when Gregory was arranging with his nephew Paolo to conclude the terms of alienation with Rodolfo Varano, the envoy of Ladislas.

This evidence may all be dismissed as partisan, but one further important piece of testimony may be adduced to support it.   On 4 October 1408 Paolo Correr, Gregory's nephew, passed through Rome on his way to Naples, returning through Rome on 27 October (Pietro dello Schiavo, *Diarium*, 18).   In November or December of the same year Jacopo Salviati, the Florentine ambassador to Naples, asked the Neapolitans for support for the forthcoming Council of Pisa.   He was told in reply that King Ladislas could not now abandon Gregory XII, since Ladislas had recently made an agreement with Paolo Correr, in which the king had for a large sum been conceded Rome, and many other lands of the Church (J. Salviati, 'Cronica, o memorie', in *Delizie degli eruditi Toscani*, xviii, 307).

These statements concord broadly with those of the chroniclers.   The Florentine Anonymous, who is followed by the *Historia fiorentina* of M. Pietro Buoninsegni, and again through Buoninsegni by Sozomenus, states that 'si (*scil.* Ladislao) fece dare al detto papa Ghirigoro la città di Roma liberamente e tutta la Marca e più terre del Patrimonio e del Ducato.   Poi diede al detto papa Ghirigoro fiorini ventimilia d'oro, e il detto papa diede a lui Bologna e Faenza e Forlì e tutte le terre della Chiesa' (*Chron. volgare di Anon. fior.*, 378; Cutolo, *Re Ladislao d'Angiò-Durazzo*, i, 328 and ii, 165 quite mistakes the source and context of this statement).   Other chroniclers allude in a more or less confused way to the same accusation against Gregory XII (Dietrich of Niem, *De Schismate*, 255, and *Nemus Unionis* (1609), c. iv, 2; Martin de Alpartil, *Chronica*, 166; and see also *Chron. volgare di Anon. fior.*, 364, 369–70; Valois, *La France et le Grand Schisme d'Occident*, iii, 578–9).

While not absolutely conclusive, the weight of evidence against Gregory XII seems to be telling.   A striking parallel between the wording of the charges made against him at Pisa and that of the Florentine Anonymous suggests that there were perhaps *two* alienations of Church lands to Ladislas—one made before Ladislas' occupation of Rome in April 1408, and one afterwards, perhaps when Paolo Correr visited Naples in October of the same year.   The 'terras notabiles, ut Romam, Perusium, Beneventum, et alias in Marchia et alibi existentes, ac provincias Campaniae et Maritimae' in the articles of Pisa corresponds to 'la città di Roma liberamente e tutta la Marca e più terre del Patrimonio e del Ducato' in the Florentine Anonymous.   '*Poi* [continues the Anonymous] diede al detto papa Ghirigoro fiorini ventimilia d'oro, e il detto papa diede a lui Bologna e Faenza e Forlì e tutte le terre della Chiesa'.   When Gregory saw that the Romagna was held firmly by the opposition Cardinals, he may have concluded that he could lose nothing by granting it to Ladislas in return for cash, and this was perhaps the occasion of a second alienation.

D

CHAPTER II

THE RESTORATION OF THE PAPAL STATE UNDER MARTIN V

I. *From the Council of Constance to the Peace of Florence*

§ 1. ODDO COLONNA was elected Pope on 11 November 1417, and took the title of Martin V.[1] The many embarrassments of his position at Constance must have made him anxious to leave the city at the earliest possible moment, and to return to Italy to the See of Peter. The Council of Constance had resembled in some respects a Congress of the European powers, and in others a Parliament of the whole ecclesiastical estate. It had created Martin Pope by a new conciliar procedure, and, as long as the Council continued, he was bound to find himself to some extent subordinate to the body which had elected him. The influence used in the papal election by the English and German nations had aroused deep distrust in Italy and Spain, and Martin was by no means free from the threat of a restoration of Benedict XIII as anti-Pope. Alfonso of Aragon's emissary reported the new Pope to be 'un home de poch sentiment e es governat per Cardinals Ytaliens', and the King later delivered the opinion that Martin ought to leave quickly for Avignon or elsewhere, since he was generally supposed to be no longer a free agent.[2]

The prince most under suspicion of making the new Pope into a tool was Sigismond. It was known that his Italian ambitions had re-awakened as soon as the affairs of the Council began to end, and that he planned to descend into Italy and to have himself crowned Emperor in Rome.[3] But it was less known that Martin V was in fact very far from falling in with this design. At the time of his election the tenacity and firmness of purpose, the ruthless will to dominate, which were at the basis of Oddo Colonna's nature, were hidden beneath an exterior of shifty affability. Only slowly did his real powers make themselves known. In January 1418 the Pope assured the Florentine emissaries that he had no close understanding with Sigismond, and added that he was anxious to leave Constance as soon as the reform of the Church was completed, which would not be long. He did not wish another Florentine embassy to be sent until he arrived in Italy.[4]

The restoration of the temporal power was bound to be one of the main concerns of the new Pope, for the whole patrimony of the Church was occupied by usurpers. A second consideration made the temporal power doubly important. The Schism

---

[1] Fromme, 'Die Wahl des Papstes Martin V', *RQ*, x (1896); Finke, *Acta*, iv, 200 f.

[2] Finke, *Acta*, iv, no. 349, p. 156; no. 361, at p. 181, 'multi murmurant . . . quod dominus noster non est hodie in libertate'. Cf. K. A. Fink, *Martin V. und Aragon* (1938), 23.

[3] O. Schiff, *Kaiser Sigismunds italienische Politik*, 73 f. In July 1418 Sigismond promised F. M. Visconti not to enter Italy with a force of more than 500 horse, Romano, *ASL*, 3rd ser., vii (1897), 114.

[4] *Commissioni*, i, 293.

had deprived the Papacy of all its financial reserves, and the legislation and con-cordats of Constance had also cut off several of the 'spiritual' revenues; 'spoils' and some other revenues were now denied to the Apostolic Chamber. The general financial control of the Papacy over the clergy had been much weakened during the Schism, when the national states had thrust their influence deeper and deeper into ecclesiastical preserves. Some sources of papal revenue, such as crusading tenths, never again gave a yield comparable with that of previous centuries, and the share of the princes in such taxes was always on the increase.[1] It therefore became even more important that the Popes should enjoy peacefully the income of the temporal power.

At Constance, Martin V could do little for his Italian lands. He recognised Isolani as Vicar-General in spirituals and temporals, and ordered the subjects of the Church to obey him.[2] A truce was proclaimed for the warring Roman baronage,[3] and letters were sent to the communes of the State of the Church to announce Martin's election.[4] The news was treated with caution; in January 1418 Braccio still forbade Orvieto to celebrate or recognise the election, on the ground that the papal ambassadors still had not announced it to him, and at the same time the free commune of Macerata continued to date its letters 'Ecclesia Romana pastore vacante'.[5] Naples, however, recognised the new Pope at once. The Pope sent his brother Giordano Colonna to the Queen, who in turn despatched an embassy to Constance.[6] Isolani's hand was strengthened in Rome, and the Roman district submitted to the Cardinal and Giordano Colonna,[7] but the Neapolitans retained the papal strongpoints of Castel Sant' Angelo, Ostia, Marino and Terracina;[8] and

---

[1] Cf. A. Gottlob, *Aus der Camera apostolica des 15. Jahrhunderts*, 197 f.

[2] Petracchi, *Vita di M. I. Isolani*, 23. Letters to towns in Campania and Maritima, the Patrimony, Sabina and Umbria, ordering them to obey Isolani, and confirming his actions in matters of rebellion, Reg. Vat. 352, fols. 9, 28v. Raynaldus, ad a. 1417, par. vi, is wrong in saying that Isolani was created Cardinal Legate by Martin V; he was merely made Vicar-General.

[3] Theiner, iii, no. 153, p. 220.

[4] E.g. to Corneto and Viterbo, Theiner, iii, no. 152, p. 219. Cf. Finke, *Acta*, iv, 201–2. Pandolfo Malatesta asked Venice to confirm the news of the election 'quia est homo et vicarius ecclesie', ibid.

[5] For Macerata, Riformanze, vol. 11, fol. 204v. Braccio prohibited Orvieto from recognising the election because 'noi aspectiamo d'ora in hora ambaxadori da nostro signore lo Papa, homini d'autorità . . .' (*BSU*, xxvi, 1923, no. 53, p. 181). For traces of this embassy in the Marches, *Cronache della città di Fermo*, 47; in February 1418 'venerunt ambasciatores Summi Pontificis per terras Ecclesie, confortando ad bonum statum Ecclesie'. On 10 January 1418 the commune of Macerata congratulated Migliorati on the letters he had received from the Cardinals and the Pope, Riformanze, vol. 11, fol. 204v. For the formula in use at Perugia see Campano, *Vita Braccii*, 126, n. The news of the election was, nevertheless, known on 24 November at Spoleto (Zampolini, *Annali di Spoleto*, 147), and on 27 November in Bologna (Piero di Mattiolo, 291).

[6] Faraglia, *Storia della Regina Giovanna II d'Angiò*, 123–4.

[7] Infessura, *Diario della città di Roma* (1890), 22–3.

[8] They held these places until November 1418, Faraglia, 125. There is some doubt whether Terra-cina was returned in 1418 or 1419. Silvestrelli, *Città Castelli e Terre della Regione Romana* (1940), 40, is certainly wrong in stating that Terracina was returned in 1417. But I have not been able to determine whether or not the documents in Contatore, *De historia Terracinense*, 105–6, are correctly dated 1419, as printed (12. Indict.). It is very probable that their date should be 1418, especially as the bull of absolu-tion is dated in Mantua, in 1418 (Contatore, 107–11).

Muzio Attendolo Sforza, with the consent of Martin and Giovanna, continued to hold Benevento.[1]

Only one of the reform measures passed at Constance concerned the temporal power, a decree proposed by the Pope in January 1418, that the rule of the lands and cities of the Church should in future be given only to Cardinals or other ecclesiastics, and that the apostolic vicariate of such lands should not be granted for a term of more than three years, and then only with the consent of the Cardinals.[2] Both these principles Martin was, in general, to adhere to, and they were to be of much importance for papal government.

Martin began, even at Constance, to appoint officers to govern the Italian lands. The Cardinal de Challant was appointed Legate in the March of Ancona, but he fell ill; a Lieutenant was appointed for him in July 1418, and he died early in September, probably without ever having begun his legation.[3] Officials were appointed for the March of Ancona, Romagna, Benevento, Campania and Maritima, and the Patrimony,[4] but in Romagna and the March their authority was small, and Braccio's huge dominions in Umbria continued to split the Papal State down the back. Some of the subject communes, Bologna and Perugia in particular, sent embassies to Constance, but with neither of these important cities did the Pope reach an agreement; to the Perugians he brusquely declined to give the vicariate to Braccio, to Bologna he refused the terms which they demanded.[5] Two other documents also show that he meant to rule with a firm hand: one revoked all concessions, infeudations and alienations of the property of the Roman Church which had been

---

[1] Bonincontri, *Annales*, 116; Minuti, *Vita di M. A. Sforza*, 222. Sforza held Benevento until his death, and on 29 January 1424 Martin V ordered the city to obey his son, Francesco Sforza (S. Borgia, *Memorie istoriche della pontifizia città di Benevento*, iii [1769], 346–53). The grant to the elder Sforza did not prevent Martin V from naming some of the officials there, unless the nomination of the Roman Jacopo de Surdis as Rector (29 November 1417) and of a layman of Benevento as Treasurer (2 January 1418) were made before the agreement with Giovanna. See Reg. Vat. 348, fols. 39, 83v.

[2] Mansi, *Sacr. concil. nova et ampliss. collect.*, xxvii, 1181. Martin violated the first of these principles almost immediately, by naming Malatesta Rector of Romagna and the Count of Montefeltro Duke and Rector of Spoleto. But as Martin's power increased, the administrators whom he named became almost exclusively clerical.

[3] Marino de Tocco, Bishop of Recanati and Macerata, was appointed Deputy ('locumtenens') of the Cardinal on 18 July 1418 (Reg. Vat. 352, fol. 139). The Legate ('mes. de Celanate') was on 12 August 1418 said to be at Argenta, north of Ravenna, with 600 horse (*Carteggio di Paolo Guinigi*, no. 1279, p. 421). But it is probable that this report confuses the Legate with his Deputy.

[4] Marino de Tocco had already been appointed Treasurer of the March of Ancona on 20 December 1417 (Reg. Vat. 348, fol. 28v). He was at this time Bishop of Teramo, and his translation to the see of Recanati and Macerata followed. Ginattano Francisci of Viterbo was made Treasurer of the Patrimony of St. Peter in Tuscia on 2 April 1418 (Reg. Vat. 348, fol. 49). Delfino de Gonzadinis, Abbot of the Monastery of S. Silvestro at Nonantola, was made Treasurer and 'Receiver General' of Romagna on 30 April 1418 (Reg. Vat. 348, fol. 73). He was also Apostolic Collector of the ecclesiastical revenues in the collectorates of Romagna and Ravenna, Div. Cam. 3, fols. 47v; Div. Cam. 5, fols. 134v, 208v. Enrico, Bishop of Feltre, and at this time one of the three Treasurers of the Roman Church (see p. 137 below), was on 3 May 1418 made Rector of Campania and Maritima, and of the Duchy of Benevento, with powers to recover those rights of the Roman Church which had been alienated in the Schism, Reg. Vat. 352, fols. 110v, 114v, 115.

[5] P. Pellini, *Istoria della città di Perugia*, ii, 231–2; G. Zaoli, *Libertas Bononie e Papa Martino V* (1916), 21–2.

made in the Schism,[1] and another revoked all the impositions and assignments of tallage for the benefit of mercenaries in the March of Ancona.[2] The second of these documents complained bitterly of the devastation which the provincials had suffered at the hands of these mercenaries, and was aimed particularly at Braccio, whose brigandage was usually excused by the assignments of tallage which at various times had been made to him by the Church in payment of his *condotta*.[3]

In Naples the election of Martin V was immediately welcomed. It provided valuable support for a régime torn by civil war and weakened by the Queen's quarrel with her husband, the Count of March, and by her general moral debility. Already, in October 1417, the Queen had begun to negotiate for an alliance with Carlo Malatesta and Ludovico Migliorati against Braccio which was later to act as the fulcrum for the return of papal government in the March.[4] It is scarcely surprising that on 14 July, while he was on his way to Italy through Switzerland, Martin was reported as 'molto gratiosamente disposta verso la Maestà di madama'.[5]

But when Martin left Constance, on 16 May 1418, the rebuilding of papal authority had hardly begun. The temporal power could never be re-affirmed until Martin reached Rome, and between Martin and Rome lay the new and hostile state of Braccio, embracing the greater part of Umbria. The financial power which was the nerve of papal war and diplomacy was still disabled; Martin was only beginning to fill the empty treasury which he had inherited from the Council, and the re-establishment of the Collectories and the re-imposition of Chancery taxes still produced only a trickle of money.[6] The powers of Europe were presenting long *rotuli*, asking him to confirm the benefices granted in the Schism, and to grant new favours. The pressure of these demands, and the reforms of clerical taxation decreed in the national concordats, meant that there was little hope of an immediate recovery of the income enjoyed by John XXIII.[7] No effective war could therefore be waged against Braccio, who was securely straddled across central Italy.

---

[1] Biblioteca Angelica, Cod. 1426, fol. 151v (cf. E. Narducci, *Catalogus codicum manuscriptorum praeter graec. et orientales in bibliotheca Angelica*, 1893). The document is without a date, but was issued at Constance ('cum itaque in hoc sacro constantiencis concilio pro statu universalis ecclesie prospere conservando . . .') and may be the same as that referred to by Contelori, *Vita Martini V*, 48, dated 5 non. Martii anno II (? for anno I).

[2] Theiner, iii, no. 154, p. 221.

[3] In September 1417 Braccio had, in spite of Isolani's prohibition, exacted a tallage from the cities and clergy of Umbria and the Patrimony. His demands appeal to the authority of Tartaglia as 'Rector' of the Patrimony (Valentini, *BSU*, xxvi (1923), pp. 31–2 and no. 43, p. 177.

[4] C. Minieri Riccio, *Saggio di Codice Diplomatico* (1879), ii, pt. 1, no. 41, p. 50; Faraglia; *Storia della Regina Giovanna*, 101; the treaty of alliance which was concluded against Braccio in April 1418 is printed by Tonini, *Storia civile e sacra Riminese*, v, pt. 2, no. 30, p. 120.

[5] L. Frati, 'Il "Diario" di Cambio Cantelmi', *ASI*, 5th ser., xlviii (1911), 119.

[6] F. Miltenberger, 'Versuch einer Neuordnung der päpstlichen Kammer in den ersten Regierungsjahren Martins V', *RQ*, viii (1894); Some types of income, e.g. the taxes from the Registry and the 'bullatores', immediately regained the level they had under John XXIII. In IE 379, fols. 3–5, the total of these taxes for July–August 1418 is over 4,000 florins. But annates had hardly begun to come in, and first fruits had been abolished. The 'total' income for this period is unknown, as the relevant volume of the Exitus is missing.

[7] Cf. K. A. Fink, *Martin V. und Aragon* (1938), 39 f.; idem, 'Die Sendung des Kardinals von Pisa nach Aragon', *RQ*, xli (1933); 47 f.; J. Haller, 'England und Rom unter Martin V', *QF*, viii (1905);

Martin had, therefore, to re-establish himself in Italy by means of diplomacy, and to make the best terms with Braccio he could find, and he began to prepare the ground by offering his services as a mediator for the warring Italian powers. When the Venetian ambassadors arrived in Constance in 1418, Martin immediately proposed himself as mediator between the Signory and Sigismond, and a five years' truce was agreed on 28 March 1418. But the enmity of the two powers, which had shown itself in a trade war during the preceding two years, was too strong to be contained: fighting broke out in Friuli on 10 May, and it is doubtful if the truce was ever ratified.[1]

On 29 July 1418 the Pope was in Geneva, and his representatives took part in the truce arranged between his vicar and feudatory, the Marquis of Ferrara, and the Duke of Milan.[2] Filippo Maria Visconti was very willing to use the support of the Pope and Emperor in the final stages of his reconstructing the Visconti lands. On 2 April 1418 he had already concluded an agreement with Sigismond by which he was to be invested with the Duchy, and to be assured of Imperial support in his enterprise against Genoa; a series of trade pacts followed, and in July he was named Captain of the Imperial Troops against Venice, although he was careful, in fact, never to take the field.[3] The main remaining enemy inside the Visconti lands was Pandolfo Malatesta, the *signore* of Brescia. From 12 to 19 October 1418 Martin was in Milan, and on 23 October he reached Brescia; on 2 November 1418 Visconti authorised his emissary to treat for peace with Pandolfo Malatesta under Martin's mediation. Sentence was pronounced by the Pope between Visconti and Malatesta on 18 January; the peace did not last long, but it gave Visconti time to turn all his forces against Genoa.[4]

On 24 October 1418 Martin arrived in Mantua, and during his three months' stay there he began to know who were his friends and who his opponents in Italy. Braccio had not despoiled central Italy for twelve years without making enemies. When Braccio came out of winter quarters in 1418 he had made an expedition into the March, demanding arrears of the tallage which had been assigned to him. The coalition formed against him in the March by the Neapolitans failed; Ludovico Migliorati was defeated and perhaps captured in April after the fall of Falerone, and 8,000 florins were exacted from him; while the lesser communes of the March were,

---

N. Valois, *La France et le Grand Schisme d'Occident*, iv, 426. France seems not to have made such demands. For the *rotuli* of the Universities of Vienna, Cologne and Heidelberg, see *AKöG*, xv (1856), 66–9. For the *rotulus* of Louis Duke of Bavaria, presented in April 1418, see Reg. Suppl. 120, fols. 84, 125.

[1] Sanudo, *Vite de' Duchi*, 920; Schiff, 69; Cusin, *Il confine orientale d'Italia*, i, 306 f. For Sigismond's attempts to close the trade routes through Venice and divert German trade to the east through Genoa and Hungary, *Deutsche Reichstagsakten*, vii, no. 210, p. 319.

[2] Romano, *ASL*, 3rd ser., vii (1897), no. 389, p. 115.

[3] Schiff, 71–3; cf. Romano, 114 n.

[4] Romano, nos. 393–4, pp. 116–7; Arm. 34, vol. 4, fol. 118. Peace was pronounced before the Pope on 18 January. For the itinerary see Miltenberger, 'Das Itinerarium Martins V von Constanz bis Rom', *MIöG*, xv (1894); for his agreement with the Gonzaga prior to his entry into Mantua, dated 7 October 1418, Div. Cam. 14, fol. 41.

in spite of the papal prohibition, compelled to pay Braccio tallage.[1]   In June the Florentines gave Braccio passage through their lands to allow him to attack Lucca, and after he had devastated the countryside of Lucca he made her tyrant, Paolo Guinigi, pay an immense sum to buy immunity.   To Florence Braccio was a friend beyond price; not only was he a bar to the resurgence of a strong Papal State, but his presence impeded the intervention of any other Italian power in the area between Tuscany and the Kingdom of Naples.   He was not in formal alliance with Florence, although rumours to this effect continually circulated; he had been her *raccomandato*, as had been his allies the Trinci, since 1413,[2] and the Florentines made it their business to plead his case before Martin V.   The Varano of Camerino were also Braccio's allies; in spite of their connexion by marriage with Paolo Guinigi they refused to stir in the latter's favour in the summer of 1418,[3] and on Braccio's return from Tuscany in August, Berardo Varano was pleased to help him in an attack on the traditional enemy of Camerino, Norcia.[4]

During the course of 1418 the opposition to Braccio began to take shape.   Count Guid'Antonio of Montefeltro had sent an embassy to Martin as early as December 1417.   In July 1418 it was reported that the Pope had 'novamente contrata buona fraternitade' with the Count.[5]   As the friend and guarantor of Carlo Malatesta, and as the lord of Assisi, an enclave in Braccio's stronghold of Perugia, Guid'Antonio could expect little affectation from Braccio.   The Count travelled to Mantua to meet the Pope, and in January 1419 he was created Duke of the Duchy of Spoleto, with the powers of Rector.[6]

Papal diplomacy found a fruitful field in the granting of papal vicariates and fees to the *signori* and barons of the Papal State.   To none of the petty tyrants was the grant of a vicariate a matter of indifference.   Their rule was often a precarious one; they thought it important to have a legal title from the Papacy and were willing to pay for it.   They therefore sent ambassadors to the Pope as he moved south. From the March of Ancona the Varano of Camerino sent an embassy to Martin even before he left Constance.   Their position in Camerino was a particularly delicate one; they had never been elected by the assembly of the commune as tyrants of the city, and they therefore lacked the quasi-democratic basis for their régime which most of the other *signori* possessed.   They exercised a sort of tempered tyranny or protectorship, and they obtained from the Pope, not a vicariate, but a guarantee that they should enjoy the same rights and dominion over Camerino that their

[1] Campano, *Vita Braccii*, 126–30; Valentini, *BSU*, xxvi (1923), 39 f.   Braccio demanded the current instalment of tallage from Macerata in July 1418, and although the commune grumbled that the Pope ought to provide for the peaceful state of the March; the money was paid.   Macerata, Archivio Priorale, Riformanze, vol. 11, fol. 259.

[2] *Capitoli del Comune di Firenze*, i, no. 28, p. 551, by which Braccio becomes *raccomandato* to Florence for ten years.   Ibid, nos. 26–7, p. 550, by which the Trinci brothers become *raccomandati* of Florence for five years from 30 October 1418, but will not be required to fight against Martin V.

[3] *Il Carteggio di Paolo Guinigi*, no. 1248, p. 414.

[4] Campano, Valentini, loc. cit.   Norcia had attacked the countryside of Camerino as recently as 7 March 1418, R. Arch. di Stato in Lucca, *Regesti*, iii, pt. 2, no. 128, pp. 22–3.

[5] Frati, *ASI*, 5th ser., xlviii (1911), 121.

[6] Theiner, iii, no. 162, p. 233; *Cronaca di Ser Guerriero di Gubbio*, 40.

ancestors had had.[1] Most of the *signori* of the March followed suit while Martin V was in Mantua or Florence, and papal vicariates were given to Ludovico Migliorati of Fermo,[2] besides to such lesser *signorotti* as the Brancaleone of Castel Durante[3] or the Cimi of Cingolì.[4] In Romagna the vicariate was given to the Alidosi in Imola,[5] to the Ordelaffi in Forlì,[6] to the Polenta in Ravenna,[7] and to Malatesta de Malatestis in Pesaro.[8] The Manfredi of Faenza offered obedience, and paid considerable sums for their lands, but it is doubtful if they received the vicariate of Faenza.[9] In

[1] Reg. Vat. 348, fol. 59v. As the brothers Varano have ruled and defended the city of Camerino, and as Gregory XI issued certain letters in favour of their family, 'declaramus nostre intencionis existere quod status ac regimen civitatis comitatus et districtus predictorum, quo ad gubernationem statum preheminenciam et honores eorum toto tempore vite ipsorum, et quoad idem Rodolphus et eius filii prefati vitam duxerint in humanis, in aliquo non mutentur, sed in eisdem terminis et condicionibus quibus utebantur predecessores eorum ante exortum scisma in ecclesia sancte dei et gaudebant etiam perseverent' (22 April 1418). Other bulls in favour of the Varano, Reg. Vat. 348, fols. 60v, 63, 66. Their payments to the Apostolic Chamber, IE 379, fol. 11v; Div. Cam. 4, fol. 214. For the relation of the Varano to Camerino see also J. Guiraud, *L'Etat Pontifical après le Grand Schisme* (1896), 202–3. Cf. also the relation of the March of Ancona of 1371 (Theiner, ii, no. 527, at p. 536), 'tamen dominus Rodolphus [Varanus] et sui fratres merentur pocius dici Rectores quam Commune'.

[2] He went to Mantua to submit to the Pope in January 1419 (*Cronache della città di Fermo*, 48), but the bulls of his vicariate were not issued until the following August (Reg. Vat. 348, fol. 138v); ibid., fol. 143v, the *tallia militum* of his lands is reduced by a quarter, to 2,250 florins. Arm. 34, vol. 4, fol. 136v, on 21 August 1419 Migliorati's representatives promise to make a payment of 1,400 florins for arrears of *census* due before 1 August 1419.

[3] Florence, Biblioteca Nazionale, xix, 82, 'liber capitaneorum', fol. 109, which contains a number of rough notes of vicariates granted in 1419/20, with the dates of the bulls of appointment. This volume is described below, p. 203. Thus, 'Brancaleone Gentilis de Brancaleon' Rector Masse Trabarie, Mantue 4 non' Jan' anno II'; 'Galeottus miles et Albericus de Brancaleonibus vicarii in castris et terris castri Durantis, Sascorbarii, Montislochi, Lonani et Petrelle Massanorum ad triennium, census consuetus, Florentie VII kal' Aprilis anno tercio'.

[4] On 24 May 1419 Giovanni Cimi had his assessment of tallage reduced to 450 florins, Reg. Vat. 352, fol. 252. In the same month he paid the arrears and current payments of his *census* of 50 florins a year, Arch. Cam. pt. i, no. 824, fol. 54v; Div. Cam. 5, fols. 64, 106; IE 379, fols. 19, 25v. Guiraud, *L'Etat Pontifical*, 211, overlooks the existence of this vicariate, and refers to Cingoli as a free city. The Cimi had in fact held Cingoli in vicariate since 1406 and earlier, cf. Theiner, iii, no. 87, p. 151.

[5] In bulls of 11 and 14 November 1418 they were forgiven their arrears of *census*, were granted the vicariate of their lands for three years, while at the same the vicariate was in another bull extended beyond the triennial period for the duration of the Pope's good pleasure (Theiner, iii, no. 157, p. 229; Reg. Vat. 353, fols. 293, 294). Ludovico Alidosi took the oath for the vicariate on 24 November, and two days later a Florentine banker guaranteed the payment of 1,500 florins of *census*, on the security of the bulls of vicariate (Div. Cam. 3, fols. 125, 126).

[6] On 28 November Giorgio Ordelaffi was granted the vicariate of Forlì for three years, and on the same day the vicariate was extended beyond this three years, for the period of the Pope's good pleasure (Theiner, iii, no. 158, p. 229; Reg. Vat. 348, fols. 81, 96v, 98v).

[7] On 29 January 1419 Obizzo da Polenta was granted the vicariate of Ravenna on the same terms as it had been granted to his predecessors by Boniface IX, viz., for a term of ten years. As a composition for the *census* owed for the vicariate the Chamber accepted 2,000 florins, which he had paid by 31 May 1419 (Reg. Vat. 348, fol. 109v; Reg. Vat. 352, fol. 249v; IE 379, fols. 13, 19v; Div. Cam. 5, fols. 21, 109v; Arch. Cam. pt. i, no. 824, fol. 36v). Boniface IX's bull of vicariate is printed by Fantuzzi, *Monumenti Ravennati de' secoli di Mezzo*, iii, no. 124, p. 235.

[8] Malatesta de Malatestis of Pesaro seems to have submitted early in 1418. His *census* for the vicariate was reduced on 29 January 1418 from 1,800 to 1,200 florins, Theiner, iii, no. 163, p. 234; Reg. Vat. 352, fol. 223. On 1 February he paid 3,200 florins as *census* for the two years following the accession of Martin V (IE 379, fol. 13v, Arch. Cam. pt. i, no. 824, fol. 37; Div. Cam. 5, fol. 17v).

[9] They paid 100 florins *census* for a part of their lands on 15 December 1418, IE 379, fol. 9. Cf. Florence, 'liber capitaneorum', fol. 109, 'Carolus Guidantonius, Astorg' et Johannes Galeaz' de Man-

Umbria, Città di Castello obtained the vicariate for the commune,[1] and the Atti of Sassoferrato offered their obedience.[2] Among the barons of the Roman District, the Conti of Segni submitted,[3] and the Orsini and Savelli were made to accept a papal judge to settle their quarrel.[4] By mid-1419 all the major barons and *signori* of the Papal State had submitted to the Pope save for Braccio and his closest allies, such as the Trinci of Foligno or the Carrara of Ascoli.

These submissions were of financial as well as of political importance, since the vicariates were invariably granted against a considerable *census*. Besides *census*, large sums were often exacted as tax on the bulls of vicariate,[5] and the apostolic vicars also became liable to pay the tallage or *tallia militum*.[6]

Every step of this kind increased Martin's bargaining powers in the negotiations with Braccio. But Braccio's military position was extremely strong. Papal authority, assisted by Sforza's garrison troops, held the country south of Rome as far as the Kingdom of Naples, and the Patrimony of St. Peter as far north as Viterbo and Corneto (now Tarquinia). Up the Tiber, papal rule went as far north of Rome as Orte and, for a time, Amelia, but at Bagnorea Braccio's domains began. He and his allies, the Trinci, ruled directly or indirectly almost the whole of Umbria, save for Amelia, Assisi, and Spoleto. His other associate, Tartaglia, ruled in Toscanella, Castro and the lands round the lake of Bolsena, save for Montefiascone, which for the time being held for Sforza and the Church.[7]

In the March of Ancona the depredations of Braccio inclined most of the *signori* and the communes to the obedience of the Pope, to whom even Braccio's allies the Varano had rendered formal obedience. On 4 September 1418 preparations were being made to receive the new Vice-Legate, Marino de Tocco, Bishop of Macerata and Recanati, and to prepare his palace for him in Macerata. At the same time the commune of Macerata appointed representatives to go to his first provincial Parliament at Ancona. On 27 September 1418 the Vice-Legate was in Recanati, whence he wrote to Macerata ordering various 'reforms' to be made in the statutes of the commune. On 16 October he was in Macerata. The March was at this time

fredibus solverunt florenos MM et habuerunt remissionem de censibus presentis, VIII kal' Aprilis anno II, Florentie', and doc. 2(a) below.

[1] Representatives of the city paid arrears of *census* to the Chamber on 6 December 1418 (Div. Cam. 4, fols. 180v–183, IE 379, fol. 9; Arch. Cam. pt. i, no. 824, fol. 28v).

[2] Florence, 'liber capitaneorum', fol. 109, 'Franc' Aluisi militi et Carolus Joachini de Actis domicelli Camerinen' in terra Saxiferrati vicarii, Florentie, 2 id' Jan' anno 3, ad beneplacitum'.

[3] On 5 May 1418 Ildebrandino Conti received the vicariate of Segni, and of the *castra* of Palliano and Serrone, for three years, Reg. Vat. 348, fol. 76v.

[4] Giovanni of Soana was sent by the Pope to compose discords among the Roman barons and princes on 12 April 1419, and the Savelli and Orsini were at the same time ordered to compose their feud and to send proctors either to the Pope or to Giordano Colonna, Reg. Vat. 352, fols. 261–5.

[5] See preceding notes. Although the Chamber accepted only 400 florins from Giorgio Ordelaffi instead of the thousand which were due, he had to pay 2,000 florins tax on the bulls of vicariate (Div. Cam. 3, fol. 128, ibid., 4, fol. 192v; Reg. Vat. 348, fols. 91, 96v, 98v).

[6] See pp. 113–14, 188–9 below.

[7] Valentini, Campano, loc. cit. The loyalty of Amelia was recognised by the Pope on 29 January 1418, and the privileges of the town confirmed, Reg. Vat. 352, fols. 37v, 42v. Later, however, the town fell to Braccio.

exhausted by war; 1416 and 1418 were bad harvests in most of Italy, and the communes were ill able to pay the tallage which was demanded by both the Church and Braccio.   In February 1419 there was a meeting of representatives of the various towns of the March of Ancona at Recanati, to discuss the sending of ambassadors to the Pope to ask for the reduction of taxes.[1]   In March of the same year Ancona secured a reduction of tallage to 1,000 florins,[2] and in another bull the Pope announced, on account of the impoverishment of the March by war, a general reduction by a quarter in the amount of tallage due from Ancona, Macerata, Recanati and a large number of smaller communities.[3]

§ 2.   The Pope had not gone far toward the recovery of the temporal power until he had retrieved Bologna.   It was the richest of the papal provinces, and one which would not only guarantee him a hold on Romagna, but also immensely increase his strength as against Venice, Florence and Milan.   But the city, still very conscious of its present riches and its past liberties, stood out for stiff terms.   A first embassy went to Constance and demanded the vicariate of Bologna for twenty years for the commune, the recovery of numerous lands and strong places from the Este, the Manfredi, the Alidosi and others, and the payment of 200,000 florins as compensation for the monies paid by the commune to redeem the castles given in pledge by John XXIII to Braccio, and those bought back from the Marquis of Este.   Finally, the commune did not wish to pay a *census* of more than 5,000 florins a year.   To this the Pope replied that he would grant a vicariate of three years for a *census* of 15,000 florins a year, of which 5,000 would be assigned to the University.   A second embassy found him at Geneva; they repeated the same demands, and added that Martin should not send a Legate, but should concede the vicariate to the commune as was done by Gregory XI and Urban VI.   No agreement was found; on 29 July 1418 it was reported from Geneva that the Pope still would not leave for Italy, because Bologna would not receive him.[4]   On 9 November, while the Pope was in Mantua, the papal ambassadors entered Bologna 'e domandono lo dominio e la signoria de la detta citade al Regimento del puovolo e de le arti che regeva allora . . .'[5] As a result, a Bolognese embassy went to Mantua and replied 'ch'erano contenti de darli el spirituale et che voleano guardare Bologna per loro'.   Again no agreement was reached; to this embassy Martin offered the same terms, and added that he wished the commune to nominate four candidates for the office of *podestà*, of whom he would accept one.[6]   On 20 December the Bishop of Bologna, Nicolò Albergati, was

[1] Macerata, Riformanze, vol. 11, fols. 262, 263v, 268; Compagnoni, *La Reggia Picena*, 306–7.

[2] Reg. Vat. 352, fol. 237.   See Ancona, Atti Consigliari, vol. 29, fol. 10; the Vice-Legate asks them to send ambassadors to Mantua, fols. 14v, 16v.   The *podestà* went to Florence, and returned with news of the reduction of the tallage (ibid.).

[3] Reg. Vat. 352, fol. 244.

[4] Zaoli, *Libertas Bononie e Papa Martino V*, 21, 36 f., and the appendix, p. 131 f., where he prints the instructions given to the various embassies sent to Martin V.   See also *Corp. Chron. Bonon.*, iii, 560–1; Frati, *ASI*, 5th ser., xlviii (1911), 122, 129–30, 134.

[5] Piero di Mattiolo, 293–4; *Corp. Chron. Bonon.*, 560.

[6] Zaoli, 146 f., P. de Töth, *Il beato cardinale Nicolò Albergati e i suoi tempi*, i, 338; *Corp. Chron. Bonon.*, 561.

summoned by the Pope to Mantua; this proved a decisive move, for Albergati's sanctity and force of character were to be of immense value to the papal cause.[1]

The moment for forcing the hand of the free commune was approaching; the finances of the city were in a critical state, and in the countryside a bad harvest, many years of war, and the wanton devastation which Bologna had herself carried out to punish S. Giovanni in Persiceto, had all produced a dangerous and universal discontent. The police reports for the *contado* discovered such sentiments as 'le cose non sono per durare in questo stato . . . lo stato de bologna no pò durare nell essere che gliè . . . e noi semo tanti che faremo venire lo papa e mutarimo questo stato in altra forma . . .'. The commune had to distribute free corn, and since the spring of 1418 an extraordinary wine tax, the 'imbottato' had been imposed.[2]

Having returned once to the city, on 18 January 1419 Albergati left Bologna again for Mantua, 'as ambassador of the Commune of Bologna' says the clerk Piero di Mattiolo, but it is very doubtful if he had formal powers from the commune. He carried with him a schedule of the demands of the commune, which still exists, with annotations in Albergati's hand. To the demand for the vicariate he wrote: 'Dominus papa respondet quod vult approbare regimen vestrum populare etiam in perpetuum . . . sed non sub titulo Vicariatus et dicit quod est melius pro nobis, et etiam alii dicunt viri docti'. Martin also required the commune to supply a hundred lances for six months if there should be war with Braccio, but the Bishop added that it was unlikely that these lances would ever be needed, since Braccio now appeared to be humbly disposed towards the Pope. At the end of the document the Bishop wrote that 'De eius adventu ad civitatem Bononie dicit quod non vult venire vobis invitis, nec ullo modo veniet vobis invitis . . . Et dixit mihi quod iretis ferrariam'.[3] The last sentence refers to Martin's progress south from Mantua to Ferrara : he left Mantua on 6 February.

The Bolognese ambassadors therefore also left for Ferrara on 6 February, and were already in the city when Martin arrived on the ninth. Their instructions[4] were almost in the form in which Martin eventually granted the popular régime to the city, save that the ambassadors at first refused the hundred lances against Braccio, and then were compelled to give way. They dropped the demand for a vicariate under that precise name, and expressed themselves willing if necessary to accept Martin's compromise, by which he should appoint a *podestà* out of three candidates proposed by the commune, when he was within a hundred leagues of the city. At other times the *podestà* was to be appointed by the Bishop. The matter was

[1] De Töth, i, 339. His contemporary Flavio Biondo, *Italia Illustrata* (Italian translation, Venice, 1543) calls Albergati 'persona prudentissima, e santa'.

[2] Zaoli, 28–9; 39–40; 77.

[3] De Töth, i, 340 He prints a facsimile of the document, facing p. 344. De Töth reads 'quod est melius pro vobis' where Zaoli, p. 49, reads 'quod est melius pro nobis'. In the fascimile the 'v' in the word 'vobis', later in the document, is quite different from 'n' and 'u', and I have no doubt but that Zaoli's reading is the correct one. The Bishop was, of course, a Bolognese. Cf. Longhi, *AMDR*, 3rd ser., xxiv (1906), 159, who also reads 'nobis'.

[4] De Töth, i, 345; Zaoli, 150, 154 f.

agreed in February, and after further discussion of detail, the bull was issued on 13 May.[1]

The agreement was uneasy and unfriendly, and, as the passage quoted above suggests, Martin was probably refused entrance into the city; he avoided Bologna when he went on from Ferrara to Florence on 15 February, and Leonardo Bruni claims to have pointed out to him in Florence a year later that he was compelled by the refusal of Bologna to admit him to make a long detour through Ravenna and Forlì.[2] It was a hard thing for a sovereign pontiff to be refused entry into a city which had just made its formal act of submission to him, but the hard bargain which the Bolognese had just driven with the Pope, and their general stiffness and intransigence toward the Roman court, are typical of the stiff-necked independence of Bologna. The city had bitterly resented the so-called tyranny exercised there by John XXIII, and was determined not to permit it to recur. The citizens preferred a native to a foreign tyranny, and during the course of the fifteenth century the papal superiority over the city dwindled every year, until the papal Legate in Bologna was finally withdrawn and the Bentivoglio family were granted the vicariate. But in essence Martin's position was saved; Bologna was granted to the commune for three years, but only under a form of administration, and not as a vicariate. The city was to dispose of its own finances, and to elect its own officials, save for the *podestà*. The formal recognition of the Pope, however grudgingly granted, was of the utmost importance. Martin could now move south to Florence and Rome with his eastern flank covered.

§ 3. On 23 November 1418, Pietro Morosini, Cardinal of S. Maria in Domnica, was appointed Legate to Naples and given faculties to crown Giovanna.[3] Already, before this, Giani Carraciolo had on 13 November left Naples with Antonio Colonna to hand over Ostia, Castel Sant' Angelo, Marino and Terracina to the papal representatives, the Colonna.[4] The Cardinal, accompanied by Giordano Colonna, arrived in Naples on 24 January 1419, and on 27 January Martin wrote to Giovanna, asking that

---

[1] Theiner, iii, no. 166, p. 236; the ancients of the commune were appointed 'in temporalibus Rectores, administratores et gubernatores' of Bologna. Zaoli, 59, prints parts of two minutes of the bull which are preserved in Bologna. Cf. R. Arch. di Stato in Lucca, *Regesti*, iii, pt. 2, no. 302, p. 54; in a letter from Bologna dated 19 February 1419 'Arete sentito come messer Gozadino e messer Marcho andonno a Ferara per concludere l'accordo fra il Santo Padre e questa Comunità. Il che, mediante la gratia di Dio, è seguito, e in questa vi mando copia de la conclusioni'. The absolution of the commune is in Reg. Vat. 348, fols. 128, 129 (7 June 1419). The first payment of *census* was made on 22 June, IE 379, fol. 20v. The first *podestà* to be appointed by the Pope was Paolo de Leone of Padua, on 2 September 1419, Reg. Vat. 348, fol. 146.

[2] *Commentarii* (Muratori, *RRIISS*, xix, pt. 3), 446, 'Bononia quoque parere abnuente, ut tibi necessariam fuerit, cum ex Ferraria Florentiam venire velles, per ravennatem et foroliviensem agrum longo ambitu iter deflectere'. Buoninsegni (p. 13) and Sozomenus (p. 9) follow Bruni from the other relevant passage at p. 44 'Bononiam vitans, quae se per id tempus in libertatem vindicaret'. That he avoided Bologna because of the plague there, as Frati suggests, *ASI*, 5th ser., xlviii (1911), 130, seems unlikely, especially so early in the year.

[3] Raynaldus, ad a., par. xxix; Reg. Vat. 352, fol. 180v, which has the date 9 kal. decembris and not 4 kal. decembris as in Raynaldus; Faraglia, *Storia della Regina Giovanna II d'Angiò*, 124–5.

[4] Faraglia, loc. cit.

Sforza should take the field against Braccio by March of the same year.[1] The Colonna in the meanwhile had risen to greatness in Naples; Antonio became in August 1418 Vice-Regent of the Duchy of Calabria, Lorenzo, already Duke of Alba, became Grand Chamberlain in February 1419, and Giordano in 1420 became Prince of Salerno, all being given appropriate grants of lands and rents with these dignities.[2] Sforza was informed on 6 March that he had been named Standard-Bearer of the Church, but the political crisis caused by the freeing of the Count of March from captivity prevented his leaving the Kingdom, and he did not finally march north until May.[3] The promise of Sforza's army was of very great importance. The Pope could not at this early stage of the pontificate afford to pay a whole army of mercenaries, but the alliance of Naples promised for the first time to give him a powerful army to put into the field against Braccio.

The first embassy from Braccio had found Martin while he was still at Constance. Of its proceedings little is known, save that Braccio's second embassy, which went to the Pope in Mantua in November 1418, complained to the Florentines that Martin's attitude towards Braccio had considerably cooled in the interval between the two embassies. Taxed with this by the Florentines, Martin denied it, but added that while he was willing to concede anything to Braccio which he honestly could, Braccio's demands were excessive, and principally so in that he wanted the vicariate of Perugia, which had formerly never been granted by the Popes except to the commune.[4] This is the first pointer which we have to the conduct of the negotiations, and it shows them at an early stage of bargaining, as Martin was eventually to concede the vicariate of Perugia and a very great deal more.

Early in January 1419 Florence sent a second embassy to Mantua, this time expressly to negotiate on Braccio's behalf.[5] Later in the month it was noted by Bishop Albergati on the text of the settlement proposed between the commune of Bologna and the Pope, that although the Pope asked for 100 lances from the commune in the event of war with Braccio, this contingency was not thought likely by the Roman Court, since Braccio was now 'humbly disposed' towards Martin V.[6] From the time of Martin's arrival in Florence on 26 February the pace of negotiations increased. The Pope had appointed a commission of two Cardinals to deal with the

---

[1] Minieri Riccio, *Saggio di Codice Diplomatico*, ii, pt. 1, no. 47, p. 58. The brief is transcribed in a letter to Sforza from Giovanna dated 6 March 1419; in the brief Martin asks that Sforza may be 'in campis Romanis' by March. Cf. Faraglia, 128.

[2] Faraglia, 145 f. The date of the grant of the principate of Salerno to Giordano Colonna was March 1420 and not August 1419, as stated by Faraglia, 145–6. The concession printed by Minieri Riccio, ii, pt. 1, no. 50, p. 64, of 3 August 1419, is not the concession of the principate, but the confirmation of a promise to concede it which the Queen had made to Lorenzo and Giordano Colonna earlier in the year. Cf. Pastor, *History of the Popes*, i, 227; Coppi, *Memorie Colonnesi* (1855), 168; Bonincontri, *Annales*, 117.

[3] Faraglia, 128 f.

[4] *Commissioni*, i, 308–9. Braccio's first embassy to Martin V is probably that referred to by P. Pellini, *Dell'Historia di Perugia* (1664), ii, 231. It was headed by Braccio's ally, Berardo Varano of Camerino.

[5] R. Arch. di Stato in Lucca, *Regesti*, iii, pt. 2, no. 236, p. 44.

[6] De Töth, *Il beato cardinale Nicolò Albergati*, i, 340.

affair[1]—at every turn he used the Sacred College as advisers and assistants. The two Cardinals were probably Giordano Orsini and the venerable Raynaldo Brancaccio, but on his return from Aragon in April 1419 direction seems to have passed to the powerful Cardinal of Pisa, Alamanno Adimari.[2] On 14 March Bindaccio da Ricasoli had arrived in Florence as Braccio's ambassador to the *signoria*; he was probably also accredited to the Pope.[3]

At this stage of the negotiations the time factor became all-important. In the early spring of 1419 all the papal diplomacy of the past year and a half was coming to fruition. The agreement with the commune of Bologna was being concluded, Guid'Antonio of Montefeltro was almost certainly enlisted as a papal mercenary, the Duke of Milan was being secured as a powerful friend. Most important of all, Sforza had been asked to be in the Roman district by March 1419. On this last the whole of papal policy depended. But it was not easy for Sforza to move from a court seething with intrigues against him, under a Queen who would always obey the latest of her favourites and lovers. In March Sforza was still in Naples, but was organising his army to move north, and sending advance supplies to Rome.

Braccio was no man to wait while the scales were being tipped against him, and he set about redressing the balance in a short and brilliant campaign. On 6 March 1419, on the pretext of the 12,000 ducats for which he had stood guarantor to Carlo Malatesta when the latter was released from captivity in 1417, Braccio struck hard and with immediate effect at the Count of Montefeltro. He attacked Gubbio and narrowly missed having the town. Having devastated the countryside he marched back to the Count's other possession of Assisi and almost immediately captured it; the defeated Montefeltro was forced before the end of March to conclude a truce through the mediation of Florence.[4] Without respite, and with the extraordinary speed which he could always command in war, Braccio marched straight from Assisi to Spoleto, the last papal stronghold in Umbria, and one of the most powerful and important fortresses in central Italy. Besides being the centre of the Duchy, Spoleto commanded the only remaining line of communications between Rome and the March. Braccio had the town on 15 April, but the castle, the strongest of all Albornoz' castles, held out. A few days later Braccio himself was wounded in an attack on the tower which protected Matteo Gattaponi's great aqueduct.[5] At the same time as their chief campaigned in Umbria, his chancellor Giovanni della Rocca

---

[1] In November 1418, *Commissioni*, i, 308.

[2] The two Cardinals originally appointed were probably two of the three Cardinals present when Corrado Trinci was received as Braccio's ambassador in May 1419 (doc. 25 below). They were therefore Cardinal Giordano Orsini, the Bishop of Albano, and Cardinal Raynaldo Brancaccio. The third Cardinal present was Alamanno Adimari, who had returned from Aragon to Florence only on 20 April (K. A. Fink; 'Die Sendung des Kardinals von Pisa nach Aragon', *RQ*, xli, 1933, 59). Adimari was mainly responsible for the second and definitive peace with Braccio in 1420 : see the letter of Nicolò Uzzano and others in L. Fumi, *Codice diplomatico della città di Orvieto*, 674–5, and the instrument of peace, in *ASR*, lii (1929), 348.

[3] R. Arch. di Stato in Lucca, *Regesti*, iii, pt. 2, no. 342, p. 61.

[4] A. Pellegrini; 'Gubbio sotto i Conti e Duchi di Urbino', *BSU*, xi (1905), 176; R. Valentini, ibid. xxvi (1923), 54; Campano; *Vita Braccii*, 131. For the truce, R. Arch. di Stato in Lucca, *Regesti*, iii, pt. 2, no. 372, p. 67. [5] Campano, loc. cit.; Zampolini, *Annali di Spoleto*, 147–51.

and his lieutenant Nicolò Piccinino were ravaging the March of Ancona, demanding money from the towns and spoiling the countryside.[1]

Braccio had up to this point made an elaborate pretence of devotion to papal interests; his attack on Spoleto was his first open attack on the Papacy, and as Valentini has justly remarked,[2] it marks the real beginning of his great duel with Martin V. But the successful resistance of the garrison of Spoleto meant that it was not the decisive blow which Braccio had intended; he had not succeeded in crushing all resistance in central Italy before Sforza could move north, and the issue of the struggle continued to depend upon the movements of Sforza. Nicolò da Uzzano wrote from Florence on 6 May that if Sforza reached Rome, either the peace between Braccio and the Pope would not be made, or it would be made on terms more favourable to the Pope.[3] As early as 27 April it had been expected in Rome that Sforza would be there by 1 May;[4] that he did not arrive was probably due to the escape from prison of Queen Giovanna's husband the Count of March. Early in May the Count's intrigues caused Sforza, having set out from Naples with his army, to turn back to deal with the political crisis there.[5]

On 15 May Carlo Malatesta was made Rector of Romagna, and it was made clear to the *signori* of the province that they should obey him.[6] Nor was Martin's diplomacy inactive in northern Italy. In April Francesco Pizzolpassi was sent to assist in the negotiations between the Marquis of Este and Filippo Maria Visconti, principally over the return of Parma and Reggio to Milan. On 5 May Visconti showed himself willing to accept the arbitration of the Pope in this matter.[7] On 10 May 1419 Visconti again used Martin V as arbitrator, and the Pope pronounced sentence in a settlement of his quarrel with Genoa.[8] On 1 May Constantino della Pergola, the Bishop of Apt, was empowered to arrange a truce in the quarrel between the Manfredi and the Counts of Cuni.[9]

The war in Umbria had never held up the course of negotiations in Florence. On 22 March 1419 a Florentine embassy had found Braccio in Assisi, and his ambassadors had returned with the Florentines to seek the Pope in Florence.[10] On

---

[1] Ancona, Atti Consigliari, vol. 29, fol. 20.   [2] In *BSU*, xxvi (1923), 56.

[3] R. Arch. di Stato in Lucca, *Regesti*, iii, pt. 2, no. 446, p. 83.

[4] G. Franceschini, 'Memorie ecclesiastiche di Urbino', *AMSM*, 7th ser., v (1950), 55–6.

[5] Minuti, *Vita di M. A. Sforza*, 232. Cf. Faraglia, *Storia della Regina Giovanna*, 134, and R. Arch. di Stato in Lucca, *Regesti*, iii, pt. 2, no. 449, p. 84.

[6] Theiner, iii, no. 167, p. 239; ibid. no. 168, p. 240. Malatesta's oath for his office, Arm. 34, vol. 4, fol. 121v. He was authorised to hear all cases of appeal arising between cities and communes of the Romagna, Reg. Vat. 348, fol. 116. He was also enabled to appoint one or two judges of appeal there, ibid. fol. 117.

[7] R. Arch. di Stato in Lucca, *Regesti*, iii, pt. 2, no. 429, p. 80; Romano, *ASL*, 3rd ser., vii (1897), no. 399, p. 118.

[8] Ibid. no. 400, p. 118. This is dated 10 May 1419, but the final declaration of peace was in the bull of 15 August 1419, published by the Pope in the presence of the Genovese and Milanese envoys on 18 August, and ratified by them on the following day: Arm. 34, vol. 4, fol. 131v. Cf. G. Salvi 'Galeotto 1° del Carretto e la Repubblica di Genova', *Atti della R. Dep. di Storia Patria per la Liguria*, n.s., ii (1937), 11–12.

[9] Reg. Vat. 352, fol. 256v.

[10] Campano, *Vita Braccii*, 131 n. The report from Florence, given the date 20 February 1419, that an agreement between the Pope and Braccio was imminent, must be wrongly dated in R. Arch. di Stato

12 May, while Braccio continued to direct the siege of the castle of Spoleto, he sent to Florence his ally Corrado Trinci and his proctor Rogiero Nicola of Perugia, to treat for peace on his behalf.[1]   On 19 May a final agreement was reached, the instrument being concluded between Trinci and Nicola for Braccio, and Louis Aleman the Apostolic Vice-Chamberlain for the Pope.[2]   Braccio was to return to the Holy See Orvieto, Narni and Terni, the town and district of Spoleto, and certain other places and fortresses.   The Pope thus regained the Patrimony of St. Peter in Tuscia, while leaving Braccio in possession in most of his conquests in Umbria.   It may safely be assumed that a reciprocal agreement promised to grant Braccio the vicariate of all or most of the lands he held.[3]   The treaty represented very great concessions on the part of the Holy See; no such carving up of the Papal State had taken place since the time of Ladislas of Durazzo, in the very worst days of the Schism.

The Pope proceeded to make arrangements to take over the areas ceded by Braccio, and on 22 May, three days after the conclusion of the agreement, he named Antonio Casini, the Apostolic Treasurer, as Governor of Órvieto and of the various places concerned, giving him full power to punish and absolve rebels, and to reduce the lands to order.[4]   On the same day a second bull was issued, empowering Casini to receive these lands from Braccio, and to give Braccio or his representatives a binding receipt for their transfer.[5]

That such an agreement could have been concluded while the siege of Spoleto was continuing, and while Sforza was on the march to Rome, suggests that Martin V was not anxious for a full scale war with Braccio.   No doubt the papal treasury was not yet in a position to face such a war; more important was to clear the Pope's path to Rome.   On 25 May Bartolomeo Valori wrote from Prato that the Pope was eagerly awaiting Braccio's arrival in Florence.[6]

§ 4.   But Braccio did not go to Florence that year, and it is improbable that he ever ratified the agreement.   On 20 May Braccio learned that Sforza was in Rome.[7] He moved north-west from Spoleto to effect a junction with his ally Tartaglia, who was based at Toscanella near the lake of Bolsena.   At the same time Sforza moved rapidly north of Rome up the Via Cassia to prevent the junction.   At a point half way between Rome and Viterbo, in the last days of May, there was a parley between the two captains.   Sforza, according to the story sustained in the Roman Court, offered peace, and was willing to give his son as a hostage.   Braccio had just been

---

in Lucca, iii, pt. 2, no. 304, p. 54.   It refers to Braccio's being allowed to keep Assisi, but in February he did not hold Assisi; it was only in March 1419 that he seized it from Guid'Antonio di Montefeltro.

[1] R. Arch. di Stato in Lucca, *Regesti*, iii, pt. 2, no. 456, p. 86, and doc. 25 below.

[2] Cf. doc. 25 below, 'ea que venerabilis frater Ludovicus episcopus Magalonen' noster vicecamerarius in eisdem capitulis promiserat . . .'

[3] Ibid.   '. . . in omnibus civitatibus terris . . . que etiam suo regimini per concordiam huiusmodi dimicteremus . . .'

[4] Reg. Vat. 348, fols. 117v–120.

[5] Doc. 24 below.

[6] R. Arch. di Stato in Lucca, *Regesti*, iii, pt. 2, no. 469, p. 88.

[7] Zampolini, *Annali di Spoleto*, 151.

notified by the papal envoy Antonio Baldinotti of the agreement reached in Florence, but he hesitated, and then refused to seal it so long as Sforza's army remained in the Papal State.[1]   In that era of bad faith, it was perhaps too much to expect Braccio to trust Sforza's and Martin's word, when he was in the presence of a powerful army raised expressly to crush him.   The Pope was anxious to carry out the agreement, and probably the more so because Sforza's army would enable him to pacify and re-organise the Papal State.   Nothing would have been less to Braccio's taste.

The parley broke down, and in early June Sforza moved north of Viterbo.   But Tartaglia frustrated him by taking his force across the lake of Bolsena by boat, and joining Braccio.   The long delayed conflict could now take place, and the result was less bloody, and more favourable to Braccio, than anyone had expected.   The papal army experienced a double defeat; first the body of levies which the Gatti of Viterbo sent to Sforza's aid was ambushed and destroyed, then Sforza and the main army met Braccio on 14 June between Montefiascone and Viterbo, and experienced a sharp though not a decisive defeat.[2]   It was not a great battle, and the reverse was probably caused by the treason of Nicola Orsini, but it seems to have completely crippled Sforza's offensive power; he never again sought an open engagement with Braccio's main force.   From the time of that rather minor action Martin V seems to have given up hope of defeating Braccio with a papal army—remarkably enough, the army with which Caldora defeated and killed Braccio in 1424 was intended only to cover the provisioning of the besieged city of Aquila.

Sforza was shut up and besieged until August in Viterbo, and little was left to the Pope except to have recourse to spiritual fulminations.   On 24 July, on the advice of a commission of cardinals consisting of Antonio Corrario the relative of Gregory XII, of the important Pierre de Foix, and of the Spaniard Alfonso Carrillo, the Pope at a public and general consistory issued a citation against Braccio and his followers and allies, calling on them to appear in consistory on 8 August following, to answer for their crimes against the Church.[3]   On 8 August the consistory was

---

[1] Campano, *Vita Braccii*, 133.   For the sending of papal emissaries to notify Braccio of the peace, doc. 25 below, and R. Arch. di Stato in Lucca, *Regesti*, iii, pt. 2, no. 476, p. 89, 'Ieri ci furono nuove che Sforza e Braccio ànno fatto accordo insieme, cioè tregua per alcuno tempo, per praticare accordo . . . Mess. Antonio Baldinotti vi andò ier mattina a Braccio e poi a Sforza e fine a Roma a mes. Giordano a raffrenarlo uno poco ecc. Da Braccio non s'e auto risposta se verra lui o se mandera a suggiellare' (from Florence, 1 June.   'Mes. Giordano' is probably Giordano Colonna).   Ibid. no. 498, p. 93, '. . . l'acordio da Braccio al papa era fato et conchiuso; de che vedendo lui Isforza essere venuto cum grande potentia, Braccio non l'ha voluto seguire, mentre che Isforza sia in paese, ne vuole rendere alcuna cosa.'   Campano's version (loc. cit.) of the parley is that Sforza told Braccio that he had come only to attack Tartaglia, and not Braccio, and that Braccio thereupon refused to desert his ally.   This is a curious but not impossible story.   It fits rather ill with the fact that Tartaglia had since December 1418 been negotiating to betray Braccio and go over to the Pope, a step which he finally took a few months later (see Reg. Vat. 352, fol. 202v, and *Cronache e statuti della città di Viterbo*, 51–2).

[2] Campano, *Vita Braccii*, 133–4; Minuti, *Vita di M. A. Sforza*, 233–40; *Cronache e statuti della città di Viterbo*, 114.

[3] Doc. 25 below.   For the form of such consistories, see H. Schröder, 'Die Protokollbücher der päpstlichen Kammerkleriker, 1329–1347', *Archiv für Kulturgeschichte*, xxvii (1937), 165–92.   For the function of the *procurator fisci* as a public prosecutor in consistorial proceedings (doc. 25 below), see E. Göller, 'Der Gerichtshof der päpstlichen Kammer und die Entstehung des Amtes des Procurator fiscalis im kirchlichen Prozessverfahren', *AKKR*, xciv (1914), 612–19.

E

duly held, and, somewhat to the surprise of the Roman Court, Braccio's previous proctor, Rogiero Nicola of Perugia, with one Giovanni of Montone, appeared to answer the citation.   With what motive they had been sent it is hard to say; probably Braccio hoped to gain time, and to delay the undoubted inconveniences of an interdict.   Be this as it may, they lacked the essential legal powers to treat on Braccio's behalf.   They could not produce the notarial *publicum instrumentum* giving them powers to act, and the Pope therefore offered to accept, instead of the full and formal *publicum instrumentum*, the imbreviature or *nota extensa*, the notary's brief preliminary summary of the full public act.[1]   But they lacked even this, and were not, therefore, allowed to speak further.   The Pope proceeded to pronounce the definitive sentence of excommunication against Braccio and his party, and to declare an interdict in the lands which he held.[2]

Sforza's defeat had brought utterly to naught any hopes which Martin may have had of crushing Braccio in battle, and even in the lesser aim of clearing his own path to Rome the Pope was for the moment baffled.   There was one rather faint hope, that a junction between Sforza and Guid'Antonio of Montefeltro might still make Braccio's defeat possible, and on 6 August Martin wrote to Count Guid'Antonio, exhorting him to co-operate with the other papal forces and to attack Braccio.[3] Impotent and exasperated, the Pope relates how he has spent many sleepless nights in seeking ways of subduing Braccio, and has gone so far to conciliate him as to offend his own conscience.   Now that all else has failed he has cited Braccio to appear to answer a legal process.   But the Count Guid'Antonio may have been far from encouraged by the rather vague mention of payment for his services which the bull contained, and was in any event much chastened by his losses of that spring.   He therefore determined on the more prudent course of seeking a truce with Braccio, and on 24 August the Pope directed a further bull to him to protest against this defection.[4]

Although Martin failed to unite all his forces for a decisive battle against Braccio, the strength of those forces grew steadily.   On 14 August 1419 Angelo della Pergola agreed to serve in the March of Ancona for the year and a half following February 1420, with a force of three hundred lances and a hundred foot.[5]   During the summer of 1419 Tartaglia, whom Martin had been attempting to corrupt since December 1418,[6] deserted his employer Braccio and agreed to serve the Pope.   On 11 September

---

[1] Cf. O. Redlich, *Die Privaturkunden des Mittelalters* (1911), 217–24.

[2] The chronicle of Urbino printed in *Zibaldone* (i, 1889, 52) gives the date 8 August 1418 for this excommunication, instead of 1419.

[3] Printed by L. Fumi, 'Il conte Guidantonio di Montefeltro e Città di Castello', *BSU*, vi (1900), 377–8, from Arm. 60, vol. 21, fol. 86.   Fumi's indication of MS. reference is faulty.

[4] Theiner, iii, no. 170, p. 242.

[5] Div. Cam. 14, fol. 3, quoted also by Fink, *Martin V. und Aragon*, 63 n.   The original agreement was made on 14 August; the *condotta* itself is dated 9 September, and is due to come into force on 1 February 1420.   A further agreement, dated 2 January 1420, and confirming the former one, is on fol. 15v of the same volume.

[6] A bull of 13 December 1418 authorises Giordano Colonna to grant Tartaglia a *condotta* for the Church, Reg. Vat. 352, fol. 202v.   The intermediary between the Pope and Tartaglia is said to have been Giovanni Gatti of Viterbo (*Cronache e statuti della città di Viterbo*, 51–2).   He and his brothers were

he agreed to accept a papal *condotta*, and was promised besides his salary the grant of Toscanella, Canino, Sipicciano, Cincelle and other lands in vicariate[1]—that is to say, most of the lands which he already held. This was a defection of the utmost importance, not only because of the military force at Tartaglia's command, but because he ruled the whole north-western part of the Patrimony of St. Peter in Tuscia.

The loyalty of the Roman barons continued to be sought by confirmations and grants of lands : in September Piero and Ranuccio Farnese were confirmed in the tenure of their lands,[2] and Francesco, Carlo and Orsino Orsini were granted Bracciano and Stroncone in vicariate.[3] In the same month the Chiavelli, the tyrants of Fabriano in the March, accepted a group of lands in vicariate,[4] and the tyrant Raynaldo Alfano of Rieti accepted the vicariate of his native city.[5] Braccio's allies the Varano of Camerino appeared to fall under papal influence; they steered a very tortuous course between Braccio and the Pope, seeking to offend neither one nor the other, and having, in appearance, a great deal of success in this design. On 5 June 1419 Martin confirmed the truce arranged between Rodolfo Varano and Norcia, by the two Cardinals of St. Clement, Gabriel Condulmer (who was also Legate in the March of Ancona) and Branda de Castillione.[6] On 9 October Constantino della Pergola, the Bishop of Apt, was appointed Rector of the Patrimony of St. Peter;[7] he joined Sforza's army and proceeded to undermine the loyalty of the countryside of Orvieto to Braccio's régime, by granting exemptions to the villages subject to Orvieto against the taxes which they owed the city.[8] Yet another

---

granted Celleno, which his family had held since Urban VI's time, in vicariate on 12 December 1419; see Reg. Vat. 348, fol. 193, IE 379, fol. 43v. Cf. also Silvestrelli, *Città Castelli e Terre della regione Romana*, 772.

[1] The *condotta* is in Theiner, iii, no. 172, p. 245, with mention of the places to be granted to him. He was granted Montalto di Castro, Marta and other strong points in the dioceses of Castro, Montefiascone and Toscanella, for three years' vicariate, with a *census* of a pound of silver a year, Reg. Vat. 348, fol. 166v (7 October 1419). The grant of the vicariate of Toscanella was registered in the 'liber II bullarum domini Martini pape V', now lost. Its presence there is noted in a fifteenth century list of vicariates in Arm. 35, vol. 5, fol. 378.

[2] Theiner, iii, no. 173, p. 249; no. 174, p. 250. The Farnese are to be restored to those lands of which they have been unjustly deprived, ibid.

[3] Theiner, iii, no. 171, p. 242, Bracciano; Reg. Vat. 348, fol. 152, Stroncone. Carlo Orsini takes the oath for himself and his brothers for these grants, Div. Cam. 3, fol. 138v, 13 September 1419. Guiraud, *L'Etat Pontifical*, 120 f., does not notice Stroncone among the Orsini lands. The head of another branch of the Orsini family, Bertoldo Count of Soana, gave the Apostolic Chamber two hunting dogs in August 1419 for *census* of the vicariate of Proceno and Abbazia de Ponzano (*ad pontem*) in the diocese of Castro, Div. Cam. 5, fol. 188 (cf. Guiraud, 124 f.); but he later lost Abbazia de Ponzano to the Conti. Nicola Orsini remained all this time in the service of Braccio.

[4] In the grant of the vicariate of Serra S. Quirico and Domo to Tomasso Chiavelli, and the reduction of tallage for these lands and Fabriano to 1,853¼ florins (Reg. Vat. 348, fols. 179v, 186, 187v) Chiavelli is referred to as vicar in Fabriano. Cf. Guiraud, 198. His proctors swore obedience for Serra S. Quirico and Domo on 25 October 1419, Arm. 34, vol. 4, fol. 138v.

[5] Arm. 34, vol. 4, fol. 137. Cf. M. Michaeli, *Memorie storiche della città di Rieti*, iii, 215–16.

[6] Theiner, iii, no. 169, p. 241.

[7] Theiner, iii, no. 177, p. 251. He was authorised to pardon rebels, except those condemned in the process against Braccio and his adherents, Reg. Vat. 348, fol. 176v. He took the oath for his office on 15 October 1419, Div. Cam. 3, fol. 70v.

[8] Valentini, *BSU*, xxvi (1923), p. 80, and nos. 89, 90, p. 194.

important *signore*, the Count of Carrara, the tyrant of Ascoli, was in December 1419 granted the vicariate of Ascoli;[1] shortly after this he joined Angelo della Pergola as a papal mercenary.[2]

The war continued during the autumn of 1419 without decisive moves on either side. Assisi, having been taken by Sforza, was recaptured by Braccio in October, but Braccio's further attempt against the castle of Spoleto failed, and the papal troops there succeeded in recapturing the town. He failed also in his second attack on Gubbio, in the New Year of 1420.[3] In Umbria the movements against Braccio in the countryside and the seditions against him in the towns witnessed to a progressive weakening of his rule; in September 1419 there were abortive negotiations to hand back Orvieto to the Pope,[4] and the defection of Tartaglia carried with it Montefiascone, Corneto and the whole district of the north-west of the Patrimony.[5] Sforza in October operated against Amelia and in this district made several minor gains,[6] but Braccio's recapture of Assisi fended off the worst of the threat. Nevertheless the initiative remained with Sforza. Early in November Martin made a fresh appeal to Guid'Antonio of Montefeltro to assemble Braccio's enemies in a military coalition.[7]

It was evident to the Pope that Sforza was unlikely to inflict a major defeat on Braccio, the less so because in Naples Sforza's position was almost completely undermined by Gianni Caracciolo. Sforza's troops, moreover, were causing little less damage in papal lands than those of an enemy.[8] The pressing need was for the Pope to enter Rome, and to win the immense advantages of power and prestige which actual occupation of the See of Peter carried. Until the Pope was in Rome it could scarcely be said that the Great Schism was over, and great sacrifices were warranted to end the humiliating wait on the doorstep of his own capital. The increasing strength of the forces aligned against Braccio and the growing current of sedition within his lands, made Braccio also willing to accept peace, in return for the recognition of his rule in Umbria. His state was ruled more piratically than politically, and the pressure of war and arbitrary taxation threatened to disintegrate it. The main

---

[1] The vicariate of Ascoli, see Florence, Biblioteca Nazionale, xix, 82, 'liber capitaneorum', fol. 109, 'Comes de Carraria in civitate Esculan' vicarius ad beneplacitum propter census f.M in festo apostolorum etc. Littera dat' Florentie kal' Decembris anno 3' (1 December 1419). The vicariate of Offida was granted on the same day, also at the Pope's good pleasure, for a *census* of 60 florins a year, Reg. Vat. 348, fol. 197v.

[2] Valentini, *BSU*, xxvi (1923), 71.

[3] Ibid. 79–80; Campano, *Vita Braccii*, 137–41.

[4] On 17 September the Pope authorised Nicolò de' Medici to treat for peace with Orvieto, which points to the existence of a papal party within the city, *BSU*, xxvi (1923), 74; Fumi, *Codice diplomatico della città di Orvieto*, 676. The city had a truce with Sforza from 22 September to 15 October, *BSU*, loc. cit.; Campano, *Vita Braccii*, 139.

[5] On 24 September 1419 Romano de Abiamonte of Viterbo was appointed as *podestà* to receive Corneto for the Church from Tartaglia, under an agreement made with the latter. Reg. Vat. 348, fols. 160v, 161v. At the same time a castellan of the fortress of Corneto was appointed, ibid. fol. 161.

[6] *BSU*, xxvi (1923), 75–7; Minuti, *Vita di M. A. Sforza*, 244. Reg. Vat. 348, fol. 189, where Ugolino de Alviano is appointed Rector and Governor of S. Restituta, Melezzole and Toscella in the diocese of Todi, as a reward for his services in recovering these places from the rebels.

[7] Valentini, *BSU*, xxvi (1923), 81.

[8] 'Non defendendo sed offendendo partes alias ecclesie devastat', R. Arch. di Stato in Lucca, *Regesti*, iii, pt. 2, no. 780, p. 144. Martin is said to be therefore anxious for peace.

questions unresolved with the Pope were Spoleto and the assignments of tallage in the March. Martin refused to grant Braccio Spoleto, and refused, probably, to countenance his further collection of tallage in the March.[1] In the first he was in a strong position, for he still held the town and the castle. The second was probably a question of prestige, but our ignorance of the text of the agreements of May 1419 and of the subsequent negotiations, makes it hard to be certain of what was at issue. Braccio had collected tallage in the March in direct defiance of papal orders, and his tyranny in so doing was one of the main rallying points of the papal party; it was hard, therefore, for Martin to acknowledge his rights there. But in the first agreement of May 1419 Martin is said to have granted Braccio this tallage, and in any event it was almost inevitable that this should be used as security for the immense payments due to him under his new papal *condotta* which was part of the terms of peace. On 20 November 1419 Carlo Malatesta entered Florence, and began to take part in the peace negotiations.[2] By December the peace was at last virtually agreed : on the question of Spoleto Martin held firm; he assigned the tallage of the March to Braccio to pay his *condotta*.

During these events the régime headed in Naples by the royal favourite Gianni Carraciolo caused much alarm in the Papal Court by its determination to disgrace and dismiss Sforza. This amounted to an anti-papal policy, and it had already weakened Sforza to such an extent that it can probably be blamed for his late arrival in Rome, and perhaps for his defeat in June. It was forced on Martin that only a complete change of régime in Naples could make the Kingdom into a really effective ally. His actions were correspondingly drastic. On 4 November 1419 he issued a bull to invest Louis of Anjou with the Kingdom as soon as Giovanna II should die.[3] The Angevin claim was thus revived, with momentous results for the future of Italy. The investiture was not intended to disturb the legal *status quo* in Naples; Giovanna had been crowned by a papal Legate and she remained Queen. But it caused an early rupture between Martin and the Queen : at the beginning of 1420 arrangements had already been made with Florentine bankers in Naples to pay the Pope 29,000 florins for the annual *census* of the Kingdom, and 11,200 florins for the bulls of investiture; the news of the Angevin investiture must have caused these payments to be stopped at the last minute, for in June 1421 they still had not been made.[4] Muzio Attendolo Sforza entered Florence on 7 January 1420 to take

[1] For these final negotiations, see R. Arch. di Stato in Lucca, *Regesti*, iii, pt. 2, nos. 595, 636, 673, 714, 840. See especially no. 636, p. 117 : the main obstacles to peace are now Spoleto (the writer here relates a proposed arrangement different from that finally reached) and the tallage of the March. 'La seconda differenza erano le taglie della marcha : a questo il Papa avere nelli primi patti consentito a Braccio, e hora dava certa intenzione' (there seems to be a gap or an error in the text at this point).

[2] Ibid. no. 766, p. 141.

[3] Raynaldus, ad a. 1420, par. viii; Faraglia, *Storia della Regina Giovanna*, 158 f.; Fink, *Martin V. und Aragon*, 62–3.

[4] Div. Cam. 5, fols. 245–6. Two letters (one fragmentary), both dated 8 January 1420, from the Vice-Chamberlain to the bankers Spini and Sardi, and Bonciani and Baroncelli. The Spini and Sardi have promised to pay 10,400 florins on account of the *census* of the Kingdom of Sicily, and they are asked to pay this to Angelotto Bishop of Anagni and Loysio Corsini. The Bonciani and Baroncelli are bound on behalf of the Neapolitans for a further sum of 10,500 florins due on the same count, and are to

part in the conclusion of the peace.   On his reception by Martin, the Pope asked him in whose lands he was quartered; when he replied, in those of the Church, Martin claimed his obedience and engaged him to serve the Angevins and the Church.[1] Sforza was made Viceroy and Grand Constable of the Angevin, and Berardo Varano of Camerino swore homage on Sforza's behalf to the King.[2]

§ 5.   The agreement with Braccio was signed on 26 February 1420.   Its terms fall into four main divisions.[3]   First, Braccio promises obedience, and promises to return to the Church the cities and counties of Orvieto, Narni, Terni, Orte and other places in the Tiber valley, and all he holds in the Duchy of Spoleto, that is to say, the same lands which he promised to return in May 1419.   The Church agrees, in return, to absolve him and his adherents from their offences, and to confirm the legality of the laws and statutes he has enacted in the cities subject to him.   It is guaranteed that Sforza will not attack him.   He is to be granted for three years a series of vicariates in Umbria and the March—Perugia, Todi; Gualdo Tadino and other lands between Assisi and Foligno; Iesi, Rocca Contrata, Staffolo and Montebodo in the March.   In all these lands Braccio is to be quite exempt from the jurisdiction of provincial Rectors;[4] he rules a virtually independent state.   Third, Braccio promises to maintain 300 lances in the March at the orders of the Pope, and, when he is so required, to lead 600 lances in papal service anywhere in the lands of the Church, and 800 lances— a huge force, representing his main armed strength—in papal service to the Kingdom or elsewhere in Italy.   In return he is to be given a provision of 52,000 florins for the first eighteen months after the beginning of the agreement, and 60,000 florins for the second eighteen months.   The methods by which these sums are to be paid are specified :   8,000 florins are to be paid immediately, 16,000 are assigned from the tallage of the lands of Special Commission and of the Duchy of Spoleto, 16,000 are to be paid in two monthly instalments, and the remaining 12,000 he is to withhold from the sums he owes the Pope for his vicariates.   The whole of the second sum of 60,000 florins is to be paid from the tallage of the March of Ancona.   The details of the second *condotta* for 600 lances are not mentioned in this agreement but the second *condotta* in fact came into effect at the same time as the first.   To the second *condotta*

---

pay it to the Bishop of Anagni and Giovanni de' Medici.   The Bishop of Anagni was used by the Pope to receive various extraordinary forms of income, see Von Hofmann, *Forschungen zur Geschichte der kurialen Behörden*, i, 88.   Francesco da Montepulciano, the Bishop of Arezzo and papal secretary received 5,000 florins for the taxes on the bulls of investiture for the Kingdom, on 29 January 1420, Div. Cam. 6, fol. 28.   At the same time it was promised that a further 6,000 florins due on the bulls should be paid in the following August.   But evidently this payment was the only one made, since on 29 June 1421 Martin complained that the first annual payment of 48,000 florins due for *census*, and a part of the sum due for the bulls of investiture ('reliquum investiturae') had never been paid (Raynaldus, ad a. 1421, par. i).

[1] Faraglia, 159-60.   [2] Ibid.

[3] The 'capitula Braccii' are printed by Valentini, 'Lo Stato di Braccio e la guerra aquilana nella politica di Martino V (1421-1424)', *ASR*, lii (1929), app. i, p. 341 f.   The bulls of investiture for the vicariates are referred to in Theiner, iii, nos. 183-4, pp. 255-6.   Braccio took the oath for his vicariates on 14 March 1420, Valentini, ibid. 228.

[4] This privilege is the subject of a separate bull, Reg. Vat. 349, fol. 121v.

was attached a salary of 54,000 florins for the six months following 27 March 1420.[1] The total sum to be paid to Braccio in the first year was therefore something like 90,000 florins, an immense sum.   Fourth, Braccio promises to submit to arbitration in his quarrel with the Duke of Montefeltro.   The judgement in the arbitration, which was in the court of Marcello Strozzi the governor of Spoleto, allotted Assisi to Braccio, and compensated Montefeltro with Porcaria and S. Gemini in the county of Narni.[2]

The result of the agreements was to confirm Braccio in his control of a new state embracing the whole of the centre of Umbria, with outposts allowing him to penetrate into the March whenever he wished down the valley of the Esino.   Contiguous with his frontiers was the allied signory of the Trinci, controlling the vitally important junction of Foligno.   Further south was the allied signory of the Varano, a daughter of whose house he married in November of the same year.   It is true that Braccio swore to return the vicariates to the Holy See at the end of three years, but it was most unlikely that Martin would possess the military force to enforce this clause, and in the event he was unable to do so.

When Braccio appeared before Martin V at Florence, the Pope gave only a cold and short reply to his address.   Leonardo Bruni has depicted fairly his bitterness against the favour shown by Florence to Braccio, and his impotent rage at his own weakness.   The treaty, although in form a peace, was in fact a truce, and during the next few years the whole temporal power of the Papacy was made to submit to the fortunes of war.   Braccio's new state was by its very nature aggressive, and Martin was unable, through his own nature and the very innermost springs of his policy, to countenance a new signory placed in the backbone of the Papal State. Yet the Pope was offered, for the moment, solid advantages.   He could at last go to Rome and re-organise the government, the military power and the finances of the Papacy.   The Duchy of Spoleto had been saved, the authority of the Pope in the Patrimony of St. Peter in Tuscia was re-established.   The battle with Braccio was not ended but was only now beginning.

II.   *The Climax of the Struggle with Braccio, 1420–1424*

§ 1.   The re-establishment of papal power in 1420 is attested by a long series of appointments of papal officials in Umbria, Spoleto, and the Patrimony of St. Peter in Tuscia.[3]   Gabriel Condulmer was appointed as Cardinal-Legate of the March of

---

[1] Florence, Biblioteca Nazionale, xix, 82, fol. 4.

[2] Valentini, 'Lo Stato di Braccio', 346–7; Reg. Vat. 349, fol. 122v; Fumi, in *BSU*, vi (1900), 383.

[3] On 7 March 1420 Marcello Strozzi was made Governor of Spoleto, Terni and the 'Terra Arnulphorum', Theiner, iii, no. 189, p. 261; he took the oath for his office on 4 April, Div. Cam. 3, fol. 145v.   On 8 March 1420 Francesco Pizzolpassi was appointed Vice-Rector in spirituals and temporals in Narni, Orte, Amelia, Magliano, Calvi in Umbria, Otricoli, Collescipione, Lugnola, Monte d'Oro and Lugnano, with the power to summon general congregations of cities and territories, to act against rebels, and to receive these cities from Braccio (Reg. Vat. 349, fol. 39, quoted by Fumi, *BSU*, v (1900), 383, but with errors in the transcription of the place names).   Cf. also Theiner, iii, no. 181, p. 255.   A Treasurer of the Duchy of Spoleto, a nominee of the Count of Montefeltro, who continued to be Duke, was appointed on 20 March, Reg. Vat. 349, fol. 57v.   On 11 March Giovanni Coniger, Baron of Castrignano, of the

Ancona, and on 7 February he left Florence to take up his legation.[1] The Breton mercenaries were at last bought out from their tenure of the castle of Sutri, which commands the Via Cassia on the main road to the north, and which they had held since the beginning of the Schism : on 28 February and 20 July agreements were sealed with the castellan, de Grammont, by which, for a payment of something over 10,000 florins, he was to hand over the castle to the Pope.[2]

The Pope continued to recognise various *signorotti* and to cultivate their support. Antonio Smeducci of San Severino was granted the vicariate of the city ;[3] no doubt this submission was not unconnected with the marriage, arranged in Florence that spring, between Polissena di San Severino and Michelotto, the bastard son of Sforza.[4] In 1420 Martin granted Luca Monaldeschi, leader of one of the two dominant parties in Orvieto, the vicariate of a group of castles and lands centred round Bolsena.[5] Tradita di Giovan'Andrea di Colonna was given in marriage to Achille Monaldeschi. Francesco Monaldeschi was made Bishop of Orvieto.[6] Such liberality did not fail of its aim ; Pietro Monaldeschi fought for Martin at the battle of Aquila, and the Monaldeschi became the dominant and papal faction in Orvieto and a guarantee of the city's loyalty. Battista Savelli and his brothers Pandolfo, Jacopo, Leonardo and Giovanni were absolved for their offences against the Holy See and confirmed in all their lands and privileges,[7] and further grants were made at the same time to the Farnese.[8]

On 26 January 1420 there was a rebellion in Bologna. The occasion was a dispute among the ruling oligarchy; Antonio Bentivoglio and Cambio Zambeccari

---

Neapolitan family of Picholino, was appointed Governor and *podestà* of Orvieto, Reg. Vat. 349, fol. 27v. He took the oath on 14 March, Div. Cam. 3, fol. 144v. He named as his vicar there Stefano de Branchiis of Gubbio, Valentini, *BSU*, xxvi (1923), 95. Conigner was a partisan of the Colonna, and the husband of Tizia Colonna the daughter of Fabrizio Colonna. Cf. G. Pardi, 'Serie dei supremi magistrati e reggitori di Orvieto', *BSU*, i (1895), 408; Lanciani, *ASR*, xx (1897), 399; Silvestrelli, *Città Castelli e Terre della regione Romana*, 154. During the same few weeks the Pope also named the *podestà* of Viterbo, Terni, Montefiascone, Orte, Calvi in Lazio and other towns, Div. Cam. 3, fol. 71v; Reg. Vat. 348, fol. 205; Reg. Vat. 349, fols. 20, 31v, 33v, 52, 55, 142v; Arm. 34, vol. 4, fol. 144. Jacopo, Prior of the Church of S. Nicolo of Bagnorea, was appointed Treasurer of the Patrimony of St. Peter in Tuscia, the lands of special commission, and the 'terra arnulphorum', Reg. Vat. 349, fol. 34; he took the oath for this office on 29 March 1420, Arm. 34, vol. 4, fol. 147. Castellans were appointed at Narni (Theiner, iii, no. 180, p. 254) and Orte (Reg. Vat. 349, fol. 29).

[1] Div. Cam. 3, fol. 144; Arm. 34, vol. 4, fol. 141.

[2] Theiner, iii, nos. 186, 194, pp. 257, 264; cf. Flavio Biondo, *Italia illustrata* (1543), 92–3.

[3] On 9 May 1420, Reg. Vat. 349, fol. 45; his proctors took the oath on 28 May, Div. Cam. 3, fol. 73. The vicariate was for three years, with an extension *ad beneplacitum*.

[4] A. Minuti, *Vita di M. A. Sforza*, 247.

[5] *ASI*, 3rd ser. ii, pt. 2 (1865), 21; Guiraud, *L'Etat Pontifical*, 161; Fumi, *Codice diplomatico della città di Orvieto*, 679–80. He was also made castellan of Rocca Ripescena, with the right to convert the income of the castle to his own use, and a salary of 100 florins a year payable by the Apostolic Chamber, Reg. Vat. 349, fol. 55.

[6] Fumi, ibid.

[7] On 28 October 1420, E. Celani, 'Le pergamene dell'Archivio Sforza-Cesarini', *ASR*, xv (1892), 236; Raynaldus, ad a. 1420; Reg. Vat. 353, fol. 123v.

[8] Reg. Vat. 349, fol. 93, grant of half the *castrum* of Cassagnano, in the diocese of Toscanella, to Giorgio Antonio Farnese, who says the property is not worth more than ten florins a year, and has to pay the *census* of a hawking dog.

were jealous of the power of the faction of the family of Canetoli. The mediation of a moderate party on the day of the rebellion prevented bloodshed, but the upshot was the expulsion of the Canetoli, and the appointment of sixteen *reformatori*, among whom Bentivoglio and Zambeccari were the effective rulers. Although the revolt was at first not specifically directed against the Church, the revolutionary party within a few weeks denounced the treaty made with Martin in the previous year, on the excuse that he now wanted to come personally to Bologna, and that his arrival would be the occasion of his destroying the popular constitution and seizing the *signoria* [1]—by no means, it must in fairness be said, a fantastic prediction, although against it must be set Bentivoglio's own hankering to become *signore* of the city. [2]

On 28 February an Archbishop and an Abbot arrived in Bologna from the Pope to try to secure the obedience of the new régime; they promised prosperity as the reward of obedience—'se lo acceptasseno che la terra se faria molto bona, et si serveno tucti richi'. The following day another embassy arrived from Carlo Malatesta, Ludovico Alidosi, Obizzo da Polenta, the Manfredi of Faenza, and Giorgio Ordelaffi— in fact, from all the tyrants of Romagna, an impressive proof of Martin's success in dominating the *signori* of his lands. This second embassy delivered a threat, advising the city to yield and saying that these *signori* were soldiers of the Pope and obliged to obey his orders. They were rebuffed: the city declined to answer them and reserved its reply for the ambassadors of the Pope.

On 3 March the papal ambassadors were sent for and obedience to the Pope was refused—'che gli dovesse piasere de lasare el comun de Bologna come steva'. The Pope replied that 'al tucto volea Bologna'. On 6 March Nicolò Albergati left Bologna a second time to mediate with the Pope, together with two ambassadors of the Commune, but on this occasion he failed, and, instead of terms of peace, brought back with him the draft of an interdict. [3] The bull was dated 20 March [4] and on 9 April, the Tuesday after Easter, Martin published it. It declared that he wished to go to Bologna with his court, and that the city refused to receive him. On Thursday 11 April two ambassadors from Bologna arrived at the Roman Court in Florence to attempt a last minute settlement, probably through the mediation of Florence, as is suggested by the fact that Florence was at first laid under an interdict

[1] *Corpus Chron. Bonon.*, 561 f.; Matteo Griffoni, 105–6; Piero di Mattiolo, 298 f.; Zaoli, *Libertas Bononie e Papa Martino V*, 81 f.; de Töth, *Il beato cardinale Nicolò Albergati*, i, 352 f. When the revolution was first effected it was said in Florence that it was not directed against the Church, 'De Ecclesia nil locutum seu attemptatum fuit, licet per omnes rem Ecclesie secus predicetur', Arch. di Stato in Lucca, *Regesti*, iii, pt. 2, no. 845, p. 156.

[2] Cf. Calvalcanti, *Istorie fiorentine* (ed. de Pino, 1944), 5, 'Con tutto potere che messer Antonio sapeva, operava le ragioni del padre a racquistare la signoria di Bologna : con la bentivoglica parte, francamente contendeva Bologna alla volontà di Martino sommo pontefice'.

[3] De Töth, i, 355.

[4] Printed by Zaoli, 102 n., with the date XII kal. Aprilis Anno III, which is thus 20 March and not 27 March as it is said to be by Zaoli. The occasion of the interdict is said in the bull to be the refusal of the city to receive Martin and his court—'ad dictam civitatem nostram Bononie cum eadem nostra curie vellemus, uti voluimus, nos personaliter transferre'. Such a transfer would have had the effect of invalidating his agreement with the city, which took effect only as long as he did not take up residence there.

on account of their presence.[1]   The course of their negotiations is unknown, but they appear to have begun by refusing to produce their credentials, an inauspicious start, and they left Florence by 14 April without reaching any agreement.[2]   The Pope and his Cardinals were reported as being utterly determined to have Bologna. The Pope was 'neither prattling nor asleep', but he and the Cardinals were willing to spend all they possessed on the recovery of the city.[3]   Loans were raised and subsidies imposed, and later in the year a subsidy was demanded in Germany, in part occasioned by the expenses of recovering these lands for the Church.[4]

Martin was now able to command an overwhelming force of mercenaries.   On 15 May Ludovico Alidosi declared war on Bologna; two days later Braccio, in obedience to the agreement of 26 February, took the field on behalf of the Pope and arrived in the Bolognese *contado*.[5]   The issue of the campaign was never in doubt, and was made the quicker by the universal desertion of the inhabitants of the Bolognese countryside, the 'tradituri villani', who rather than see their crops spoiled and their women raped, preferred immediate surrender.   All the castles of the Romagna, and those north of the city, including the key points of Castel Bolognese, S. Giovanni in Persiceto, and Medicina, yielded without resistance.[6]   On 15 July

---

[1] Div. Cam. 6, fol. 67, 'interdictum ecclesiasticum cui civitas Florentin' occasione presencie certorum oratorum Bononien' supposita fere dinoscitur usque ad tres dies videlicet veneris sabbati et dominicam (sic) proxime venturas . . . suspendimus per presentes.'

[2] Div. Cam. 3, fol. 145, printed in part by Fantuzzi, *Notizie degli Scrittori Bolognesi* (1781), i, 29.   'Die Jovis X Aprilis presentibus dominis Jacobo de Calvis Aymone priore Magdalen' et magistro Roberto Atlow, in capella reverendissimi domini vicecamerarii, idem reverendissimus dominus vicecamerarius allegando, quamodo dominus Nicolaus de Corbellis et Gratiolus de Achariis de Bononia legum doctores oratores Bononiensium ac procuratores et syndici, ex parte requisiti fuerint, me notario internuntio, iam bis vel ter, quod iidem iuxta promissionem alias sanctissimo domino nostro pape in publica eius audiencia per eos factam, procurationem sive originalem sive mandatum procurationis eorum ipsi reverendissimo domino vicecamerario traderent, quod non fecerint per subterfugiam transeundo.   Idem ergo dominus vicecamerarius nunc presentialiter dictum dominum Nicolaum requisivit ut dictum mandatum originalem statim sibi tradat.   Super quibus venerabilis dominus Johannes de Sarmon', procurator fisci etc. sibi petiit instrumentum, prefatus dominus Nicolaus respondit quod ipse dictum mandatum tradere vellet inquantum de iure tenetur et alias non, nisi a dominis suis aliud super hoc receperit in mandatum, et eo tunc se dixit traditurum nedum copiam sed et originalem.   Actum florentie quo supra.'   Zaoli, *Libertas Bononie*, 107, also found the 'instrumentum sindicatus' for this embassy.   His remark on the preceding page (p. 106), that there is no record of an embassy after the interdict, must be a slip.   The Bolognese ambassadors are said to have left Florence by 14 April, Div. Cam. 3, fol. 74v.

[3] R. Arch. di Stato in Lucca, *Regesti*, iii, pt. 2, no. 921, p. 172, 'pono pro constanti Bononienses venire ad dictionem Ecclesie statim; statim, idest, ista estate; nam papa nec dormit neque sermonizzat, neque vilis est in isto facto, ymo et cardinales omnes unanimiter volunt expendere quicquid habent et etiam mori, ut asserunt, antequam reportare de isto facto conclusionem'.

[4] On 29 April 1420 the Apostolic Chamber borrowed 1,500 florins from Carlo Malatesta (Div. Cam. 6, fol. 90) and on 2 May 500 florins from Berardo Varano of Camerino (ibid. fol. 90v).   Other loans were raised from Florentine merchants for a total of 5,800 florins, between February and July 1420 (ibid. fols. 42, 77v, 89v, 103v, 141).   On 3 May Paolo Guinigi, the tyrant of Lucca, authorised his Representatives to pay out loans at every demand of the Holy See (L. Fumi and E. Lazzareschi, *Carteggio di Paolo Guinigi*, no. 508, p. 97).   This loan had been requested in March 1420 (ibid. no. 495, p. 94), but it does not seem to have been paid out until 1421, see p. 69 below.   For the subsidy of 6,000 florins each demanded from Cologne, Trier and Mainz, partly on account of the 'occupationes Patrimonii ejusdem Romanae ecclesiae, et nuperimme pro recuperatione civitatis nostrae Bononiensis', see Raynaldus, ad a. 1420, par. xxviii.

[5] Matteo Griffoni, 106; Campano, *Vita Braccii*, 149.

[6] Griffoni, 106; Piero di Mattiolo, 306–7; *Corpus Chron. Bonon.*, 565–7; Zaoli, 109–13.

the general council of Bologna was called, and it was decided to submit to the Church. On the following day a peace was proclaimed, the terms of which are now lost, but which enabled Cardinal Gabriel Condulmer, the Legate of the March, to enter the city on 21 July.[1]

Bologna had lost the war, but its leader, Antonio Bentivoglio, had not. The peace was made through his good offices, and as a reward he was not merely pardoned, but he, the instigator of the rebellion, was in August 1420 granted the vicariate of Castel Bolognese, and made papal Rector of the provinces of Campania and Maritima,[2]—the last was probably less of a reward than a means of keeping him in the south and away from Bologna.

The terms of peace for the city provided that the offices remain in the power of the commune, save for the treasurer and the office of the 'bolete', by which orders for payment were made to the treasurer.[3] On 4 August a Treasurer was appointed; on 20 August a Legate, the Cardinal Alfonso Carrillo of the title of S. Eustachio, who arrived in the city on 25 August.[4] On 19 August the Perugian, Matteo Ubaldo, Braccio's ambassador to Martin V, was appointed podestà of Bologna and made Count of Fiorentiola, no doubt as a gesture towards his master.[5] Castellans were appointed at strongpoints,[6] and by the end of August Bologna was held firmly for the Pope. The suppression of the revolt had the effect of strengthening papal rule in the city, and at no time during Martin's pontificate was Bologna more firmly governed than during the legation of Carrillo.

§ 2. The way to Rome was open, and on 9 September the Pope left Florence and travelled by way of Aquapendente and Viterbo to Rome, where he arrived on 28 September 1420.[7] The date is a memorable one. The liberties of the commune of Rome were long dead, the anarchy of the Schism was at last over; from this year until 1848 the history of the City is only a reflection of the history of the Popes. These changes in its heart were recorded on the face of Rome; the Renaissance

---

[1] Zaoli, 114.

[2] Reg. Vat. 349, fol. 74 (21 August); ibid. fol. 64v (22 August). The latter appointment was short-lived; on 28 November 1420, Jacopo Buccii, Bishop of Aquino, was appointed Vice-Rector in spirituals and temporals in Campania and Maritima, and all previous appointments were cancelled, Reg. Vat. 349, fol. 155v. Cf. Cavalcanti, *Istorie fiorentine* (ed. de Pino), 7, 'ed e' tennesi (scil. Bentivoglio) Castello Bolognese, e, per sospetto del papa, non andò in Campagna, perchè era nel seno delle pontificali forze'.

[3] *Corp. Chron. Bonon.*, 568.

[4] The bulls of his legation are in Reg. Vat. 353, fols. 33v–48; the bull of his appointment is printed by Zaoli (p. 178) dated 20 August. The register copies are dated 19 August. The appointment of the Treasurer of Bologna, the Florentine Pietro Bartolomeo de' Borromei di San Miniato, Reg. Vat. 349, fol. 63v; Div. Cam. 3, fol. 74. Borromeo was a banker who lent money to the Chamber, and Paolo de Caputgrassis of Sulmona, clerk of the Chamber, was appointed for a time to supervise him (cf. Reg. Vat. 349, fol. 79v).

[5] Reg. Vat. 349, fols. 73, 73v; cf. Pellini, *Historia della città di Perugia*, ii, 250.

[6] Luce Dellante, relative of the cameral clerk Bartolomeo Dellante, was made Governor and podestà of S. Giovanni in Persiceto on 1 September, Reg. Vat. 349, fol. 80v, the bull being marked 'gratis pro socio'. Cento, another strongpoint in the Bolognese contado, had had a vicar appointed on 24 July 1420, ibid. fol. 61v. Giovanni Vitelleschi, of Corneto, 'notarius noster', and probably identical with the future Cardinal, was appointed castellan of Bologna on 25 October, ibid. fol. 294.

[7] Miltenberger, *MIöG*, xv (1894), 664.

Popes imposed a new unity on the jumbled pagan and Christian buildings, the 'mirabilia urbis Romae' of the Middle Ages, until the street plan effected by Sixtus V made Rome inescapably a papal city.[1]   No longer a medieval camp among classical ruins, Renaissance Rome began to devour and destroy ancient Rome; at the same time as the humanist scholars accomplished the 'restoration' of ancient Rome in their books, the classical city was being fed into the lime kilns.   Martin V was not a builder, and he confined himself to tidying the chaos into which the City had fallen during the Schism; but he was the restorer and founder of Renaissance Rome as the capital of a Renaissance state.

On his way to Rome and soon after his arrival there the Pope received numerous deputations from the cities newly acquired from Braccio, absolved them for rebellion, issued and confirmed privileges, appointed officials.[2]   Orvieto asked, and was granted, that its *contado* should remain subject to the city—the communes were continually thus having to defend their hegemony over the countryside from the papal Rectors.[3]   To provision Rome against the arrival of the papal court, a series of agreements was made to import grain from the provinces, and, through the agency of Florentine merchants, from Sicily.[4]

Both in its immediate results for papal policy, and in its ultimate effect on Italian politics, the return to the old curial policy of the Angevin candidature proved to be nothing less than a disaster.   In the summer of 1420, the Queen's attempt to dissuade Martin from this new move having failed, Malizia Carafa was sent to Florence, whence he left in August to go to the young Alfonso of Aragon, off Bonifacio in Corsica.   By whose suggestion Alfonso was approached, whether the move was spontaneous, or prepared beforehand from Naples, is now unknown.   In the event Carafa was completely successful; the ties of blood and alliance which Alfonso had with Duke Louis were, as Minuti wrote, many times outweighed by 'l'animosità signorile et la cupidità de gloria temporale et del stato'—a cupidity which had behind it the economic and political pressure of the Aragonese drive to the east in the Mediterranean.   Alfonso accepted Giovanna's offer to adopt him as her son and as her heir to the throne, and the agreement was ceremonially recognised in Naples on 7 September.[5]   With this set-back for the Pope went another, for him perhaps even more serious, the granting to Braccio during the winter of 1420/21 of an Aragonese

---

[1] Cf. P. Tomei, *L'Architettura in Roma nel Quattrocento* (1942); S. Giedion, 'Sixtus V and the planning of Baroque Rome', *Architectural Review*, April 1952.

[2] Otricoli and Veroli were absolved for offences against the Holy See, Reg. Vat. 353, fols. 75, 57; Veroli's privileges were confirmed, and the town given permission to hold a fair, ibid. fols. 58, 59v. *Podestà* were appointed for Narni, Amelia, Velletri, Bagnorea, Castrum Griptarum, 'terra Gradularum', Castro, Calvi in Lazio and Montefiascone.   Orders were given to repair the castle of Montefiascone, Arch. Cam., pt. 1, Tes. Prov., Patrimonio, B.1, vol. 1, fols. 96, 97.

[3] Valentini, *BSU*, xxvi (1923), 103–5.   The request was granted 'nisi de exemptis per nos', a reservation meant to protect the privileges of such as the Monaldeschi.

[4] See below, p. 123.   To help pay for these imports the College of Cardinals lent the Apostolic Chamber 2,000 florins (Reg. Vat. 353, fol. 83v, 21 December 1420, with the marginal notation 'fuit solutum sacro collegio.   A[ntonius] thesaurarius', in the autograph of the Apostolic Treasurer).

[5] Faraglia, 175 f.; Fink, *Martin V. und Aragon*, 63 f.; Valentini, 'Lo Stato di Braccio', 230 f.; Minuti, *Vita di M. A. Sforza*, 258.

condotta, for a payment of 200,000 florins, a large part of which was guaranteed by Florence.   The Papal Court thereupon retreated from the aggressive Angevin policy begun a few months before; the Cardinal Ludovico Fiesco was sent to Naples, and the Bishop of Coria to Alfonso, to try to undo the harm done.

The engagement of Braccio as an Aragonese mercenary made it doubly necessary for the Roman Court to increase the military help given to Sforza, who was holding Aversa, to the north of Naples, for the Angevin.   The Church still held the western passes to the Kingdom, and to go there Braccio was forced to pass east through the March and the Abruzzi.   But, after Braccio had been promised the lordship of Capua, and installed as Governor in the Abruzzi, to supply Sforza in Aversa with men and arms was far from easy.   The burden of financing the Angevin army fell largely upon the Apostolic Chamber, and, with so much at stake, it is evident that during the spring and summer of 1421 a supreme effort was made to raise troops and money. Tartaglia di Lavello with 300 lances and Angelo della Pergola with a further 300 were already in the Pope's pay; their contracts of service were renewed, and in April 1421 the Duke of Sessa, an important Neapolitan baron, agreed to accept whoever should be created King of Sicily by the Pope, and to make war at the Pope's behest.   Later in the year he took the field in the Kingdom with several hundred lances.[1]   Carlo Malatesta and Aloisio de Verme were each engaged with 100 lances, and several other minor mercenaries were taken into service.[2]

To raise money to pay and supply such a force, drastic measures had to be taken. Mercenaries were engaged by the Apostolic Chamber between January and September 1421, for salaries which amounted to an annual total of over 170,000 florins a year.[3] To this must be added a further 90,000 florins a year, which continued to be due to Braccio.   The castle of Spoleto had already in September 1420 been pledged to Jacopo Ciotti, Count of Palazolo of Siena, for 11,000 florins, and his brother-in-law Bindo de' Tolomei had assumed control of the castle.[4]   Loans were raised in June and July 1421 of 6,000 florins each from the Guinigi of Lucca and the Gonzaga of Mantua, of 10,000 florins from the Chamberlain of the Roman Church, the Governor of Avignon, and of a total of almost a further ten thousand florins from various officials of the Roman Court, including 2,000 florins from Antonio Colonna.[5]   In May 1421 Carlo and Pandolfo Malatesta paid the *census* for their vicariates for two years,

[1] Sienese report of 19 September 1421, 'el duca di Sesse con 800 cavagli e più di mille de suoi vassali a piedi', Fink, *Martin V. und Aragon*, 152.   Martin's agreement with the Duke of Sessa, and various other *condotte*, are noted by Fink, 71–2, from Div. Cam. 14, fol. 63 f.

[2] Fink, 71–2.

[3] This sum has been calculated from Div. Cam. 14 and the 'liber capitaneorum', Florence, Biblioteca Nazionale, xix, 82.   The former records the agreements with captains, the latter the sums paid to them. My total is the total amount due under the *condotte*, and not the sum actually paid.

[4] Theiner, iii, no. 195, p. 267.   Giovanni de la Petra of Siena, Bishop of Grosseto, was appointed castellan of Spoleto on 5 September 1421 (Reg. Vat. 349, fol. 84), but the castle was later handed over by him to Bindo de' Tolomei.

[5] Fink, 72.   Also IE 379, fols. 44–6, long lists of loans made to the Apostolic Chamber by members of the Roman Court between 6 and 31 July 1421.   Giovanni de Astallis, the banker and Treasurer of Rome, lent 1,000 florins, Hermann Dwerg, apostolic protonotary (see Pastor, *Geschichte der Päpste*, 8/9 Edn., i, 256–7), 1,000 florins, Giordano Colonna Prince of Salerno, 1,000 florins, Cardinal Orsini the Cardinal of Brancaccio, 500 florins.   The total borrowed was 9,598 florins.

the year past and that to come, a total of 20,000 florins.[1] The Cardinal Legate of
Bologna was on 8 March 1421 authorised to raise loans of up to 20,000 florins to meet
the expenses of his vicariate, pledging any town in which there was no castle or
fortress.[2] Gabriel Condulmer, the Legate in the March, was on 24 June 1421
authorised to raise up to 6,000 florins in loans from the provincials, pledging such
revenues as he saw fit.[3] The Bishop of Aquino, the Vice-Rector of Campania and
Maritima, was on 31 July given power to raise a forced loan in the province from
any persons secular or ecclesiastic, in order to provide against the wars imminent in
the province.[4] The Bishop of Macerata and Recanati, Treasurer in the March of
Ancona, was on 11 August told to impose a caritative subsidy on the regular and
secular clergy in the March, the amount being left to his discretion.[5] Antonio Nerli
the Abbot of Mantua and papal referendary, was at the beginning of August told to
impose a caritative subsidy on the clergy in the lands subject to Venice, Florence,
Siena, Mantua and Ferrara, to be collected within the next two months.[6]

By these means Martin was able, early in 1421, to send reinforcements to Sforza.
The Count of Carrara, who had been attacked and forced to submit to Braccio when
Braccio first marched south to the Kingdom, was for a few months won over by
Martin to the Angevin cause; on 29 April Martin wrote to the Legate in the March
instructing him of the Count's loyalty, and ordering that he be allowed to keep any
lands which he won in war.[7] Having already released many nobles from their fealty
to Giovanna, Martin went further, and after Alfonso had arrived in Naples in June,

---

[1] IE 379, fol. 140. This sum was transferred to the secret account of the Pope (ibid. fol. 162), but
this does not preclude its being used to pay mercenaries.

[2] Reg. Vat. 353, fol. 131. He was also given a faculty to raise further loans in his vicariate, and to
pledge 'villas rochas aliasque terras et fructus redditus' against these loans; this is dated 19 September
1421, Reg. Vat. 353, fol. 255. A recognition of a loan to the Chamber of 5,000 florins from Pietro
Bartolomeo de' Borromei, Treasurer of Bologna, and the Florentine Gino Capponi, made on 31 August
1421, ibid. fol. 148. Borromeo also lent the Chamber 10,000 florins when he assumed the office of
Treasurer in August 1421 (Reg. Vat. 354, fol. 43); it is not clear if this is an entirely different loan from
the other.

[3] Reg. Vat. 353, fol. 197. There is a marginal annotation, 'Cassata de mandato reverendissimi
domini vicecamerarii domini nostri pape die XV mensis novembris 1424 per me Antonio de Sarzana'.

[4] The loan is to be 'certam pecuniarum quantitatem discrete et juste personarum qualitate pensata',
and the Hospitallers of St. John of Jerusalem are to be exempt. Reg. Vat. 353, fol. 215v. Cf. IE 379,
fol. 54 (11 October 1421), 'ab hominibus et civitate civitatis Terracinensis ratione caritativi subsidii
auctoritate apostolica imposita per manus providi viri Bartolomei Pistis de Terracina, florenos trecentos'.

[5] Reg. Vat. 353, fol. 232v. He is as soon as possible to send accounts of the amount collected to the
Apostolic Chamber.

[6] Ibid., fol. 223. For Nerli, see B. Katterbach, *Referendarii utriusque signaturae* (1931), 12. The
administration of the subsidy in Venice was afterwards transferred to Marco Lando, Bishop of Castello,
and the amount to be collected there fixed at 4,000 florins, Reg. Vat. 354, fols. 103, 21 August 1422.
For Florence, cf. *Commissioni*, i, 318, 'supplicherete il santo Padre, che si degni i cherici del nostro terreno
non richiedere nè gravare a uno certo caritativo sussidio, che si dice vuole loro imporre' (25 September
1421).

[7] Doc. 29 below. The Aragonese protested at this suborning of the liegeman of Giovanna II, see
Fink, *Martin V. und Aragon*, 154-5. But Martin's expectations were disappointed; on his return from
Aversa to Ascoli in 1421 the Count renounced his Angevin obedience, and agreed to join Braccio, cf.
Minuti, *Vita di M. A. Sforza*, 264, 'el conte de Carrara se partì de campo dal re et de Sforza quando
andorono ad Aversa, et andò ad Ascoli homo del re Aluisi: da lì a pochi mesi se condusse con Brazo'.
The count was ordered under pain of excommunication to recede from Braccio's service, Reg. Vat. 353,
fol. 205, 14 July 1421.

the Pope on 29 June forbade the ecclesiastics and barons of the Kingdom to pay any further taxes or *census* to the Queen.[1] From being secret, his military support of Sforza and the Angevin became open, and Tartaglia and the Duke of Sessa were both despatched openly to join Sforza in August.[2] The Aragonese, who in their embassy to the Pope in April had merely justified Alfonso's intervention in Naples, returned in a further embassy in September 1421 to protest strongly, even fiercely, against Martin's open encouragement of civil war in the Kingdom. He is accused of stirring up war, of sending Tartaglia, the Duke of Sessa, Paolo and Berardo Celano, and the Count of Carrara with hostile intent into the Kingdom. Martin who should be the fervent upholder of peace is the author and promoter of war, and the treasury of the Church, instead of being used for the poor and for the Divine Offices, has become the spoil of tyrants. Further, Braccio's salary in the March, the Duchy of Spoleto and the lands of special commission has been withdrawn, in contempt of Martin's promise—a somewhat ingenuous protest, following as it does the charge that the treasury of the Church is being used to pay mercenaries.[3] In reply Martin denied any sentiment of hostility towards the King of Aragon,[4] and on 28 September he despatched the Spaniard Pietro Fonseca, the Cardinal of Sant' Angelo, to return to Naples with the Aragonese ambassadors to renew practices of peace.

§ 3. Against the Aragonese portrait of Martin V as mischievous and warlike must be set the piracies of Braccio in the Papal State. Here a state of war had prevailed from the beginning of 1421, and few places were safe from the marauding of Braccio and his lieutenants. In March Piccinino was spoiling the countryside of Rieti and Amelia.[5] At the same time, in the March of Ancona, Ser Giovanna de Rocca, Braccio's chancellor, was demanding tallage from Macerata.[6] In an attempt to restore order a general truce was proclaimed in the Patrimony on 1 April 1421.[7] Spoleto, Narni, Terni and Amelia had already been placed under the government of the Vice-Chamberlain, Cardinal Louis Aleman, of the title of St. Eusebius.[8] Strong-points were strengthened and placed in reliable hands; Agapito Colonna was made Governor of Orvieto, and Antonio Colonna Governor and *podestà* of Orte.[9] At this

---

[1] Raynaldus, ad a. 1421, par. i.

[2] Campano, *Vita Braccii*, 169, 'Occulte enim Pontifex, quasi non ipse gerendi belli auctor esset, ante id tempus [the arrival of Alfonso in Naples] auxilia miseret; nunc, cognito Regis adventu, confirmandum exercitum et peditatu equitatuque augendum ratus, manifestius omnia facere, magnas undique belli vires moliri . . .'

[3] Printed by Fink, *Martin V. und Aragon*, 153 f.

[4] The brief printed by Fink, 'Politische Korrespondenz', no. 332, is probably of the autumn of 1421, 'nullam rationabilem causam habes odii et querelarum adversus nos, qui te libenti et benigno animo in sinu nostre caritatis ut filium carissimum retinemus . . . te caritative requerimus et rogamus, ut deponas iracundiam hanc iniuste conceptam, nec odio nostri ecclesiam persequaris'.

[5] Campano, 160 n.; Michaeli, *Memorie storiche di Rieti*, iii, 323–4, where it also appears that Martin advised Rieti not to resist, but to make the best terms with Braccio that it could obtain.

[6] Macerata, Riformanze, vol. 12, fols. 5v, 23 (March 1421). The tallage was paid to Braccio on 1 May.

[7] Reg. Vat. 353, fol. 136v.

[8] Ibid. fol. 179v, 3 February 1421.

[9] On 5 May 1421, Reg. Vat. 349, fol. 151v and see fol. 159v. Cf. G. Pardi, *BSU*, i (1895), 408–9.

period the Colonna began to lay hands on a large number of castles and lands, whose possession made them almost into the rulers of a state within the Papal State. The important castle of Ardea, which commands the southern approach to Ostia and Rome, passed into the direct control of Prospero Colonna, who bought it from the monastery of S. Paolo fuori le Mura.[1] In August, Corrado Trinci rebelled against the Pope, marched into the Duchy of Spoleto and seized Assignano and Trevi.[2] In the March of Ancona the punitive raids of Braccio and his faction continued, especially those of his henchman Jacopo dei Arcipreti, lord of Iesi. In November 1421, after various punitive expeditions, Jacopo laid siege to Ancona to demand tallage, in spite of the commune's having already paid the tallage which he demanded to the papal Treasurer of the March.[3]

In September 1421 Braccio marched south to Naples through the heart of the Papal State, passing within a few miles of Rome. He was reported to have with him a force over seven thousand strong, and the nervous rulers of Rome strengthened the guard on the gates. In the autumn he took two papal towns on the borders of the Abruzzi, Castella Nuova and S. Lucia, and went on to seize a number of the lands of the monastery of Montecassino.[4]

The arrival of the Aragonese Cardinal Fonseca in Naples was rightly reckoned as a portent of peace; the Genoese Cardinal Fiesco—who nevertheless remained in Naples—had up to this date carried out a frankly Angevin and anti-Aragonese policy, and Alfonso had several times asked for his removal. On 13 October 1421 the Florentine ambassadors arrived in Rome, and agreed with the Pope the essentials of a compromise over the Neapolitan question. Both the Kings were to withdraw from Italy, Alfonso was to be compensated with the principate of Calabria, and Braccio was to return north and re-enter Martin's service as a mercenary on the terms already agreed. The question of the succession of the throne of the Kingdom was to be left open.[5] At the end of November the Florentines and the Cardinal succeeded in concluding a truce between the Angevins and Aragonese, and both Braccio and Sforza adhered to the agreement. Aversa was to be given over by Sforza into the hands of the Pope. Early in 1422 things began to go in favour of Alfonso. Two Aragonese embassies at the Roman Court renewed their master's

---

[1] On 7 June 1420 Raymondo Orsini agreed to restore Ardea to the monastery of S. Paolo fuori le mura, in a treaty to which Giordano Colonna was also a party, Div. Cam. 14, fol. 47v. On 17 June 1420 Piero Giovanni Palozzi de Fuscis de Berta of Rome was ordered by the Pope to receive the place from Orsini, and govern it for the monastery, Reg. Vat. 349, fol. 58v. In 1421 Giordano Colonna finally took possession of Ardea, receiving it in exchange for other lands which he gave the monastery (Tomassetti, *La Campagna Romana*, ii [1910], 452, quoting from the Colonna archives, and from some of the notarial acts of Venettini which escaped Lanciani, in *ASR*, xx). Cf. Silvestrelli, *Città Castelli e Terre della Regione Romana*, 617.

[2] Reg. Vat. 353, fol. 233v, a citation for rebellion against Corrado Trinci, addressed to Cardinal Louis Aleman as Rector of Spoleto, dated 27 August 1421. But evidently the Trinci submitted quickly, for little more than a fortnight later, on 13 September 1421, Corrado Trinci was confirmed in all his privileges, so long as he remained obedient to the Holy See, Reg. Vat. 353, fol. 253v.

[3] Ancona, Atti Consigliari, vol. 30, fol. 65v, 'non obstante quod ista communitas solverit domino Thesaurario Marchie Anconitane dictos ducatos, et habet quietationem a dicto domino Thesaurario'.

[4] Campano, 173; A. de Tummulillis, *Notabilia Temporum* (ed. A. Corvisieri, 1890), 33.

[5] Fink, *Martin V. und Aragon*, 88; *Commissioni*, i, 323 f.

complaints against Martin's previous conduct, and demanded the final transfer of Aversa and Castelmare di Stabia to the Queen, a transfer which took place at the end of March. Sforza, harassed and long unpaid, in May 1422 met Braccio near Benafro, and not only concluded peace with him, but accepted a *condotta* from Alfonso of Aragon at a stipend of 45,000 ducats a year.[1]

In June of 1422 an agreement must have been reached between the Roman Court and Braccio, although the text is now lost. In May Braccio had moved north through the Abruzzi and the March and the Legate Condulmer concentrated his forces near Ancona, raised additional levies, and prepared to resist. But agreement was reached in Rome before any fighting began in the March. Braccio passed near Fermo at the end of June or the beginning of July. He was met by the Marshal of the March of Ancona, who arranged for the payment to him of assignments ordered by the Pope,[2] probably those due under a lost bull of 24 June 1422. By 7 July he was between Gubbio and Montone, and shortly after he arrived at Città di Castello. Here the city had been conceded in vicariate to the commune by Martin V in August 1420,[3] but Braccio had in 1422 exacted from the Pope the grant of the vicariate for himself, in return for the restoration of some of the towns which he had captured in the autumn of 1421. The arrangement has been said to be not lacking in ingenuity on the part of the Roman Court, since Città di Castello commands the passes into Tuscany, and whoever holds the city threatens—and thus may alienate—Florence. But Braccio received Florentine aid to enter his new possession, which he took in September after a two months' siege. He then accepted a *condotta* from Florence and Siena against the Duke of Milan : any hopes entertained by the Pope that the grant of Città di Castello would embroil him with Florence were thus proved illusory.[4]

§ 4. The second phase of the struggle with Braccio had ended very much in favour of the *condottiere*. The attempt to reverse the situation in Naples by calling in the Angevin had been more than countered by the appearance of Alfonso of Aragon. Martin had been compelled to accept the new *status quo* in Naples, and to see Braccio

[1] Fink, 97–8; Minuti, *Vita di M. A. Sforza*, 273. The text of the agreement between Braccio and Sforza is printed by D. José Amettler y Vinyas, *Alfonso V de Aragon en Italia y la Crisis Religiosa del Siglo XV*, i (1903), 495 f.

[2] Arch. Cam., pt. i, Tes. prov., Marca, B. 1, vol. 1, fol. 159, 'Cole Quarto marescallo necnon et ser Marcho qui iverunt ad magnificum dominum Braccium in primo eius adventu in provinciam ad sciendum de intentione sua et si erat in concordia cum domino nostro, et requiendandum sibi terras ecclesie. Cole Quarto marescallo et Ser Marcho notario qui iverunt secunda vice ad dictum dominum Braccium post receptionem bulle assignationis facte dicto domino Braccio ut dimitteret pecunias receptas per dominum thesaurarium Marchie—iverunt usque Eugubium' (10 July 1422). Printed by Fumi, 'Inventario e spoglio dei registri della Tesoreria Apostolica della Marca', *Le Marche*, iv (Fano, 1904), 109, but with some omissions and errors. Before Braccio's arrival the Legate had been preparing to resist; in a letter of 25 May he informed Macerata that he intended to unite the forces of the Church into one, Compagnoni, 310. The bull of assignment to Braccio mentioned in the passage quoted above no longer exists, but it is probably that of VIII kal. julii anno V, referred to in a later bull of 9 January 1423, Reg. Vat. 354, fol. 165.

[3] Reg. Vat. 349, fol. 67, 26 August 1420. This folio has been sewn in in the wrong order, and should be folio 68.

[4] Campano, 186–90; Valentini, 'Lo Stato di Braccio', 245–6.

F

become one of the greatest powers of the Kingdom.   Sforza had abandoned the papal party.   It was a bleak outlook for papal diplomacy.

Tartaglia, who had since the summer of 1421 been with Sforza in the Kingdom, had towards the end of the year shown signs of renewing his acquaintance with his former master Braccio.   At the end of 1421 Sforza seized him, and after trial before the papal commissioner in Aversa he was executed—justly, as Braccio confessed to Sforza in their meeting in the following year.[1]   His lands were seized for the Pope by Ludovico Colonna and the Rector of the Patrimony early in 1422.[2]   In March 1422 the much favoured Luca Monaldeschi of Orvieto, whose daughter Agnesella had married Tartaglia, was guaranteed by the Apostolic Chamber the repayment of her wedding portion of 3,000 florins.[3]

The lands which Braccio had seized from the monastery of Montecassino in 1421 probably formed part of the exchange which he made for Città di Castello.   But before papal forces could re-enter Montecassino, in July 1422 the local brigand, Cicco Bianco of Piedemonte, invaded the abbey itself, expelled the Abbot Tomacelli, and seized what remained of its lands, which were then divided between Cicco Bianco, Braccio, Alfonso and the Queen.[4]   This fresh invasion was dealt with from Rome. On 31 July 1422 the Bishop of Aquino, Rector of Campania and Maritima, was told to take over and administer all the fortresses and lands of the monastery, and on 2 August Antonio Abbot of the monastery of S. Lorenzo fuori le Mura at Rome was appointed Reformer of the monastery, to be obeyed by the monks as though he were their Abbot.[5]   Only after the efforts of a series of papal officials was Cicco Bianco finally in November 1423 driven out, and conciliated with grants of land.[6]

Formal relations between Martin V and Braccio were normal from the summer of 1422 to the spring of 1423.   Two instruments of January 1423 recognise a debt of over 76,000 florins to Braccio by the Apostolic Chamber, and make assignments towards its satisfaction.[7]   But in March 1423 the three year term of the vicariates which Martin had granted in Florence expired, and Braccio became bound by his

---

[1] Minuti, *Vita di M. A. Sforza*, 274.

[2] Ludovico Colonna as a papal commissioner subdued the castle of Montefalco, Reg. Vat. 354, fol. 22. Ulisse Orsini of Monterotondo, by order of Giordano Orsini the Cardinal Bishop of Albano, seized Sipicciano from Cristoforo di Lavello, Tartaglia's brother.   Ulisse was ordered on 12 February 1422 to restore the village to the Rector of the Patrimony, Reg. Vat. 353, fol. 326v, C. de Cupis, *BDA*, 3rd ser., i (1910), 70.   For the action of the Rector of the Patrimony against Toscanella, Campano, 182 n.

[3] Reg. Vat. 354, fol. 147, 6 November 1422.   This sum was secured on the village of Marta, which had been seized from Tartaglia, and which was granted to Monaldeschi either for five years, or until the sum of 3,000 florins had been repaid him by the Apostolic Chamber.

[4] A. de Tummulillis, *Notabilia Temporum*, 34.

[5] Reg. Vat. 349, fol. 228v and Reg. Vat. 354, fols. 109, 124, dated 31 July and 2 August 1422.

[6] On 28 July 1423 Antonio Giovanni Cenci of Rome was appointed to recover the lands of the monastery and to come to terms with Cicco Bianco of Piedemonte, Reg. Vat. 354, fol. 256.   Domenico d'Anglona, Bishop of Sutri, was appointed Visitor and Reformer of the monastery and Governor in temporals, ibid. fols. 267v, 268 (27 August 1423); Reg. Vat. 349, fol. 285v (10 October 1423).   Cicco Bianco was granted certain fees in Piedemonte belonging to the monastery, and absolved for his offences, 8 November and 3 December 1423, Reg. Vat. 355, fols. 10, 11.   Giovanni Conigner was appointed Captain of the territories of the monastery, with powers of *merum et mixtum imperium*, Reg. Vat. 350, fol. 13v.

[7] Reg. Vat. 354, fol. 169v.

oath of 1420 to return his lands to the Pope. The obligation was bound to lead to a crisis; in March Braccio sent an embassy to the Pope under Bindaccio de' Ricasoli to know 'whether he was to treat him as an enemy or a friend'. Only one document survives which throws any light on these negotiations, a contract for the marriage of the daughter of Lorenzo Colonna and of Braccio's son Carlo, dated 23 March 1423, and sealed for Bindaccio de' Ricasoli acting as proctor for Braccio.[1] But evidently, if any agreement on general questions was reached, it did not satisfy Braccio, for on 27 April he moved threateningly from Perugia toward Rome with all his forces, and it has been suggested with much probability by Valentini, that this threat forced the Pope to renew the vicariates.[2] Braccio was soon after reported by the Florentines as having promised not to offend any of the lands immediately subject to the Holy See.[3]

How superficial any agreement was bound to be, appears from the ceaseless attempts of Braccio to stir up rebellion against Martin in Spoleto, and of Martin to undermine Braccio's position as Governor of Aquila. Bindo de' Tolomei, the Sienese castellan in Spoleto, quarrelled with the inhabitants of the town in December 1422, and as a result the Pope seems to have decided to redeem the fortress from pledge.[4] On 4 and 12 February 1423 the Pope wrote to Jacopo Ciotti, Count of Palazolo, to tell him that the money owed him on the security of the fortress of Spoleto would shortly be paid at Siena, and that he was to transfer the fortress from his castellan Bindo de' Tolomei to the papal commissioner Jacopo Bishop of Aquino; the latter was appointed castellan by a bull of 13 March.[5] The money was paid to the commune of Siena on 26 February—the principal of 11,000 florins, together with 615 florins interest.[6] On 1 March Bindo de' Tolomei was given a safe conduct to leave Spoleto.[7] But the transfer of the fortress did not assure the fidelity of the town. The Governor and Priors of the town complained at this period that the withdrawal of the mercenary Pietro Navarrino left the town undefended.[8] In April there was a plot to betray the fortress to Braccio; it was detected and suppressed.[9] On 5 July Albertoni, the Governor, was ordered to look to the manning of the fortresses and strongpoints of Spoleto,[10] and on 13 August there was an open rebellion

[1] Lanciani, *ASR*, xx (1897), 395–6. This document, which was overlooked by Valentini ('Lo Stato di Braccio', 255), indicates that Ricasoli had made some progress towards an agreement with the Pope before Braccio left Perugia.

[2] Valentini, ibid.   [3] Ibid.   [4] Docs. 26, 27, 28 below.

[5] Docs. 26, 28 below; I have re-edited these documents, as the texts in Bandini, *La Rocca di Spoleto*, pp. 313 f., are corrupt. The appointment of the Bishop of Aquino as castellan is in Reg. Vat. 349, fol. 261v, 'Mandantes dilectis filiis nobilibus viris Jacobo quondam Marti militis ad presens dicte arcis castellano, et Bindo de Tholomeis eius genero, domicellis Senen', quatenus possessionem vacuam dicte arcis, cum municionibus universis, tibi traddere et assignare debeant'.

[6] G. C. Marri, *I documenti commerciali del fondo diplomatico mediceo nell'Archivio di Stato di Firenze* (1951), no. 71, p. 38.

[7] Reg. Vat. 354, fol. 194, 'Cum . . . Bindo de Tholomeis . . . de arce nostre Spoletan' de proxime recessurus . . .'

[8] Spoleto, Riformazioni, anno 1423, fol. 7.

[9] 'Lo Stato di Braccio', 251 n.

[10] Brief, transcribed in the Riformazioni of Spoleto, 1423, fol. 23v. Battista Piero Mattei de Albertonis of Rome had been appointed Governor on 25 November 1422, Reg. Vat. 349, fol. 246.

of the nobles of Spoleto. Far from unprepared, Martin sent a large force under Ludovico Colonna which arrived on 20 August and immediately subdued the town. With Colonna was a new Governor, Marino Bishop of Macerata and Recanati.[1] Peace was fairly quickly restored; on 30 October Mastino de Burgo, who had been Senator of Rome, was appointed Governor, *podestà* and Deputy in Spoleto; he entered the town on 8 November.[2] The exiles were re-admitted and terms signed with them, and rebellion was at an end. In the following year Braccio tried to magnify and support a minor rebellion which had occurred in Ancona, but again without success.[3]

Martin and his allies had far more success in Aquila than Braccio in Spoleto. On 31 April 1423 Aquila submitted its conditions to Louis III, who accepted the obedience of the city on 5 May. Martin's part in this move is not clearly documented, but may fairly safely be assumed.[4] At the beginning of May, Braccio entered the territory of Aquila and began the siege which was to end a year later in his defeat and death. In the same month the legal position of Braccio in Aquila suffered an important change; after the arrest of Caracciolo by Alfonso, Giovanna broke with the King and appealed to Sforza for protection. The Queen went to Benevento with Sforza and completed the revolution by disowning Alfonso and adopting Louis in his stead. The Papal Court found its hand strengthened overnight, the Angevin candidate suddenly secured the Queen's support, and Braccio, from the legitimate governor of the Abruzzi, became the mercenary of a foreign invader. Martin immediately wrote to Sforza to express—albeit in guarded terms— his satisfaction.[5]

§ 5. At the same time, events were taking place in Romagna which were to have important effects on the war of Aquila and the condition of the State of the Church. Giorgio Ordelaffi, the tyrant of Forlì, died in 1422, leaving Teobaldo Ordelaffi, a ten-year-old boy, and a wife, Lucrezia, daughter of Lodovico Alidosi, the tyrant of Imola. In his will Giorgio is thought to have recommended the child to the protection of Filippo Maria Visconti and Nicolò d'Este.[6] The vicariate of Forlì was granted to Teobaldo by the Church on 17 September 1422,[7] and he ruled under the

---

[1] Spoleto, Riformazioni, 1423, fol. 33, confines the narrative of the revolt to the mention of 'novitas et tumultus maximus' between the Guelph and Ghibelline factions of the city. Zampolini, 163, claims that the Bishop of Aquino, the castellan, himself incited the Ghibelline nobles to move against the Guelphs. The appointment of Marino, Bishop of Macerata and Recanati on 19 August, is in Reg. Vat. 349, fol. 279; this important cameral official was sent only to tide over the crisis, and on 30 October 1423 Mastino de Burgo of Città di Castello, ex-Senator of Rome, was appointed Deputy, Governor, and *podestà* in Spoleto, Reg. Vat. 349, fol. 296. Cf. Salimei, *Senatori e Statuti di Roma*, 166, 169.

[2] Spoleto, Riformazioni, 1423, fol. 71.

[3] *Commissioni*, i, 569.

[4] Valentini, 'Lo Stato di Braccio', 249 f.

[5] Fink, 'Politische Korrespondenz', no. 498.

[6] *Annales forolivienses*, 86; L. Cobelli, *Cronache forlivese*, 166 f.; Giovanni di M° Pedrino, *Cronica* (ed. Borghezio and Vattasio, 1929), 65–6; P. Bonoli, *Istorie della città di Forlì* (1661), 207 f.; *Commissioni*, i, 399 f.; Flavio Biondo, *Hist. ab inclinatione Romanorum*, or *Decades*, Basel, Froben, 1569, pp. 401 f.; Hieronymous de Forlivio, *Chronicon*, 33–4.

[7] Reg. Vat. 349, fol. 234v.

guardianship of his mother.   But the jackals were not long in appearing; a party of
sedition against the rule of Lucrezia came rapidly to strength inside the city, and,
thinking to further a future revolution there and profit by it, Caterina Ordelaffi,
the wife of the Genovese grandee Bartolomeo Fregoso, in March 1421 bought the
nearby castle of Castel Bolognese from its papal vicar, Antonio Bentivoglio, for 8,000
florins.   From March 1421 Milanese troops were assembling near Forlì to await
events, and in Florence the fear of a Milanese invasion of Romagna caused something
little removed from panic.

Among these conflicting interests Martin V moved with prudence and duplicity.
His policy had two faces, one for Florence, and a very different one for Milan.
Between the ambitions of Filippo Maria Visconti in Romagna, and Florence, which
feared encirclement by Milan, lay the neutral city of Bologna, a useful counter in the
hands of the Pope.   From Florence Martin wished for support against any move
which the Visconti might make against Bologna.   From Visconti he wanted support
against Braccio in the campaign of Aquila, and he hoped to obtain by his mediation
between both parties an extension of the direct rule of the Church in Romagna.

The understanding of Martin with Filippo Maria Visconti dated from the beginning of his pontificate; Martin had given Visconti diplomatic help in all the last
phases of the reconstruction of the Visconti *signoria*, in the recovery of Parma and
Brescia, and in the seizure of Genoa.   In 1422 there had been negotiations for a
marriage alliance between the Colonna and the Visconti, and an alliance of Milan
and the Church.[1]   In the same year the Legate of Bologna, Alfonso Carrillo, had
proclaimed an open alliance with Milan.[2]   But from the beginning of the troubles in
Forlì Martin played a double game.   While, in Rome, Martin encouraged Visconti
to send troops to the Romagna, in Bologna the Legate Carrillo assured the Florentines
that he had no understanding with Visconti, and that the troops would not be
allowed to go into papal territory.[3]

On 14 May 1423 the attempt of Lucrezia Ordelaffi to execute an agitator touched
off the long-expected rebellion.   Immediately the troops of the Marquis of Este,
having previously sworn allegiance to the Church between the hands of Carrillo,
occupied the city in the name of Teobaldo Ordelaffi and the Duke of Milan.   In
Florence the Dieci di Balìa were immediately appointed, an act amounting to a
declaration of war against Milan.   The Legate assured Florence of his goodwill, and
instanced as a proof his recovery of Castel Bolognese, which he had on 11 June.
He discussed, but never concluded, a defensive league with Florence, a league which
Martin told the Florentine ambassadors he would not oppose.[4]   In August Martin
gave permission to Pandolfo Malatesta to accept the *condotta* of Florence, but
expostulated to the Visconti that this permission was extorted from him against
his will.[5]   Martin removed the Legate Carrillo early in July; vicars were appointed

---

[1] L. Osio, *Documenti diplomatici tratti dagli archivi Milanesi*, ii (1869), nos. 56, 58, pp. 98, 105.   The
marriage was never concluded, and in 1424 Caterina Colonna married Guid'Antonio of Montefeltro.
[2] Valentini, 'Lo Stato di Braccio', 239–40.   [3] *Commissioni*, i, 410.   [4] Ibid. 449–55.
[5] Ibid. and Fink, 'Politische Korrespondenz', no. 402.

in his stead on 7 July,[1] and a new Legate, Condulmer, the former Legate in the March, was appointed to Bologna in August. The new Legate was openly pro-Florentine, and in September went so far as to conclude a defensive league with Florence, but Martin promptly disavowed the league to the Visconti, claiming, perhaps justly, that it was made against his express wishes.[2] At the same time Martin achieved a most important success for his affairs in the south, by arranging for Filippo Maria Visconti to grant Sforza a *condotta* for 4,000 troops, to fight against Braccio in the Kingdom. In September active hostilities began between the mercenaries of Florence and Milan in the Romagna. Martin preserved his neutrality and that of Bologna, and he ordered the Marquis of Este to deliver up Forlì, either to Teobaldo Ordelaffi or to the Legate Condulmer, although he can hardly have expected this order to be obeyed.[3]

The Florentines wished to engage Braccio for the war of Romagna, but Braccio remained before the obstinately defended walls of Aquila, held there in a struggle which would decide the future of all Italy south of Tuscany.[4] In January 1424 Sforza was drowned at the crossing of the Pescaro, and it became evident that the Church must now gather all its forces to save Aquila. Visconti, who had already despatched a fleet, was asked to send two thousand men and to enter into open alliance. In March three briefs were despatched to Aquila to encourage the town to resist and the papal mercenary Pietro Navarrino was sent with a small force to its aid, the first act of open war made by the Roman Court against Braccio since the agreements of June 1422. In March the mercenary Giacomo Caldora was bought over for the Angevin, and in April two forces moved against Braccio at Aquila, one from Rome under Ludovico Colonna, and one from Naples under Caldora. The aim of the expedition was not to seek a decisive battle, but merely to re-victual Aquila, although the forces used were numerically larger than those of Braccio. There was also the hope that the Milanese army would at last march south from Romagna, and, to prevent this junction, Braccio sent Count Ardizzone of Carrara north to Ascoli to hold the passes. On 25 May Caldora and Colonna arrived in the *contado* of Aquila. Braccio, instead of attacking before the enemy had time to recover from the march, refused the advice of his captains and preferred to allow Caldora's whole army to deploy into the plain below the city, so that his victory might be complete, and the enemy forbidden the chance of escape. On 2 June the battle took place, one of the most savage, bloody and tenacious of the fifteenth century. The issue was in doubt for many hours, but before midday the desertion of Pier Gianpaolo Orsini and the entry into battle of the soldiery of Aquila finally turned the scale. Braccio's main force was annihilated, and its captain, captured unhurt, but then cut down by the Perugian exiles, died in Caldora's camp two days after the battle. Martin V was almost unable to believe his own good fortune, and demanded that his enemy's body

[1] Reg. Vat. 349, fol. 272v. The vicars were Jacopo, Bishop of Spoleto, and Didacho Martini, Archdeacon of Cuenca.
[2] Fink, 'Politische Korrespondenz', no. 404.
[3] Brief of 1 September 1423, in *Commissioni*, i, 488.
[4] For what follows, see Valentini, 'Lo Stato di Braccio', 300 f.; W. Block, *Die Condottieri* (1913).

be brought to Rome. In Braccio's defeat by Caldora it was felt that *virtù* had succumbed to mediocrity, and that, if not unworthily defeated, Braccio had at least succumbed to an unworthy foe.[1]   After six years of humiliation Martin V now found himself a victor, able not only to recover the States of the Church but to turn the scales of the balance of power in Italy.

III.   *The Recovery of the Lands of the Church in Umbria, the March and the Patrimony*

§ 1.   The government of Braccio's dominions did not survive his death for more than a few weeks.   Guid'Antonio of Montefeltro and Francesco Sforza were told to recover all Braccio's lands for the Church, and in the March of Ancona Ludovico Migliorati and the communes in the south of the province were ordered to close the passes against the survivors of the enemy army.[2]   Perugia, the capital of Braccio's state, elected his bastard son Oddo, a boy of fifteen or sixteen, as *signore*, and prepared in a somewhat half-hearted way for defence.   But when Malatesta Baglioni, one of the defeated, arrived from Aquila and Rome on 18 June with letters from the Pope, he was given a hearing, and three days later a Perugian embassy left for Rome.   Without resistance Oddo Fortebraccio gave up the fortresses of the *contado* into the hands of the commune, and in mid-July he left the city.[3]   The ambassadors had meanwhile found the Pope in his summer quarters at Gallicano, and while they negotiated there the Papal army under the young Francesco Sforza approached Perugia.   The towns of Umbria offered no resistance, and Todi submitted to the Pope in the person of his commissioner Luca Monaldeschi; the town's ambassadors arrived at Gallicano on 17 July.[4]   On the following day peace was signed with the Perugian ambassadors.   The capitulations of peace were approved by Martin in the bull of absolution which he issued for the city on 29 July; they take the usual form of a series of demands by the commune, to which the replies of the Pope are attached.[5]   The terms are extremely liberal.   The city is to accept a Legate and *podestà* from the Pope and to submit to certain restrictions in its jurisdiction of appeal, and 'plenum dominium' of the city is resigned into the hands of the Pope. The other officials of the city are to be elected according to the statutes, the present

[1] See Piero Candido Decembrio, quoted by Valentini, 'Lo Stato di Braccio', 223 n.

[2] The bull to Guid'Antonio in Theiner, iii, no. 225, p. 287.   For the March, see the documents printed by Fumi, Le Marche, iv (1904), 112 f.

[3] Graziani, *Cronaca*, ed. Fabretti, in *ASI*, 1st ser., xvi, pt. 1 (1850), 286 f.; Pellini, *Dell'Historia di Perugia*, ii, 279 f.   Baglioni was rewarded by the grant of Cannara in vicariate on 21 November 1427, and in 1428 by a grant of an annual pension of 400 florins payable by the Apostolic Chamber, Reg. Vat. 356, fols. 20, 23v.

[4] Todi's agreement with Monaldeschi is printed by Leonii, 'Document tratti dall'Archivio segreto del Comune di Todi', *ASI*, 3rd ser., ii, pt. 2 (1865), 21.   He was appointed Deputy of Todi, which is said to have returned to the obedience of the Holy See 'mediantibus laudabilibus operationibus tuis', on 23 July 1424, Reg. Vat. 350, fol. 53.   Cf. *Commissioni*, ii, 114.   A *capitaneus* was also appointed for Todi on 5 August 1424, Reg. Vat. 350, fol. 49.

[5] The capitulations are printed by Fumi, *Inventario e Spoglio dei Registri della Tesoreria Apostolica di Perugia e Umbria* (1901), xxx f.   The bull approving the capitulations and absolving Perugia in Fumi, liii f., and Valentini, 'Lo Stato di Braccio', no. 32, p. 373.

officials remaining until the expiry of their terms of office. The ordinances which Braccio's government made up to the date of his death are to remain in force; those who acquired the rents of ecclesiastical properties under his régime are to continue to enjoy them, the privilege of minting money is to continue, the taxes are not to be immoderately increased beyond their amount when the Church last ruled in Perugia. The Legate will consult with the priors and *camerarii* of the city over political matters. Finally the Pope agrees to support the same political faction which Braccio had placed in power when the popular party, the Raspanti, were proscribed in 1416. The Michelotti, who had fought for Martin at Aquila and who had cut down Braccio on the field, remained in exile, and the sequestration of their property was confirmed. In the capitulations Martin agreed to accept a list of twelve exiles, but in a treaty between the commune of Perugia and Guid'Antonio of Montefeltro which was in force in November 1425, the list of exiles covers many pages, and is said to be the same as that compiled in the city on 26 July 1424.[1] Perugia thus, as the chronicler Graziani comments, went flatly against the principle that 'mai sbandito fe buona terra'.

Antonio Corrario, Cardinal Bishop of Porto, was appointed Vicar-General in Perugia on 6 August, although he was prevented from coming by the plague, and his place taken until 29 August by the papal commissioner Didacho Rapado, Bishop of Tuy.[2] The first papal *podestà* arrived in the city on 19 November.[3] Assisi submitted to the Church after Oddo Fortebraccio left the town in October to serve Florence as a mercenary. This Florentine connexion gave Martin considerable annoyance, and he more than once protested against the support given by Florence to the exiles, and to such allies of Braccio as Corrado Trinci.[4] But with the submission of Città della Pieve in the spring of 1425, the reconquest of Perugia may be considered complete.[5]

§ 2.   The Trinci of Foligno had been close allies of the dead Braccio, and a daughter of their house was the wife of Oddo Fortebraccio.[6] It is not therefore surprising that there was a rebellion of the Trinci in the summer of 1424. By the beginning of

---

[1] Perugia's correspondence with Guid'Antonio about the exiles is in A. Fabretti, *Documenti di Storia Perugina*, i (Turin, 1887), 189 f.

[2] The Cardinal's appointment was as Vicar-General in temporals in Perugia, Todi and the Duchy of Spoleto, Reg. Vat. 350, fol. 50. The Bishop of Tuy had been made Nuncio, Commissioner and Rector-General in Perugia on 29 July 1424, ibid. fol. 44v. Paolo de Caputgrassis of Sulmona, cameral clerk, was appointed Treasurer of Perugia, Todi, Orvieto and the Duchy of Spoleto on 25 July 1424, ibid. fol. 41. See also Graziani, 296 f.

[3] Graziani, 302. The first papal nominee to this office never assumed it. He was Francesco Ferretti, of the powerful family of that name of Ancona; Reg. Vat. 350, fol. 57v. The salary of the post was immense, 2,000 florins, the salary of the Governor of a province.

[4] Valentini, 'Lo Stato di Braccio', no. 28, p. 371; *Commissioni*, ii, 96–7; 185–6.

[5] Graziani, 299 f., 308; Pellini, ii, 284. Città della Pieve was handed over to the papal forces by its castellan, Cherubino de Hermanno of Perugia, and in recognition of these services he was awarded a pension of 150 florins a year, chargeable on the revenues of Città della Pieve, Reg. Vat. 355, fols. 161, 264. Jacopo de Burgo was appointed *podestà* of the town on 12 October 1424, Reg. Vat. 350, fol. 64. But he could not have entered the town until it surrendered, in April 1425, Graziani, 308.

[6] Pellini, ii, 232.

September Francesco Sforza was in the field, with the papal commissioner the Bishop of Tuy, against Corrado Trinci.[1] He had complete success; he occupied Trevi, Nocera and Montefalco, the three most important points of the Trinci lands outside Foligno itself, and when Corrado Trinci came to make his peace with the Pope in November 1424, that formidable tyrant had to agree to give up all the lands conquered from him, and to see them taken under the direct government of the Holy See.[2] His submission was followed by the marriage of his daughter Faustina to Giovan'Andrea Colonna, son of Antonio Colonna of Riofreddo.[3]

Braccio left, besides his bastard son Oddo, a widow, Nicola Varano, and an infant son, Carlo. Martin was at first conciliatory, and he granted Carlo Fortebraccio the vicariate of Gualdo and Montone,[4] and undertook to leave Madonna Nicola undisturbed in the possession of Città di Castello.[5] But Filippo Maria Visconti immediately began to intrigue to secure a foothold in Città di Castello,[6] and by the late spring of 1425 the Cardinal Vicar of Perugia had been instructed to include the city in his jurisdiction, and take what measures he saw fit for its welfare.[7] In September the Cardinal was told to make arrangements with Mazzancollo the castellan of Gualdo to seize Gualdo, either in the event of Carlo Fortebraccio's death, or as soon as his vicariate expired.[8] The intentions of Filippo Maria Visconti were shown with perfect clarity in a letter seized by the Florentines and shown by them to the Apostolic Treasurer. It was intended in October 1425 that, through the mediation of her family, the Varano, Madonna Nicola be asked to provide Città di Castello as a base to re-victual Milanese troops.[9] But neither this design, nor that of the Pope, came to any fruition, and this lady continued to hold Città di

---

[1] Simonetta, *Rerum Gestarum Francisci Sfortiae Commentarii* (Muratori, *RRIISS*, xxi, pt. 2), 20. The appointment of the Bishop of Tuy as commissioner is in Reg. Vat. 355, fol. 77v. The latter was under the orders of the Cardinal-Vicar of Perugia; but papal mercenaries were ordered to obey him.

[2] The absolution of Montefalco, Nocera and Trevi for offences committed while under the rule of Corrado Trinci, Reg. Vat. 355, fols. 84, 91, 125. The last is printed by M. Morici, *BSU*, xi (1905), 260 f. Montefalco and Nocera were declared to be under the immediate rule of the Holy See, and the castle at Trevi was ordered to be destroyed. In a list of the Trinci possessions made in 1421 these three towns take pride of place after Foligno; in each the *podestà* was paid 200 florins a year (D. M. Faloci Pulignani, 'Il vicariato dei Trinci', *BSU*, xviii (1912), 14 f.). The absolution of Corrado Trinci on 17 November 1424, Reg. Vat. 356, fol. 5v. He is restored to his rule in the lands which he at present holds, 'et non ad alia civitates terras castra et loca que non tenes et possides, sed nos tenemus et possidemus, et in quibus nullum ius vigore presentium tibi acquiri volumus'. Cf. *Commissioni*, ii, 282. For Trinci's attempt to recover these lands under Eugenius IV, Guiraud, *L'Etat Pontifical*, 182 f.

[3] D. Dorio, *Istoria della famiglia Trinci* (1648), 251.

[4] Reg. Vat. 355, fol. 54, where the vicariate of Gualdo is granted for three years to Carlo and Oddo Fortebraccio; ibid. fol. 57v, Carlo is granted the vicariate of Montone, 27 July 1424. Oddo must soon after have been deprived of his share in the vicariate; in Reg. Vat. 350, fol. 105v, the Cardinal-Vicar of Perugia is made curator of Gualdo, on account of the infancy of its holder, Carlo Fortebraccio (10 May, 1425).

[5] *Commissioni*, ii, 398.

[6] *Commissioni*, ii, 309, 314, 360.

[7] Reg. Vat. 350, fol. 104v, 'tibi faciendi, mandandi, ordinandi et disponendi, quod pro illius (scil., the city) felici regimine, ac statu pacifico et tranquillo ad honorem nostram et ipsius Caroli fore cognoveris pro futura, potestatem plenariam concedentes', 8 May 1425.

[8] Reg. Vat. 355, fol. 225.

[9] *Commissioni*, ii, 360, 364–5, 397, 401, 431–8, 447–9. Cf. Graziani, *Cronaca*, 313; *Cronaca di Ser Guerriero di Gubbio*, 43.

Castello freely until the three-year vicariate of her son's lands Gualdo and Montone had expired. In December 1427, after Madonna Nicola had suppressed an attempted rebellion in Montone, the Cardinal-Vicar of Perugia put into effect the instructions given him in 1425, and required her to deliver up Gualdo and Montone to the Church.[1] On her refusal she was declared a rebel, and a strong force was sent against her. The discontented elements in Città di Castello came out for the Church, and in January 1428 the city fell to the Cardinal, and Madonna Nicola fled to Camerino.[2] A Governor was appointed, and for the rest of Martin's pontificate the city was ruled directly for the Church.[3]

§ 3. To subdue and govern the March of Ancona Martin chose Pietro Emigli, the Abbot of Rosazzo, whom he had already so distinguished by his friendship as to permit to use the surname of Colonna.[4] In June 1424 Emigli was appointed Governor in temporals of the March of Ancona, of Massa Trabaria and of the Presidency of Farfa, with the full powers of a Legate *a latere*, to recover those places which had been seized from the Church.[5] In early June, before he even arrived in the March, the communes ruled by Braccio and his satellites were in rebellion against their late masters. Rocca Contrata and Staffolo capitulated to the Treasurer of the March almost immediately after the battle of Aquila, and at the same time Iesi rose against its Perugian ruler Jacopo dei Archipreti.[6] With an army of local levies the Treasurer secured the city's submission on terms; the Pope agreed that the rock of Iesi be destroyed, and promised not to grant the city away in vicariate.[7] The new Governor entered the March in mid-July; he was at Rocca Contrata on the 21st and he required the commune to swear obedience in his court at Macerata on the 22nd.[8] With him he brought the forces of Antonio Colonna and of the mer-

---

[1] Graziani, 325–6.   [2] Reg. Vat. 351, fol. 25v, printed in *BSU*, vi (1900), 385 n.; Graziani, ibid.

[3] Reg. Vat. 351, fol. 83, 9 January 1429. The first Governor appointed was Gaspar, Archbishop of Benevento; he was followed on 6 June 1429 by Francesco, Bishop of Pavia 'Cubicularius noster', ibid. fol. 121.

[4] B. Katterbach, *Referendarii utriusque Signaturae*, 2.

[5] Reg. Vat. 355, fol. 38v, 27 June 1424. Together with Astorgio, Bishop of Ancona, the Treasurer of the March, he was charged with the recovery of the lands of the Church in the March of Ancona, and authorised to make agreements to that end (Reg. Vat. 355, fol. 42, 14 July 1424). But Lapiro, which had been seized in March 1424 by Antonio Smeducci of Sanseverino, was excluded from his cognisance (ibid.). Cf. Arch. Cam., pt. i, Tes. Prov., Marca, B.1, vol. 3, fol. 118, and G. C. Gentile, *Sopra gli Smeducci vicarii per Santa Chiesa in Sanseverino dal secolo XIV. al XV.* (Nozze Servanzi-Valentini, Macerata, 1841), 17–19. The Bishop of Urbino, the former Deputy in the March, had in June 1424 been ordered to bring a process against Antonio Smeducci for this seizure, Reg. Vat. 355, fol. 28. Cf. also I. Schuster, *L'Imperiale Abbazia di Farfa*, 415–6.

[6] Arch. Cam. pt. i, Tes. Prov., Marca, B.1, vol. 3, fol. 123 f. Help was requested against Iesi on 10 June from Pausola ('Mons Ulmi'), S. Iusto, Monte Santo, Ripatransone, S. Maria in Lapide, and Ludovico Migliorati of Fermo, 'ut micterent pedites, quia comunitas Exii miserat unam licteram domino thesaurario, ut iret ad succurendum eis, quia fecerunt novitatem contra Jacobum dominum Francisci . . .' Cf. Fumi, *Le Marche*, iv, 113.

[7] Ibid. The brief published by G. Baldassini, *Memorie istoriche dell'antichissima e regia città di Jesi* (1765), app. 47, p. lxxvii, refers to the destruction of the fortress, but the date should be 'anno septimo' instead of 'anno sexto'.

[8] Arch. Cam. pt. i, Tes. Prov., Marca, B.1, vol. 3, fol. 127v, and cf. Fumi, *Le Marche*, iv, 116. Macerata, Riformanze, vol. 13, fol. 97v.

cenary Gattemelata, and he proceeded to lay siege to Cingoli, which had been ruled for Braccio by Anselmo Montemelini. In September 1424 the town submitted, and its ruler was expelled.[1]

Antonio Colonna remained in the March until July 1425; he recovered Apiro from the Smeducci of San Severino, and was laying siege to Arquata, on the Tronto, when the Pope recalled him so that he might replace Ludovico Colonna as Viceroy of Apulia.[2] Pietro Emigli spent 1425 in re-ordering the administration of the March. In February he was ordered by the Pope to revise all the assessments of tallage of the towns and *signori* of the March according to the 'dispositio et qualitas moderni temporis', as the continuous wars of the past decade had impoverished a good many of the communes. The re-assessments were duly made, and no doubt the provincial Parliament which he held in Macerata in March 1425 assisted him in making them.[3] Emigli's government seems to have been benevolent and beneficial. The towns no longer had to raise forced loans in order to pay their tallage, and Ancona, which had for some years been on the verge of revolt, relapsed into quiet.

In the spring of 1426 Jacopo Caldora was sent into the March with a strong force, and Emigli was able to resume his main task, the suppression of the *signorotti*. In May he moved against the Smeducci of San Severino, who had already two years before fallen into bad odour with the Holy See by their seizure of the disputed territory of Apiro, and whose vicariate, even supposing its renewal in 1423, must have expired in May 1426.[4] The cities in the March sent levies and supplies to the siege of the city, which fell after a few weeks. The Smeducci were expelled and their goods expropriated, and Antonio Smeducci was sent into captivity at Narni.[5] From this successful action Caldora and Emigli moved immediately to a more difficult and important task, the recovery of Ascoli.

Commanding the valley of the Tronto, the Via Salaria, and the passes south to the Kingdom of Naples, Ascoli was the most important centre in the March remaining in the hands of tyrants. The Count of Carrara, who was both feudatory of Queen Giovanna and vicar of the Church, had died in 1421, and his sons Obizzo and Ardizzone had not commended themselves to the good graces of the Holy See. Their conversion to the papal cause in 1422 had lasted only a few months; they had thereafter fought with Braccio, and were under his command at the time of the battle of Aquila. Passing into the service of Florence, they were both captured,

[1] Arch. Cam. quoted above, B.2, vol. 1, fol. 156, and B.2, vol. 3, fol. 282v (cf. Fumi, *Le Marche*, iv, 163 f.); Compagnoni, *La Reggia Picena*, 313; Macerata, Riformanze, vol. 13, fol. 101v. The expulsion of 'quidam Anselmus de stirpe Brachii' is referred to in a letter of Francesco Sforza, dated 1434, and printed by O. Avicenna, *Memorie della città di Cingoli* (Iesi, 1644), 153–5. He had married Rengarda, one of the two daughters of Giovanni, last of the Cimi rulers of Cingoli (ibid.); cf. Pellini, *Dell'Historia della città di Perugia*, ii, 283. At Iesi, although the fortress was destroyed, it was rebuilt a year later; in September 1425 a thousand workmen were engaged by the Treasurer to excavate the moats, Arch. Cam. pt. i, Tes. Prov., Marca, B.2, vol. 2, fol. 171 (cf. Fumi, *Le Marche*, iv, 169).

[2] Arch. Cam. quoted above, B.2, vol. 2, fol. 158 f.   [3] Reg. Vat. 355, fol. 154, 1 February 1425.

[4] The first vicariate of the Smeducci was issued on 10 May 1420, Reg. Vat. 349, fol. 47.

[5] Arch. Cam. volume quoted above, fols. 160v, 178 f. (cf. Fumi, *Le Marche*, iv, 168–71); G. C. Gentile, *Sopra gli Smeducci vicarii in Sanseverino*, 19; *Cronache della città di Fermo*, 55. Nicolò, Bishop of Tropea, was made Deputy in Sanseverino on 29 December 1426, Reg. Vat. 350, fol. 276.

with Carlo Malatesta, at the rout of Zagonara in 1424.[1] In Milan Ardizzone was reported to have accepted a *condotta* from the Duke on terms which obliged him, if Visconti so desired, to fight against the Pope. In August 1425 Martin told the Florentine ambassadors that only his friendship for Florence (whose *raccomandato* the Count of Carrara still was) prevented him from sending an army against Ascoli.[2]

On what grounds Martin suppressed the vicariate of Ascoli, which had been renewed for three years in April 1425,[3] I have been unable to discover, but the most likely seem to be the entering of Milanese service without papal permission. On some pretext Obizzo (his brother Ardizzone being still in Milan) was commanded in July 1426 to deliver Ascoli to the Pope, and on his refusal Caldora moved against the city. Obizzo received no more support from his subjects than did other tyrants of the March under like circumstances. On the appearance of Caldora and Emigli before the city there was an almost immediate revolt within the walls. Obizzo da Carrara made terms with the Governor, giving up the city and district of Ascoli and its fortresses, and receiving a few hundred florins to cover the cost of the munitions in the castles.[4] On 8 August the commune of Ascoli made its own peace with the Governor, and returned to the direct obedience of the Holy See. Once one of the most independent and democratic towns of the March, Ascoli attempted to re-assert its liberties, and it obtained that the city be governed according to its statutes and privileges, and be not taxed arbitrarily. But in essentials the agreement merely replaces the *signoria* of the Church for that of the family of Carrara. The Governor reserves for the Church the rights to appoint what officials it pleases, declines to destroy the fortresses and promises that the statutes be observed only in so far as they do not run against the liberties of the Church.[5] In the event the Church appointed both *podestà* and treasurer of Ascoli, and the finances of Ascoli became no more than a department of the Apostolic Treasury of the March.[6]

Early in September 1426 Offida, the last of the fortresses of the *contado* of Ascoli, was handed back to the Church. But Pietro Emigli hardly survived this last of his successes; he died in Macerata on 25 September.[7] He was succeeded in the effective government of the March by the Treasurer, Astorgio Agnesi, Bishop of Ancona, who in the spring of the following year was appointed Deputy in the March.[8] Astorgio spent his winter of 1426/27 in completing the military work of his predecessor. The continued resistance of Obizzo da Carrara's castle of Macchie, near San Ginesio, was broken after a siege, revolts were put down in San Severino and Montefiore,[9]

---

[1] The grant of the vicariate to the Carrara brothers in Reg. Vat. 350, fol. 1, 1 September 1423. For the capture of Ardizzone at Zagonara, G. Pedrino, *Cronica*, 87.

[2] *Commissioni*, ii, 217, 373.

[3] Reg. Vat. 350, fol. 137v, 5 April 1425.

[4] *Cronache della città di Fermo*, 56; Arch. Cam. pt. i, Tes. Prov., Marca, B.2, vol. 2, fol. 161v.

[5] The agreement is below, doc. 23.

[6] For the treasurer of Ascoli see below, p. 181. A *podestà* was appointed there on 22 October 1426, Reg. Vat. 350, fol. 268.

[7] Macerata, Riformanze, vol. 13, fol. 13v; Arch. Cam. volume quoted above, fol. 273.

[8] Reg. Vat. 350, fol. 295, 30 April 1427.

[9] Arch. Cam. pt. i, Tes. Prov., Marca, B.2, vol. 3, fol. 279 f. (cf. Fumi, *Le Marche*, iv, 175–6); ibid., Tes. Prov., Ascoli, B.1, vol. 1, fol. 119 f.

and in March 1428 the Deputy seems to have attempted to forbid the *signori* of the March to maintain armed men.[1] It would have been too much to expect the petty tyrants to obey such a command, which would have meant their immediate ruin, but the military force which enabled the Church to attempt even to issue such a revolutionary order was displayed again in the summer of 1428. Ludovico Migliorati the tyrant of Fermo died in June of that year. Some years earlier, when Migliorati had been captured by the Milanese at the siege of Brescia in 1420, Martin V had attempted to secure Filippo Maria Visconti's assent to the Pope's seizing Fermo for the Church.[2] The assent was not given, and Martin took the matter no further, but Migliorati's death and the consequent ending of his vicariate gave the Deputy of the March a chance which he was quick to take. The towns of the March sent him their levies, and with these he moved against Fermo, which was held by the brothers Gentile and Firmano Migliorati. On 4 August 1428 Fermo revolted in favour of the Church, and on 10 August papal troops entered the city. The Gerfalcon, the great fortress of the Migliorati which stood beside the Cathedral, held out. A siege train was set up, and in November the brothers Migliorati agreed to capitulate on terms, and to accept a large money provision in return for their withdrawal. The Gerfalcon was returned to the Church early in 1429.[3]

Although the revolt of Fermo against the Migliorati was made to the cry of 'viva lo popolo e la libertà', the attempts of the commune to recover its ancient liberties were suffocated by the Church just as those of the commune of Ascoli had been. The request that the Gerfalcon be destroyed was refused, a Governor and a Treasurer were appointed by the Church, and the monies of the city were disposed of freely by the agents of the Apostolic Chamber, just as they were in the other subject cities. The subjection of the city was complete; the general court of the March visited Fermo and heard pleas there, and the protests made by the city against the rate of taxation in 1429 met with a firm, if not a contemptuous refusal.[4] The only *signori* of any importance in the March who remained independent were the wily Varano of Camerino and those more or less faithful allies of the Holy See, the Montefeltro and the Malatesta.

§ 4. In the Patrimony of St. Peter in Tuscia the echoes of Braccio's defeat were as long in dying away as they were elsewhere in the Papal State. In the spring and autumn of 1425 two of Braccio's former satellites, Ulisse Orsini of Mugnano and Raynaldo Alfani of Rieti, were driven out of their petty dominions. The vicariate

---

[1] Arch. Cam. pt. i, Tes. Prov., Marca, B.3, vol. 1, fol. 169, 'Antonio . . . misso cum littera domini locumtenentis ad dominis de Marchia ut deberent cassare et removere omnes gentes armorum que essent ad eorum stipendia' (cf. Fumi, *Le Marche*, iv, 283).

[2] *Commissioni*, ii, 166.

[3] For the capture of Fermo, see *Cronache della città di Fermo*, 57–9; Arch. Cam. pt. i, Tes. Prov., Marca, B.3, vol. 2, fols. 240–248 (cf. Fumi, *Le Marche*, iv, 285–91). The brief welcoming the letters of submission from the commune of Fermo is dated 15 August 1428, Fermo, Archivio Priorale, no. 1451. Nicolò Guinigi, Bishop of Lucca, was appointed castellan of the Gerfalcon on 11 February 1429, Reg. Vat. 351, fol. 88.

[4] Fermo, Archivio Priorale, no. 471. See pp. 181–2 below.

of Raynaldo Alfani in Rieti was suspended in March 1425, on the pretext of a quarrel which he had had with a neighbouring commune. Alfani was promptly expelled from the city by papal troops, and the Bishop of Todi appointed Governor.[1] The commune sent ambassadors to Rome to attempt to secure favourable terms for its future government, but they met with short shrift. To the request that they be allowed to present three candidates to the Pope for the office of *podestà*, of whom he would choose one, it was curtly answered that the Pope would give them the same treatment as Bologna and Perugia—that is, he would appoint whom he pleased. Requests for a reduction of taxes met with an equally stern front in Rome, and in the end Rieti had to be content that the revenues of the city fall into his hands, and accept what was said to them of Martin V by his nephew Jacopo Colonna, 'che Papa Martino al denaro non ce remedio'.[2]

In June 1425 Orlando de Orlandis of Genazzano, familiar and commissioner of the Pope, attacked Ulisse Orsini in his castle at Mugnano with a mixed force of levies and mercenaries based on Viterbo; the pretext for the attack I have been unable to discover. Antonio Colonna assisted at this siege, which lasted until September, and ended in Orsini's being betrayed by his men and captured, and in the fall of Mugnano.[3] Mugnano was then granted to Antonio Colonna in vicariate; he held it until it was taken from him by Eugenius IV and regranted to Matteo Orsini, the son of Ulisse.[4] The attack on Ulisse Orsini demonstrated how far from united was the Orsini family; Cottanello, which was his fief, was granted by Martin V to Jacopo Orsini of Tagliacozzo—a grant which was again reversed by Eugenius IV in favour of Matteo Orsini.[5]

IV. *Romagna and the rebellion of Bologna,* 1424–1431

§ 1. The chastisement of Braccio's faction, the rooting out of petty tyrants in the March, the general work of pacification which was carried out in the two or three years following the battle of Aquila, were all part of the internal machinery of the Papal State. But in Bologna and Romagna the Papacy had to defend itself against the cupidity of several Italian powers, and to fight in the general arena of Italian politics. Martin's first intention was to exploit the discomfiture of Florence in the

---

[1] Michaeli, *Memorie storiche della città di Rieti,* iii, 220 f.

[2] Michaeli, iii, 327–8, in the text of the letter relating the reception of the embassy of Rieti in Rome. The absolution of the city for rebellion, 13 November 1425, Reg. Vat. 355, fol. 231v. The Apostolic Chamber sent commissioners to Rieti to confiscate the goods of the Alfani in November 1425, Div. Cam. 9, fol. 161, and on 29 December Jacopo of Bagnorea, notary of the Apostolic Chamber, was sent to Rieti to investigate what revenues were owed to the Pope there (ibid. fol. 181). Jacopo Trinci, Abbot of Sassovivo, was appointed Rector of Rieti on 2 April 1426, Reg. Vat. 350, fol. 236.

[3] Arch. Cam. pt. i, Tes. Prov., Patrimonio, B.1, vol. 2, fol. 52 f., shows many of the expenses for the campaign against Mugnano. On 7 July Johannes de Visco, 'magister bombardum', was required to move various cannons to make them available in the war against Ulisse Orsini, Div. Cam. 3, fol. 169. See also *Commissioni,* ii, 400.

[4] Contelori, *Vita Martini V,* 10; Silvestrelli, *Città Castelli e Terre,* 681.

[5] Silvestrelli, 467; De Cupis, *BDA,* 3rd ser., i (1910), 90, with date 1424 for 1425. The grant of the vicariate to Jacopo Orsini is in Reg. Vat. 351, fol. 149v, 30 July 1430.

war in Romagna in order to strengthen the rule of the Church there, without thereby delivering himself into the hand of Filippo Maria Visconti. Aquila was counted in Florence as a defeat for the Republic, and it was followed, in July 1424, by the disastrous defeat of Carlo Malatesta and all the Florentine troops at Zagonara, and by the capture of most of their leaders. Martin said in August that but for this defeat he would have given Florence immediate peace;[1] he held out beyond this the hope of an Italian league of the Pope, Florence, Milan, Venice and the Kingdom, a project which was to appear many times in the papal diplomacy of the fifteenth century.[2] He continued to cultivate a close understanding with Milan, and granted Visconti a very large sum in the proceeds from a tenth on the clergy there.[3] He was not impressed by Florentine attempts to turn him against Visconti on account of Milanese intervention in the Kingdom of Naples;[4] that Milanese influence was at work there he knew, but he counted it far more urgent to exclude Florentine influence from Romagna and the March, where she had a traditional sphere of influence among the *signori*, and had the habit of using this influence so that papal power over its subjects should not grow too effective. The range of this influence may be read in the list of Florentine *raccomandati* : it included the Trinci, the Malatesta, the Count of Montefeltro, the Manfredi of Faenza. The Manfredi, particularly, were unwilling subjects of the Church and willing mercenaries of Florence. Faenza is described by Leonardo Bruni as, after the battle of Zagonara, the only real defence of Florence. But Manfredi was unwilling to pay the Pope *census* for his state, and only Florentine intervention prevented a papal expedition being sent against him in 1426.[5] When Visconti proposed as part of the terms of peace that Florence should cut the ties of friendship and obligation which bound her to these *signori*—'che noi lasciassimo tutti gli accomandati sottoposti alla Chiesa nella loro libertà'—Albizzi refused and replied that to do so would be lack of faith on the part of Florence.[6] Few better illustrations could be given of the importance which Florentine statesmen attached to those subtle ties which bound the *raccomandato* to the protecting power. The *raccomandato* was an ally below stairs, a secret friend who imposed on his protector none of the public responsibilities of open alliance. Through him Florence could foment trouble without moving a soldier or spending a florin—and that she did so encourage trouble in the States of the Church is beyond question. The supreme trouble-maker, the linchpin of the Florentine system of protected *signori*, had been Braccio, and after his death Martin was determined to overturn this typically Florentine policy.

[1] *Commissioni*, ii, 156, 167.
[2] Ibid. ii, 213, 383–4.
[3] Ibid. ii, 347 n., 455–6.
[4] Ibid. ii, 211, 213.
[5] See the documents published by C. Monzani, 'Di Leonardo Bruni Aretino', *ASI*, 2nd ser., v, pt. 2 (1857), 32–3. Leonardo Bruni and Francesco Tornabuoni protested to Martin against the despatch of Caldora and Michelotto da Cotignola into Romagna, whereupon he replied that they were to act against Manfredi, on account of his disobedience. But the Florentine protest prevented this threat from being carried out. Florence was at this time already pledged to pay the *census* due from Manfredi to the Church, see p. 189 below.
[6] *Commissioni*, ii, 214, 'non ci pareva onesto mancare la fede del Comune a'suoi accomandati'.

§ 2. Throughout the complex peace negotiations which were conducted at Rome, Visconti continued to express his willingness to restore Forlì and Imola to the Church, and Albizzi was probably not far wrong in concluding that 'in segreto il Papa s'intende col Duca *per omnia*'.[1] The understanding of Martin V with Filippo Maria Visconti was a singular instance of two formidable foxes running together. It was founded on a certain practical identity of interest. Martin V needed a free hand to deal with his feudatories in Romagna and the March, and both Florence and Venice wished to keep that area as troublesome and rebellious as it had always been. Filippo Maria Visconti was on the defensive against the new aggressive policy of Venice on the *terra ferma*, and anxious to weaken Florence as much as possible, perhaps in preparation for a future move into Tuscany. Both Milan and Rome had at this time a vague concept of an alliance of the great Italian powers, which corresponds to the idea of the Italian league and the balance of power in Italy, as it was conceived after the peace of Lodi.[2] To this may be added a certain affinity of spirit between Oddo Colonna and Filippo Maria Visconti, a common thread of cunning and perhaps a common pleasure in the hazards of the political game. Certainly they respected one another, and Visconti gave Martin good words after his death.[3]

But there was no room for good faith in the political world which Martin V and Visconti shared, and it seems doubtful if the Church would ever have recovered Forlì and Imola from the Duke, had it not been for the Florentine success in concluding an alliance at the end of 1425 with Venice and Savoy, the alliance which completely turned the scales against Milan and led to her defeat at Maclodio. This alliance immediately restored Martin to his position as arbiter between the warring powers, and led in Romagna to the almost immediate return of Forlì and Imola to the Pope, since Visconti could no longer spare the troops to hold them. The Legate of Bologna accepted the cities in May 1426,[4] and in June the brilliant young Bishop-elect of Fermo, Domenico Capranica, was appointed Governor of the two cities; he entered Forlì in July.[5]

---

[1] *Commissioni*, ii, 502.   [2] See Cipolla, *Storia delle Signorie*, 346.

[3] A. Billii, *Historia* (Muratori, *RRIISS*, xix), 141–2.

[4] *Corp. Chron. Bonon.*, iv, 3; Giovanni di M° Pedrino, *Cronica*, 152.

[5] His appointment is in Reg. Vat. 356, fol. 13v, dated 6 June 1426. For the biography of Capranica see M. Morpurgo-Castelnuovo, 'Il cardinale Domenico Capranica', *ASR*, lii (1929), who errs, however, in saying (p. 9) that his family was obscure. He was a relative ('germanus') of the apostolic secretary, Paolo Capranica, Bishop of Embrun and later Archbishop of Benevento, concerning whom see Von Hofmann, *Forschungen zur Geschichte der kurialen Behörden*, ii, 81, 110, 186, and my article in *JEccH*, iv (1953), 66–7. The parentage is established by references in Div. Cam. 12, fol. 30v (22 October 1430, a compromise over the goods of the dead Paolo, in which Domenico Capranica, the 'germanus' of Paolo, acts for himself and his brothers and nephews) and Arm. 34, vol. 4, fol. 155v (23 August 1420, in which the same word 'germanus' is used to describe the relationship between the two). Domenico Capranica is described as a clerk of the diocese of Palestrina in a petition of his of 7 February 1419, Reg. Suppl. 120, fol. 223v. This confirms that he came from Capranica in Lazio, which was a territory of the Colonna. Another member of the family was Bartolomeo Capranica, or Bartholomeus quondam Nicolai de Capranica, secretary of Giordano Colonna (Theiner, iii, no. 272, p. 249) and also a scriptor of apostolic letters (Von Hofmann, ii, 186). Bartolomeo was appointed to rule in the principate of Salerno and Duchy of Venosa after his master's death, see below, p. 100. For the later history of the family of Capranica, see U. Camelli, 'Il monastero di S. Bartolomeo de "Campo Fullonum" e i prelati di casa Capranica', *Studia Picena*, xi (Fano, 1935).

These events do not indicate complete concord between Milan and Rome. At the same time as the league with Venice was in preparation, Visconti was abandoning his Angevin alliance, and planning a league of Milan, Sigismond and Aragon, which should lead to the simultaneous descent of the two kings into Italy, and the forcing of the Pope to call a general Council.[1] He was therefore prepared to intervene in the Kingdom of Naples in the opposite interest to the one favoured by the Pope, and when the completely dominant position of the Colonna in Naples is considered, this can only be seen as a direct threat to the whole papal position. But the negotiations for the Milanese league dragged slowly, Sigismond supplied no aid, and as Bergamo and Brescia fell Visconti's situation became desperate.[2]

Peace was negotiated through the papal Legate Nicolò Albergati, and signed in Ferrara in 1427. During the negotiations the Florentines pressed for the release of Ludovico Alidosi and his restoral to his state in Imola. But they had no success in the latter demand, and when peace was signed the Church retained Forlì and Imola, without showing the slightest disposition to return the Ordelaffi or the Alidosi to power in their former vicariates.[3] At the same time as peace was concluded, Martin obtained from Filippo Maria Visconti an undertaking that he would not interfere in the affairs of the Kingdom of Naples, or in those of the State of the Church, either during Martin's lifetime, or for a year after his death.[4]

§ 3. The Peace of Ferrara seemed to mark a high level in the influence of papal diplomacy and in the stability of the Papal State. But papal rule was still unsteady at one important point. Bologna was the richest of all the papal provinces, and strategically vital to papal domination in Romagna and Emilia, but the city was an unruly subject, as hard to govern as difficult to conquer. Martin's first Legate, the Spaniard Carrillo, ruled there firmly,[5] but his successor Condulmer was, on account of his Florentine sympathies, withdrawn after less than a year of office. It was decided to replace Condulmer by a Legate of neutral sympathies acceptable to both Milan and Florence, and the choice of Louis Aleman must then have seemed in every way admirable.[6] As Vice-Chamberlain of the Roman Church, Aleman had already been the principal minister for the government of the temporal power, and his appointment as the most important of the provincial Legates must have appeared

---

[1] K. A. Fink, 'König Sigismund und Aragon', *Deutsches Archiv*, ii (1938), 152 f.; D. José Amettler y Vinyas, *Alfonso V de Aragon y la Crisis Religiosa del Siglo XV*, i, 264 f.; O. Schiff, *König Sigismunds italienische Politik*, 94 f.

[2] See the famous letter to Sigismond, Osio, *Documenti diplomatici*, ii, no. 152, p. 260.

[3] In 1425–6 Florence was pressing to have Ludovico Alidosi released from captivity and restored to his state in Imola, *Commissioni*, ii, 496 f.; *ASI*, 2nd ser., v, pt. 2 (1857), 27; De Töth, *Il beato cardinale Nicolò Albergati*, ii, 38 n., 50. But so far as Alidosi's claims to Imola were concerned, Florence had not the slightest success.

[4] Printed in Lünig, *Codex Italiae Diplomaticus*, iv (1735), no. 92, p. 175.

[5] Cf. A. S. Piccolomini, *De Viris Illustribus*, in *Bibliothek des literarischen Vereins in Stuttgart*, i (1843), 34, 'Bononiam aliquando rigide gubernavit'.

[6] G. Pérouse, *Le Cardinal Louis Aleman, Président du Concile de Bâle, et la fin du Grand Schisme* (1904), 19 f., 51 f. The brief explaining Martin's motives in appointing him, Fink, 'Politische Korrespondenz', no. 437.

G

most logical.   But although he governed the city with competence and in apparent
tranquillity for almost four years, he was too much the civil servant and too little the
man of action to withstand the sudden and murderous gales of violence which could
arise among the political factions of Bologna.

The magnates of Bologna had acquired during this period all the aggressive self-
satisfaction of successful war-profiteers, for the war of Florence and Milan offered
the neutral city great opportunities for gain.[1]   Of the three factions dominant in
the city, one was without its leader, Antonio Bentivoglio, who was kept in the south
by the Pope.   The Canetoli and the Zambeccari therefore came to have a monopoly
of influence and office, and by the beginning of 1428 their power had reached such a
point of open defiance of the law that Bologna was in a state little removed from
anarchy.[2]   Aleman failed to resist the factions, and instead humoured and favoured
them.   For this he was reprimanded severely by the Pope.[3]   But either ineffectively
or too late, for at the beginning of August, while the Legate was preparing fresh
honours for the Canetoli, they broke into open rebellion against him.   Even so,
Aleman might have held out against them in his barricaded palace, had he not made
the error of parleying with the leaders in the opened doorway.   This final error undid
him ; the Canetoli rushed the doors, and led the Legate prisoner while they sacked
the palace and assumed the government of Bologna.   The faction of Bentivoglio
was deprived of its leaders and had not been supported by the Legate in time to
create an opposition.   The Bishop Nicolò Albergati, far from being able to mediate,
had to escape from the city disguised as a monk.[4]

The revolution accomplished, sixteen 'reformers' appointed, and Aleman expelled the city, there followed a long and bitter struggle.   Martin V's diplomacy
secured one major triumph, in that no Italian power would offer assistance to
Bologna.   Martin had profited immediately from the success of his diplomacy at the
peace of Ferrara : Filippo Maria Visconti had just undertaken not to interfere in the
State of the Church, and even had he been minded to do so, he was in no political or
military position to undertake such an offensive.   His treasury was still empty from
the war,[5] and his attempt to align Aragon and Sigismond on his side in Italy still fell
short of realisation.[6]   Florence was too tired from war, and also too divided in her

---

[1] A. Billii, *Historia*, 110 ; Flavio Biondo, *Decades*, 446.

[2] Filelfo, *Epistolae* (Spier, 1506), fol. 11 ; F. Biondo, *Decades*, 447 f. ; Billii, *Historia*, 111–12 ;
Pérouse, 78.   Pérouse is too lenient in his judgement of Aleman, who evidently allowed the Canetoli to
practise open violence for political ends.   The texts speak insistently of failure to do justice ; see the
Pope's reproach to Aleman, Fink, 'Politische Korrespondenz', no. 434, 'propter tepiditatem tuam et
mollitiem in multis rebus . . . et precipue circa administrationem justitie', and no. 435, 'unicuique
justitiam ministrando'.   [3] Fink, 'Politische Korrespondenz', no. 434.

[4] 'Prefatus Nicolaus cardinalis coactus est clandestine et tamquam incognitus recedere de civitate et
diocese supradicta, necque eo modo quo decebat cardinalem incedere', Biblioteca Angelica, Cod. 1426,
fol. 9.   This is the bull of interdict against Bologna, dated Genazzano 6 kal. Septembris Anno 11, which
no historian appears so far to have used.   It contains a full recital of the circumstances of the rebellion,
which, while it supplies no new information, is important as confirming at every point the narrative of
Flavio Biondo, *Decades*, 447 f.   Biondo is therefore not only the fullest, but the most reliable historian
of these events.

[5] See the letter to Sigismond, Osio, *Documenti diplomatici*, ii, no. 152, p. 260.

[6] Fink, *Deutsches Archiv*, ii (1938), 170 f. ; idem, *Martin V. und Aragon*, 132 f.

counsels, to carry out aggression in central Italy. In the Kingdom of Naples the Colonna continued to be the absolutely dominant party, and, by agreement with Queen Giovanna, Jacopo Caldora, the Constable of the Kingdom, was permitted to march north to assume the general command of papal forces against Bologna.[1] Venice, from whom the Canetoli had in particular hoped for support, would not move an inch from neutrality, even when tempted by hints that she would be offered the dominion of Bologna.[2] The Republic was on the contrary angling to induce the Pope into a league against Milan, and this was the last moment at which she would consider offending Rome. She would do no more for Bologna than offer her mediation, and instead of supporting Bologna's action in employing her *condottiere* Ludovico di San Severino, she attempted to recall him.[3]

In spite of these diplomatic successes, the conduct of the war against Bologna fell far short of what was hoped in Rome. The number of mercenaries employed was very large, and cannot have fallen short of several thousand. Caldora seems to have been idle and ineffective, and although all the castles of the district of Bologna fell to the Pope in the early stages of the siege, the city itself seemed in the spring of 1429 to be no nearer capture than it had been when Caldora arrived. It is true that the threat of a general rebellion in Romagna had been averted, but this was as much due to the early and capable action of Domenico Capranica the Governor of Forlì and Imola, as to Caldora.[4] Bologna would not succumb to a direct assault, and while the Pope faced a ruinous bill to pay his troops,[5] the Bolognese will to resist declined but little.

In the end, the crushing cost of the war forced Martin to grant Bologna terms very far from an unconditional surrender. Through the mediation of Venice and Ferrara, peace was signed at the beginning of September 1429.[6] The city was forgiven its rebellion, the instigators of revolt, including the renegade abbot and pseudo-Bishop Zambeccari, remained unpunished, and the sixteen 'reformers', who were the effective government of Bologna, remained in office, while the Bentivoglio remained in exile. The future Legate was to have power only to confirm the election of the ancients and other high officials, but he was to nominate two treasurers and two officials of the 'bollete',[7] one in each case to be a citizen of Bologna, and the other not. Both the Legate and the ancients were each allowed to maintain a stated number of soldiers and no more. The Pope agreed even to undertake to pay the arrears of salary of the mercenaries whom Bologna had employed to fight him, a clause of which he complained bitterly to his Legate, the Cardinal de Foix.[8] Besides this, he agreed to pay the ransoms of prisoners captured by his own troops.[9]

---

[1] Faraglia, *Storia della Regina Giovanna*, 353–5.
[2] For these and the following incidents, Fink, 'Martin V. und Bologna', *QF*, xxiii (1931/2).
[3] Ibid. 192–3.   [4] Giovanni di Mᵒ Pedrino, *Cronica*, 170 f.
[5] Fink, 'Martin V. und Bologna', 203 n.   [6] Fink, 199. The instrument of peace, ibid. 213.
[7] The latter officials were those who transmitted orders for payments to be made, to the Treasurers.
[8] Raynaldus, ad a. 1429, par. xix.
[9] Martin agreed to release Tomasso and Carlo Zambeccari freely (see the instrument of peace, 'Martin V. und Bologna', 217), and in order to do this he had to pay their ransom to their captor, Nicolò of Tolentino. Eugenius IV had to redeem this pledge; see Arm. 39, vol. 7a, fol. 163v, a brief to the

Although the document talks in the beginning of the Pope being restored to full power ('plenum et liberum dominium') over the city and its revenues, his resumption of power was encumbered by so many qualifications, and the revolutionary government treated with such remarkable softness and respect, that it is impossible to talk of a full restoration of papal power in Bologna, and Filippo Maria Visconti seems nearer the truth, in a letter written in the same week that the peace was signed, in talking of the settlement as an equal partition of powers between Pope and commune.[1] It is difficult to admit Professor Fink's contention that Martin effectively restored his power, merely because he had successfully refused to grant the vicariate to the commune,[2] although it is true that a vicariate would have meant certain and secure self-government for the city, and would have been a definite victory for the rebels. The truth was that the Pope had not gained a victory, but had merely avoided a defeat. The arrangement of 1429 was full of traps and ambiguities, a truce rather than a peace; both sides were sick of war, but neither had abandoned their pretensions, and so the subsequent history of the city was to prove.

The new Cardinal Legate of Bologna, Lucido Conti, entered the city in the same month that peace was signed. Unhappily, he proved no stronger than his predecessor. In April 1430 the Canetoli committed a series of brutal political murders which went unpunished save in form, and began to terrorise all the adherents of the Bentivoglio and of the Church.[3] Conti withdrew immediately from the city to Cento, and thence to Ferrara, and the Bishop of Tropea was sent to the city as Governor. Quite unable to obtain any kind of satisfactory obedience, he also withdrew, and in June 1430 the state of war between Bologna and the Church recommenced. Further large forces of mercenaries were raised, including the lord of Mantua, and the siege laid again; in July there was an attempt to force the walls of the city, in which the

---

Governor of Bologna (? July 1433). 'Cum felicis recordationis Martinus papa quintus predecessor noster solvere et dare promiserit dilecto filio nobili viro Nicolao de Tolentino, tum in suis stipendiis militanti, mille et quingentos florenos auri de camera pro redemptione dilectorum filiorum Thomasii et Caroli de Zambeccariis, civium Bononiensium, quos idem Nicolaus belli jure captivos detinens ad voluntatem prefati predecessoris iuxta (sic) consignavit et tradidit post modum de mandato predecessoris ipsius libere relassatos . . .' and as Nicolò of Tolentino was not paid as promised, Eugenius makes an assignment from the revenues of Rome for the satisfaction of the debt (see another brief, ibid. fol. 165v).

[1] Osio, *Documenti diplomatici*, ii, no. 288, p. 421. Almost exactly the same language was used by Flavio Biondo, who was one of Capranica's secretaries at Forlì at this time, and so in an excellent position to observe (see also above, p. 90, n. 4). *Decades*, 448, 'Tandem anno vixdum exacto fessi Bononienses civitatem umbra potius quam re pontifici dediderunt; pacti nanque Antonium Bentivolium cum studiosis ut ante fore exulem, ius creandorum in urbe magistratum praetore excepto, et civitatis pari cum pontifice praesidio tenendae, sibi reservantes, caetera illi permiserunt'.

[2] 'Martin V. und Bologna', 202, 'Die Revolution, wohl zur Unzeit begonnen, hatte nicht den erwünschten Erfolg gebracht; aus dem erstrebten Vikariat war nichts geworden. Nach wie vor war der Papst der eigentliche Herr der Stadt, und wenn der Herzog von Mailand in einem Brief an den deutschen König von einer gleichen Teilung der Gewalten spricht, scheint er aus politischen Motiven Verhältnisse zugunsten Bolognas doch etwas zu verschieben'.

[3] *Corp. Chron. Bonon.*, iv, 21-3; Giovanni di Mº Pedrino, *Cronica*, 243-4; Flavio Biondo, *Decades*, 449; Billii, *Historia*, 119-20; *Annales Forolivienses*, 89.

army of the Church was assisted by a Milanese force which was on its way to support Guinigi in his war against Florence.[1] In September there was a brief truce, and through the mediation of the Marquis of Ferrara the papal representatives made a peace with the city, but this peace was repudiated by the Pope, while at the same time, in defiance of it, the Canetoli ambushed a large papal force. So the war began again, and was continuing without respite at the time of Martin's death in February 1431. Had he lived he might have finally broken the rebellious factions in Bologna,[2] but the acceptance by Eugenius IV of the *status quo* in Bologna was to lead, instead, to the gradual installation of the *signoria* of the Bentivoglio.

§ 4. More successful was Martin V's action against the Malatesta. Although the Malatesta of Rimini had maintained, under Martin V, their tradition of loyalty to the Holy See, this did not protect them from Martin's policy of resuming the grants made to the *signori*. Carlo Malatesta went to Rome in 1428,[3] and is said to have come to an understanding with the Pope about the disposal of the lands of his house, since his brother, Pandolfo Malatesta *signore* of Fano, had died in 1427, leaving three illegitimate sons, all minors, while he himself was now childless.[4] Carlo Malatesta himself then died in 1429.[5] Whatever the agreement of 1428 had been, the Malatesta heritage was at once challenged by both Malatesta of Pesaro and by the Pope—perhaps the latter acted at the instance of the former,[6] although the main excuse for resuming the vicariates was non-payment of *census*. The Pope declared the vicariates forfeit, and agreed to restore them to the three brothers only in return for the cession of large and important tracts of territory. The new vicariates were eventually issued to the brothers (Galeotto Roberto, Sigismondo Pandolfo, Domenico Malatesta) on 1 July 1430.[7] The Pope granted Senigaglia, which had belonged to Carlo Malatesta, to the Malatesta of Pesaro.[8] For the Apostolic See he took Cervia (important for its salt pans), Osimo, Borgo San Sepolcro,

[1] Giovanni di M° Pedrino, *Cronica*, 256, 261; *Corp. Chron. Bonon.*, iv, 23-5; Biondo, *Decades*, loc. cit.; Billii, loc. cit.

[2] Cf. *Cronica* of Giovanni di M° Pedrino, 252.

[3] The *Cronaca Malatestiana del secolo XV* (Muratori, *RRIISS*, xv, pt. 2, 59) has 1427, but the chronology of the chronicle is confused at this point. Cf. Clementini, *Raccolto istorico della fondatione di Rimino* (1617), ii, 222; Giovanni di M° Pedrino, *Cronica*, 164.

[4] For Pandolfo's death, *Cronaca Malatestiana*, 59, where the date is again wrong; *Annales Forolivienses*, 89; Giovanni di M° Pedrino, *Cronica*, 161-2; P.-M. Amiani, *Memorie istoriche della città di Fano*, i (1751), 356. Cf. the genealogy in Zonghi, *Repertorio dell'antico archivio comunale di Fano*, facing p. 162.

[5] *Cronaca Malatestiana*, 60; Giovanni di M° Pedrino, *Cronaca*, 217.

[6] Cf. Billii, *Historia*, 116; for the hostilities of the branch of Pesaro against that of Rimini, Arch. Cam. pt. i, Tes. Prov., Marca, B.4, vol. i passim.

[7] Rimini, Biblioteca Gambalunga, Sched. Garampi, Apografi Riminesi, no. 762, contains this vicariate. Cf. Amiani, *Memorie istoriche della città di Fano*, i, 361-3; ii, lxxiv-v; *Annales Forolivienses*, 89; Giovanni di M° Pedrino, *Cronica*, 248.

[8] The vicariate was granted to Carlo Malatesta, son of Malatesta de Malatestis, on 16 September 1430. It was for Senigaglia and its *castra*, which are listed as Scapezzano, Monte Rado, Ripe, Roncitelli, La Tomba and Perozzone, and was for an annual *census* of 100 florins (Reg. Vat. 351, fol. 166).

Mondavio, Pergola, besides a large number of minor *castra*. These places were received for the Pope by the Deputy of the March, Astorgio, Bishop of Ancona, in August of 1430,[1] and their transfer, made without resistance, was a heavy blow to the *signoria* of the Malatesta.

[1] The instructions to the Deputy of the March to take over these places are dated 8 May 1430, Reg. Vat. 351, fol. 148. Their transmission to him is described in Arch. Cam. pt. i, Tes. Prov., Marca, B.4, vol. 4, fols. 26–7. Cf. his quittance for their receipt, of 5 August 1430, printed by F. G. Battaglini, *Della vita e de'fatti di Sigismondo Pandolfo Malatesta*, doc. vii, p. 607, from Div. Cam. 13, fol. 113; see also P. Compagnoni, *Memorie istorico-critiche della chiesa e de' vescovi di Osimo*, iii (1782), 351; Giovanni di M° Pedrino, *Cronica*, 253; Bonincontri, *Annales*, 137. *Podestà* and other officers in the newly-acquired cities were appointed by the Vice-Chamberlain on 3 September 1430, Div. Cam. 13, fol. 107. Guiraud, *L'Etat Pontifical*, 224, in treating of Cervia forgets what he has said above, p. 220, of its transfer to the Pope, and overlooks the re-occupation of Cervia by the Malatesta in 1433 (*Annales Forolivienses*, 91).

CHAPTER III

PROVINCIAL GOVERNMENT

I. *The Territorial Divisions of the State of the Church*

§ 1.   THE State of the Church was still, under Martin V, divided into the provinces which had taken shape during the thirteenth century or before—the March of Ancona, Romagna, the Patrimony of St. Peter in Tuscia,[1] Campania and Maritima,[2] together with some smaller divisions such as Sabina, Massa Trabaria, S. Agata, the Presidency of Farfa, the Duchy of Spoleto and the 'Terra Arnulphorum et specialis commissionis'.

The territorial scheme of government at the end of the pontificate of Martin V is a half-way house between the medieval divisions and the system of 'legations' which emerged in the sixteenth century.   Under Martin V the Legates of Bologna and Perugia had absorbed in their jurisdiction some provinces which had formerly possessed their own papal Rector; Romagna came under the legation of Bologna, and Sabina, the Duchy of Spoleto and Todi under Perugia.   Practically the whole Papal State outside the present province of Lazio was thus brought under one of the three 'legations'—although it must be added that these posts could be held by 'Governors' instead of by Legates.   A second development of the later fourteenth century was the appointment of 'Rectors' or 'Governors' to rule many of the more important towns, possessing authority of a kind much resembling that of the *signori* whom they had often supplanted.   Such Governors were usually subject to the Rector or Legate of the province, but they were also supervised directly from Rome.

§ 2.   In practice, the supreme head of the government of Rome in Martin V's time was the Apostolic Vice-Chamberlain.   It was only during the pontificate of Eugenius IV, however, that it became customary for the Vice-Chamberlain to hold also the office of Governor of Rome, and in Martin's time the Vice-Chamberlain governed the city without the aid of any such additional grant of authority.   The government of Rome extended also to the Roman District, a rather ill-defined area which represented the old supremacy of the commune of Rome, extending for about 40 kilometres or more round the City.   If the District be taken as the area which paid the salt and focage tax to the Chamber of Rome and sent tribute or men to

---

[1] I preserve 'Tuscia' in its original form; it has been wrongly designated 'Tuscany' by some English authors.   The region of Tuscia (which once extended as far as Perugia) dates from the early Christian centuries, and is mentioned by Gregory the Great.   Cf. Ficker, *Forschungen zur Reichs- und Rechtsgeschichte Italiens*, ii, 301–2.

[2] I have used the older Latin spelling.   The modern Italian form is Marittima.

95

the games on the Testaccio,[1] it is evident that it overlapped considerably with the jurisdiction of the provincial Rectors on either side, but the area involved was too poor to give rise to dispute.

The province of Campania and Maritima, which stretched down the coast to the east and south of Rome as far as the frontier of the Kingdom of Naples at Terracina,[2] was at first treated by Martin V as a single unit,[3] but later split by him into the two separate provinces of Campania and Maritima,[4] although with what motive I have been unable to discover. The whole region was miserably poor, paralysed economically by malaria, by the lack of any system of drainage, and by the ruinous internecine warfare of the Roman nobles—not excluding that of Agapito Colonna during his tenure of the office of Rector.[5]

To the north of Rome lay the far richer province of the Patrimony of St. Peter in Tuscia, which extended north through the *tufa* hills to Castro and Radicofani.[6] The Rector had his seat in Viterbo, and was paid 100 cameral florins a month.[7] His jurisdiction included Narni, Terni and Amelia, strategically important cities in the Tiber valley,[8] Sabina and its main city Rieti,[9] and the 'terra Arnulphorum', the group of villages round Cesi, to the south of Spoleto.[10] Of these, Sabina and the 'terra Arnulphorum' were lands usually referred to as 'specialis commissionis', with the meaning that they were attached to the jurisdiction of the Patrimony only by a special appointment. Many of these districts had local Governors. Francesco Savelli was made Rector of Narni, Terni and Amelia in May 1424, just before the battle of Aquila,[11] although it is doubtful if he continued to hold this post in the re-

---

[1] A map of the area which Rome claimed to administer in the fourteenth century is given by de Boüard, *Le régime politique et les institutions de Rome au Moyen Age* (1920). Cf. Tommasseti, 'Sale e focatico a Roma nel Medio Evo', *ASR*, xx (1897).

[2] The limits of the provinces are defined by Guiraud, *L'Etat Pontifical*, 47 f.

[3] Rectors and Vice-Rectors were appointed in 1418 and 1420, Reg. Vat. 352, fol. 110v; Reg. Vat. 349, fols. 64v, 155v.

[4] The provinces were split at the beginning of 1423, when Stefano de Branchiis of Gubbio was appointed Commissioner in Campania with the powers of Rector (Reg. Vat. 349, fol. 254v), while Agapito Colonna was made Governor of Maritima (ibid. fol. 256). A Commissioner was appointed to pacify the united provinces, for a few months in 1425 (Angelotto Bishop of Anagni, 'te . . . commissarium et nuntium nostrum ac in spiritualibus et temporalibus visitatorem et reformatorem tanquam pacis angelum destinalus', Reg. Vat. 350, fol. 98v), but the provinces were again separate by August 1425, and a series of Rectors or Commissioners are recorded for Campania (Reg. Vat. 350, fols. 138v, 236v, 274v; Div. Cam. 3, fol. 181v; Reg. Vat. 351, fol. 45), although none are recorded for Maritima.

[5] Cf. p. 186 below.　　　　　　　　　　　　　　[6] Guiraud, 85–88.

[7] This is the salary assigned to Henry, Bishop of Feltre, as Rector, in 1420 (Reg. Vat. 349, fol. 131, his appointment as Rector is on fol. 129).

[8] From 1419–24 these cities were united in a single jurisdiction (Reg. Vat. 348, fol. 117v; Reg. Vat. 349, fols. 39, 204; Reg. Vat. 350, fols. 8v, 24), but this arrangement was abandoned in the subsequent pacification. Cf. Guiraud, 165 f. In 1426 these cities were reckoned a part of the Patrimony for the purposes of an assessment of tallage, Arm. 33, vol. 11, fol. 6, but later they were for financial purposes lumped together in a special commission for the exaction of tallage exercised by Bartolomeo da Toscanella in 1429 in Otricoli, Narni, Rieti, Terni, Ritaldo, Cassia, Norcia and Spoleto (Fumi, *Inventario e Spoglio dei Registri della Tesoreria Apostolica di Perugia e Umbria*, 36).

[9] A Rector was appointed for Sabina in March 1424, Reg. Vat. 350, fol. 20; he was the Trinci Abbot of Sassovivo (cf. D. Dorio, *Storia della famiglia Trinci*, 195–6). In 1427 jurisdiction over Sabina had returned to the Commissioner of the Patrimony, Div. Cam. 11, fol. 61v. Cf. Guiraud, 89 f.

[10] Guiraud, 163 f.　　　　　　　　　　　　　　[11] Reg. Vat. 350, fol. 24v.

organisation which followed Braccio's defeat. Sabina for a time had its own Governor, and after the expulsion of the Alfani in 1425 Rieti had a 'commissioner in temporals' who served the same office as a Rector, and who probably ruled the whole of Sabina.[1]

The Legate or Governor of Perugia ruled the city and its district, the Duchy of Spoleto, Todi, Assisi, Nocera, Spello, Montefalco, Gualdo Cattaneo and the other districts round Foligno which the Church had seized from Corrado Trinci or the Fortebraccio.[2] The Legate was given a monthly salary of 400 cameral florins, and the Governor one of 200 florins.[3] The Treasurer of Perugia had jurisdiction over a rather different area, which excluded Cassia, Norcia and the rest of that rather turbulent area of the Duchy of Spoleto which bordered on the Marches,[4] and some-times included Orvieto. Spoleto was ruled by a Governor or Deputy ('locumtenens') with a monthly salary of 50 florins.[5] His appointment was not for the Duchy, but for the city and district of Spoleto, with authority also in the northern territory of Cassia and Norcia.[6] Although formally subject to the Legate of Perugia, he seems in fact to have dealt direct with Rome.[7] Other areas under the Legate of Perugia which were ruled by Governors or Commissioners of the Church were Montone, the former fief of Carlo Fortebraccio,[8] Bettona, Gualdo Cattaneo and the area between Assisi and the Duchy of Spoleto,[9] and Todi.[10] Orvieto was a city apart, never assimilated by the Patrimony although the Rectors of the province always claimed authority there. Under Martin V it was ruled, with Todi, by a special Rector. Its financial administration was usually under the Treasurer of Perugia.

---

[1] Reg. Vat. 350, fol. 181v, but this appointment of Matteo the Abbot of Subiaco was cancelled on account of his being sent as nuncio to Queen Giovanna on 27 April 1426 (Reg. Vat. 350, fol. 240v), and Jacopo Trinci, the Abbot of Sassovivo and former Rector of Sabina, was appointed in his place on 2 April 1426, ibid. fol. 236. 'Commissioners' were appointed to govern Rieti in 1428 and 1430, Reg. Vat. 351, fols. 29v, 142, 160.

[2] The appointment of the Cardinal Bishop of Porto as Legate in Perugia, Todi and the province of the Duchy of Spoleto is in Reg. Vat. 350, fol. 50. The extension of his jurisdiction to Assisi, ibid. fol. 238v. That he ruled over the lands seized from the Trinci and Fortebraccio is almost certain; see Fumi, *Inventario e Spoglio dei Registri delle Tesoreria Apostolica di Perugia e Umbria*, 18–19.

[3] Reg. Vat. 350, fol. 52v.

[4] Ibid., fol. 133. The towns excepted from his jurisdiction were Cassia, Norcia, Cerreto, Visso and Monte Santo. For the violence of this area, which was in the sphere of influence of the Varano, see Guiraud, 188–90.

[5] Reg. Vat. 353, fol. 288.

[6] The extension of the authority of the Governor of Spoleto to Cassia in October 1422, Reg. Vat. 354, fol. 136v. In 1428 the Deputy of Spoleto was ordered to condemn Norcia to pay 1,000 florins for its aggression against Arquata, Reg. Vat. 351, fol. 70v.

[7] In the correspondence of Domenico Capranica as Governor of Perugia (Div. Cam. 12), there is no trace of his exercising authority over Spoleto.

[8] The Abbot Jacopo Trinci was appointed Governor in 1429, with powers to convert the revenues of the place to his own use, until a loan of 600 florins which he had made the Apostolic Chamber had been repaid, Reg. Vat. 351, fols. 123, 123v.

[9] Luca de Tartarinis de Nepe, Archpriest of the Church of S. Tommaso a capo delle Mole of Rome, was appointed in July 1428 as Commissioner in temporals in Bettona, Gualdo Cattaneo, Castagnola, Montefalco, Monticello ['Monticuli'] and Fano in Umbria, Reg. Vat. 351, fol. 62v.

[10] Johannes de Tomariis, Auditor of the Rota, was made Deputy of Orvieto and Todi in 1426, Reg. Vat. 350, fol. 260v. The Bishop of Montefiascone, Antonio of Anagni, was appointed Deputy of Todi in October 1428, Reg. Vat. 351, fol. 69, and he was shortly afterwards translated to the bishopric of Todi.

The March of Ancona, Massa Trabaria and the Presidency of Farfa were delimited under Martin V as under Albornoz, and the Governor or Legate of the March ruled this group of lands as the Rector had done in the past.[1] The salary of the Legate at the later period is not recorded, but that of the Governor was 100 cameral florins a month.[2] The appointment of the Governor of the March was made without prejudice to the rights of Guid'Antonio of Montefeltro as Rector of Massa Trabaria,[3] a post which gave the Count virtual exemption from the Governor's jurisdiction, as the province was composed mainly of his own dominions. The adjoining district of S. Agata Feltre was assigned to the Governor or Deputy of the March, but the Malatesta of Rimini were Rectors of the commune of S. Agata itself, and of its dependent *castra*.[4] The Presidency of Farfa possessed its own President and court, as is provided in the *Constitutiones Egidiane*.[5] The two other Presidencies mentioned in the *Constitutiones*, Camerino and S. Lorenzo in Campo,[6] had by Martin V's time been swallowed up by *signori*, the first by the Varano, and the second by the Malatesta of Pesaro.

Several cities of the March were given papal Governors after they were recovered for the Church from their former *signori*, notably San Severino,[7] Fermo and Ascoli.

In March 1430 Vallariano de Mutis of Rome was appointed Deputy ('locumtenens'), but only for six months, and with the powers given by the statutes to the *capitaneus* of the city. This last appointment therefore amounts to no more than that of a *podestà*. In the parlance of the Chamber 'locumtenens' sometimes seems to have meant a person taking the place of someone else, in a specific office. But on other occasions 'locumtenens' was used as a vague term of dignity, and the person so termed was not in fact taking the place of anyone in particular.

[1] Guiraud, 191 f.

[2] Reg. Vat. 355, fol. 40v.

[3] Ibid. fol. 38v. Montefeltro had been appointed Rector in May 1424, Arm. 60, vol. 21, fol. 97. His predecessor had been his enemy, Gentile Brancaleone, appointed on 2 January 1419, Florence, Biblioteca Nazionale, xix, 82, fol. 109.

[4] S. Agata is mentioned as a separate jurisdiction in the *Constitutiones Egidiane* (ed. P. Sella, 1912), lib. i, c. 9. The appointment of the Deputy of the March in July 1418 mentions separately his jurisdiction in the *castra* of the commune of S. Agata, Reg. Vat. 352, fol. 139. So the area must have been a small one. In 1430 the brothers Malatesta, Galeotto Roberto and Sigismondo Pandolfo, were appointed Rectors in temporals for three years of S. Agata and the surrounding villages—'dicte comunitatis [sancte Agathe] necnon Sapigni, Fragheti, Maciani et aliorum castrorum terrarum villarum locorum et iurisdictionum que sub cura regimine superioritate comunitatis prefati tenentur et gubernantur . . . cum mero et mixto imperio . . . rectores seu gubernatores usque ad triennium . . . facimus constituimus et etiam deputamus' (Reg. Vat. 351, fol. 152). The whole area of S. Agate Feltre (see Sella's map, attached to the *Rationes Decimarum Italiae: Marchia*, 1950) was a great deal larger than the comparatively small area subject to the commune of S. Agata itself.

[5] Lib. ii, c. 2, 6, 7, 8. In July 1423 Antonuccio de Appogio de Monte S. Maria in Lapide sent his proctors to swear for the office of President of Farfa, to which he is said to have been appointed by letters of XIII kal. Julii anno VI (Div. Cam. 7, fol. 254). A judge was appointed for the Presidency of Farfa in July 1429, Reg. Vat. 351, fol. 129v. Guiraud, *L'Etat Pontifical*, 93–5, makes the unfortunate error of supposing the Presidency to be near the Abbey itself, in Sabina, and goes on to suppose that jurisdiction was shared between the Pope and the Abbot of Farfa. In fact, the Presidency of Farfa was the area round Montalto nelle Marche, and had no administrative connection with either Sabina or the Abbey of Farfa.

[6] Lib. ii, c. 2.

[7] Nicolo de Acziapaziis, Bishop of Tropea, was appointed Deputy in Sanseverino in December 1426, Reg. Vat. 350, fol. 276.

The last two were placed under a single Governor, and finally, in 1430, reverted to the direct rule of the Deputy of the March.[1]

The Treasurer of the March possessed jurisdiction throughout the March, and although Ascoli (and perhaps also Fermo) had a Treasurer appointed by the Apostolic Chamber, the Chamber of Ascoli was considered to be part of the Chamber of the Treasury of the March.[2]

The province of Romagna had only a short independent existence under Martin V; Carlo Malatesta was appointed as its Rector in 1419,[3] and retained the office only until Alfonso Carrillo, on being created Legate in Bologna in 1420, was also given jurisdiction over Romagna.[4] Carrillo's salary was 650 florins a month,[5] and his successor Condulmer is said to have bickered over the amount offered him, which the Florentines reported to have been 4,000 florins a year, instead of the 6,000 for which he asked.[6] The main business of the Legate was always to govern the city of Bologna and its large and rich county; the rest of Romagna was full of tyrants, and it was only after the recovery of Forlì and Imola by the Church in 1426 that any considerable part of the province was ruled directly for the Holy See. A Governor was appointed for both these cities, and they were ruled in substantial independence of the Legate. The Chamber of Forlì, where the Governor lived, appears to have been separate from the Chamber of Bologna.[7]

The Exarchate of Ravenna gains a mention in the official title of the Legate of Bologna,[8] but there is no sign that it ever had, at this period, a separate administrative existence.

Finally come Città di Castello, which was acquired from Braccio's widow in 1428, and Borgo San Sepolcro, which Martin had from the heirs of Carlo Malatesta in 1430. Città di Castello was ruled by a Governor, who was assigned 300 florins a year in the list of salaries laid down for the city in 1429.[9] Under Eugenius IV the two cities were ruled by a single Governor, with his seat in Città di Castello.[10] There was also a 'thesaurarius generalis' in Città di Castello.

§ 3. Certain papal enclaves and spheres of influence in the Kingdom of Naples remain to be discussed. First is Benevento, which for some centuries had been governed directly by the Popes. During the Schism it had come into the possession of Muzio Attendolo Sforza, and although Martin V began by appointing a Governor and Treasurer of Benevento, Sforza was too valuable to the Church to offend by

---

[1] Matteo, Abbot of Subiaco, was made Deputy of Ascoli in 1426, Reg. Vat. 350, fol. 272v. After the fall of Fermo to the Church in 1428, Iacopo Cerretani, Bishop of Teramo, was sent to govern Ascoli and Fermo, *Cronache della città di Fermo*, 61; Fermo, Archivio Priorale, no. 1457. On Cerretani's recall, both cities were in October 1430 returned to the direct rule of the Deputy of the March, who became Governor there, Reg. Vat. 351, fol. 160v.

[2] See below, pp. 181, 207.   [3] Theiner, iii, no. 167, p. 239.

[4] Reg. Vat. 353, fol. 33v.   [5] Ibid. fol. 255.

[6] *Commissioni*, ii, 122 (20 July 1424).

[7] This was so in 1399; see Arch. Cam. pt. i, Tes. Prov., Forlì, B. 1, vol. 1.

[8] See Carrillo's appointment, printed in Zaoli, *Libertas Bononie e Papa Martino V*, 178 f.

[9] Div. Cam. 11, fol. 250v (12 March 1429).   [10] Guiraud, 172.

reclaiming the city from him.   He therefore remained in uncontested possession of the city, and his son Francesco after him.[1]   His title to the city was never clearly defined; he was not Apostolic Vicar there, but merely exercised a personal rule with the consent of the Pope.   Montecassino, on the other hand, was treated for some years as papal territory, although it had never been part of the Papal State, because of the decadence of the monastery itself and of the seizure of its lands and castles by Braccio and a local brigand, Cicco Bianco.   But although the Governor of Campania was for a time also the temporal administrator of Monte-cassino,[2] this action was only taken on account of the inability of the monastery to manage its own affairs, and when the Abbot Tomacelli finally returned to rule the convent his lands were given back to him.[3]   The Apostolic Chamber was, however, careful to charge the monastery for the expenses it had had to bear in administering and recovering the monastic lands.[4]

The intervention of Martin V in the Kingdom of Naples on behalf of his family and his allies was of a rather different nature, and was made in the capacity of feudal lord and 'protector' of the Kingdom.   After the death of Giordano Colonna in 1424, Bartolomeo Nicolò of Capranica was appointed as Commissioner, on behalf of the sons of Giordano, in the Principate of Salerno, the Duchy of Venosa and Castelmare di Stabia.   He was given powers under a papal bull to collect money and regulate the accounts of officials, and a monitory clause in the bull stated that his sentences would be upheld with papal authority.[5]   A similar appointment was made for Francesco de Itro of Fondi in the following year, to serve under Salvatore Zurlo, Count of Sant' Angelo, 'pro nobis et Romane ecclesie in temporalibus Gubernator'.[6]   Other commissioners were appointed in 1426 for Bitetto and other towns in the province of Bari, which is said, with the consent of the Queen, to have been taken under papal protection.[7]   A further document which trespasses heavily on the independence of

---

[1] See p. 44 above, n. 7.

[2] Reg. Vat. 349, fol. 228v.   This appointment of Jacopo, Bishop of Aquino and Rector of Campania and Maritima is to administer, not the monastery itself, but Pontecorvo and the other lands and fortresses belonging to the monastery (31 July 1422).   At the same time Domenico d'Anglona, Bishop of Sutri, was made Governor in temporals of the monastery itself (ibid. fol. 285v).

[3] Reg. Vat. 353, fol. 242, 28 December 1425.

[4] In January 1427 the Abbey paid the Apostolic Chamber 500 florins, the second part of a payment of 1,000 florins, on account of the money spent in defence of the Abbey, IE 385, fols. 19, 127.

[5] Reg. Vat. 352, fol. 72, 9 September 1424.   Cf. the appointment of Stefano de Branchiis of Gubbio as Commissioner in the principate of Salerno, 24 January 1425, Reg. Vat. 350, fol. 80v.   'Te in civitate Salernitan' eiusque principatu territoriis et districtibus usque ad kalendas Septembris proxime futuri, cum mero et mixto imperio ac omnimoda iurisdictione temporali et gladii potestate ac pleno ac libero officio Straticonis inibi diutius exercere consueto, et sallario per nos declarando, familia officialibus equis honoribus et oneribus consuetis, commissarium pro nepotibus nostris auctoritate apostolica tenore presentium facimus constituimus et etiam deputamus . . . Alioquin sententias sive penas quas rite tuleris seu statueris in rebelles, ratas habebimus, et illasque faciemus auctore et nepotes prefati faciant auctore domino, usque ad satisfactionem condignam (MS. indignam) inviolabiliter observari'.

[6] Reg. Vat. 350, fol. 103v.   For the family of Zurlo, see Faraglia, *Storia della Regina Giovanna*, 238–9; 325–6.

[7] Reg. Vat. 350, fol. 262.   The Commissioners were Cola Quarto of Trevi and Ulisse Capograssi of Narni, but the bull states that in these territories Lorenzo Count of Cotignola and his nephew Dominico de Attendolis are already Commissioners.

the Kingdom of Naples is the privilege granted to the county of Celano, which was held by Odoardo Colonna, Count of Alba. This bull, besides granting many other privileges, completely exempts the Count and Countess of Celano from the jurisdiction of the royal officials of the Kingdom of Naples.[1] Martin V regarded the association of the Colonna family with the Church as an alliance which ought to be of profit to both parties, and there are few better illustrations of his somewhat domestic treatment of the Papacy than these bulls.

II. *Provincial Officials: Parliaments*

§ 1. The administration of a papal province is clearly set out in the *Constitutiones Egidiane*, which continued in the fifteenth century to be the basis of public law in the State of the Church. The fundamental text of the Constitutions is that issued at Fano in 1357, which was applied to all the provinces of the State of the Church.[2] After the reception of the first set of amendments from Albornoz, at which all the provincial Rectors were present, each province preserved its own text of the Constitutions, adding to them the additional decrees pronounced by its own Rectors. Papal bulls of Martin V refer, not to the Constitutions in general, but to the Constitutions of each particular province.[3] But it is clear from the surviving manuscripts of the Constitutions that the text in use in Sabina, Campania and Maritima, and in the March, was essentially the same, and that the only important variations are the constitutions issued by Rectors after the death of Albornoz.[4]

The Rector was the supreme head of the province, with the full powers of 'merum et mixtum imperium cum gladii potestate' and the control, with one

[1] Reg. Vat. 355, fol. 190v. 'Item quod comes et comitissa Celani qui inibi pro tempore fuerint habeant et habere debeant sicut dicti olim comites habuerint in terris et locis predictis merum et mixtum imperium. Item ut ipse comitatus iurisdictione quorumlibet officialium regalium et reginalium etiam sunt exempti'. Guiraud, 47–8 is wrong in thinking Celano a part of the State of the Church. Jacovella, daughter of Nicolò Count of Celano who died at some time near 1418, married Odoardo Colonna and brought him the County of Celano in dower; thus both she and her husband are referred to in the bull (cf. T. Brogi, *La Marsica antica, medioevale* [1900], 380). The marriage was never consummated, and Odoardo afterwards married Grata dei Conti (Coppi, *Memorie Colonnesi*, 216), but he retained the county of Celano, which remained in Colonna hands until 1459, Coppi, 212. The same error as that of Guiraud is made by Corsignani, *Reggia Marsicana* (1738), i, 475, 478. Cf. also Contelori, *Vita Martini V*, 20.

[2] 'Ipsas ad omnes dictas provincias prorogamus', *Constitutiones Egidiane*, ed. Sella, xi–xii; 2. Cf. E. Besta, *Storia di diritto italiano*, i, pt. 2, *Fonti* (1925), 705; Vito la Mantia, *Storia della legislazione italiana*, i, *Roma e Stato della Chiesa* (1884), 463.

[3] Mastino de Burgo was made Governor of Spoleto with the powers accorded to the *podestà* according to the constitutions of the province, Reg. Vat. 349, fol. 296. The constitutions said to have been issued by Albornoz for the province of Spoleto are referred to and quoted in the bull against the Trinci, on account of their rebellion in 1421, Reg. Vat. 353, fol. 233v. 'Dudum siquidem bone memorie Egidius episcopus Sabinen' . . . inter ceteras provinciales constitutiones per eum in provincia nostra Spoletan' ducatus . . . statuit et etiam ordinavit quod nullus cuiuscumque status vel condicionis . . .' (follows as in *Constitutiones Egidiane*, ed. Sella, lib. iv, c. 18, p. 160).

[4] E.g. Cod. Ottob. lat. 741 is headed (fol. 100) 'Incipiunt Constitutiones Generales Campanie et Maritime', but it differs in no essential way (albeit it is a rather mutilated version) from the accepted text as received in the March of Ancona—such as that written for Domenico Capranica as Legate there, Cod. Vat. lat. 6742.

exception, of the whole papal administration there.[1] The Treasurer, however, although subordinate in rank, was almost independent in his powers. The Rector was forbidden to intimidate the Treasurer in order to obtain unjust favours,[2] and was compelled to obtain the presence of the Treasurer when revenues or castles were farmed or put out to the highest bidder,[3] or when compositions were made with offenders.[4] Three copies of the accounts of the revenues of the province were kept, one of which went to the Rector, one to the Treasurer, and one eventually to the Apostolic Chamber.[5] But apart from this independence of the Treasurer, which was also a dependence on the Apostolic Chamber, the Rector's powers were very full. He was empowered to appoint and remove officials, both those of the Court of the Rector [6] and of the communes,[7] to pardon communes and officials for offences and to absolve them from sentences of excommunication,[8] to impose and execute sentences for any offences.[9] He impressed troops from the communes and nobles,[10] or accepted a money payment for exemption;[11] he raised mercenaries for the Church and had powers of command over them.[12] On his arrival in the province he was supposed to call a Parliament and take the oath there.[13] He no longer, in the fifteenth century, exacted procurations from the communes of the province.[14] He had the power of calling the Parliament when he saw fit.[15]

In the main the practice of the fifteenth century followed the pattern which had been laid down in the *Constitutiones*. In one instance the pattern was not followed: in the *Constitutiones* the Rector is the supreme power in spiritual causes, and he has an auditor or 'judex in spiritualibus' to exercise this power;[16] the whole of Book III of the *Constitutiones* is devoted to this spiritual jurisdiction. Under Martin V the Rector of the province was not usually a Rector in spirituals, and it was in some instances expressly laid down that he should exercise spiritual jurisdiction only so far as it was needed for his temporal jurisdiction[17]—meaning that he must confine

---

[1] The formula of appointment of the Rector of the Patrimony in 1419, Theiner, iii, no. 177, p. 251. Cf. *Constitutiones Egidiane*, lib. ii, c. 1, and see also Calisse, 'Costituzione del Patrimonio di S. Pietro in Tuscia nel secolo XV', *ASR*, xv (1892), 8–12; Eitel, *Der Kirchenstaat unter Klemens V* (1907), 62–66; G. Ermini, 'I Rettori provinciali dello Stato della Chiesa da Innocenzo III al Albornoz', *RSDI*, iv (1931).

[2] *Constitutiones Egidiane*, lib. i, c. 13.   [3] Ibid. lib. i, c. 11.   [4] Ibid.

[5] Ibid.   [6] Ibid. lib. ii, c. 2.   [7] Cf. lib. ii, c. 20.

[8] Theiner, iii, no. 177, p. 251. For such an absolution, see the absolution and removal of interdict accorded by Marino, Bishop of Macerata and Recanati, to Castignano in April 1419, Colucci, *Antichità Picene*, xvi, 101.

[9] Theiner, loc. cit.   [10] *Constitutiones Egidiane*, lib. ii, c. 23.

[11] Ibid.   [12] Theiner, loc. cit.

[13] *Constitutiones Egidiane*, lib. ii, c. 1.

[14] Anzilotti, *ASR*, xlvii (1919), 352; cf. Calisse, *ASR*, xv (1892), 30 f.

[15] Lib. ii, c. 23. Cf. Theiner, loc. cit. where he is empowered to call 'generales sive particulares convocationes'.

[16] Lib. ii, c. 5. The judge in spirituals is to deal with 'omnibus causis pertinentibus ad forum ecclesiasticum et de omnibus appellationibus interpositis et interponendis ad eum seu rectorem sive auditorem super spiritualibus' (ibid.). Cf. lib. iii, c. 2. See also F. Ermini, *Gli ordinamenti politici e amministrativi nelle Constitutiones Aegidianae* (useful, but on the subject of spiritual jurisdiction somewhat confused, pp. 99 f.). Better Aloisi, in *AMSM*, n.s., i (1904), 349 f. and v (1908), 289 f. and cf. doc. ix, ibid. p. 308.

[17] Theiner, iii, no. 177, p. 251, 'ita tamen quod spiritualem jurisdictionem et fulcimentum dumtaxat emporalis jurisdictionis et non alias valeas exercere'. The same proviso is to be found in the appoint-

himself to the imposition or remission of spiritual penalties for temporal offences. Instead, there was appointed in all provinces where there was no Legate a Vicar or Commissioner in spirituals, to whom belonged all the jurisdiction in spiritual matters which is given to the Rector or his Auditor in the *Constitutiones*; he had, that is, jurisdiction over all Bishops, Abbots and lesser persons and bodies in matters relating to the *forum ecclesiasticum*, both ordinary and in appeal.[1]   Where the Rector acted in spiritual causes, it was always under a special commission from the Pope.[2]   Under the Vicar in spirituals the 'judex in spiritualibus' continued in the March of Ancona to carry out his duties.[3]   But where a Cardinal Legate was appointed, he was always granted the extensive powers of spiritual jurisdiction which a Cardinal Legate normally enjoyed.[4]

There is no trace under Martin V of the quarrels between Treasurer and Rector which were typical of the Avignonese period, and, indeed, now that the Pope governed from only a short distance away, and that both Rectors and Treasurers were drawn from the same body of papal officials, the probability that a Rector would forcibly impose corrupt practices on his Treasurer was relatively slight. Rome was able to survey her Italian Rectors far more closely than Avignon had ever been able to do, and the Apostolic Chamberlain supervised the Rector closely in matters of administration, justice and finance.   The Rector was forbidden to pledge or alienate the property of the Church, and when such alienation was thought necessary to raise money, special direction was given from Rome.[5]   Although his bull of appointment promised that his sentences would be upheld,[6] this did not prevent appeal being made to Rome, which could result in their being quashed.[7] On the other hand, the practical discretion in political matters which lay in the Rector's hands continued to be very great, and it could be made the greater, where a province was disorderly or newly conquered, by the grant of the powers of a Legate *a latere*.   Such powers were given to Pietro Emigli as Governor of the March of Ancona,[8] to Pietro Donato, Archbishop of Crete, as Governor of Perugia in 1425 [9]— a year after the city had been recovered—and to Domenico Capranica on his appointment as the first Governor of Imola and Forlì.[10]   The Legate *a latere* was the most

---

ment of a Vice-Rector 'in spirituals and temporals' for Campania and Maritima (Reg. Vat. 349, fol. 155v), and in the appointment of a Vice-Rector of Viterbo (Reg. Vat. 352, fol. 242v).

[1] In the March of Ancona and Campania and Maritima this officer was termed a Vicar-General in spirituals (Reg. Vat. 348, fol. 163; Reg. Vat. 350, fol. 303v); in the Patrimony he was termed a 'spiritualis' (Reg. Vat. 349, fol. 131; Reg. Vat. 351, fol. 71v).

[2] E.g. when Astorgio the Deputy of the March acted as executor for a decision of the Pope concerning the *jus praesentandi* of the commune of San Ginesio to the college of S. Costanzo, he did so as 'commissarius specialiter deputatus', T. Benigni, *San Ginesio illustrata* (1795), ii, no. 45, p. 507.

[3] Cristofono of Vicenza was 'judex super spiritualibus' in the March: Arch. Cam. pt. i, Tes. Prov., Marca, B. 1, vol. 3, fol. 97; cf. Fumi, *Le Marche*, iv, 111.

[4] Cf. G. Durandus, *Speculum Juris* (1566), pt. i, 'de legato', lib. i.

[5] Theiner, iii, no. 177, p. 251.   For instances of permission to pledge the properties of the Holy See, see p. 70 above.

[6] Theiner, loc. cit.   [7] See below, pp. 147 f.
[8] Reg. Vat. 355, fol. 38v.   [9] Reg. Vat. 350, fol. 172.
[10] Ibid. fol. 261, 'cum plena potestate et auctoritate ac plene legationis officio'.

dignified of the three kinds of papal Legate,[1] and, although a Legate not a Cardinal could not claim the privileges of a Cardinal Legate *a latere* in matters of benefices and spiritual privileges, he nevertheless enjoyed certain legal exemptions, such as, for example, that no one could bring a process against him.

§ 2. After the Rector, the Treasurer was the second officer of the province. He entitled himself 'Apostolic Treasurer', and was appointed for the period of the Pope's good pleasure.[2] He was often a clerk of the Apostolic Chamber, and only exceptionally was he quite unconnected with the Chamber. He controlled the revenues of the province and rendered account of them to the Apostolic Chamber;[3] he investigated all frauds in the revenue; he superintended the farming or auction of the revenues of the Chamber,[4] assisted when compositions were made with offenders,[5] and supervised all the financial offices of the province, such as the taxing of pasture and pannage, or the salt monopoly. He had to be consulted by the Rector before monies owed to the Apostolic Chamber were remitted,[6] or before any process was cancelled.[7] He had his own notaries,[8] and he issued letters in his own name and on his own authority.[9] He had his own seals,[10] and he also had the custody of two of the four seals of the *curia generalis*.[11] He made payments at the behest of the Rector and the Apostolic Chamber. In Perugia and Bologna the Rector's mandate was a written *bullecta*; in the other provinces it may have been merely verbal. The Treasurer received payments, and gave quittances under his own seal.

The office of Treasurer was of considerable political importance. He would take charge of military operations, as did Astorgio, Bishop of Ancona, when he assisted the Governor in the subduing of the March; he would also negotiate agreements with communes on behalf of the Church, as did Astorgio when he accepted the submissions of Cingoli and Iesi in 1424. The Treasurer also seized and sold the

---

[1] G. Durandus, loc. cit.; Hostiensis, *Summa Aurea* (Lugduni, 1568), 73 f.; Sägmuller, *Lehrbuch des katholischen Kirchenrechts* (1904), 334–5. Durandus says that legates are 'alii laterales, alii constituti, alii nati'.

[2] Theiner, iii, no. 175, p. 250. Both his office and that of the Rector came to an end on the death of the Pope.

[3] *Constitutiones Egidiane*, lib. i, c. 11.   [4] Ibid. lib. i, c. 11, 15, 16.

[5] Ibid. lib. i, c. 11.   [6] Ibid. lib. i, c. 14.

[7] Ibid. lib. i, c. 16.   [8] Ibid. lib. i, c. 11; lib. ii, c. 2, 9.

[9] E. Re, 'Il "Tesoro" di Gregorio XII e la sua divisione', *AMSM*, 3rd ser., i (1916), passim.

[10] The three seals are described by E. Re, 'Il "Tesoro" di Gregorio XII', 13, one 'nostri maioris sigilli appensione muniri [fecimus]', one 'sub nostro parvo sigillo', and one 'sub nostro parvo signeto quo utimur'. Cf. Ascoli, Archivio Comunale, Pergamene, R. 1.8, a document in which the Bishop of Alatri, Treasurer of the March, informs the commune that the penalties recorded against it in the 'liber maleficiorum et condemnationum' of the province have been expunged—'In quorum omnium testimonium cautelam et fidem patentes nostras litteras per infrascriptum cancellarium nostrum scribi et subscribi mandavimus, nostri pontificalis sigilli appensione munitas'. Dated from the Gerfalcon at Fermo, 10 February 1429, the original seal has disappeared. Subscribed 'Antonius de Alatro cancellarius de mandato subscripsi'. The wafer seal described below (doc. 6 below) is therefore in all probability a fourth seal.

[11] *Constitutiones Egidiane*, lib. ii, c. 10. One seal is that of the Rector. The two held by the Treasurer are those of the 'curia spiritualis' and 'curia generalis'. The fourth seal is that of the 'curia malleficiorum'.

goods of rebels. In the absence of the Rector of the province the Treasurer of the Patrimony was given special powers to try criminal cases, this particularly to combat highway robbery.[1] The Treasurer of Perugia was made judge of appeals in civil and criminal cases in the district of Bettona and Gualdo,[2] merely as a convenient means of filling a gap in the hierarchy of justice. Other additional powers could be freely given. Bartolomeo de Bonitis of Orvieto was in 1424 made both Treasurer of the Patrimony and Commissioner there with the powers of Rector.[3] His successor, Giovanni of Rieti, was in the following year appointed Treasurer, and given in addition the powers of a Rector, whenever he saw fit to use them.[4] The office of Apostolic Collector, the official appointed by the Chamber to collect all the spiritual dues of the Papacy, was quite distinct from that of the Treasurer, but on some occasions one man might combine the two offices.[5] The Treasurer's normal jurisdiction included the supervision of the revenues from pasture (*dogana pecudum*), but on at least one occasion he was also appointed as official of the *dogana pecudum*, and thus his control was made direct.[6] Equally, it was his permanent duty to investigate frauds in the salt monopoly, and he did so, but the Treasurer of the March of Ancona was also on one occasion appointed as Commissioner of the *salaria*, in order to reform and improve the salt revenues in general.[7] He was, in fact, the faithful watchdog of the rights of the Apostolic Chamber, and when those rights were thought to have been infringed he would follow the scent into any department of government.

§ 3. The officials of the *curia generalis* of the province continued, on the whole, to be appointed as was laid down in the *Constitutiones*. In the March of Ancona there was usually one judge of spiritual causes, one of criminal and civil causes, and one of appeal.[8] Albornoz had also ordered that the other provinces should retain their own judicial arrangements. In Martin V's time there was in Campania and Maritima

[1] Reg. Vat. 354, fol. 141, 8 November 1422.

[2] Div. Cam. 11, fol. 70, 12 March 1427. Cases involving the shedding of blood were excepted.

[3] Reg. Vat. 350, fol. 46.

[4] Ibid., fol. 142v. 'te . . . in casibus quibus expedire videris officio et potestate quibus rectores qui fuerint pro tempore in eadem provincia dumtaxat usi sunt, seu uti quomodolibet potuerunt, uti possis et valeas in omnibus et per omnia, ac si verus rector existeres plenam et liberam concedimus tenore presentium facultatem' (3 September 1425).

[5] E.g. Delfino de Gonzadinis in Romagna, see n. 4, p. 44 above. Giovanni of Rieti both Treasurer and Collector in the Patrimony in 1425, Reg. Vat. 350, fols. 141v, 142. Astorgio Bishop of Ancona was both Treasurer and Collector in the March in 1424, Reg. Vat. 355, fol. 123v.

[6] This again was Giovanni of Rieti, who thus united all the financial offices in the province save for the *salaria* (Reg. Vat. 350, fol. 137).

[7] Reg. Vat. 350, fol. 39v, Astorgio Bishop of Ancona, the Treasurer of the March, is appointed Commissioner of the *salaria* of the March, 'cupientes igitur ut salaria . . . que per diversos hactenus in eiusdem camere prejudicium distracta et occupata fuit salubriter dirigatur et etiam gubernetur et in suis membris debite reformetur' (13 February 1424).

[8] Lib. ii, c. 2, 5. For the growth of this system of judges see G. Ermini, 'I giudici provinciali della Monarchia pontificia nel medio evo', *Studi Economico-Giuridici publicata per cura della facoltà di Giuris-prudenza*, Cagliari, 1931, anno 18/19. At some times only a single judge seems to have been appointed in the March for both civil and criminal causes. Giovanni Mazzancoli of Terni was on 5 February 1424 appointed 'iudex generalis causarum civilium et criminalium' in both the March and

H

merely a single *judex generalis in temporalibus* ;[1] no doubt this was all the poverty of the province would permit.   In the Patrimony of St. Peter in Tuscia there was a judge of civil and criminal causes [2] and a judge of appeal.[3]   In the March of Ancona an additional judge was appointed in the Presidency of Farfa.[4]   A vicar in spirituals was appointed, and the judge in spiritual causes may be presumed to have come under his jurisdiction rather than that of the Rector.[5]

The *curia* had a host of minor officials.   There was a considerable number of notaries, of the *camera rectoris*,[6] of the bench of judges,[7] of the Treasurer,[8] of the Presidency of Farfa.[9]   A tariff was laid down in the *Constitutiones* for the charges they might make for their services.[10]   The notary's office was important and lucrative, since he formed the main channel of communication between the government and its subjects.   Thus, when Macerata obtained a decision from the *curia generalis* in favour of its exemption from sending its officers to 'sindicate' in the court of the province, a copy of the decision of the *judex malleficiorum* of the province was made and authenticated for the benefit of the commune by the notary of the court, Filippo Jacopo of Monte S. Maria in Lapide.[11]

Beneath the judges were other curial officials : the *procurator fisci* or *procurator camere*, whose duty it was to look to the rights of the Apostolic Chamber,[12] to note the names of those who failed to answer citations, and to give witness in cases concerning the audit (*syndicatio*) of the officials of the province.[13]   Another *procurator ad negocia* is named in the *Constitutiones*, with the duty of protecting the rights of the fisc and administering its goods,[14] but this title does not appear in the list of the provincial *curia* under Martin V.[15]   He and the *advocati fisci* acted as *advocati pauperum*.[16]   The advocates and procurators of the *curia generalis* were

---

the Presidency of Farfa, thus combining offices which the Constitutions allot to three separate judges, Reg. Vat. 350, fol. 13.   A 'judex appellationum curie generalis', ibid. fol. 12.   There was not always only one judge of civil and criminal causes for the March; in 1420 there was a separate appointment of a 'judex generalis maleficiorum', Reg. Vat. 349, fol. 164.

[1] Reg. Vat. 349, fol. 278; Arch. Cam. pt. i, Tes. Prov., Campania, B. 1, vol. 1, fol. 32, payment of Giovanni Bishop of Alatri, the Vicar in spirituals.

[2] Reg. Vat. 349, fol. 220v (17 June 1422) ; Theiner, iii, no. 243, p. 299.

[3] Reg. Vat. 352, fol. 249; Div. Cam. 3, fol. 132 (April 1419).

[4] The *Constitutiones* (lib. ii, c. 5) provide for a judge in each of the three Presidencies of Farfa, Camerino and S. Lorenzo in Campo, but only the first of these jurisdictions continued to exist.   A judge in civil and criminal causes was appointed for the Presidency of Farfa on 20 June 1429, for a term of six months, Reg. Vat. 351, fol. 129v.   See also the payments to a judge of the Presidency recorded in Arch. Cam., pt. i, Tes. Prov., Marca, B. 1, vol. 3, fol. 93 (1423/4).

[5] In the Patrimony and Campania and Maritima there was a vicar in spirituals, but there is no trace of a judge in spirituals.

[6] *Constitutiones Egidiane*, lib. ii, c. 2, 8.

[7] Ibid. lib. ii, c. 2, 4, 10.   [8] Ibid. lib. i, c. 11 ; lib. ii, c. 2, 9.

[9] Ibid. lib. ii, c. 2.   [10] Lib. ii, c. 8, 9, 10.

[11] The original notarial instrument is in Macerata, Archivio Priorale, Cart. Grande, no. 3, dated 1 October 1424.

[12] Lib. ii, c. 14.   Cf. the appointment in Theiner, iii, no. 243, p. 299.

[13] Lib. ii, c. 22 (p. 98, lines 10–17).

[14] Lib. ii, c. 14.   [15] Cf. Fumi, *Le Marche*, iv (1904), 110–111

[16] *Constitutiones Egidiane*, lib. ii, c. 14.

united in a college, possessing its own statutes and privileges, and there was a tariff establishing the charges which they might make.[1]

For the execution of justice there was a Marshal,[2] who was to have three lances and sufficient men-at-arms. For these he was paid 33 florins monthly, and he also had a provision of 12 florins a month for his own person.[3] In the Patrimony the Marshal's police duties are indicated in the terms of his appointment, which calls him also the 'custodis viarum et stratarum'.[4] He was assisted in the execution of justice by messengers (*nuntii curie generalis*), by couriers (*cabalarii*), and by bailiffs (*bayuli*).[5]

The *Constitutiones* give the Rector the right to appoint his own officials, but under Martin V many of them, including the judges, *procuratores* and Marshal, seem to have been appointed from Rome.[6]

§ 4. The 'castelries' (*castellanie*) which are mentioned so often in the thirteenth and fourteenth centuries [7] had by the fifteenth century lost most of their importance, and the revenues from them play little part in the accounts of provincial Treasurers.[8] The castle (*rocca, arx*) had become under Martin V a military rather than a governmental unit, and there are many appointments by the Pope to castellanships of an obviously military importance.[9] Traces of the older system remain; Antico in Sabina, after forming part of the vicariate of the brothers Besaccione in 1421,[10] is found in 1424 granted to a 'castellanus et officialis', and in 1427 to a 'castellanus rocche et gubernator castri', the latter appointment being for a term of five years.[11] The castle of Ancona is said in 1421 to have an income of something under 100 florins a year; a castellan is no longer appointed but the rents are granted to the Legate of the March.[12] But of the system of letting out castelries to farm to the highest bidder there is little trace.[13]

---

[1] Ibid. lib. ii, c. 10.

[2] Ibid. lib. ii, c. 12.

[3] Div. Cam. 6, fol. 24v, 14 February 1420.

[4] Div. Cam. 9, fol. 73, 31 May 1425.

[5] *Constitutiones Egidiane*, lib. ii, c. 17; Arch. Cam. pt. i, Tes. Prov., Marca, B. 1, vol. 3, fol. 93; B. 2, vol. 1, fol. 144v, 'nuntii curie generalis', 'cabalarii', 'bayuli'. Cf. Fumi, loc. cit.

[6] Theiner, iii, nos. 242, 243, 245, pp. 298, 299, 300.

[7] G. Ermini, *La libertà comunale nello Stato della Chiesa*, ii (1927), 23–31; Calisse, *ASR*, xv (1892), 37–9.

[8] In the March there is little trace of the *castella*. In the Patrimony the rents from this source were still handled by the Treasurer, Anzilotti, 'Cenni sulle finanze del Patrimonio di S. Pietro in Tuscia nel secolo XV', *ASR*, xlii (1919), 358–9.

[9] Theiner, iii, no. 180, p. 254, to the castle of Narni. Evidently there was no appreciable income from the castle, since the salary of the castellan is to be paid from the revenues of the province. See also Reg. Vat. 348, fol. 161, appointment of Francesco Pauluctii of Perugia as castellan of the 'arx seu fortillicia' of Corneto.

[10] Reg. Vat. 349, fol. 171. The main possessions of these brothers were in Feltre. They were 'ex comitibus de Piagnano', and they held Piagnano, Pian di Meleto, Pirlo, Pietro Cavola, Petrella, and other nearby territories.

[11] Div. Cam. 8, fol. 254, an order addressed to 'nobili viro Petro Jannis Raynaldi de Sublaco castellano et officiali rocche de Antiquo Sabinen' diocesis' to release the family of Cicheti, whom he has imprisoned for certain offences, 17 December 1424. Armaleo of Ascoli was appointed castellan of the castle and Governor of the *castrum* for five years on 17 July 1427, Reg. Vat. 351, fol. 5.

[12] Reg. Vat. 353, fol. 264. The rents are those 'qui olim castellani sive gubernatores arcis in civitate nostra Anconitan' tunc existentes tamquam ad ipsam arcem seu cameram apostolicam pertinencia possidebant'.

[13] The system is described in the *Constitutiones*, lib. i, c. 11; cf. Ermini and Calisse, quoted above.

Associated with the Treasurer for the exaction of certain revenues were the officials for the supervision of pasture (*dogana pecudum*), for the customs control of grain (*tracta frumenti*) and other customs dues on foodstuffs (*grascia*) and for the administration of pannage. These officials were appointed by the Pope, and their accounts were submitted to the Apostolic Chamber.[1] They were not appointed in every province; in the March of Ancona and Romagna agricultural conditions were different from those of the west, and there was not the annual move of animals down from the hills in search of pasture. Consequently there was no *dogana pecudum*, and the *tracta* of grain and foodstuffs was controlled directly by the Treasurer.[2] But in the Roman District and the Patrimony of St. Peter there was every autumn a tremendous influx of beasts from the hills of Sabina and the Abruzzi, with great profit for the owners of pasture from benefit done to their soil,[3] and for the Apostolic Chamber from the taxes imposed on the transit of the animals. Both Rome and the Patrimony had in consequence an official of the *dogana*, whose duty it was to receive and control the profits of the Apostolic Chamber from this source in accordance with the statutes of the *dogana*. This official also controlled the pannage,[4] and the patrimonial and fiscal profits of the demesne lands of the Apostolic Chamber.[5] The *tracta grani* was not always in the hands of a special official, but in 1422 there was appointed in the Patrimony a commissioner 'pro fienda recollecta grani'.[6]

The administration of the salt tax fits rather ill into the scheme of provincial government, for although the provincial Rectors and Treasurers took a lively interest in its collection, most of the arrangements with the officials of the *salaria* were made direct from Rome. The *saline* or manufactories of the salt must be distinguished from the *salarie*, the organisations for its compulsory sale, although both can be comprehended in the term *salaria*. The salt was manufactured at Corneto, Ostia, Terracina and Cervia. Officials of the *salaria* were appointed by the Pope for Rome

[1] Anzilotti, *ASR*, xlii (1919), 375; Gottlob, *Aus der Camera apostolica*, 136-7.

[2] See the heading 'tracta grani' in the accounts of the Treasury of the March, Arch. Cam. pt. i, Tes. Prov., Marca, B. 1, vol. 1, fol. 73. 'Die quintodecimo mensis Martii supradictus reverendus pater Geminianus thesaurarius prefatus, nomine dicte camere apostolice, habuit et recepit a Silvestro Angeli de Montefortino, pro licencia sibi concessa extrahendi de terris ecclesie et illas conducendas ad Montem Fortinum salmas quindecim frumenti, bol' triginta : solvent' ad rationem duorum bolen' pro salma, duratura dicta licencia pro totum mensem Aprilis proxime futuri—duc'—bol' xxxᵗᵃ'.

[3] De Cupis, *Delle vicende dell'agricoltura e della pastorizia nell'Agro Romano* (1911).

[4] Reg. Vat. 351, fol. 59v, the appointment of Nucio della Fonte of Aquila as the official of the *dogana* of the Patrimony, 'cum eius glandibus, videlicet Ardee, Marini, Solforate, Bellipasi et Fassignani, Falconagni, Frascati cum casalibus in saleo, Casamara, Pretaporci, Casali, Lelli, Stinchi et aliorum casalium inter catario dicti Frascati existentium, et insuper Fiani, Civitelle, Morlupi, Montis Guardie, Vicarelli, Porciliarii, Decimi, Casteluccie Castelli domini Romani, Turris de Cinciis, Turris de Valtea', Larnarozii, Maranelle, Montis sancte Marie, necnon medietatis Salforate, quarti Pali, quarti Galere, tertie partis aliarum terrarum quartorum dicte Galere . . .' It is extraordinary that none of these places are in the province of the Patrimony of St. Peter in Tuscia; they are all in the Roman District.

[5] Anzilotti, *ASR*, xlii (1919), 365 f.

[6] The commissioner was Stefano de Branchiis of Gubbio, Reg. Vat. 354, fol. 97v. He was told to provide guarantees for the safe movement of the animals through the Patrimony to their pastures, lest the fear of political disorders prevent their owners from sending them, ibid., fol. 101v, 15 August 1422.

and the Patrimony of St. Peter (including the *salina* of Corneto), Terracina, the March of Ancona, and Perugia and Umbria.[1] Commissioners[2] and 'custodians' (*custodes*)[3] were appointed from time to time to assist in the supervision of the salt monopoly and the prevention of frauds there.

§ 5. The Parliament, which in the *Constitutiones Egidiane* appears as an integral part of the provincial government, by the time of Martin V had been reduced to a very minor rôle, and that only in a single province. The *Constitutiones* lay down that a Rector on appointment shall hold a Parliament at which he shall take the oath, and this rule appears to have been followed in the March of Ancona. On 4 September 1418 the commune of Macerata appointed its *podestà* as proctor of the commune to go to the first Parliament of the new Vice-Legate, Marino Bishop of Macerata and Recanati, to swear obedience to the Church if this was needed, and 'ad promictendum obligandum et realiter observandum et ad implemendum omnia et singula que pro statu Ecclesie sacrosancte matris et domine nostre et dicti domini nostri necnon pro universali pace quieta bono et commodo totius huius provincie Marchie et provinciarum ipsius'.[4] Of the general business conducted at this Parliament nothing is known, but at Macerata the result was the issuing of a series of amendments or 'reformations' to the communal statutes, which were duly submitted to the Vice-Legate and approved by him.[5] The meeting of the Vice-Legate with the provincials at Recanati in February 1419 to discuss the lowering of the rates of tallage does not appear to have been a Parliament, since the representatives of the towns were not summoned in the accustomed form, nor were their proctors furnished with the usual powers.[6] When the Legate Gabriel Condulmer arrived in the March in 1420 he proceeded to call a Parliament at Ancona, at which he published a series of reforming constitutions.[7] There is no record of a Parliament held by Thomas Bishop

---

[1] See pp. 143 f. below.

[2] Reg. Vat. 349, fol. 176, appointment of Cola Quarto of Trani as Commissioner in the March of Ancona, with the powers usually accorded to a Marshal. Ibid. fol. 184v, instructions to him to apprehend those guilty of frauds in the *salaria*, and to bring them to justice before the Treasurer of the March, 23 August 1421. Reg. Vat. 350, fol. 39v, a commission to the Treasurer of a similar nature. Reg. Vat. 354, fol. 32, confirmation, dated 26 March 1422, of Nicolò Cola Quarto's previous appointment, which is here referred to as being to investigate frauds in the monopolies of salt and grain ('tracta tam salis quam saluche' or 'tracta salis et frumenti').

[3] These 'custodes' were appointed by the merchant to whom the *salaria* had been granted (Theiner, iii, no. 208, p. 275) and were confirmed by the Pope. Jacopo of Anagni was appointed in June 1423 (Reg. Vat. 354, fol. 237v) and Stefano de Manentis of Genazzano in June 1425 (Reg. Vat. 355, fol. 189v).

[4] Doc. 15 below. See, in general, G. Ermini, *I parlamenti dello Stato della Chiesa dalle origini al periodo albornoziano* (1930), and A. Marongiu, *L'Istituto parlamentare in Italia* (1949), especially pp. 172–6. I was also able to consult briefly the thesis of Professor Marongiu's pupil, Dante Cecchi, *Il parlamento nella Marca di Ancona dal 1357 alla fine del secolo XVIII*, of which there is a typescript copy in the Biblioteca Comunale at Macerata. Dr. Cecchi deals more with the later 'congregazione provinciale' than with this earlier period, but the thesis is based on unpublished material, and is of much interest.

[5] These amendments are dated 19 November 1418, and are collected in vol. 11 of the Riformanze of Macerata. They are also referred to by the Legate in a letter dated 27 September 1418, ibid., fol. 268.

[6] See above, p. 50.

[7] *Liber constitutionum marchie anconitane* (Iesi, 1473, Hain-Coppinger no. 106), 'Lecte et approbate in generali parlamento omnium provincialium in civitate ancone celebrato anno domini MCCCCXX indictione xiii pontificatus eiusdem domini nostri anno [tertio] die vi novembris in festo sancti leonardi.'

of Urbino, who became Deputy in the March after the recall of Gabriel Condulmer in the summer of 1423,[1] nor is any Parliament known to have been held by the Deputy who assumed office in 1426, Astorgio Bishop of Ancona. As the Deputy was only in the place of the Legate or Governor, whose original appointment remained in force,[2] he would not have been obliged by the *Constitutiones* to hold the Parliament required of a new Rector.

Pietro Emigli, the Governor of the March appointed in 1424, was under such an obligation, and he proceeded to hold his Parliament at Macerata in March 1425. It is probable that the revision of the assessments of tallage in the March were discussed there;[3] that the communes were made to enter into any important obligations there seems unlikely, since the mandate given by Macerata to her representatives in this Parliament was a *post factum* one, not issued until four days after the Parliament had taken place.[4] It is noticeable that Emigli held his Parliament, not when he entered the March, which was both the time at which he was strictly required to call it, and also at a time when the feudal army of the province was required to fight against rebels, but only when the province had been reduced to peace and order, and the only questions to be discussed were administrative ones.[5] His not calling a Parliament earlier had not prevented him from summoning the levies of the March, and most of the communes and some of the *signori* had sent their soldiers to serve in the Governor's army.

Thus the political function of the Parliament, its use as a rallying point for the loyal supporters of the Pope in time of crisis, was on the wane, and its function tended to be reduced to that of receiving the constitutions of the Rector, or supplying him with information for administrative purposes. But the political value of Parliament must have tended to re-appear at the times of the greatest weakness of government; no doubt the Parliament of 1418, at a time when the organisation of resistance to Braccio was in its earliest and weakest stages, had a certain political importance. When Antonio Casini, in the premature expectation of a peace with Braccio, was in 1419 appointed Rector to recover the lands held by Braccio in the Patrimony, the faculties granted him included one to hold a Parliament against rebels.[6]

In one of its most important functions the provincial Parliament was atrophied,

---

[1] Condulmer returned from the March to go to Bologna, p. 78 above. There is a letter of the Deputy dated 3 February 1424 in Compagnoni, *La Reggia Picena*, 311.

[2] The appointment of Emigli cancels that of both the former Legate and his Deputy, Reg. Vat. 355 fol. 38v.

[3] See above, p. 83.

[4] Doc. 16 below. Cf. the letter convoking a Parliament in the Patrimony, in Fabre, 'Un Registre caméral du Cardinal Albornoz', *Mélanges*, vii (1887), 182–3. The only similar mandate of the later period I have found is that of 1432, doc. 22 below.

[5] Compagnoni states, p. 312, that Emigli (Colonna) held a Parliament in Macerata on 22 July 1424, but this is not so. In the Riformazioni, vol. 13, fol. 99, there is a copy of the mandate given to the syndics of Macerata to swear obedience in the court of the Governor. The scribe has put 'in parlamento', and then struck this through and substituted 'in curia'. On fol. 97 is Emigli's letter, requiring the cities of the province to appear in his court at Macerata, to swear fidelity.

[6] Doc. 24 below. Cf. Theiner, iii, no. 177, p. 251, which empowers the Rector to call 'general or particular convocations'.

since it was no longer necessary, in the fifteenth century, to call a Parliament in order to impose the *tallia militum*.[1] From being an especial tax, imposed occasionally at a Parliament called especially for the purpose, the *tallia* had become the 'tallia sive subsidium', an annual tax, imposed by the Rector either on his own authority or at the orders of the Apostolic Chamber.[2] The possibility of calling a Parliament for such a purpose continues to be referred to in the documents, just as the annual order to impose a tallage was worded as though this were still an exceptional measure. In 1423 the Treasurer of the Patrimony was ordered to impose a 'tallia sive caritativum subsidium' 'sive in generali parlamento dictorum provincie ducatus et terris (*sic*) specialis commissionis quando et ubi placuerit convocando seu per alium modum prout discrecioni tue videtur expedire'.[3] But if any Parliament were called it escaped mention in all the existing records, and in fact it does not appear that a Parliament was convoked under Martin V in any province save the March of Ancona. Similarly, when Innocent VII ordered a hearth tax to be imposed in the province of Campania and Maritima, he ordered that it be imposed at a general Parliament,[4] but when the same tax was re-imposed in 1420, the Apostolic Chamber ordered its collection to be made, without any reference to Parliament.[5]

III. *Provincial Revenues*

§ 1. The Treasurer of the province was responsible for the finances of that province, and sometimes for some areas which lay outside it. His Chamber was the Chamber of the Province, and he might have subsidiary Chambers, where a city was governed directly for the Church, which administered the finances of that city, but were counted as a part of the Chamber of the province. Such was the relation between the Chamber of the March and the Chamber of Ascoli.[6] All payments were made on the Treasurer's instructions by his notary,[7] and the money was under his supervision; there was no provincial *depositarius*, and the Rector did not order payments to be made except through the Treasurer. In Bologna and Perugia, however, the Legate issued the *bullecte* ordering the Treasurer to make payments, and in Perugia there was a *depositarius*. The Treasurer had to account to the Apostolic Chamber and to submit his books to the Chamber for audit, and he was held personally responsible for any deficiencies.[8] When a substantial surplus appeared, or when he was so ordered, he paid money into the Apostolic Chamber,[9] or, on some occasions

---

[1] Ermini, *I parlamenti dello Stato della Chiesa*, 98 f.; Calisse, *ASR*, xv (1892), 30–1, does not mention a Parliament as necessary to impose this tax in the Patrimony. The relation of Romagna and the March of 1371 mentions that the consent of the provincials of the March was at first needed for this tax, but adds that it has now become an annual impost, Theiner, ii, no. 527, p. 538.

[2] Cf. doc. 3 below. In the March of Ancona the tallage seems to have been imposed by the Rector and Treasurer. In Perugia and the Duchy of Spoleto it was imposed annually, on the orders of the Vice-Chamberlain, who sent the Treasurer a list of the towns concerned and the amounts fixed. See p. 113 below, and doc. 5.

[3] Reg. Vat. 354, fol. 233.

[4] Theiner, iii, no. 72, p. 139.

[5] Div. Cam. 6, fol. 216v.

[6] See Appendix of Sources below, p. 207.

[7] *Constitutiones Egidiane*, lib. i, c. 11.

[8] See pp. 141–2 below.

[9] Anzilotti, *ASR*, xlii (1919), 360–5.

into the secret account of the Pope.[1]   Very frequently, assignments were made from Rome for the provincial Treasurer to pay monies to objects specified by the Chamberlain : to mercenaries, to the *depositarius* of the Chamber in Rome.[2]   He was responsible for all the payments for the normal running of the province.   He paid his own salary, that of the Rector, and that of all the officials of the *curia generalis provincie*.[3]   Where they were not paid by the Apostolic Chamber or out of local revenues, he paid the salary of castellans.[4]   With mercenaries the situation is not clearly defined; he paid the salaries of all smaller forces raised within the province, and, in the case of larger forces, the onus of payment might be divided between Rome and the provincial treasury.[5]   When the local levies of the cities were retained beyond the time customary he became responsible for their payment, or else had to release them and take on other mercenaries.[6]   For the salaries of the *podestà* appointed by the Pope or the Rector he was not responsible; these were paid by the commune concerned, as were the salaries of all the officials of the communes.   The salary of the Rector or Governor of a city was usually paid by that city.

The Treasurer collected all the revenues of the province with the exception of the indirect taxes controlled by the *doganerius pecudum* and *conductores salarie*, and of the *census* paid by the holders of an apostolic vicariate.   It was usually placed in the terms granting a vicariate that the *census* for it should be paid directly to Rome, and this was done.[7]   Only under special instructions did the Treasurer of a province collect such *census*.[8]   On the other hand, he did collect from the *signori*, the vicars, all the other dues which they owed, the tallage, *affitti* and so on.

§ 2.   The most important of the revenues of the provinces was the *tallia militum*. This tax had in the thirteenth and fourteenth centuries been imposed from time to time as a special levy to provide soldiers to protect the province in time of disorders. The Rectors in the March of Ancona and Romagna imposed it usually by agreement with the provincials, at a provincial Parliament.   In the Patrimony of St. Peter it seems to have been exacted in the fourteenth century without convoking Parlia-

---

[1] Arch. Cam. pt. i, Tes. Prov., Umbria, B. 2, vol. 2b, fols. 27, 28, 28v, 30, a series of payments to the Pope by the hand of Angelo Massii de Genezzano, his agent of the secret treasury, totalling 6,400 florins between November 1425 and April 1427.   Similar payments from the Treasurer of the March to the Pope, April 1424, ibid., Marca, B. 1, vol. 3, fol. 107v.

[2] E.g. doc. 4 below.   Such assignments could extend to the whole profits of a province; on 3 June 1429 the Treasurer of the March of Ancona is ordered to consign all the monies arising from his office to Giovanni Cavalcanti of Florence, who will receive them on behalf of Cosimo and Lorenzo de' Medici. A receipt is to be secured for each payment, and the Apostolic Chamber is to be informed that it has been made (Div. Cam. 11, fol. 280).

[3] Fumi, *Le Marche*, iv (1904), 110–111, 283.

[4] Arch. Cam., pt. i, Tes. Prov., Marca, B. 2, vol. 1, fols. 139–40, salaries of the castellans of Rocca Contrata, Piri, Barbara.

[5] Fumi, ibid. 163, 169.

[6] Ibid. 295–6, 'Quia pedites missi per comunitates provincie jam serviverant (sic) per duos menses, et prefate comunitates revocaverant (sic) eos et non solvebant predictos peditibus, prefatus d. conduxit Andream Caponum et infrascriptos, quia aliter fuisset magnum periculum'.

[7] Theiner, iii, nos. 157, 158, pp. 224, 229.

[8] The Cardinal Legate of Bologna was given a special faculty in 1421 to collect the *census* of the Este of Ferrara, Reg. Vat. 353, fol. 255.   Later the Este paid their *census* direct to Rome.

ment.[1] But rapidly enough this occasional and variable levy became a fixed and permanent one.   First the amounts due from each city became fixed by custom, then the imposition of the tax became more frequent, and was made often without reference to Parliament, then finally it emerges in all the provinces as an annual tax.[2] At the same time it suffered a change of name which indicates its change of character; it became in Umbria and the Patrimony a 'subsidy', and is referred to as a 'talea sub nomine et vocabulo subsidii'.[3] When the tyrant of Rieti was expelled in 1425 and the city submitted to the Holy See, its ambassadors came to Rome to discuss with the Pope what should be the amount of the 'sussidio' which they were in future to pay;[4] by this was meant this direct tax owed to the Holy See.   The incidence of the tallage or subsidy was on all cities, towns and *castra* which were of sufficient importance to be assessed; the amounts paid range from several thousand florins a year for the large towns to twenty or thirty florins for the villages.[5] These assessments were all based on the traditional figures.   In the March of Ancona the many wars caused a reduction of tallage to be made for many towns in 1418, and there was a complete re-assessment of the whole province in 1425, made, probably, after consultation with the provincial Parliament.   When the Apostolic Chamber ordered the Treasurers of Perugia or the Patrimony to collect tallage, the instructions often included a list of the amounts due from each city, compiled in accordance with lists kept in the Apostolic Chamber.[6] The priors or council of each commune or *castrum* were responsible for collecting the tallage and transmitting it to the provincial Treasurer.[7] Where the Apostolic Chamber found that there was no competent body to collect taxes in an area, it ordered the provincial Treasurer to arrange for their collection himself.[8] The Treasurer of the province gave quittances in due form to the communes paying their tallage.[9]

Tallage was not paid by the barons and *signori* as a personal liability, but only

[1] Ermini, *I parlamenti dello Stato della Chiesa*, 98 f.; Calisse, *ASR*, xv (1892), 30–1.

[2] Anzilotti, *ASR*, xlii (1919), 351–5.

[3] Reg. Vat. 353, fol. 259v, referring to the tallage of Spoleto.

[4] Michaeli, *Memorie storiche della città di Rieti*, iii, 324–32.   It is called 'subsidio consueto pro gentibus armorum', ibid. 325.

[5] There are three contemporary lists of tallage under Martin V: one of the March of Ancona and the Patrimony in 1426, Arm. 33, vol. 11, fol. 6; and one of the Patrimony alone, copied from the former, and dated 1430, Div. Cam. 13, fol. 20.   A third list, dated before 1426, in Florence, Biblioteca Nazionale, xix, 82, fol. 107.   A small part of the first of these lists is printed by Guiraud, *L'Etat Pontifical*, 206–7, but with some errors, e.g. 'Casignanum' for 'Castignanum'.

[6] For the Patrimony, Reg. Vat. 354, fol. 233 (1423); Div. Cam. 8, fol. 229v (1424); Div. Cam. 11, fol. 61v (1427), and cf. doc. 3 below.   For the province of Perugia, doc. 5 below, and similar mandates in Div. Cam. 9, fol. 203v (1426); Div. Cam. 11, fol. 40 (1427); ibid. fol. 273 (1429).   For Spoleto, Div. Cam. 7, fol. 38v (1421/2); doc. 5 below; Div. Cam. 11, fol. 71v (1427); ibid. fol. 184v (1428).

[7] *Constitutiones Egidiane*, Const. adiecte, p. 243.

[8] In November 1427 it was reported to the Vice-Chamberlain that in the *castra* of Cesaro, Porcaria and San Gemini, immediately subject to the Holy See, 'non sint iurum redditum et perventium sive tallearum et subsidiorum collectores'.   The Rector of the Patrimony was therefore ordered to collect the lay and ecclesiastical taxes in this district himself, Div. Cam. 8, fol. 229v.

[9] See doc. 6 below.   The Treasurer of the March later gave similar quittances, but without the wafer seal, on a parchment roll which was made to last for several payments, e.g., Macerata, Archivio Priorale, Cass. 8A, 'solutio tallearum'.   This is a roll giving quittances from December 1431 to June 1432.   Each quittance is signed by the Treasurer.

so far as they possessed towns and villages liable to the tax. Apostolic vicars in temporals were required to pay, save those such as Guid'Antonio of Montefeltro who possessed special papal privilege.[1] The vicars each paid a lump sum for the whole tallage of their lands; thus only the territories immediately subject to the Church paid tallage direct to the provincial Treasurer, and the others paid through their vicar.

Tallage was not paid in all the possessions of the Church, but only in the March of Ancona, in the Patrimony, in Sabina, the *terra Arnulphorum* and lands of special commission, the Duchy of Spoleto, and the lands governed from Perugia, including Città di Castello. Thus Bologna and the county of Bologna, Romagna, and Campania and Maritima do not appear to have been subject to it. It may be hazarded that Bologna had always been in a good enough bargaining position with the Popes to fend off this impost; that equally it had been impossible to make the tyrants of Romagna pay it; and that Campania and Maritima had always been too poor to pay.

The collection of tallage was made in three annual instalments in the Patrimony, and in three or six in the March of Ancona.[2] In the March the Treasurer usually accepted three payments a year, giving in return a quittance authenticated by his autograph signature.[3] Normally its collection for a particular year was made in the course of that year, but in at least one case collection was anticipated. In the spring of 1429, when the papal purse was strained to the utmost by the war to recover Bologna, the Treasurer of the March was ordered, because of the exhaustion of the monies at his command, to collect next year's tallage, or a part of it, in advance.[4] But it may be doubted whether such an attempt would have much practical effect.[5]

In Umbria and the Patrimony not only the laity but the clergy were obliged to pay the subsidy or tallage. Under the name of a caritative subsidy, or 'tallia caritativi subsidii', the bishops and clergy of these areas were taxed every year for a considerable sum.[6] This was collected not by the Apostolic Collector but by the Treasurer of the province concerned, and the assessments of the clergy for this subsidy, and the orders to the Treasurers to exact it, were made in such a way as to leave no doubt that the clerical subsidy was the exact complement of the lay subsidy.

---

[1] Reg. Vat. 355, fol. 175 and Arm. 60, vol. 21, fol. 102. Guid'Antonio of Montefeltro has refused to pay the assignments of tallage to Braccio—'tu tamen vigore cuiusdam exceptionis per quondam Bonifatium VIIII in eius obedientia nuncupatum super hoc tibi concesse et postea per sedem apostolicam confirmate, ad solutionem huiusmodi tallearum nec etiam aliorum subsidiorum stipendiorum vel onerum, te asserens non teneri supradicta prefato thesaurario vel cuiquam alteri, solvere non curasti'. The Pope now grants him exemption against payment of tallage and subsidy for 15 years, provided he continues to pay his *census* of 1,300 florins for the vicariate, 'necnon etiam afficus fumantarias et alios census antiquos et alia regalia beati petri' (25 October 1424).

[2] See doc. 3 below, for the Patrimony. Cf. Ancona, Atti Consigliari, vol. 30, fol. 4, 'Le talghe per la gente darme, comenza a kal. de Septembre, de pagare sextaria per sextaria'. Macerata paid two-sixths at a time, doc. 6 below; Riformanze, vol. 12, fol. 92. In the Duchy of Spoleto the tallage was to be collected 'de sextaria in sextariam usque ad completam solutionem', Div. Cam. 7, fol. 38v.

[3] Doc. 6 below.   [4] Doc. 7 below.

[5] Cf. Fumi, *Le Marche*, iv (1904), 292, where 1428 is to be read for 'mcccviiij'.

[6] See doc. 5 below. The clergy of Perugia itself are not recorded as paying a subsidy. The Treasurer of the Patrimony was told that no exemptions of ecclesiastics or religious were valid against the collection of this subsidy, Div. Cam. 7, fol. 46v, 26 May 1422.

The bishop and clergy of Rieti refused to pay this subsidy, alleging certain decrees of the Council of Constance, although which decrees remains unknown; but they were excommunicated as a result.[1] The only trace of a caritative subsidy being imposed on the clergy in the March of Ancona is in 1421, at the same time as the Pope tried to exact a similar subsidy in Venice and other parts of Italy outside the Papal State.[2] In the March the Treasurer was made responsible for collecting the subsidy, and the amount he was to impose on the clergy there was left to his discretion.[3] This clerical subsidy, exacted for temporal purposes, accords very ill with the loud appeals to ecclesiastical liberties when the clergy were made to pay taxes to communes in the State of the Church—a strenuous attempt to deny that what is sauce for the goose is sauce for the gander. The paradox did not escape the Reform Commission of Cardinals which sat in 1429–30.[4]

In theory the total annual amount of the tallage was enormous; the March of Ancona was reckoned in 1426 to provide a total of 34,286 florins a year,[5] while the Patrimony provided the modest total of about 13,000 florins a year,[6] the Duchy of Spoleto about 3,000,[7] and the area ruled from Perugia, excluding Città di Castello, about a further 3,000 florins.[8] Because it was such a large single source of income, the tallage was particularly liable to be pledged as security or even assigned outright to meet liabilities of the Apostolic Chamber, and particularly the salaries of mercenaries. In the very troubled early period of the pontificate the tallage was assigned outright to the mercenaries, giving them the right to collect direct from the towns concerned and to give binding quittances—even in some cases to use force against the towns in the event of non-payment.[9] Such a system opened the door to malpractice, intimidation and lawlessness, as was only too evident from the assignments made to Braccio. A slightly less painful method, from the point of view of the Holy See, was to assign to mercenaries the tallage due from tyrants, and allowing one lawless gentleman to collect his money from the other if he could.[10] How much Braccio and the other *condottieri* in practice collected from assignments is doubtful, but it was certainly a great deal less than the nominal total. The matter was raised

---

[1] They were absolved from excommunication on this account on 31 August 1425, Div. Cam. 9, fol. 120. Their resistance was not fruitless: the clergy of Sabina were forgiven all arrears of 'talleas subsidiorum caritativorum' up to 1 January 1425, ibid. fol. 41.

[2] See above, p. 70.

[3] Reg. Vat. 353, fol. 232v. The subsidy is to be imposed on all the regular and secular clergy of the March, the amount being left to his discretions. Accounts of the amount collected are to be sent to the Apostolic Chamber as soon as possible (11 August 1421).

[4] Haller, *Concilium Basiliense*, i, 177, where it is said that as the exemption of the clergy from the impositions of lay rulers will be demanded at the future Council, 'videbatur necessio expedire, quod in curia Romana et in terris ecclesie clerici essent immunes a predictis gabellis et aliis oneribus secundum iuris dispositionum'.

[5] Arm. 33, vol. 11, fol. 6.   [6] Calculated from Div. Cam. 13, fol. 20 et seq.

[7] Ibid.   [8] Doc. 5 below.

[9] In the assignment made to Braccio in 1423, Reg. Vat. 354, fol. 165, the Treasurer is told to collect the tallage on Braccio's behalf, but if he fails to do so, Braccio is himself authorised to collect the money from the provincials.

[10] E.g. the assignment of the tallage due from Guid'Antonio of Montefeltro to Braccio, n. 1 above, p. 114.

in the Apostolic Chamber after the defeat and death of Braccio, when it was wished to recover for the Church all the tallage which Braccio had been assigned, but had not succeeded in collecting.[1]   There is no doubt that he collected a great deal from the communes of the March in the early part of the pontificate, when his army was there to enforce payment.   But whether the later assignments took very much effect, after 1421 when the Papacy was far stronger, is extremely doubtful, and Giovanni de la Rocca, Braccio's former chancellor, asserted in 1426 that his master had never had more than four or five ducats from this source.[2]   The assertion is a striking one, when it is considered that the total assignments were in the region of 40,000 florins a year.[3]   When the Pope appointed a special commissioner of his own to collect tallage to pay a mercenary, as he did when he appointed Stefano de Branchiis of Gubbio to collect the subsidies of the Patrimony to pay to Tartaglia, the result was far more impressive; this commissioner collected 11,820 florins in two years.[4]

This raises the further question, how far the provincial Treasurers succeeded in collecting the tallage due.   It is as hard a question to answer as all questions are which impose modern arithmetic on medieval accountancy.   But it seems, even allowing for concealed assignments and for payments of tallage by the *signori* direct into the Apostolic Chamber,[5] that only in exceptional circumstances was even a third of the amount due actually collected.[6]   The total income from all sources of the Chamber of the March was in most years between eleven and thirteen thousand florins.[7]   Yet the amount due annually from tallage alone (which, admittedly, was the main income of the Chamber) was between thirty and forty thousand florins.   There was in all provinces frequent action to recover arrears of tallage.[8]

---

[1] Reg. Vat. 355, fol. 43, the Treasurer of the March is told to collect all the tallage which had been assigned to Braccio, and which he had not succeeded in collecting, 21 July 1424.

[2] Div. Cam. 3, fol. 176v. 'Die VIIII Januarii [1426] Ser Johannes de la Roccha olim cancellarius quondam Brachii de Montone, constitutim im presencia dominorum locumtenentis et thesaurarii predictorum, et interrogatus per ipsum dominum thesaurarium, se ipse tempore quo exigebat pecunias tallearum Marchie pro domino Brachio, habuit capita solidorum a solventibus aliquot, dixit quod de exactis per eum numquid habuit ultra ducatos quatuor auri.   Et si plures reperirentur autem vult restituire duplicem.   Et insuper dixit quod forsan Andreas Prativinus qui exegit de dictis pecuniis (sic) habuit usque quatuor vel quinque ducatos de dictis pecuniis.' He did, however, admit to receiving 1,600 florins from Malatesta of Pesaro, by reason of the *census* of his vicariate which had been assigned to Braccio.

[3] See p. 116 above.

[4] Arch. Cam. pt. i, Tes. Prov., Patrimonio, B. 1, vol. 1a, fol. 64v.

[5] Rodolfo Varano, after making various compositions with the Apostolic Chamber for his tallage (Reg. Vat. 349, fol. 212v; Reg. Vat. 354, fol. 92), paid at least 400 florins of the 3,500 he owed, direct into the Apostolic Chamber, IE 379, fol. 78, 25 April 1422.

[6] Cf. D. P. Waley, 'An Account-Book of the Patrimony of St. Peter in Tuscany, 1304–1306', *JEccH*, vi (1955), 19–20.

[7] Cf. Fumi, *Le Marche*, iv (1904), passim.   One of the totals is misprinted, and 31,897 on p. 167 should be read as 13,897.

[8] In 1425 the tallage of the Duchy of Spoleto is said not to have been paid since 1419, Div. Cam. 9, fol. 21v.   The Governor is therefore told to collect the arrears, the 'residuo tallearum' which figures in the accounts of all the provincial treasurers.

§ 3. The *regalia beati Petri*, the older taxes which the Papacy had inherited in the March from the Imperial administration in the twelfth century, were by this period shrunk to amounts little more than negligible. The hearth tax in particular, the 'fumantaria' of Romagna and the March, or 'focaticum' of Campania and Maritima and the Patrimony, had shrunk from a major tax to a very minor impost indeed.[1] Only in the Roman district and in Campania and Maritima did the hearth tax continue to have any importance. The area subject to the commune of Rome paid this tax to two commissioners appointed by the Chamberlain of the City 'pro sale et focatico', together with a group of other small taxes and the salt tax.[2] In Campania and Maritima there was a hearth tax of one *bolognino* from each hearth, which in theory served to pay the salary of the Rector.[3] In the Patrimony of St. Peter in Tuscia there was also a special levy for the salary of the Rector, made at the rate of one florin for every hundred paid by a commune as subsidy.[4] The communes also continued to make yearly gifts (*exennia*) to the Rector, as they had done in the fourteenth century.[5]

How far the *fumantaria* had sunk in amount, can be seen from the complaint of a certain Gabriele de Lambardis that the amount of this tax in Imola which had been granted to him in a half share was negligible and not worth the cost of collecting.[6] The 'census' and 'affictus' payable still in the March of Ancona and the Patrimony of St. Peter represented a complex of demanial and regalian rights which had been transformed during the thirteenth century into fixed annual taxes.[7] The amounts of these taxes had not changed a great deal since the compilation of the *Liber Censuum*, and they were by fifteenth-century values small, a matter of a few florins even for towns of a considerable size.[8] The two taxes were quite separate one from the other, although they are usually referred to together.[9] They were payable by the holders of vicariates, as were the *focaticum* and *fumantaria*. But this type of *census* must be clearly distinguished from the *census* payable by the holder of a temporal vicariate, which was a payment of a quite different nature.

The only other direct tax was the subsidy of the Jews, an annual tax which was

---

[1] Calisse, *ASR*, xv (1892), 30–31; Anzilotti, ibid., xlii (1919), 352–3.   [2] See pp. 145–6 below.

[3] See p. 111 above. The tax was still in force in 1429, when Castro, in the diocese of Veroli, was exempted from it, Reg. Vat. 356, fol. 31v.

[4] Arch. Cam. pt. i, Tes. Prov., Patrimonio, B. 1, vol. 1, fol. 34, 'Pecunie solute per comunitates pro provisione rectoris, ad rationem unius floreni pro quolibet centinario florenorum subsidii impositi dictis comunitatibus'.

[5] Macerata, Riformazioni, vol. 13, fol. 215.

[6] Reg. Vat. 354, fol. 84, the tax was therefore granted him in its entirety (30 April 1422). The original grant to him in Theiner, iii, no. 159, p. 231, and Div. Cam. 4, fol. 192, where the Bishop of Imola is told to help in collecting the tax. Cf. Reg. Vat. 348, fol. 104, where 50 florins a year are assigned from the *fumantarie* of Faenza and Romagna; Reg. Vat. 353, where Giovanni de Orlandis of Genazzano is granted 200 florins a year, assigned on the same source. The same man was assigned 100 florins a year, secured on the 'census redditi affitti et fumantarie' of the March of Ancona, Reg. Vat. 352, fol. 52. It is much to be doubted if the money assigned in Romagna was ever collected.

[7] Calisse, *ASR*, xv (1892), 24–26.

[8] Ancona paid no *census* and 36 duc. 12 sol. in *affictus*; San Severino paid 77 duc. 12 sol. in *census* and 22 duc. 24 sol. in *affictus* (Arm. 33, vol. 11, fol. 7).

[9] The number of towns in the March which paid *census* was fairly small, but practically all paid *affictus* (ibid.).

imposed on the considerable colonies of Jews resident in the March and the Patrimony, colonies protected both by the Papacy and the larger communes. A particularly large group was attracted by the maritime trade of Ancona.[1]

In every province the proceeds of justice in the *curia generalis* were an important source of income, and particularly the proceeds of criminal justice. From time to time orders would be given from Rome for a general beating-up of unexecuted sentences, so that the condemned persons would make compositions with the provincial Treasurer. Such a systematic search for compositions was made not only for offences tried in the *curia rectoris*,[2] but also for offences tried in the courts of the communal *podestà*. Papal commissioners were appointed to go round the communes and make such compositions, in concert with the Chancellor of the commune concerned.[3] Not only individuals but communes were subject to punitive fines, and Norcia in particular was subject to an immense fine for its aggression against Arquata.[4] Smaller in amount, but more regular in payment, were the *capita solidorum*, the taxes paid by litigants before the provincial court, in theory to contribute to the salary of the judges.[5] A related source of revenue was that from the confiscation of the goods of rebels.[6] It was not the policy of the Apostolic Chamber to accumulate property, and orders were usually given to sell confiscated property at the best price obtainable.[7] The rights of third parties were on some occasions respected in such transactions; when the goods said to have been seized by Raynaldo Alfani, the erstwhile tyrant of Rieti, were returned to their original owners, third parties who had purchased such goods from Alfani were compensated with money from the sale of the property of rebels.[8]

§ 4. The supervision and taxing of pasture, the *dogana pecudum*, was extremely important to the revenues of Rome and of the Patrimony of St. Peter. One

[1] Cf. Ancona, Atti Consigliari, vol. 31, fol. 33v, a proclamation that no one 'presuma de fare alcuna iniuria o villania o dispiacere o dire alcuna parola sirza o obbrobriosa contra alcuno de' dicti Judey' (3 June 1427).

[2] *Constitutiones Egidiane*, lib. i, c. 11.

[3] Angelo of Todi, notary of the Apostolic Chamber, was appointed to review and investigate all sentences passed by 'potestates et officiales' in the county of Perugia, Todi and the Duchy of Spoleto (Div. Cam. 13, fols. 30v, 31v, 9 February 1430). A similar commission was given to Ser Baldinotto of Sarzana to act in the March of Ancona, the Presidency of Farfa and Massa Trabaria. The latter was also to obtain information about the moveable and immoveable goods belonging to the Apostolic Chamber (Div. Cam. 13, fol. 107, 5 September 1430). Ser Baldinotto was allotted the same duties in Orvieto, Narni, Terni and Rieti, Div. Cam. 13, fol. 77.

[4] See p. 97 above, n. 6, and cf. IE 389, fol. 7.

[5] *Constitutiones Egidiane*, lib. ii, c. 13. 'Capita solidorum' had a variety of meanings. It could mean any sort of payment, as a generic term. It could also mean a second kind of tax, a sort of percentage charge on all sums paid to the provincial Treasurer. In the latter sense, see, for the Patrimony of St. Peter in Tuscia, Anzilotti, *ASR*, xlii (1919), 362–3, and for the March of Ancona, doc. 6 below.

[6] *Constitutiones Egidiane*, lib. iv, passim. Such confiscations were frequent. In 1420 the Bishop of Montefiascone was ordered to arrest rebels from Bologna and confiscate their goods, Div. Cam. 6, fol. 140v. Similar orders referring to a rebel in Offida in 1430, Div. Cam. 13, fol. 119v.

[7] Div. Cam. 8, fol. 184, on account of the confiscation of goods of rebels in Stagino, the castellan of Spoleto is to sell the goods at the best possible price, and either to transmit the money to the Chamber or to employ it in the execution of his office, 21 June 1424.

[8] Div. Cam. 9, fol. 241v.

doganerius was appointed for the Patrimony, and another for Rome, the latter having jurisdiction also in the Roman District and in Campania and Maritima.[1]   The two organisations were of quite different types; the *doganerius* of the Patrimony was a papal official pure and simple, sometimes a cameral clerk, appointed at the Pope's good pleasure, held to render the accounts of his office, and to turn over all the monies he collected to the Apostolic Chamber.[2]   The *doganerius* of Rome, on the other hand, was a private person who bought the *dogana* for a term of months from the Chamber of the City and administered it for his own benefit—in other words, it was put out to farm.[3]   Each *dogana* probably had its own statutes, but only a later and very mutilated abstract of those of the *dogana* of Rome still exists.[4]

The income of the *dogana* from cattle and sheep came from two sources, one fiscal, one of a more patrimonial kind.   First, all beasts which were brought down from the hills in the autumn to winter in the plains had to be registered by their owner, marked and checked, and a payment, known as the 'fida', had to be made for them to the *doganerius* at a fixed rate per head.   Second, once they entered the plains, the beasts needed pasture, and the Apostolic Chamber had a monopoly in granting such pasture to the owners of the animals, known as the 'herbaticum', in return for a payment made for each head of cattle.

This system applied to all cattle, sheep and goats; they were known according

---

[1] C. de Cupis, *Delle vicende dell'agricoltura e della pastorizia nell'Agro Romano*, 86; Anzilotti, *ASR*, xlii (1919), 365 f.; *Statuti della città di Roma* (ed. Re), 274–81.

[2] Reg. Vat. 350, fol. 37, appointment of Bartolomeo Onofrii of Perugia.   'te officialem generalem doane sive pascuorum provincie nostre patrimonii beati Petri in Tuscia, cum potestate arbitrio familiaribus ac salario per nos declarando, honoribus et oneribus consuetis, usque ad beneplacitum nostrum, auctoritate presentium facimus constituimus et etiam deputamus.   Tibi nichilominus quascumque personas cuiuscumque status preeminentie vel condicionis extiterint, cum eorum animalibus grossis et minutis pascendis in ipsis pascuis ad illa venire volentes, nostre [et] Romane ecclesie eiusdem camere nominibus affidandi et assecurandi, ipsisque personis . . . ad dicta pascua veniendi et per quecunque civitates terras et loca prefate ecclesie transeundi ibique standi et ad propria redeundi pro earum beneplacito voluntatis salvum liberumque conductum et plene securitatis licentiam in opportuna forma per annum dumtaxat duraturum concedendi, et cum eisdem personis . . . sub illis pactis modis et condicionibus de quibus discrecioni tue videbitur conveniendi componendi et concordandi, et super hiis quecumque conventiones et pacta tractandi firmandi et concludendi occasione pascuum predictorum iuxta consuetudinem antiquam, ipsisque personis eodem nomine pollicendi et promittendi quod ex aliqua causa non convenientur coram aliquo potestate . . . plenam et liberam potestatem harum serie concedentes . . .'   Other appointments of *doganerii* are in Reg. Vat. 350, fol. 137 (Giovanni of Rieti, in 1425); ibid. fol. 309 (Bartolomeo Dellante of Pisa, 1427); Reg. Vat. 351, fol. 59v (Nucio della Fonte of Aquila, 1428); ibid. fol. 119 (Bartolomeo Onofrii de Cini, again, 1429); Reg. Vat. 355, fol. 279v (Bartolomeo Onofrii of Perugia, 1426).   See also Theiner, iii, no. 265, p. 315.   The quittance to Bartolomeo Onofrii for his first year's administration of the *dogana* is in Reg. Vat. 355, fol. 257.   In the year beginning 24 August 1424 he received 5,620 flor. 3 bonon. and spent 5,840 flor. 29 bonen.   That he should have such a separate quittance suggests that he sent his accounts straight to the Chamber, and did not give them to the provincial Treasurer.

[3] Div. Cam. 7, fol. 167.   The conservators of the Chamber of the City are told to sell the 'gabellam dohane pecudum et aliorum animalium ad dictam dohanam pertinentium, et gabellam carnium casei et lane urbis' to Antonio Colonna, for one year, for the price of 10,500 florins current in the City, 15 March 1423.   This *dogana*, of sheep, meat, milk, cheese and wool was known as 'lo gruosso', Arch. Cam. pt. i, Mandati Camerali, no. 825, fol. 141v, no. 826, fol. 3.   Cf. Malatesta, *Statuti delle Gabelle di Roma*, doc. 33, pp. 152–3.

[4] An eighteenth-century abstract of the statutes of the *dogana* under Nicholas V, now Cod. Vat. lat. 8886, printed by de Cupis, 549 f.

to their size as *bestie grosse* or *minute*. When they came down from the hills, especially if this were from the Abruzzi, they often had safe conducts from the Pope or Vice-Chamberlain,[1] or from the *doganerius*, who was sometimes given special instructions to afford such safe conducts.[2] Before their arrival the owner was held to notify their number and kind to the *doganerius*, and also to mark them on the ear and on the body with a personal mark which was notified at the same time.[3] They were then checked on their arrival by the *numeratores*, who in the case of Rome are said in the Statutes of the City to be officials of the City, elected at the same time and by the same methods as the other officials,[4] though there is reason to believe that by the fifteenth century they were merely nominees of the *doganerius*.[5] The checking points for the beasts were at Tivoli, at Sant'Antimo, near Aversa, in the Kingdom of Naples, and at the bridges of Rome;[6] evidently a large part of the beasts dealt with by the Roman *dogana* was pastured inside the walls. No similar information is available for the *dogana* of the Patrimony; although the procedure was probably very similar, it may have been much more difficult to deal with the numbering and registering of the beasts, since there was no central point to pasture them comparable to Rome, and they might arrive from any point over a very wide frontier. It seems probable that the operation of the *dogana* of the Patrimony was far less automatic than that of Rome; the faculties given to the *doganerius* of the Patrimony included authority to make agreements with the owners of beasts, and it may be that each large-scale movement of animals was the occasion for a separate contract. At Rome both registration of the beasts and payment for them had to be carried out in the Chamber of the City. There was one rate of payment per hundred beasts for Romans and inhabitants of the District, that is to say, those who paid the 'sal et focaticum', and another for 'forenses'.[7] The authority of the *doganerius* of Rome extended also to the whole province of Campania and Maritima; the beasts which came to pasture there came not only from the Papal State, but also in very large numbers from the Kingdom of Naples—hence the necessity for a checking point at Sant'Antimo. The *doganerius* had a notary and assistants, the 'superstites' and 'numeratores', who have been described above.[8] He had judicial power in civil and criminal cases which concerned the *dogana*.[9]

When the beasts entering the *dogana* had paid the *fida* they needed pasture for the winter, and this pasture was granted them by the *doganerius* in return for a payment known as the 'herbaticum' or 'pascuum'. In this it is necessary to dis-

---

[1] Div. Cam. 6, fol. 213v, safeconduct for the lords of Celano and some citizens of Aquila, Celano and Sulmona to lead their beasts into the Roman District; ibid. fol. 240, safeconduct for Ancio della Fonte of Aquila to lead his beasts to pasture on the lands of Antonio Colonna in the Roman District. Div. Cam. 7, fol. 90v, safeconduct for Carlo Orsini to take 2,000 sheep and 300 other beasts to pasture from Apulia and the Kingdom of Naples (15 September 1422), followed by a long string of safeconducts issued to others for the same purpose.

[2] Reg. Vat. 354, fol. 101v.

[3] S. Malatesta, *Statuti delle Gabelle di Roma*, prints one of these registrations, doc. 20, p. 144.

[4] *Statuti della città di Roma*, 277–8.

[5] Cf. de Cupis, 555.

[6] *Statuti della città di Roma*, loc. cit.

[7] *Statuti della città di Roma*, 274–5.

[8] De Cupis, 549 f.

[9] Ibid.

tinguish between the *herbaticum* which was owed to the commune, that which was owed to private persons or to the Apostolic Chamber on account of their demesne lands, and that which was owed to the *doganerius*. The earlier history of the *herbaticum* is already a confusing one. It derived from the ancient rights of common for their beasts which all the inhabitants of the commune had possessed. The early Middle Ages had seen two rights of common; one possessed by the inhabitants of the commune, and the other treated as a *regalia* by the Prince. The second was frequently granted to barons or ecclesiastics, and a situation arose in which private and communal rights of pasture existed at the same time, and sometimes over the same land.[1] In the later Middle Ages a further complicating factor arose, when the feudatories began to usurp the common rights of pasture enjoyed by the inhabitants of the communes, and to treat them as seignorial rights.[2] At the same time the pastures became, from a simple privilege of pasture, a source of income for the communes no less than for the feudatories. The communes would sell the 'pascua' to the highest bidder, and he would then exact the *herbaticum* which was charged to those who came from outside the commune to use the pastures.[3] But the inhabitants of the commune, even as late as the seventeenth century, continued to have the right to use the pastures without charge.[4] To this already complicated situation, in the fourteenth and fifteenth centuries the growing powers of the Papacy brought a fresh group of interests to be conciliated, those of the *dogana pascui*. The main concern of the Apostolic Chamber was to see that the *doganerius* had enough pasture to rent for all the beasts which paid the *fida*. The demesne lands of the Apostolic Chamber were not enough for this purpose, and the *doganerius* had to rent other rights of pasture both from feudatories and from communes. Particularly important under Martin V were the pastures of Abbazia de Ponzano, for which the Apostolic Chamber paid large sums every year to the Conti and the Prefect of Vico.[5] Besides this, the Apostolic Chamber would encroach on the former rights of the communes, and treat the communal pastures as its own, as appears to have happened in the case of Ceprano.[6] This increasing pressure of the central power was also reflected in the way in which, during the fifteenth century, communes tended to have their communal rights of pasture confirmed as privileges by the Holy See. After the death of Tartaglia di Lavello, Toscanella tried to obtain such a confirmation from the

---

[1] C. Calisse, *Gli Usi civici nella Provincia di Roma* (1906), 10 f.; idem, in *ASR*, xv (1892), 23; A. Doren, *Italienische Wirtschaftsgeschichte* (1934), 236–8.

[2] Calisse, *Gli Usi civici*, 33 f. An example is the success of the Orsini, by 1311, in exacting the *herbaticum* from the commune of Saccomuro (V. Federici et al., *Statuti della Provincia Romana* [*Fonti per la Storia d'Italia*, 1930], 357–63).

[3] Calisse, *Gli Usi civici*, 72.

[4] Giovanni Battista Cardinal de Luca, *Theatrum veritatis et iustitiae* (Rome, 1669–77), iv, De Serv., disc. 38–43.

[5] In 1426 the Apostolic Chamber paid Alto Conti 1,000 florins for the use of these pastures, Div. Cam. 3, fol. 189. Cf. IE 383, fols. 10v, 46v. The pastures of Abbazia de Ponzano were a source of considerable profit to the Papacy as early as 1304; cf. Baumgarten, *Untersuchungen und Urkunden über die Camera Collegii Cardinalium*, no. 247, p. 162.

[6] Theiner, iii, no. 207, p. 274. The commune is granted for four years the right to half the proceeds of the 'pascuis et herbaticis' belonging to the Apostolic Chamber there.

I

Pope for its rights of pasture in S. Sabino.[1] But this did not exhaust the pastures round Toscanella; there were others, and very extensive ones, which had belonged to Tartaglia as Count of Toscanella,[2] and which after his execution as a rebel were annexed to the Holy See and used by the *doganerius*.[3] Under Eugenius IV similar apostolic confirmations of communal rights of pasture were sought by Vetralla, Corneto and Nepi.[4]

In the Patrimony of St. Peter the *doganerius* also was responsible for the system of restrictions on the movement of grain. The export of grain was forbidden, not only between one province and another, but even between one city and another in the same province. Two protective policies were applied at the same time, those of the communal interests which wished, as they always had done, to conserve all the food supplies of the city, and those of the papal officials, who wished to apply a similar protective policy to the province as a whole.[5] The Rector of the province, or the Vice-Chamberlain, or the Pope, would on occasion, and usually for a fee, grant licences of exemption for the export of grain (*tracta grani*). Such licences were granted to merchants,[6] to persons with influence at the papal court,[7] to *signori*,[8]

---

[1] S. Campanarii, *Tuscania e i suoi monumenti*, ii (1856), 239, 'item quod attento quod tenimentum S. Sabini est sub iurisdictione et territorio civitatis Tuscan. quod libere cives et habitatores Tuscanen. possint d. tenimento uti et frui, et in ipso tenimento pascuari facere et tenere eorum bestias sine contradictione alicuius', notwithstanding the concessions made by the Apostolic See or others to the church of St. Margaret in Montefiascone.

[2] See the grant of the county of Toscanella to Tartaglia, Theiner, iii, no. 206, p. 274, which expressly mentions the pasture.

[3] Div. Cam. 7, fol. 22, 7 April 1422. Nicolò and Cambio de' Medici, having lent the Apostolic Chamber 700 florins, are to be repayed out of the proceeds of the 'pascuis, herbis etc.' in the Patrimony, which used to belong to the dead Tartaglia, and now belong to the Apostolic Chamber. An earlier assignment of the same revenues is in Reg. Vat. 353, fol. 337, to Aldigheri Francesco de Biliottis of Florence, 26 February 1422.

[4] Theiner, iii, nos. 256, 259, 260, pp. 307, 310, 311. The bull to Corneto relates how in Martin V's time the *doganerius* had usurped the rights of the commune over the pasture of 'Rocca Jorii'. The commune's rights there are now acknowledged, but it is held to sell the pasture rights to the *doganerius* for a just price. Cf. however, Arch. Cam. pt. i, Tes. Prov., Patrimonio, B. 1, vol. 2, fol. 51v, a payment made on 11 November 1424 to the commune of Corneto, 'pro tenuta Rocche Jorii empte a dicta communitate pro camera apostolica'.

[5] See *Constitutiones Egidiane*, lib. ii, c. 30; see also, in general, U. Benigni, *Die Getreide Politik der Päpste* (Berlin, n.d.), which is, however, rather sketchy for this early period.

[6] For the form of these licences see Malatesta, *Statuti delle Gabelle di Roma*, doc. 16, p. 142. Gherardo of Pisa paid 425 florins to the Chamber on 27 November 1421, 'quos solvit pro tracta duorum millium salmarum frumenti de Marchia Anconitana extrahendi', IE 379, fol. 59v. On 13 February 1422 Leonardo de Scallionibus of Piacenza paid 100 florins 'pro solutione gabelle quingentarum grani per eum extractarum de Marchia Anconitana', ibid., fol. 70v. Cf. Reg. Vat. 353, fol. 260, an earlier licence for Leonardo of Piacenza to buy 1,200 loads of grain in the March, 3 October 1421.

[7] Jacopo de Aspicino of Piombino, relative of the Pope, is licensed to take 100 *modii* of grain to Piombino, Div. Cam. 6, fol. 35v, addressed to the priors of Corneto and the Treasurer of the Patrimony, 1 March 1420. Orlando de Orlandis of Genazzano (another of the Pope's personal suite) was licensed to import 30 *rubbra* of grain from Campania and Maritima, ibid. fol. 240.

[8] Berardo Varano of Camerino was on 28 December 1421 licensed to buy 1,500 loads of grain from any city of the March of Ancona, transporting it without further payment of gabelle, and selling it as he wished, Reg. Vat. 353, fol. 291v. He paid the Apostolic Chamber 275 florins for this licence, IE 379, fol. 65v, 31 December 1421. Pandolfo Malatesta was in the same manner licensed to buy 2,000 loads of grain in the March, Reg. Vat. 353, fol. 293, 18 December 1421.

to cities threatened with famine.[1] That these licences could clash with local protective policies appears in the refusal of the priors of S. Elpidio sul Mare to allow the export of corn from the town by a merchant of Piacenza, who had obtained a papal licence. The Vice-Chamberlain did not attempt to enforce the licence, but merely ordered the repayment of the money paid for the corn, with appropriate interest.[2] Nor were licences to export large amounts of corn granted lightly; when the floods of one year threatened Bologna with famine, the Legate had to obtain from the Pope a licence to import a stated amount of corn from the March of Ancona.[3]

Rome presented a special problem, just as it had done since classical times. One of the first actions of Martin V when he knew he was to return to Rome in 1420 was to ensure an adequate supply of corn for the city, by arranging to import from Sabina and the March of Ancona, from the Kingdom of Naples and from Sicily.[4] He also partly financed these purchases from a loan made for the purpose by the College of Cardinals. He appointed a special commissioner to buy corn for Rome in the March, and the later appointment of an official in the Patrimony 'pro recollecta grani' was probably made for the same purpose.[5] Later in the fifteenth century the *doganerius pascui* of the Patrimony had the duty of buying corn for the City,[6] and it is probable that this was no innovation. But as the registers of the *dogana pascui* under Martin V have not survived, no certain information can be had. In the Patrimony the *doganerius* also collected the payments of grain made in kind by the *terratici*, the tenants of the few remaining demesne lands of the Papacy.[7] Neither this duty, nor the control of the Annona, appear to have fallen to the *doganerius pascui* of Rome. It was the Conservators of the Chamber of the City and the *grascieri*, and not the *doganerius*, who were usually concerned in buying corn for the City.[8]

[1] On account of the damage they have suffered from war, Suriano, Orte and Aquapendente are licensed to buy grain anywhere in the Patrimony, Reg. Vat. 353, fols. 18, 25v, 24 September and 7 October 1420. A similar licence for Viterbo, Div. Cam. 6, fol. 223, 20 October 1420.

[2] Div. Cam. 7, fol. 41v, 14 May 1422. The merchant is Leonardo de Scallionibus of Piacenza, and the licence probably the same as that referred to above.

[3] Reg. Vat. 350, fols. 169, 169v, 170. The licence was for 10,000 loads (*sarcine*) of grain (24 September 1425).

[4] The merchants concerned in supplying the corn to the Chamber were Rodolfo Peruzzi (Div. Cam. 6, fol. 201v) and Nicolò and Cambio de' Medici (Div. Cam. 7, fol. 281v), all of Florence, and Bartolomeo of Pisa (Div. Cam. 6, fol. 243). The corn was to be delivered at Civitavecchia, and in the transaction with the Medici was to be imported from Sicily. In the event none of the 2,000 loads of Sicilian corn reached Rome. The fleet carrying it was broken up, one galley being captured by the Genovese, and the other three putting into Naples and selling the corn there. Many officials were appointed to buy corn for the Chamber: Marino Bishop of Recanati and Macerata, the Treasurer of the March (Reg. Vat. 353, fol. 48, 3 November 1420), and Ludovico Mazzancoli, special commissioner 'pro frumento et aliis victualibus pro nobis ac urbe et Romana curia emendis'. The latter was Bishop of Terni. He was told to raise a loan of 400 florins in the region of Terni, Narni and Amelia to buy grain, and Nicolò Trinci of Foligno was asked to lend him a certain quantity of grain (Reg. Vat. 353, fols. 59v, 60, 18 and 19 November 1420).

[5] Stefano de Branchiis of Gubbio was appointed commissioner 'pro fienda recollecta grani' on 9 July 1422, Reg. Vat. 354, fol. 97v. He also had duties connected with the *dogana* of the Patrimony, fol. 101v.

[6] Anzilotti, *ASR*, xlii (1919), 377.   [7] Ibid. 365 f.

[8] Malatesta, *Statuti delle Gabelle di Roma*, doc. 14, p. 140. Cf. IE 379, fol. 43 (June 1421), 'A grasceriis urbis deputatis super facto grani conducti pro fulcimento ipsius urbis et venditi per eos, pro parte mille florenorum quos iidem grascerii eidem domino thesaurario dare tenebantur, florenos 750'.

IV. *The Administration of Justice*

§ 1. The court of the Rector of a province enjoyed civil and criminal jurisdiction of the fullest kind. It was called by the canonists 'ordinary', that is to say it extended to all manner of cases and was not merely a 'delegated' jurisdiction to hear one or two particular cases.[1] The Rector was invested with 'plena potestas' and 'plena jurisdictio', the full powers residing in the Prince;[2] he had 'merum imperium', the fullest powers of jurisdiction.[3]

The Rector's court had ordinary jurisdiction (not in the sense used above, but in the sense of cases of first instance as opposed to cases of appeal) where the commune concerned had failed to obtain the privilege of 'merum imperium', or where the commune and the Rector had concurrent jurisdiction under the arrangement known as 'preventio', or where the commune responsible had failed to do justice. Although the papal lawyers had always refused to admit that any commune could enjoy 'merum et mixtum imperium' except by Apostolic privilege,[4] such privilege had by the time of Albornoz been granted to the vast majority of the major communes.[5] But the growing *signoria* of the Church was making the old quarrels about jurisdiction obsolete. Where the Church appointed the *podestà* of a commune, this officer was, although bound by communal statutes, a papal official. And since the *podestà* was by Martin V's time appointed by the Pope in all save a handful of the communes,[6] the earlier quarrels about the possession of 'merum et mixtum im-

---

[1] G. Durandus, *Speculum Iuris* (Venice, 1566), pt. i, de iurisdictione omnium iudicum', 'Ordinaria est, quae a Papa, vel Imperatore, vel a lege, vel ab universitate conceditur . . . Delegata est, quae a principe demandatur specialiter ad unam, vel plures causas'.

[2] Theiner, iii, no. 177, p. 251.

[3] Ibid. and Durandus, p. 203, 'est autem merum imperium quedam summa potestas, per quam ea, quae sunt iurisdictionis maxima explicantur'.

[4] Durandus, loc. cit. and cf. Baldus (cited in the edition of Durandus), 'potestates terrarum non habent merum imperium de iure communi; sed praeses provinciae; sed de consuetudine et usurpatione sic'. Durandus, who was at one time Auditor of the Apostolic Palace and at another the Rector of a papal province, gives a more incisively contrary opinion, 'Ergo potestates civitatum nostri temporis mutilantes membra, et capita amputantes, usurpant sibi merum imperium . . .' Cf. F. Ercole, *Dal Comune al Principato*, 256–264; G. Ermini, *La libertà comunale nello Stato della Chiesa*, ii, 83 f. Two interesting processes brought by the Church against communes claiming the right of *merum et mixtum imperium* are those against Fabriano (W. Hagemann, 'Fabriano im Kampf zwischen Papsttum und Kaisertum bis 1272', *QF*, xxxi, 1941, doc. 8) and Gualdo Tadino (Collectorie 402, 403, 419, resumed in R. Guerrieri, *Storia civile ed ecclesiastica del comune di Gualdo Tadino*, 1933, 96–98). See also Theiner, i, no. 528, p. 354.

[5] G. Ermini, loc. cit.

[6] The following list of communes in which the *podestà* was appointed from Rome is very far from complete, nor does it include those communes in which the *podestà* was appointed by the Rector of the province : Amelia (Reg. Vat. 349, fol. 196v); Ascoli Piceno (Reg. Vat. 350, fol. 285); Assisi (ibid. fol. 148); Bagnorea (Div. Cam. 6, fol. 213); Bologna (Reg. Vat. 348, fol. 146); Calvi nel Lazio (Reg. Vat. 349, fol. 52); Calvi nell'Umbria ('Carbium', Reg. Vat. 349, fol. 145); Castro (ibid. fol. 141); Castrum Griptarum, near Montefiascone (Div. Cam. 6, fol. 212); Città della Pieve (Reg. Vat. 350, fol. 75); Corneto (Reg. Vat. 348, fol. 36v); Forlì (Reg. Vat. 350, fol. 264); Terra Gradularum, in the diocese of Montefiascone (Div. Cam. 6, fol. 213v); Iesi (Reg. Vat. 350, fol. 282v); Imola (ibid. fol. 274); Magliano (Guiraud, *L'Etat Pontifical*, 95); Montefalco (Reg. Vat. 350, fol. 178); Montefiascone (Reg. Vat. 349, fol. 31v); Narni (Reg. Vat. 349, fol. 142v); Norcia (Reg. Vat. 350, fol. 76); Offida (ibid. fol. 286); Orte (Reg. Vat. 349, fol. 33v); Orvieto (G. Pardi, 'Serie dei supremi magistrati e reggitori di Orvieto',

perium' by the communes are by this period almost meaningless. However, in criminal cases the Rector's court continued, under the *Constitutiones Egidiane*, to have certain rights which were meant to make certain that justice was done. Communes were bound to report all criminal cases (*maleficia*) within a month of their occurrence to the judge of criminal cases of the province.[1] If by this time no action had been taken by the commune, the case was dealt with in the court of the Rector.[2] This provision was not a dead letter, and Macerata was not allowed to plead its privilege of 'merum et mixtum imperium' as a sufficient reason for refusing to comply.[3]

'Preventio' was the principle that a case be terminated in whichever court it was first begun, either the communal court or that of the Rector.[4] Where an action was begun in both courts on the same day, the Rector's court had precedence.[5] The circumstances in which *preventio* applied are by no means clear. In the fourteenth century the Rector's court in the Patrimony enjoyed the right of *preventio* only in certain towns where he possessed it by agreement or custom.[6] The *Constitutiones Egidiane* give no definite ruling on the matter, but speak as though *preventio* were the rule wherever a commune had ordinary jurisdiction,[7] and, certainly, at a much earlier period the Popes had attempted to enforce this.[8] There is, on the other hand,

---

BSU, i, 1895, 409); Otricoli (Reg. Vat. 349, fol. 249); Perugia (Reg. Vat. 350, fol. 57v); Rieti (ibid. fol. 103); Rocca Contrata (Reg. Vat. 350, fol. 308v); San Gemini (Reg. Vat. 349, fol. 20v); S. Giovanni in Persiceto (ibid. fol. 80v); Spoleto (Reg. Vat. 350, fol. 273v); Sutri (Reg. Vat. 349, fol. 141); Sanseverino (Reg. Vat. 350, fol. 273); Terni (Reg. Vat. 349, fol. 20); Todi (Reg. Vat. 350, fol. 49); Toscanella (ibid. fol. 233v); Trevi (ibid. fol. 182v); Viterbo (Reg. Vat. 348, fol. 205); all the towns taken from the Malatesta in 1430, including Senigaglia (which was in the same year granted to the Malatesta of Pesaro) and Osimo (Div. Cam. 13, fol. 107). It is curious that there are no towns in Campania or Maritima in this list. It is most unlikely that the *podestà* in this province were not appointed by either the Pope or the Rector (cf. Falco, *ASR*, xlix [1926], 282), and it is therefore to be supposed that they were appointed by the latter. The Pope or the Rector therefore appointed the *podestà* in all the major towns, save for Ancona, Macerata, Recanati and the towns granted in vicariate.

[1] Lib. iii, c. 4, corrected by *Const. adjecte*, c. 4 (p. 239 of Sella's edition).

[2] Cf. Ermini, *La libertà comunale*, ii, 62 f.

[3] Macerata, Riformanze, vol. 14, fol. 139v (February 1428), 'Item super continentia litterarum patentium presentarum communi dicte civitatis pro parte novi iudicis causarum appelationum criminalium curie generalis, mandantes deberet mitti scindicum ad referendum malificia in curia generali, quem syndicum communis dicte civitatis propter privilegium meri et misti imperii quod habet a summo pontifice mittere non consuevit nec tenetur.' Macerata's claim of privilege against this claim of the *curia generalis* was always being attacked (e.g. in 1406, Compagnoni, *La Reggia Picena*, 277; and again in 1424, see p. 106 above) but usually the Rector's court admitted it. On this occasion the commune was not so successful, and later in 1428 it had to send syndics as demanded (Riformanze, vol. 14, fol. 167).

[4] See the definition in Boniface VIII's concession to Velletri, printed by G. Falco, 'Il comune di Velletri nel medio evo', *ASR*, xxxvi (1913), doc. 5, p. 457, and also Falco's comments in *ASR*, xlviii (1925), 82–3, n.

[5] *Constitutiones Egidiane*, lib. iv, c. 6.

[6] M. P. Fabre, 'Un registre caméral du Cardinal Albornoz', *Mélanges*, vii (1887), 135–6 et passim.

[7] E.g. in lib. iii, c. 4.

[8] Theiner, i, no. 482, p. 312, where, having conceded certain communes the right of ordinary jurisdiction, Nicholas IV qualifies the concession 'Per hoc autem Rectori Marchie, qui pro tempore fuerit, nolumus aliquod preiudicium generari, quin homines communis vestri seu terre vestre possint ad eum, cum sibi expedire putaverint, tam appellationis quam simplicis querimonie causa liberum habere recursum'.

no trace of the Rector's court having exercised the right of *preventio* in such communes as Ancona and Macerata, and it may, perhaps, be taken that the right was
exercised only in the lesser communes. Moreover, with the nomination of the
podestà almost everywhere in papal hands, *preventio* must have lost all its former
importance, since in any event it was a papal official who would decide the case.
There is little trace of *preventio* in the later jurisdiction of the Papal State.[1]

All the officials of the province, both those of the Rector's court and those of the
communes, were bound at the end of their term of office to account for their function
of the office (*sindicare*) in the Court of the Rector, and there to answer any allegations
which might be brought against them.[2] This was a powerful weapon of the central
power, and one which the Church did not neglect to use. Some communes, however,
escaped the rule. Macerata was brusquely ordered by the Deputy of the province
to send the *podestà* (who was freely elected by the commune) and his officials, to
account for their office in the court of the province; but the commune successfully
pleaded its privilege of exception from this law.[3] To ensure that the officials of the
curia rectoris of Campania and Maritima accounted for their office, the Pope appointed
special commissioners;[4] it was particularly important that the notaries should be
brought to book, since these powerful officials were everywhere at this period
usurping the functions of judges, and enjoying power without proper responsibility.[5]

§ 2.   The most important part of the jurisdiction of the Rector's Court was that of
appeal. Albornoz went to extraordinary lengths in his constitutions to deal with
every conceivable subterfuge by which the communes could avoid this appellate
jurisdiction.[6] That the communes were anxious to hear appeals is evident from
their statutes; few statutes of the larger communes in the State of the Church make
no provision for appeals.[7] But under Martin V only the two great communes of
Bologna and Perugia managed to secure concessions from the Holy See which
allowed them their own jurisdiction in appeal. Two appeals were allowed by the
ius commune, and the second appeal was all-important, since it closed the case.[8]
Therefore it was the second appeal which the Rector's Court principally disputed;
in 1430 Ancona was forced to comply with the directions of the judge of appeal of
the province, and to order that anything in the statutes of the city which forbade
anyone to appeal 'in secundis causis appellationum' to the court of Rome or to the

---

[1] Giovanni Battista Cardinal de Luca, *Theatrum veritatis et iustitiae*, xv, de iudiciis, disc. xvi, par. 12,
13. Cf. Luca Peto, *De iudiciaria formula Capitolini fori* (Rome, 1610), 15, who mentions *preventio*
between the court of the Auditor of the Chamber and the Capitoline court, in cases of *obligationes in
forma Camerae*.

[2] *Constitutiones Egidiane*, lib. ii, c. 22.

[3] *Riformanze*, vol. 11, fol. 268, 27 September 1418.

[4] Div. Cam. 9, fol. 18v.

[5] Cf. G. Barraclough, *Public Notaries and the Papal Curia* (1934), 16. Further, the protests against
the corruption of the notaries in the court of the Auditor of the Chamber, Mollat, *RHE*, xxxii (1936).

[6] *Constitutiones Egidiane*, lib. iv, c. 18, 22, 23, 24; cf. lib. i, c. 7.

[7] Cf. P. Sella, *Il procedimento civile nella legislazione statutaria italiana* (1927), 149–62.

[8] Sella, 162; Fournier, *Les officialités au Moyen-Age* (1880), 219–20.

court of the province of the March be cancelled.[1] The judges of the Rector's Court in the March of Ancona appear to have travelled round the province in order to hear cases, although not, so far as I can ascertain, according to a fixed circuit.[2]

Bologna was the most successful of all the communes in keeping out the papal jurisdiction in appeal. In the minute of the draft bull by which the commune was granted the administration of the city in 1419, the right to hear appeals from the city was safeguarded for the Rector and the Pope.[3] But the Bolognese succeeded in excluding this clause from the final version of the bull, which reserves to the Pope only the usual reserved pleas of heresy and forgery of Apostolic letters. This would certainly not have prevented the papal lawyers from claiming to hear appeals, since an appeal always lay to the Pope from any of his subjects, and, in fact, Martin V did recall a case from the Bolognese courts to the Rota.[4] The city protested to the Pope, and nothing further is known of the case. But it seems most unlikely that Rome had any success in drawing appeals to itself from Bologna, since the city would not have submitted without the most vigorous of protests; under Eugenius IV the city was specifically given the right to the final judgement of appeals.[5] It is scarcely to be wondered at that such a city of lawyers should claim legal autonomy; Louis Aleman's most conspicuous failure in his rule of the city was a failure to administer justice in the courts.[6] I have not been able to discover whether the papal Legate in Bologna had his own court there and an Auditor of appeals, as he had done in the latter part of the fourteenth century,[7] or whether he merely supervised the course of justice as it was laid down in the statutes. It seems very unlikely that he did not have his own court, and hear appeals in it, and the existence of a grant of powers to the Legate to try criminal cases in Bologna, and to use torture,[8] makes it almost certain that this was so.

In Perugia the situation was better defined. The capitulations by which the city submitted in 1424 laid down that citizens of the city were not to be drawn outside the city in cases of first or second instance in appeal, which amounts to a complete exemption from the jurisdiction of Rome in appeals. The Vicar or Governor of the city was to hear appeals, but the procedure in his court was to be according to the statutes of the city.[9] The city was also to have the right to elect according to the statutes a Captain [10] who, under the statutes, was the official responsible for appeals,[11] or, if this was displeasing to the Pope, then a judge of

---

[1] Ancona, Atti Consigliari, vol. 33, fol. 16, the *iudex civilium et criminalium curie generalis*, Roberto de Bartolinis of Perugia, demands that 'fiat decretum quod omnis ordo factus per istam communitatem contra libertatem ecclesiasticam anno CCCCXXIIII circa sit cassus, et banniatur per civitatem quod in secundis causis appellationum cuilibet liceat appellare et recursum habere ad curiam generalem provincie Marchie, aliquibus in contrariis non obstantibus'. This decree was duly made as demanded, and published on 20 February 1430 (ibid. fol. 17v).

[2] The 'iudices curie generalis' sat in Fermo in 1429, *Cronache della città di Fermo*, 60.

[3] Zaoli, *Libertas Bononie e Papa Martino V*, 59, n.   [4] Zaoli, 64 n.

[5] Theiner, iii, no. 266, p. 316, 7 January 1433.   [6] See p. 90 above.

[7] O. Vancini, 'Bologna della Chiesa', *AMDR*, 3rd ser., xxiv (1906), 532 f. and xxv (1907), doc. 48, p. 105.   [8] Reg. Vat. 353, fol. 285v, 1 January 1422.   [9] See p. 174 below.

[10] Fumi, *Inventario e Spoglio dei Registri della Tesoreria Apostolica di Perugia e Umbria*, xxxviii.

[11] *Statuti della città di Perugia* (ed. G. degli Azzi), 13 f.

appeals. In practice, the Legate of Perugia had a court of appeal which was extremely independent of any pressure which the commune tried to bring, and the independence of Capranica in Perugia may be contrasted with the disastrous weakness of Louis Aleman before the commune of Bologna. The Legate of Perugia certainly at one point had his own Auditor or Vicar of appeals, although when Capranica was Governor, before his appointment as Cardinal was published, higher justice appears to have been administered either by the *podestà* or by the Governor himself.

The vicariates in temporals granted to *signori* sometimes contained a specific clause safeguarding the jurisdiction of the Rector of the province, and sometimes did not, but it is much to be doubted if this clause had any effect in practice. There is no trace of an appeal being carried to the Court of the Rector or the Pope from the courts of the Apostolic vicars; whatever the strict juridical ruling may have been, the *signori* were quite strong enough, in general, to prevent any of their subjects from prosecuting such an appeal. This is true, at all events, of the fully fledged tyrants of Romagna and the March; it is possible that papal jurisdiction in appeal may have been effective in the vicariates of the Roman barons or of other lesser fry.

§ 3. The *podestà* who were appointed by the Papacy were in form only communal officials, and they were bound by the statutes of the commune to which they were appointed. But in practice they must be treated as part of the central provincial administration; the situation is typical of the way in which, without altering a line of the communal statutes, the Papacy was creating a centralised and absolute government. In 1430 Angelo of Todi, notary of the Apostolic Chamber, was appointed to investigate and review (*remittere*) all sentences and condemnations passed by the *podestà* and officials of the Duchy of Spoleto, the county of Perugia and Todi.[1] Such action could not have been taken a century earlier without causing a revolt, and it testifies that effectively the *podestà* were no longer communal but papal officials. In Perugia the *podestà* was treated as an official of the Vicar or Legate, and he was ordered to arrest or release persons, to begin or cancel processes, at the instruction of the Vicar. This was particularly important as the *podestà* was responsible for the *inquisitio*, which has passed into modern Italian law as the *istruttoria*.

Besides his normal jurisdiction, an official might be directed by the Pope or Vice-Chamberlain to hear a case, and his authority was then, according to the canonists, not 'ordinary' but 'delegated'. Thus, one plaintiff petitioned the Pope that the Treasurer of the March be told to hear his case, a civil one concerning the occupation of certain goods and dovecotes, and, the petition being granted, the Vice-Chamberlain instructed the Treasurer of the March accordingly.[2] The high cost of prosecuting a case in Rome was responsible for other delegations of cases; thus, after a case concerning the rent of a shop had been tried in Città di Castello by the judge of appeal there, a further petition was made to the Pope to review the case. But as

---

[1] Div. Cam. 13, fol. 31v.   [2] Div. Cam. 13, fol. 117.

the plaintiff proved too poor to prosecute his case in the Roman Court, the case was committed by the Vice-Chamberlain to the Governor of Città di Castello, to try the second instance of appeal.[1]   Similarly, in a lawsuit between two brothers of Viterbo, one of whom was a scriptor and abbreviator of apostolic letters, and two spinster sisters ('virgines adultas'), of the same city; the wily scriptor brought his suit before the Auditor of the Apostolic Chamber, and was about to secure a sentence against the sisters on grounds of their contumacy, when letters arrived from them declaring their poverty, and saying that they were unable to bear the expenses of prosecuting the case in Rome.   The case was therefore transferred from the Auditor to the Vice-Chamberlain, and thence to the *podestà* of Viterbo, whom the Vice-Chamberlain directed to hear the case and give judgement.[2]   A further category of such delegated jurisdiction is that of the cases between one commune and another in which the Rector or Legate was named by Rome to judge the suit.   Thus in a quarrel between Ancona and Fermo in 1421, the Legate Gabriel Condulmer was judge, not in his own right, but as 'iudex et commissarius ad hoc specialiter delegatus'.[3]

Another important activity of the Rector's Court was its jurisdiction in cases of arbitration.   This again was largely between one commune and another, as in the quarrel between Fermo and Ripatransone in which Pietro Emigli the Governor of the March acted as arbitrator in 1425.[4]   In this work there was much competition from the *signori*, who equally wished to draw the emoluments and prestige of arbitration.[5]

§ 4.   Spiritual jurisdiction was vested in the Vicar in spirituals, as has been explained above; but the temporal Rector was sometimes employed to try particular cases by virtue of delegated jurisdiction, particularly when communes engaged as parties in the suit.   Thus the Deputy of the March was named by the Pope as a special commissioner to pronounce sentence in the matter of the *jus praesentandi* of the commune of San Ginesio to the College of S. Costanzo.[6]   In a dispute between Marino Bishop of Recanati and the commune of Recanati over a will, the Bishop excommunicated the commune for contumacy, whereupon the latter appealed to the Holy See.   The Pope appointed Pietro Emigli, the Governor of the March, to hear and decide the case as a special commissioner.[7]   Questions involving ecclesiastics and laymen could also be decided in this way; thus the Abbot of Subiaco as Governor of Ascoli was given a commission to hear all cases of appeal between citizens of Ascoli and religious persons exempt and not exempt, including the Bishop of Ascoli and his court.[8]

[1] Div. Cam. 13, fol. 112.   [2] Doc. 13 below.
[3] Fermo, Archivio Priorale, no. 1244, 29 April 1421.   [4] Ibid. no. 173, 20 November 1425.
[5] E.g. the judgement of Berardo and Piergentile Varano in the dispute between San Ginesio and Sarnano, Colucci, *Antichità Picene*, xxiv, 103–23 (1421–2); or the arbitration of Braccio between Rieti and Terni, Michaeli, *Memorie storiche della città di Rieti*, iii, 319–23 and Guiraud, *Etat Pontifical*, 168.
[6] T. Benigni, *San Ginesio illustrata con antiche lapidi, ed annedotti documenti* (Fermo, 1795), ii, no. 44, p. 487.
[7] Reg. Vat. 355, fol. 80, 25 September 1424.   [8] Div. Cam. 11, fol. 108, 5 July 1427.

Albornoz defined the forms of law in use in the State of the Church in his constitutions, declaring that first papal constitutions should be followed, then his own constitutions and those of Bernard Bishop of Embrun, then the ancient custom of the province (by which he intended the statutes and customs of the communes), then canon law, and finally civil law.[1] It is usual to deduce from this provision, and from the later treatise of the Cardinal de Luca, that canon law prevailed over civil law in the state of the Church,[2] but this statement should not be made without reservation. One conspicuous exception was Rome, where civil law prevailed over canon law.[3] It is not at all certain that the constitutions of Albornoz had any validity in Rome at the time of Martin V,[4] and it seems very probable that they did not; there is no record that he ever promulgated them there,[5] and the first Pope specifically to mention the extension of the constitutions to Rome was Leo X. The civil law also, together with traces of Lombard and other customary law, had a very considerable place in the formation of the statutes of the communes,[6] which were given precedence over canon law by Albornoz. Finally, in the formation of the *Constitutiones Egidiane* themselves, the statutes of the communes had very considerable influence; thus the term to exhaust appeal is in canon law a year and a day, but in the *Constitutiones* is a maximum of two months, after the style of the communal statutes.[7]

[1] Lib. v, c. 26.

[2] E. Besta, *Storia di diritto italiano*, vol. i, pt. 2, *Fonti*, 748. Cf. Giovanni Battista Cardinal de Luca, *Theatrum veritatis et iustitiae*, xv, 'de iudiciis', disc. xxxv, par. 24, 37. De Luca distinguishes between canon law as enacted by the Pope 'tanquam Papa, et Episcopo Ecclesiae universalis' and that enacted by the Pope 'tanquam Principe temporali Status Ecclesiastici. Ut (ex. gr.) prae caeteris est illud circa formam testandi etiam in profanis cor. parocho, et duobis testibus. Sive est constitutio Aegidiana cum similibus.'

[3] De Luca, *Theatrum veritatis et iustitiae*, xv, 'relatio Romanae curiae', disc. xlvi, par. 22; Luca Peto *De iudiciaria formula Capitolini fori* (Rome, 1610), 16. This important fact is not brought to light in the article of Menestrini, 'Il procedimento civile nello stato pontificio', *Rivista italiana di scienze giuridiche*, xliii (1907).

[4] Sella, *Costituzioni Egidiane*, p. xv.   [5] Ibid.

[6] Vito la Mantia, *Storia della legislazione italiana*, i, 401.

[7] Sella, *Il procedimento civile nella legislazione statutaria italiana*, 161; *Constitutiones Egidiane*, lib. vi, c. 13.

CHAPTER IV

CENTRAL GOVERNMENT

I. *The Organisation of the Apostolic Chamber*

§ 1. BOTH as a spiritual and as a temporal prince, the Pope had, since the twelfth century, controlled his monies through the Apostolic Chamber. Later in the Middle Ages the Chamber assumed two other important functions; it became the main organ of government of the Papal State, and also an office which wrote, registered, and despatched several of the most important classes of papal letters.[1]

The Chamberlain was one of the two or three greatest personages of the Roman Court, and his powers were extraordinarily wide and various.[2] He was at the head of all the diverse activities of the Chamber, and was the final judge in all the temporal and spiritual cases which arose from its work. He could appoint officials both in the Chamber itself and in the Papal State. He had jurisdiction in all disciplinary and police matters concerning the curialists and followers of the Roman Court,[3] and he had some administrative control over certain papal officials outside the Chamber, particularly the secretaries.[4] He administered oaths of obedience to every class of official of the Roman Court and the Papal State, including the papal vicars in temporals.[5] His powers continued when the Pope was away from the Roman

---

[1] E. Göller, *Repertorium Germanicum*, i (1916), 33*–42* and 97*–8*; G. Tellenbach, ibid., ii (1933), 69*–83*; U. Kühne, ibid. iii (1935), 27*–45*; E. von Ottenthal, 'Die Bullenregister Martin V. und Eugen IV.', *MIöG*, Ergbd. i, (1885), 484–95; idem, 'Römische Berichte IV: Bemerkungen über päpstlichen Cameralregister des 15. Jahrhunderts', *MIöG*, vi (1885); A. Gottlob, *Aus der Camera apostolica des 15. Jahrhunderts* (1889); Baix, *La Chambre Apostolique et les 'libri annatarum' de Martin V* (1947), cccxvii–cDiii; idem, 'Notes sur les Clercs de la Chambre Apostolique (xiiie–xive siècles)', *Bulletin de l'Institut historique Belge de Rome*, xxvii (1952).

[2] See the appointments in *Bullarium Romanum* (editio Taurinen.), iv, 581, 643, and the indemnity granted to François de Conziè as Chamberlain of Clement VII, printed by Göller, 'Zur Stellung des päpstl. Kamerars unter Clemens VII (Gegenpapst)', *AKKR*, lxxxiii (1903), 391–7. Further, the powers printed by Samaran and Mollat, *La Fiscalité pontificale en France au XIVe siècle* (1905), doc. xii, p. 221. See also the oath of the Chamberlain, printed by Gottlob, 86–7, n.

[3] Samaran and Mollat, 3–5; Gottlob, 80–91; cf. *RQ*, viii (1894), 396, 'Franciscus camerarius . . . ad quem et eius camerariatus officium tam in civilibus quam in criminalibus protectio, correctio, punitio, omnimodo iurisdictio capellanorum et refferendariorum ceterorumque officialium et aliorum eidem sedi immediate subiectorum pertinere noscuntur'. Further, Tangl, *Die päpstlichen Kanzleiordnungen von 1200–1500*, 365, the reforms proposed in 1429/30, 'si autem auditores rote ordinationes tangentes ipsos non servarent, corrigerentur per camerarium aut vicecamerarium domini nostri'.

[4] Von Ottenthal, 'Die Bullenregister', 471; Göller, 'Mitteilungen und Untersuchungen über das päpstliche Register- und Kanzleiwesen im 14. Jahrhundert', *QF*, vi (1904), 306–7.

[5] Gottlob, 86–9; Von Mitteis, 'Curiale Eidregister', *MIöG*, Ergbd. vi (1901). Cf. Theiner, iii, no. 158, p. 231; no. 171, p. 245; no. 177, p. 253; no. 182, p. 255. The oaths taken in the Chamber were recorded in certain registers kept especially for the purpose (von Mitteis, cited above), and also in the *Manualia* of the notaries of the Chamber. Cf. Div. Cam. 3, fol. 125, which records the oath of Ludovico Alidosi for his vicariate of Imola (Theiner, iii, no. 157, p. 224).

Court, and his appointment continued during the interregnum following the death of a Pope. He was usually a chief adviser to the Pope on all matters of high policy.[1]

Martin V's Chamberlain was François de Conzié, Archbishop of Narbonne, who had been Chamberlain of the Clementine obedience from 1383, had gone over to the Pisan obedience and remained Chamberlain for John XXIII during the rest of the Schism. The Vice-Chancellor of Benedict XIII, Johannes de Broniaco, also went over to Alexander V, and continued as Vice-Chancellor of Martin V, and these two defections form an important link between the administrative practice of the two lines of Popes.[2] De Conzié did not exercise his office, and for the whole pontificate of Martin V remained in Avignon as Vicar-General of the Comté Venaissin.[3] His office in Rome was filled by a Deputy- or Vice-Chamberlain who divided the profits of the office with de Conzié, and may for practical purposes be considered the Chamberlain. These substitutes had the titles of both Deputy- and Vice-Chamberlain, and they used either title indifferently.[4] The first was Louis Aleman, the later Legate and Cardinal, followed by the clerk of the Chamber, Benedetto Guidalotti, and, for a short time, by Oddo Poccia of Genazzano. Poccia seems to have disputed the office with Guidalotti, and even after his appointment as Apostolic Treasurer in 1426 the former sometimes appears as Deputy of the Chamberlain.[5] Neither the Chamberlain and his substitutes nor the Treasurer were Cardinals while they held these offices, and the Treasurer, Antonio Casini, gave up his office on being made Cardinal in 1426. Martin V was one of the last Popes to exclude the Chamberlain from the Sacred College,[6] and that he should have done so fits well both with his policy of using his personal servants in high office, and with his determination not to be ruled by the Cardinals.

§ 2. Although it was a highly organised and bureaucratic department, the Apostolic Chamber was far removed from the modern concept of a ministry. The Chamber enjoyed an extraordinary multiplicity of functions, because it was not a body of officials appointed to carry out a particular branch of government, but a college ('Collegium Camerae') whose members would follow what they conceived to be the interests of the Chamber into any and every aspect of government. It is not surprising that Eugenius IV, confirming the statutes of the Chamber, used words which seem to exhaust the whole field of action of the Papacy—'. . . Camerae Apostolicae, ad quam Ecclesiarum et monasteriorum omnium, necnon etiam urbium, civitatum,

---

[1] Gottlob, 89–91.

[2] Cf. E. von Ottenthal, *Die päpstlichen Kanzleiregeln von Johannes XXII. bis Nicolaus V.* (1888), xii.

[3] Baix, cccxix. The appointment to Comté Venaissin is in Reg. Vat. 348, fol. 84, dated 27 July 1418.

[4] See the appointment of Louis Aleman as 'camerarii nostri locumtenens et vicecamerarius', printed by von Mitteis, 'Curiale Eidregister', 439–44. Aleman had been de Conzié's deputy at Constance since July 1417. The Deputy of the Chamberlain was authorised to appropriate half the proceeds of the office, Reg. Vat. 350, fol. 95, dated 27 May 1424.

[5] Baix, loc. cit.; P. M. Baumgarten, 'Oddo Potii de Varris de Genazzano, päpstliche Schatzmeister, und sein Notar Laurentius Dominici de Rotellis', *Hist. Jahrb.*, xxxi (1910), 785–6.

[6] Gottlob, 80.

terrarum, castrorum, oppidorum, villarum et locorum Romanae Ecclesiae immediate subiectorum, spiritualia et temporalia negocia peragenda deveniunt.' [1]

The Chamberlain was not so much a papal minister as the chief functionary of a college, the hierarchy of the 'domini de camera'. Beneath him came the Treasurer, who is discussed below, followed by the 'consiliarii' or 'assistentes camere', able lawyers and administrators who are seldom mentioned in the existing documents, probably because the legal material which concerns them has failed to survive. They received a special salary, and would sit on special financial commissions, or assist when the Chamber sat as a court of law.[2] One of them, Stefano Geri da Prato, Bishop of Volterra, had been the confidential financial adviser of John XXIII.[3]

The main body of the 'domini de camera' was that of the clerks of the Chamber, who were responsible for all its everyday work. This hardworking and able group of men had a hand in almost every practical and financial aspect of papal government, both inside and outside the Roman Court. Within the Chamber they carried out much of the main book-keeping of papal finance, saw to the collection of spiritual dues and taxes and to the temporal revenues of all kinds, to the authorisation of payments, to the keeping and auditing of accounts. They supervised the provincial treasurers of the Papal State and the Apostolic Collectors throughout Europe, receiving their payments and auditing their accounts. In all this they worked in co-operation with the Treasurer and his notaries, and had the assistance of the scriptors and notaries of the Chamber. They drafted the bulls dealing with nominations to consistorial benefices, and many other bulls, particularly those referring to the running of the Papal State. They corrected the letters of the Chamberlain. It had been demanded at Constance that they should be doctors or licentiates in law, and most of them in fact were. They sat beneath the Chamberlain when the Chamber sat as a court of law, and they were among the few officials who attended an ordinary sitting of Consistory, although it is by no means certain that they had a monopoly in drafting consistorial acts.[4]

The clerks of the Chamber formed a corps on which the Popes drew for many of the important posts outside the Roman Court, and particularly for the financial and

---

[1] *Bullarium Romanum* (edit. Taurinen.), v, 76.

[2] Baix, cccxxxix–xliii. The *consiliarii* he names should be supplemented by the names of Damelo de Mileis (Reg. Vat. 351, fol. 37) and Angelotto de Fuschis, Bishop of Anagni (Reg. Vat. 352, fol. 197). De Fuschis was a cameral clerk, a familiar of the Pope, and often employed on business of the secret treasury, cf. Von Hofmann, *Forschungen*, i, 88; ii, 188. The *consiliarii* were paid a special retaining fee; cf. J. P. Kirsch, *Die Rückkehr der Päpste Urban V. und Gregor XI. von Avignon nach Rom*, pp. xxiv, 79; Kühne, *Repertorium Germanicum*, iii, 30*; Schäfer, *Die Ausgaben der apostolischen Kammer unter den Päpsten Urban V. und Gregor XI.*, 34,279.

[3] Guasti, 'Gli avanzi dell'Archivio di un Pratese vescovo di Volterra', *ASI*, 4th ser., xiii (1884); cf. my article, *JEccH*, iv (1953), 64.

[4] Mabillon, *Museum Italicum*, ii (Paris, 1689), 426, the fourteenth century ceremonial of Caetani, 'Die sabbato sequente dominus Papa, facta ei reverentia in consistorio per cardinales, mandat, quod aperiantur portae aulae, ubi tenetur consistorium, omnibus intrare volentibus : et ibidem debet venire ad consistorium, et infra consistorium infra sedere camerarius, et notarii, et capellani domini Papae, et auditores palatii, et clerici camerae domini Papae; alii vero debent stare pedes extra consistorium'. See H. Schröder, 'Die Protokollbücher der papstlichen Kammercleriker, 1329–1347', *Archiv für Geistesgeschichte*, xxvii (1937), 170 f.

political administration of the Papal State. Cameral clerks became Apostolic Collectors, emissaries to Italian and ultramontane powers, Rectors and Treasurers of papal provinces, Governors of towns, special financial commissioners, inspectors of fortresses and mercenary troops. The opportunities were many, and Domenico Capranica, the ablest of all Martin V's cameral clerks, became as a very young man the Governor of one province and the Cardinal Legate of another. There was also scope for the lawyers, and although there was only one post of Auditor of the Chamber, some clerks combined their duties in the Chamber with the office of Auditor of the Rota.

Such attractions, combined with the fact that Martin V had accepted cameral clerks from all three obediences, meant that the Chamber was very fully staffed, and in 1425 there were nine clerks actually drawing emoluments from the Chamber, the 'distributiones cotidiane', and considered as exercising their office.[1] This list includes some clerks who were outside the Roman Court at the time, but others who were employed outside the curia did not find a place on it. A commission of reform which sat in 1423 said that the number of cameral clerks previously employed was four, a number which had sufficed when the Chamber was three times as rich.[2] When Eugenius IV approved the statutes of the Chamber in 1438 the number was fixed at seven, and although it is probable that the work of the Chamber was heavier under Martin V than during the Schism, the number of clerks he employed still seems excessive. But the other complaint of the reform commission, that the office was given to unqualified and unsuitable persons, is at most only partly true. There may have been exceptions, but such men as Capranica, Guidalotti, Giovanni of Rieti, were able administrators and learned in the law.

§ 3.   The notary was a very important part of the machinery of the Papal Court; not only were notaries essential in the courts of justice, but they also carried out a great part of the donkey-work of administration, and many of the operations of government which, requiring a 'public instrument' to be drawn up, could not be carried out without the office of the tabellionate.[3] This was particularly true of the Chamber, which was continually drawing up contracts and agreements with merchants, mercenaries, apostolic vicars and other subjects, and which also needed

---

[1] Doc. 9 below, the purpose of which was to secure a fair distribution of the emoluments of the clerks of the Chamber. To Baix' list should be added Menimus de Agazzia of Siena, who was also appointed Commissioner in temporals in Rieti (1 January 1430, Reg. Vat. 351, fol. 142). Petrus de Ramponibus of Bologna was appointed clerk of the Chamber on 16 September 1425 (Reg. Vat. 350, fol. 189), but the appointment was probably of honour. He was one of the ringleaders of the Bolognese rebellion of 1428, and a marginal note states that he was deprived of the dignity on 31 August 1428 (ibid.).

[2] J. Haller, *Concilium Basiliense*, i (1896), 168. 'Olim non erant nisi quatuor, ut in epytaphio camere apostolice continetur, et viri insignes, et graves . . .' What the 'epytaphius' was is not clear; it may be some traditional error which had been consecrated by usage. At its most extended sense the word can mean an inscription, but here 'statutes' or 'customs' seems far more likely. For a reference under Clement VII to the statutes and customs of the Apostolic Chamber, see Göller, in *AKKR*, lxxxiii (1903), 396. Unhappily, none of the statutes of the Chamber prior to those of Eugenius IV have survived.

[3] For the work of notaries at the papal court see P. M. Baumgarten, *Von der apostolischen Kanzlei* (1908), 9–68; Barraclough, *Public notaries and the Papal Curia* (1934); Schröder, 'Die Protokollbücher', quoted above. More generally, see O. Redlich, *Die Privaturkunden des Mittelalters* (1911), 209 f.

notaries to draw up documents of political importance, such as agreements between Italian powers in which the Pope acted as mediator. Many of the clerks of the Chamber were themselves notaries, but a number were specially appointed as notaries of the Apostolic Chamber. They carried out a variety of duties; keeping accounts, drawing up and engrossing notarial acts, and keeping a record or 'Manuale' of various acts which the Chamberlain or clerks deemed to be important, and which were perhaps not registered in the cameral register or elsewhere. The practice of assigning a notary as assistant to a particular cameral clerk which had obtained in the fourteenth century was no longer continued, and the 'Manuals' of Luphard Tebold and Astolfino de Marinonibus under Martin V were compiled in the service of the Chamberlain and of the 'domini de camera' in general, and not in that of any particular clerk of the Chamber.[1] It is possible that this apparent decline in the political importance of the clerks of the Chamber may be due to the rise of the secretaries, who in Martin V's day took care of many important political transactions which in the mid-fourteenth century would have fallen to the clerks of the Chamber.

The office of the tabellionate was granted in the Roman Court by papal authority. The most usual channel for its grant was the Vice-Chancellor, who arranged the examination of candidates for the office.[2] But, where the Chamber was concerned, his authority seems in this respect to have been passed over, and the cameral notary, Petrus Imberti, was examined for the office by another cameral notary, Petrus de Trilhia, without any apparent intervention of the Vice-Chancellor.[3]

The notaries of the Chamber had important duties in dealing with papal correspondence. In the correspondence of the Chamberlain they drafted most of the cameral letters, and corrected and collated many of them. In the papal correspondence which was registered in the Chamber they engrossed the bulls which were given them by the secretaries and cameral clerks, and also registered them.[4] The work was heavy, and there were at least fifteen such notaries under Martin V.[5]

Besides notaries, the Chamber also had its own scriptors, who engrossed and registered the letters of the Chamberlain from the drafts prepared by the clerks and notaries of the Chamber.[6]

§ 4. The Auditor of the court of the Apostolic Chamber had his own organisation. He had at times a Vice-Auditor with powers equal to his own, or alternatively only a Vice-Auditor was appointed. It may be said, with rather approximate truth, that the Auditor had the same relation to the Chamberlain that a principal official had

---

[1] For these manuals see Kühne, *Repertorium Germanicum*, iii, 29*–30*, and A. Mercati, 'Una fonte poco noto per la storia di Gregorio XII', *ASR*, l (1927). The scope of the manuals appears from their titles, e.g. in *MIöG*, vi (1885), 620–1, or Arm. 34, vol. 4, fol. 111, 'Manuale mei Astolfini de Marinonibus publici imperiali auctoritate notarii, ac notarii camere apostolice, in quo obligationes contractus et alia occurentia, in quibus requisitus sum, ac iuxta commissiones reverendissimi domini domini Ludovici dei gratia electi Magalonen', domini pape vicecamerarii, et aliorum dominorum de camera michi commissa fideliter annotavi.'

[2] For the usual practice see Baumgarten, *Von der apostolischen Kanzlei*, 30–7.

[3] Von Mitteis, *MIöG*, Ergbd. vi (1901), 445–6.

[4] Von Ottenthal, 'Die Bullenregister', 488–95; idem, in *MIöG*, vi (1885), 620–1.

[5] Baix, cccxxix.   [6] Baix, cccxxviii–ix.

to a bishop.[1]　The Auditor's powers were therefore very large, and he dealt with a large body of business.　The notaries of his court were appointed by the Chamberlain, and from the beginning of the fourteenth century their number had been considerable.　He had his own seal, which was controlled by a 'sigillator'.　His court included various advocates, the *advocatus fisci*, *advocatus pauperum*, but its most important official was the *procurator fisci*, an official who, although he was described as 'procurator fiscalis curie camere' or 'procurator fisci sive camere pape', could also be called the 'procurator generalis', since his competence extended far outside the court of the Chamber.[2]　His function was to act as prosecutor in all courts of the Roman Court, not merely in that of the Chamber, and he also acted as defender whenever papal officials of the Roman Court or the Papal State were prosecuted.　He was, nevertheless, an official of the Chamber, and is described as such in the statutes issued for the Chamber by Eugenius IV.　He was required to attend, both when the Chamber sat as a court, and when the Pope held a consistory.　His action may be seen in two of the most important political trials which took place under Martin V, the process against Braccio in 1419, and that against the rebels of Bologna in 1428.[3]

§ 5.　The Apostolic Treasurer has been left aside until this point because, although he was subordinate to the Chamberlain in the Apostolic Chamber, his organisation nevertheless enjoyed a limited independence.　His own position was a little ambiguous; it was one of great dignity and responsibility, but not, when compared with that of the Chamberlain, one of extensive or well-defined powers.　His function was to receive and disburse the monies of the Holy See.　He issued quittances against the monies he received, and made payments when he was told to do so by the Chamberlain or the Pope.　He could hold his own court, but he also formed part of the court of the Apostolic Chamber.[4]

The Treasurer had his own notaries and scriptors, who kept the 'Introitus et Exitus', the main account books of the Holy See, and also issued and registered quittances, and kept certain other account books, such as those of records of payments made to mercenaries.

The mandates issued by the Chamberlain to the Treasurer for the payment of

---

[1]　Mollat, 'Contribution à l'histoire de l'administration judiciaire de l'Eglise Romaine au xive siècle', *RHE*, xxxii (1936), 899.

[2]　E. Göller, 'Der Gerichtshof der päpstlichen Kammer und die Entstehung des Amtes des Procurator fiscalis im kirchlichen Prozessverfahren', *AKKR*, xciv (1914), 612–19.

[3]　Doc. 25 below, and Biblioteca Angelica, cod. 1426, fol. 7v.

[4]　Gottlob, 95–6; Baix, cccxxii–vi.　See the annotation in Martin V's registers quoted by Miltenberger, 'Versuch einer Neuordnung der päpstlichen Kammer in den ersten Regierungsjahren Martins V', *RQ*, viii (1894), 395–6.　'Attende, quod ista non debuit exponi (scil. quitantia) per dominum thesaurarium, quia ex ignata sui officii potestate nil facere potest nisi recipere de certis et quittare, nec sigillum habet, quod debeat emolumenta recipere, quia non sunt nisi quatuor in Romana Curia sigilla tax(arum ?), non enim potest dominus thesaurarius absolvere vel excommunicare nec dispensare, aut dilationem dare, nisi ex speciali commissione pape, quod nunquam fuit visum, vel camerarii apostolici, qui habet plenitudinem totius officii et officiorum camere'.　This statement is not contradicted by anything in the appointment of Oddo Poccia as Treasurer, printed in *Hist. Jahrb.*, xxxi (1910), 782–4.　The Treasurer had his own seal, but this carried no emoluments with it.　See Miltenberger, 'Versuch', 395, n. and P. Sella and M. H. Laurent, *I sigilli dell'Archivio Segreto Vaticano*, i, nos. 698, 704.

money were more formal than they had been twenty years before, when de Conzié was Chamberlain of the Avignonese obedience. Under Benedict XIII the mandate was a brief departmental note countersigned by the autograph signature of the Chamberlain, but under Martin V, while the autograph signature was preserved, the mandate took the form of a regular cameral letter authenticated by the signet of the Chamberlain.[1]

The Treasurer was responsible for relations with the Depositary, an official who was a combination of banker and safe deposit. The Depositary was usually the head of the Roman branch of a Florentine bank, and he shared with the Treasurer the task of receiving and disbursing papal monies. The Depositary did not hold all the papal monies; both he and the Treasurer appear to have received and paid out monies. Payments were, however, made by the Depositary only on the orders of the Treasurer. One single set of accounts was kept for the money handled by the Depositary and Treasurer, the 'Introitus et Exitus'. These accounts were made out by the Depositary in Italian, then Latin translations were made, one for the Treasurer and another for the Chamberlain. If the monthly expenditure of the Holy See exceeded its income the Depositary would grant a kind of overdraft. At the end of each month a balance was struck in the 'Introitus et Exitus', and the accounts of the month audited by a clerk of the Chamber. If there was a deficit, the Chamber was shown in the audit as being the debitor of the Depositary by that amount. The book-keeping was not double entry, and each month the previous month's debit or credit of the Chamber with the Depositary was brought forward.[2]

Martin V found himself at the beginning of his pontificate with three Apostolic Treasurers, one from each of the three obediences. All three were re-granted their dignities, but only Antonio Casini, the Bishop of Siena and ex-Treasurer of John XXIII, actually exercised the functions of the office.[3] Casini was of great political importance, and the Florentine embassies regarded him as the key official of papal diplomacy.[4] Oddo Poccia (Oddo Potii de Varris de Genazzano), who succeeded Casini in 1426, was a man deep in the confidences of the Colonna family, a trusted servant who controlled the secret monies of the Pope both before and after his promotion to Apostolic Treasurer, and was after Martin's death imprisoned by Eugenius IV to discover their whereabouts.[5] Thus the practical importance of the Treasurer was commensurate with the dignity of his office, even if his formal powers were not.

---

[1] For the older formula see Göller, *Repertorium Germanicum*, i, 42*. The originals of similar mandates to those described by Göller as in a Register are in Inst. Misc. nos. 3849, 3856–8. The mandate in use under Martin V, doc. 1 below.

[2] Gottlob, 159–66, 110–11; Baix, cccxliii–iv. Cf. the 'ordo camere' projected under Sixtus IV, printed by Bauer, in *ASR*, 1 (1927), 392–8.

[3] Baix, cccxxii–iv.

[4] *Commissioni*, ii, 92, and 106, 'Veduto noi il Tesoriere esser sempre a tutti questi nostri segreti con la sua Santità, diliberamo tutto conferire con lui'.

[5] See my article, 'Camera Papae: problems of papal finance in the later Middle Ages', *JEccH*, iv (1953), 67, and Baumgarten, in *Hist. Jahrb.*, xxxi (1910), quoted above. Further, for his fall under Eugenius IV, Poggio Bracciolini, *Historiae de varietate fortunae* (Paris, 1723), 101.

K

In spite of its secrecy and comparative informality, the organisation for dealing with the Pope's secret monies should probably be dealt with as part of the Apostolic Chamber.[1] The books of the 'cubicularius secretus' of Eugenius IV were audited by cameral clerks under the supervision of the Chamberlain, although it is not known if a similar audit was carried out under Martin V—probably not, as Martin was a great deal less scrupulous and correct in dealing with papal property than was his successor. Under Martin V the secret treasury was served by several agents, of whom Poccia was the most important. These men received very large sums for the use of the Pope, both from the Apostolic Treasury in Rome, and from the various provincial treasuries in the Papal State. The agents of the secret treasury were not usually cameral clerks; under Martin V they included the secretary and registrar of apostolic letters Paolo Capranica, the registrar Nicolò Cesari of Ceciliano, the *cubicularii* Thomas de Pileo and Angelo Massii of Gennazano, and Bartolomeo Capranica.

§ 6. The growing importance and corporate power of the College of Cardinals had since the twelfth century assured it a share in the revenues of the Holy See. Under Nicholas IV this share was guaranteed by the bull 'Coelestis altitudo', which gave the College the right to a half share in certain spiritual revenues, and also to certain temporal *census* and revenues, including the profits of the temporal possessions of the Church.[2] The later interpretation of this grant, so far as it concerned the temporalities, seems to have been that the Cardinals should have half the net profits of the various provinces and half the gross amount of the *census* paid for papal vicariates such as those of Bologna or Ferrara. To collect and divide their monies the Cardinals possessed a Chamber which was closely linked to the Apostolic Chamber, whence it drew most of its income. The head of the Chamber of the College was a Cardinal-Chamberlain, and its administrative work was done by two clerks of the Chamber of the College, assisted by a few notaries and scriptors. The closeness of the connection of the two Chambers is shown by the fact that the two clerks of the Chamber of the College sat by right of their office in the court of the Apostolic Chamber.

The history of the share of the Cardinals in the profits of the State of the Church is far from clear. Boniface VIII shared some of the temporal revenues with the Cardinals, but probably not all of them, and the same seems to be true of Clement V.[3] Under John XXII the Cardinals drew a share of the profits of the Comté Venaissin,

---

[1] 'Camera Papae', quoted above.

[2] J. P. Kirsch, *Die Finanzverwaltung des Kardinalkollegiums im XIII. und XIV. Jahrhundert* (1895); P. M. Baumgarten, *Untersuchungen und Urkunden über die Camera Collegii Cardinalium für die Zeit von 1295 bis 1437* (1898); J. B. Sägmuller, *Die Tätigkeit und Stellung der Cardinäle bis Papst Bonifaz VIII* (1896); G. Mollat, 'Contribution à l'histoire du Sacré Collège de Clement V à Eugène IV', *RHE*, xlvi-vii (1951-2); K. Jordan, 'Zur päpstliche Finanzgeschichte im 11. und 12. Jahrhundert', *QF*, xxv (1933/4), 87-88; F. Schneider, 'Zur älteren päpstlichen Finanzgeschichte', *QF*, ix (1906), 13.

[3] Kirsch, 26-8; Baumgarten, 150 f.; ibid. 160 f.; F. Baethgen, 'Quellen und Untersuchungen zur Geschichte der päpstlichen Hof- und Finanzverwaltung unter Bonifaz VIII', *QF*, xx (1928/9), 166-9. Mollat, *RHE*, xlvi (1951), 71-2, sheds no new light on this problem.

but not, it seems, of the Italian lands.[1] It may be true that on balance the wars in Italy engulfed all these profits (it is difficult to define 'profits' or 'net revenues' of the State of the Church exactly, and no doubt the distinctions were equally vague in the fourteenth century), but there are many instances of payments made under John XXII from the Italian provincial treasuries to Avignon, without any corresponding indication of a share given to the Cardinals. It seems likely that the Cardinals considered that John XXII was withholding the temporal revenues from them, since they made his successor, Benedict XII, enter into a solemn agreement to pay the College its proper share of the temporal revenues, stipulating that an officer of the College be present when the officials of the lands of the Church (by which are intended the provincial Treasurers) presented their accounts for audit in the Apostolic Chamber.[2] Whether this last part of the undertaking was observed is not clear; it certainly did not pass into the established practice of the Chamber. But so far as the *census* of vicariates was concerned, both Benedict XII and Clement VI divided the temporal monies with the College.[3]

With the death of Clement VI the published sources fail, and the subject is left in total darkness; some inaccurate guesses have been made about the period of the Schism,[4] but nothing can be certainly known until the 'Introitus and Exitus' volumes and the surviving registers of divisions of the Cardinals have been examined.

Under Martin V there is no trace in the documents of any monies being paid from the State of the Church to the Cardinals; not only the profits of provincial treasuries, but also the *census* of apostolic vicariates, all remained in their entirety in the Apostolic Chamber. There is also evidence that for some considerable time before Martin V's pontificate the Popes had ceased sharing these temporal monies with the Cardinals. The reform commission of Cardinals which sat in 1423 complained that the temporal revenues of the Church ('census et alii proventus ordinarii et naturales Romane ecclesie') were no longer shared by the Pope with the Cardinals as they should have been under the constitution of Nicholas IV. Some Popes, the report suggests, had been encouraged to sell the lands of the Holy See to temporal princes, since they no longer shared the income with the Cardinals—perhaps this is a reference to Gregory XII. The report goes on to ask that the Pope should now share these revenues, and promises that if this is done the Cardinals will not fail to

---

[1] Kirsch, Baumgarten, loc. cit. Göller, *Die Einnahmen der apostolischen Kammer unter Johann XXII* (1910), 70*, remarks that part of the income drawn by the Chamber from the State of the Church was from other than administrative sources, and that another part of it seems to come from ecclesiastical tenths. In consequence he found it difficult to estimate exactly how far the Cardinals were sharing in the temporal revenues.

[2] This undertaking is printed by Kirsch, *Finanzverwaltung*, 71–2.

[3] Göller, *Die Einnahmen der apostolischen Kammer unter Benedikt XII* (1920), 42, 43, 48, 49; L. Mohler, *Die Einnahmen der apostolischen Kammer unter Klemens VI* (1931), 1, 11–12, 18, 20–21, 23, 27, 28 etc.

[4] By M. Souchon, *Die Papstwahlen in der Zeit des Grossen Schismas* (1898–9), i, 120–1, 180–1, ii, 81–2, 109–11. Souchon has no real sources on which to base his conjectures except Guasti's part-publication of Stefano Geri's accounts, and his treatment of this material leaves much to be desired. It is scarcely possible to say that John XXIII was the first Pope to organise thoroughly the division of revenue with the Cardinals (ibid. ii, 111).

contribute from these monies towards the defence and recovery of the lands of the Church,[1]—provided, a significant provision, that the defence of these lands be conducted according to their advice. In 1429 or 1430 a second commission of Cardinals, appointed as a preliminary to the Council of Basel, repeated the same request in a slightly different form.[2] A year or two later the demand for this part of the bull of Nicholas IV to be honoured appears once more, in the election capitulations of the conclave of Eugenius IV.[3] It therefore seems very unlikely either that Martin V shared the temporal revenues with the Cardinals, or that the requests of the commissions caused him to change this practice, and the notorious firmness with which Martin treated his Cardinals makes this far from surprising.

Whether the College succeeded at any time in the fifteenth century in recovering this lost ground is again far from clear. The matter is raised in several election capitulations, and is referred to in the statutes of the College of Cardinals, but there is no positive indication that the College had any success, and the demand at the end of the century that the Cardinals be assigned cash pensions makes it clear that they had by that time lost this battle.

II. *The Apostolic Chamber and the Temporal Revenues*

§ 1. As the central financial bureau of the Papal State, the Apostolic Chamber dealt with the provincial Treasurers rather than with papal subjects direct. The apostolic vicars in temporals form a notable exception. Their *census* was almost always paid direct to the Chamber and the obligation to send it to Rome was usually included in the terms of the vicariate.[4] Only by special licence did a provincial Treasurer collect such a census. The Pope thus kept his vicars under his direct control, and the compositions for arrears of *census* and tallage which they frequently made were negotiated direct with the Chamber.[5] It was also important that the

---

[1] J. Haller, *Concilium Basiliense*, i, 173. 'Pro sustentacione vero domini nostri pape et cardinalium videtur diligenter attendendum ante omnia, quod census et alii proventus ordinarii et naturales Romane ecclesie debite exigantur et non alienentur, quod hactenus non est factum, et causa videtur esse, quia nonnulli summi pontifices adeo fuerunt occupati, adeo eciam obnoxii et indigentes favoribus principum, quod facile per concessiones vel per neglectum illa dimiserunt, maxime quia in aliis proventibus spiritualibus satis habundabant et proventus illos non communicabant cum cardinalinus, quibus de constitucione N(icolai) quarti debent esse communia . . . Quare videtur, quod constitucio illa felicis recordationis N(icolai) quarti sit servanda, et supplicatur domino nostro, quod illam dignetur servare in forma sua, ut et ipse suffultus auxilio collegii maiorem et honestiorem de bonis ecclesie Romane reportet fructum . . . ut que communia sunt communiter administrentur et communia inde proveniant emolumenta, magis que et reverebitur et timebitur ecclesia in temporalibus, que ut occulatim videtur magis et magis dissipantur et pereunt. Et . . . collegium est contentum, de parte sua proveniente ex censibus et proventibus antedictis, si aliqua onera incumbant rei tam pro recuperacione quam eciam pro defensione vel gubernacione, dumtamen fiant de eorum consilio, contribuere si et quando opus sit.'

[2] Haller, i, 174.   [3] Raynaldus, ad a. 1431, par. vii.

[4] E.g. Theiner, iii, no. 158, p. 230, 'ecclesie seu camere predictis in Urbe, vel ubi nos et dicti successores nostri residebimus'.

[5] E.g. the composition which the Varano reached with the Apostolic Vice-Chamberlain in 1422 for an overall annual payment of 4,000 florins for tallage, *census* (excluding *census* of vicariates) and *afflictus*, confirmed by a bull of 27 April 1422, Reg. Vat. 349, fol. 212v. This sum was shortly after reduced to 3,500 florins, Reg. Vat. 354, fol. 92.

Pope should know when vicars fell behind in their payments, since in many cases this entailed the loss of their vicariate. Where this clause existed in the grant of the vicariate, it was always a convenient pretext where the Pope felt himself strong enough to get rid of a *signore* by force. Martin V probably used this excuse on occasion, as did Alexander VI after him.

The provincial Treasurer called himself 'thesaurarius apostolicus' and was an official of the Chamber rather than of the Rector. He made payments at the Rector's mandate, however, perhaps even on the authority of his spoken word. Besides mandates from the Rector, he also had to honour all sorts of assignments from the Chamberlain.[1] Such assignments were most often for the benefit either of mercenaries or of the Chamber's bankers.[2]

Ultimate responsibility for the finances of the province lay with the Treasurer and not with the Rector, as appears from the system of audit. The provincial Treasurer kept three copies of his accounts. One went to the Rector and another, either annually or at the end of his term of office, went to the Chamber for audit. The audit of these accounts was not always carried out promptly,[3] but one case demonstrates that it was done with thoroughness, and that the personal responsibility of the Treasurer was enforced punctiliously.

The notary of the Treasurer of the March, Marino de Tocco, was one Ser Angelo Giovanni of Recanati. Marino ceased to be Treasurer in February 1422, and retired to his bishopric of Recanati and Macerata, but on discovering that Ser Angelo had embezzled several hundred ducats from the provincial treasury, he had him sent in chains to Rome. Here he was tried by the Auditor of the court of the Apostolic Chamber, Domenico of San Geminiano, was found guilty, and was condemned to imprisonment until he restored the money. But the affair was far from ended for the ex-Treasurer. In December 1423 the Chamberlain wrote to him that since the frauds appeared in the account books which Marino de Tocco had submitted to the Apostolic Chamber, then he, the ex-Treasurer, was responsible for the loss, and must restore the money to the Chamber. At the same time he was granted all the claims which the Chamber possessed against Ser Angelo, an award which can have given him but little comfort.[4]

---

[1] See doc. 4 below, for an example.

[2] Particularly interesting are the assignments to the depositary, Antonius de Piscia, presumably to extinguish the 'overdraft' of the Apostolic Chamber, e.g. 15,500 florins on 31 March 1429, from the income of most of the provinces (Div. Cam. 11, fol. 255); 1 March 1430, 1,000 florins from Imola and Forlì (Div. Cam. 13, fol. 36v.); 21 March 1430, 3,500 florins from Perugia (ibid. fol. 47v); on the preceding day, 6,000 florins from the March of Ancona (ibid. fol. 48); 14 July 1430, 3,000 florins from Spoleto (ibid. fol. 89v); 16 July 1430, 2,000 florins from the *salaria* of the Patrimony (ibid. fol. 90v).

[3] E.g. the accounts of Bartolomeo de Bonitis de Altopassu as Treasure of the Patrimony for April 1424–September 1425 were not approved until the pontificate of Eugenius IV, 8 idus Octobris anno 11, and then without a calculation of the total income and expenditure being made. Arch. Cam. pt. i, Tes. Prov., Patrimonio, B. 1, vol. 2, fol. 57. Other volumes in this series lack any approval by the Chamber.

[4] Div. Cam. 8, fol. 58, 'Sed quia infrascriptas pecuniarum summas sic, ut prefertur, per dictum Ser Angelum defraudatas, in computis et rationibus per vos in apostolica camera exhibitis et productis, ad introitum prefate camere sub suis postis et pertitis posuistis et allocastis, vosquidem fecistis de ipsis

Marino de Tocco failed to pay the money claimed, and the Vice-Chamberlain thereupon told the Governor of the March to take action against him, if necessary sequestrating the possessions of his bishopric in order to recover the money. In February 1425 Marino was granted an extension of twenty days to pay his debt, but he still did not pay, and at some time between February and June the sequestration of the goods of his bishopric was ordered to be put into effect. Finally, on 4 June 1425, he paid the Apostolic Chamber an instalment of 500 florins. The sequestration was removed, and the legal rights arising from the process against Ser Angelo were again transferred to him. As he asserted that the notary had secretly transferred the monies he had embezzled to others ('sunt facte contractiones et translationes bonorum clandestine'), he was empowered to recover them from the third parties concerned. His claim for 91 florins for the expenses of the enquiry was refused. At the same time a commission seems to have sat in Rome to examine his accounts further, investigating not only further frauds of Ser Angelo, but also the claims of Gabriel Condulmer, former Legate of the March, who asserted that Marino had failed to pay him his salary.

The money finally claimed from Marino de Tocco on account of the frauds seems to have amounted in all to 1,200 florins, an immense sum. Marino having paid 500 florins, a further 300 being remitted by the Pope, continued to owe another 400 florins, and in 1426 was excommunicated by the Chamberlain for their non-payment. His nephew made a recognition of his debt of 400 florins in June 1426, after which no more is heard of this unfortunate official.

When they were closed, the accounts of provincial Treasurers often showed the Treasurer in debt to the Chamber. In January 1424 Geminiano da Prato, the successor of Marino de Tocco as Treasurer of the March, was ordered to pay within six days the 700 florins which he owed the Chamber from his term of office as Treasurer, and was threatened with excommunication as a penalty for non-payment.[1] The reverse occurred with the accounts of Jacopo of Bagnorea, Treasurer of the Patrimony; it was shown that the Chamber owed him 150 florins for his salary, and his successor as Treasurer of the Patrimony was ordered to pay this.[2]

The audit of a provincial Treasurer's accounts was usually made by three clerks of the Chamber, or by the Treasurer and two clerks of the Chamber. It took the form of a general examination of the accounts, closed by a form of approval which included a general balance of the gross totals of income and expenditure.[3]

---

prefate camere debitorem'. My account of these transactions is based on: Div. Cam. 8, fol. 58; Reg. Vat. 355, fol. 52; Div. Cam. 9, fols. 12v, 14, 87v, 88; IE 383, fol. 5; Div. Cam. 3, fols. 165, 166, 185. Cf. also I. Schuster, *L'Imperiale Abbazia di Farfa*, 416–7.

[1] Div. Cam. 8, fol. 73v. It is clear that the form of audit and approval was not entered into the accounts until all outstanding payments on them had been cleared. Geminiano da Prato's accounts were finally approved on 21 February 1427, Arch. Cam., pt. i, Tes. Prov., Marca, B. 1, vol. 1, fol. 180v, and ibid. vol. 2. He paid the last instalment of his debt to the Chamber on 20 March 1427, IE 385, fol. 29.

[2] Div. Cam. 7, fol. 196, dated 26 April 1423.

[3] Gottlob, 159 f., who also prints the form of audit.

§ 2.   The Apostolic Chamber concerned itself in direct taxation only in the imposition of the *tallia militum*.   The assessments for tallage were particularly the concern of the Chamber, and towns wishing to have their tallage reduced had to appeal to the Pope, and not to the Rector.   The Chamber also ordered the Governor to re-assess all the towns of the March, and approved his findings.[1]

The disposition of the tallage when it had been collected varied in the various provinces.   In the March of Ancona the tallage or subsidies were part of the ordinary income of the province, were imposed without special authority, and were treated as part of the ordinary revenues.   In Perugia and the Duchy of Spoleto these taxes were imposed annually by the authority of a special letter from the Vice-Chamberlain, in which the provincial Treasurer was told to send the money which he collected from this source direct to the Chamber.[2]   In the same area, moreover, the Chamber sometimes appointed commissioners specially to collect tallage, responsible not to the Treasurer of Perugia but to the Chamber direct.   Such commissioners might have to pay the tallage to mercenaries to whom it had been assigned, or they might transmit the money to the Chamber.

§ 3.   The salt monopoly was administered by 'officials' or 'conduttori' under agreements which they made with the Apostolic Chamber.   The provincial Rectors and Treasurers had a hand in enforcing the discipline of the monopoly, but it was primarily the concern of the central government.   The monopoly obliged all the communes of the State of the Church to buy their salt from one of these 'officials' or 'conductors', each commune being assessed for the amount it must buy.   The price was laid down by the Apostolic Chamber for the various regions.   The salt was stored at various points in the provinces in 'camere' or 'magazini', and the communes were obliged to provide these storehouses, and to allow the officials of the monopoly to transport the salt there without payment of toll or custom.

The salt monopoly fell into decay during the Schism, and was encroached on by all manner of local interests.   To restore it, the Chamber negotiated agreements with two Florentine merchants, one of whom, Bartolomeo Geri, became the 'official' of the Patrimony, while the other, Ricardo Anichini, became the 'conductor' of the March of Ancona.   The situation of these two 'salarie' was slightly different, in that the Patrimony had its own salt pans (*saline*) at Corneto, whereas the March had to import salt from outside the province.[3]   The systems adopted in the two provinces were also different.   The Geri [4] were papal officials in the proper sense.   They sold the salt at a fixed price, paid over the monies they received for it to the Chamber,

[1] See p. 83 above.   Also doc. 5 below which records, in the marginal note, the *taxatio* for tallage which was carried out in the Chamber for the district of Trevi, and for certain ecclesiastics.

[2] Doc. 5 below.   It is not clear that the Treasurer of the Patrimony had to have special authority to impose tallage; such had not been the practice of the preceding century.   But cf. p. 113 above and doc. 3 below.

[3] This is evident from the terms of the agreement with the Vice-Chamberlain.   There were, nevertheless, salt pans at Recanati; see the grant of these pans by the commune, Zdekauer, 'L'Archivio del Comune di Recanati ed il recente suo riordinamento', *Le Marche*, v (1905).

[4] Theiner, iii, nos. 187–8, pp. 258, 260.   Cf. Gottlob, 243–5.

and then received a percentage on the gross amount sold.   An element of capitalist enterprise entered in the clause which provided that the Geri should initially buy their stocks of salt with their own money.   The Chamber undertook to pay them for the stocks which remained at the end of the contract.

In the case of the Anichini [1] this agreement was reversed; the 'conductors' bought the salt outside the March, imported and transported it, and kept the proceeds of the sales, but they agreed to pay the Apostolic Chamber a percentage charge on the amount of salt which they sold.   In both cases 'officials' or 'chancellors' were to be appointed by the Chamber to supervise the loading and unloading of the salt at all stages, to hold the keys of the storehouses, and in general to see fair play. The merchants were obliged to guarantee that the monopoly did not suffer as a result of their neglecting to import or provide sufficient salt.   They were to render accounts of their administration to the Chamber whenever these were required.

The conductors of the monopoly in the March were assisted by a notary who was appointed by the Holy See, [2] and by 'custodians', appointed by them and confirmed by the Holy See, who were to investigate attempts to defraud the monopoly. [3]   The Treasurer and Rector of the province were obliged to assist the salt monopoly, and to execute justice against those attempting to defraud it. [4]   For greater efficiency in detecting and prosecuting such frauds, a special commissioner with the powers of a Marshal was appointed in the March, with orders to apprehend offenders, and to bring them before the Treasurer of the March to be punished according to the statutes of the province. [5]   Later in the pontificate, the Treasurer of the March himself was granted a similar commission. [6]   In the Patrimony there appear to have been special statutes for the *dogana salis* which laid down penalties for the infringement of its rights, but the text of these no longer survives. [7]

Anichini's administration in the March was evidently a success; he was said by the Pope to have brought considerable profits to the Chamber, and as a reward he was granted all the salt remaining in the storehouse and his appointment renewed. [8] It was renewed several times, once with a guarantee that in the event of war between the Church and any other power his goods would not be seized, [9] a stipulation which

---

[1] Div. Cam. 14, fol. 21v, 9 December 1419.   The *salaria* of the March had formerly been held by one Benedetto of Urbino, Reg. Vat. 348, fol. 104v, 10 January 1419; Div. Cam. 3, fol. 56, 13 January 1419.

[2] Nicolò Luccii Manciani de Cavis was appointed notary and official of the *salaria* of the March on 28 July 1420, at a monthly salary of 12 florins, Reg. Vat. 349, fol. 63.

[3] Jacopo of Anagni, appointed *custos* first by Anichini, then re-appointed by the Pope, with the power to investigate all frauds in the use and transport of the salt, and to denounce them to the Treasurer of the province, Reg. Vat. 354, fol. 237.   A similar appointment in 1425, Reg. Vat. 355, fol. 189v.

[4] Theiner, iii, no. 208, p. 275.   Further instructions to the Treasurer of the March to assist Anichini in the reform of the *salaria*, Reg. Vat. 354, fol. 262v, 29 August 1423.

[5] Reg. Vat. 349, fols. 176, 184v, 23 August 1421, renewed in 1422, Reg. Vat. 354, fol. 32.   The commissioner was Cola Quarto of Trani, an active papal official, and his salary was 30 florins monthly.

[6] Reg. Vat. 350, fol. 39v, 13 February 1424.

[7] Antonius of Sarzana, *doganerius* of the *salaria* of the Patrimony, was on 10 December 1430 ordered to proceed against and punish contraventions of the *salaria* in accordance with the statutes of the *dogana* and of the province, Div. Cam. 13, fol. 141.   [8] Reg. Vat. 353, fol. 310, 23 January 1422.

[9] Reg. Vat. 350, fol. 238, 21 April 1426.   He was appointed *commissarius* as well as *conductor*, ibid. fol. 241.   Cf. Div. Cam. 7, fol. 154, for a previous renewal.

must have had in mind a possible war with Florence. It was also renewed to Anichini's heirs after his death in 1426, for the duration of the two years' pact which he had made with the Vice-Chamberlain.[1]

How far the salt monopoly prevailed against the interests of the *signori* is doubtful. The Malatesta possessed the important salt pans of Cervia, until they were compelled to cede the town to the Pope in 1430. They claimed special privileges in the *salaria*,[2] and Carlo Malatesta exported salt to other *signori* of the March and Umbria.[3] The Varano imported salt and re-exported it, but only under licence from the Pope. In 1422 Berardo Varano made an agreement with the Vice-Chamberlain allowing him to import 10,000 loads of salt, and to export it to the lands of Braccio and Corrado Trinci; for this licence he paid 500 florins.[4] He was not allowed, however, to sell the salt inside the March, and he had to compensate Anichini for any loss which the latter might suffer. In Romagna the Alidosi and Ordelaffi were expressly granted the salt monopoly (*canepa salis*) within their vicariates,[5] but there is no trace at this period of a papal salt monopoly in the Romagna.[6] The commune of Bologna had its own salt monopoly, which was part of the communal finances.[7] There is even less evidence of the extent to which the free communes managed to avoid the salt monopoly. Ancona, which administered its own salt monopoly, the *membro del sale*, is almost certainly an exception.[8]

There were five *salarie* in the Papal State. Those of the Patrimony and the March have been described. The *salaria* of Rome extended to the whole of the Roman District, and was not run by an official, but was farmed to the highest bidder, as was later in the century done for all the *salarie*. The farmer of the monopoly was termed the *doganerius salis*, and he performed the same functions as the other officials and conductors of the monopoly.[9] He received the salt from the pans of the

---

[1] Reg. Vat. 350, fol. 258.

[2] Carlo Malatesta's representatives appeared before the Vice-Chamberlain in July 1420, with letters claiming such privileges, Arm. 34, vol. 4, fol. 154. For the salt monopoly of the Malatesta in the *contado* of Fano, see Zonghi, *Repertorio dell'antico Archivio comunale di Fano* (1888), 44–5.

[3] Div. Cam. 13, fol. 27, 1 November 1429. The Treasurer of Perugia is told to collect from Corrado Trinci money he owes to Carlo Malatesta (then dead) on account of the 600 loads of salt which the latter had sold him. He is to require Atto de Attis, papal vicar in Sassoferrato, to deliver up all the salt which Carlo Malatesta and his brother sent him. And he is to make Chiavelli the papal vicar in Fabriano repay to the Treasurer all the sums which he exacted for the passage of Malatesta's salt through his lands.

[4] Div. Cam. 14, fol. 86; Reg. Vat. 354, fol. 85v. He may also export the salt to Monte Santo, Cerreto or Visso. He paid 350 florins in May 1422 (IE 379, fol. 81v, 83); the rest at a later date. The salt is to be moved to Umbria 'per viam Tolentini'.

[5] Theiner, iii, nos. 157–8, pp. 224, 229.

[6] In the estimate of papal income made under Sixtus IV (Bauer, 'Studi per la storia delle finanze papali', *ASR*, 1 (1927), 377–8) the only salt revenues from Romagna are those of Cesena, Fano and Senigaglia, 'dele terre . . . che furon de Malatesta'.

[7] O. Bosdari, 'Il comune di Bologna alla fine del secolo XIV', *AMDR*, 4th ser., iv (1914), 142–3. Cf. Theiner, iii, no. 227, p. 288.

[8] Remo Roia, 'L'amministrazione finanziaria del comune di Ancona nel secolo XV', *AMSM*, 4th ser., i (1924), 180 f.

[9] Gottlob, *Aus der Camera apostolica*, 103–4, 243–5. The appointment was as 'Duanerio' or 'doganerius et officialis salarie urbis'. It was made annually for a term of four months, e.g. in 1421 Blasio Petri Cechi de Nigro was appointed (Reg. Vat. 349, fol. 159); in 1424 Paolo de Fuschis de Berta (Reg. Vat. 350, fol. 65).

campus salis near Ostia, and stored it in the Tabularium on the Capitol.[1] His work has to be distinguished from that of the two commissioners 'pro sale et focatico', who were subordinate to the Chamber of Rome. Their duties were to exact from the cities in the District which were subject to Rome the money for the salt which they received, besides a hearth tax and several other small taxes resulting from the former supremacy of the Roman commune.[2]

The salt pans and *salaria* of Terracina must have supplied the rest of Campania and Maritima; they were administered by an 'official' but I have found little trace of the arrangements for their control.[3] They were very profitable, and as it seems unlikely that large sums would accrue from the salt monopoly of so poor a province, it is probable that the salt was exported beyond the province—perhaps beyond the Papal State.

The salt monopoly of Perugia was at first administered by the Treasurer of Perugia, and then by a Governor of the *salaria*; it extended to all the lands ruled from Perugia and Città di Castello.[4] The Duchy of Spoleto, and the mountain district of Norcia and Cassia were included in the salt monopoly of the March.[5]

None of the account books of the *salarie* under Martin V have survived, and estimates of the income they rendered can be no more than a guess. The *Introitus et Exitus* volumes contain a series of entries recording payments from the *salaria* of the Patrimony (referred to in the documents as the *salaria* of Corneto), and certain minimum figures may be deduced from these entries. 35,368 florins were either paid in cash to the Chamber or assigned for other purposes during the ten years beginning in 1421. The lowest payment from this *salaria* in any one year was the 2,000 florins paid in 1429, the highest 5,540 in 1424.[6] The average annual amount received over these ten years is therefore about 3,500 florins a year. This figure is a minimum one; the real profits, when assignments not recorded in the registers and amounts paid to the secret funds of the Pope are considered, were probably far more than this.

The *salaria* of the March almost certainly yielded at least as much as that of the Patrimony, but its profits have left little trace in the account books. In 1424 it paid 4,035 florins to the Chamber, in 1429 5,508 florins.[7] Other years record no

---

[1] *Statuti della città di Roma* (ed. C. Re, 1880), 228; Tomassetti, 'Del sale e focatico del comune di Roma nel medio evo', *ASR*, xx (1897); Arch. Cam., pt. i, Camera di Roma, B. 72, vols. 1 and 2 (described by Tomassetti, in article cited).

[2] *Statuti della città di Roma*, 179, 193; S. Malatesta, *Statuti delle gabelle di Roma*, 35; Tomassetti, article cited.

[3] Giovanni Malruscio, official of the *salaria* of Terracina, was in 1428 ordered to investigate frauds in the *salaria*, Div. Cam. 11, fol. 206v.

[4] In 1429 the Treasurer of Perugia was said to be unable to deal with the *salaria* any longer, through pressure of business, and in his place was appointed Antonio Angeli de Leanto of Florence (which suggests a commercial arrangement of the same type as those with Anichini and Geri), as Governor of the *salaria* of Perugia, Todi, Assisi, Città di Castello, Montefalco, Bettona and Gualdo Cattaneo (Reg. Vat. 351, fol. 115v, 13 April 1429).   [5] Reg. Vat. 353, fols. 310v, 316.

[6] IE 379, fols. 43v, 46v, 50v, 77v, 99, 106, 118v; IE 382, fols. 18v, 26, 33v, 49, 52v, 68, 74; IE 383, fols. 24, 28v, 40v; IE 385, fols. 12v, 19, 42v, 64, 85, 104; IE 387, fols. 15v, 37; IE 389, fols. 35, 41v, 50; Reg. Vat. 353, fol. 296; Reg. Vat. 355, fol. 16v.

[7] IE 382, fols. 68, 68v, 164; IE 385, fol. 45v.

profits at all, but the commendation given by the Pope to Ricardo Anichini for his profitable administration makes it practically certain that large profits were in fact made. The *salaria* of Terracina has again left little trace, but payments from this source of 4,050 florins in 1427 and 4,856 florins in 1430 indicate that it was far from unprofitable.[1] The farm of the *salaria* of Rome was paid into the accounts of the City. Of the profits of that of Perugia I have found no trace. At a hazard, the total annual profits of the salt monopoly throughout the Papal State at this time could be put at something near 20,000 florins, a figure well below that of 34,500 florins which is given by Gottlob for a period rather later in the fifteenth century.[2]

III. *The Administration of Higher Justice*

§ 1. The supreme courts of the Papal State were also two of the supreme spiritual courts of the Papacy, the courts of the Auditor of the Apostolic Chamber and of the Roman Rota. The system in use under Martin V foreshadows that of the sixteenth and seventeenth centuries. Civil and criminal appeals from the Papal State were first brought to the Auditor of the Chamber, and then a second appeal might be permitted before the Rota. In some cases—in later centuries this was extended to all the so-called *causae maiores*—an appeal might be brought directly before the Rota.

The court of the Auditor of the Apostolic Chamber dates from the thirteenth century.[3] He could have a Vice-Auditor, with the same powers which he himself enjoyed, but there was no further increase than this in the number of judges, and no question of the formation of a college, as occurred with the Auditors of the Sacred Palace. In Martin's time the Auditor was appointed by the Chamberlain, and not, as later, by the Pope.

The relation of the Auditor to the Chamberlain suffered a great deal of change during the fourteenth and fifteenth centuries. In 1323 an Auditor of the Court of the Apostolic Chamber was appointed, specifically without prejudice to the jurisdiction of the Chamberlain.[4] In 1353 it was already necessary for the Pope to grant a special faculty to the Chamberlain to hear appeals from the Auditor, evidence of the Auditor's growing independence.[5] Under Martin V the relationship was evidently a matter of considerable delicacy. In a case already referred to above, the Chamberlain wished to transfer to the *podestà* of Viterbo the hearing of a case which had been brought in Rome before the Auditor of the Apostolic Chamber. The Chamberlain made no claim to transfer this case by his own authority, but suggested by the wording of his letter that the Auditor had voluntarily released

---

[1] IE 385, fols. 19, 42v, 65; IE 389, fols. 35, 41v, 50.

[2] *Aus der Camera apostolica*, 245.

[3] Ch. Samaran and G. Mollat, *La fiscalité pontificale en France au xiv⁰ siècle* (1905), 132–41; E. Göller, 'Der Gerichtshof der päpstlichen Kammer und die Entstehung des Amtes des Procurator fiscalis im kirchlichen Prozessverfahren', *AKKR*, xciv (1914), 605–12; G. Mollat, 'Contribution à l'histoire de l'administration judiciaire de l'Eglise Romaine au xiv⁰ siècle', *RHE*, xxxii (1936), 897–928.

[4] Göller, 'Die constitution "ratio iuris" Johannes XXII. und die Camera apostolica', *RQ*, xvi (1902), 415.

[5] Samaran and Mollat, doc. viii, p. 209.

his jurisdiction over the case, so that it could be transferred to the Chamberlain, and thence to the *podestà*—'causam et causas huiusmodi ad nos per eundem dominum Dominicum auditorem remissas . . .'[1] This independence of the Auditor grew during the fifteenth century to a point where he became a totally independent official, always appointed by the Pope, and only nominally connected with the Chamber and the Chamberlain, while the Chamberlain himself was deprived of all but the most petty jurisdiction.[2] But under Martin V this evolution was far from complete. The Auditor was appointed by the Chamberlain under Martin V, but by the Pope under Eugenius IV.[3] He continued, under Martin V, to come under the Chamberlain's direct supervision and orders. In 1420 the Vice-Chamberlain gave detailed orders to the Auditor, how he was to sit twice a week to hear the cases of criminals detained by the *soldanus* of the Roman Court, so that the prisoners might not suffer by undue delay.[4]

The jurisdiction of the Auditor of the Chamber was 'ordinary' and not 'delegated', and continued to be effective *sede vacante*.[5] He was in the first place the judge of all ecclesiastical cases in the Catholic world relating to affairs touching the Apostolic Chamber. Appeals might be brought to him straight from the ordinaries, 'omisso medio', as though the appeal were made direct to the Pope.[6] He was secondly a judge of first instance in all civil and criminal cases arising in the Roman Court itself which concerned clerics.[7] This jurisdiction caused continual battles with the Senator of Rome, since, in spite of an arrangement dating from the time of Boniface IX, the Capitoline Court was always imprisoning courtiers of the Roman Court for offences committed in the City. A particularly clear and definite statement about this jurisdiction, interesting because it shows that the Chamberlain preserved his own personal jurisdiction in these matters, was made in 1422. The Senator was told that clerks and ecclesiastical persons could be cited only before the

---

[1] Doc. 13 below.

[2] F. Grosse-Wietfeld, *Justizreformen im Kirchenstaat in den ersten Jahren der Restauration (1814–16)* (1932), 144–5. Cf. Giovanni Battista Cardinal de Luca, *Theatrum veritatis et iustitiae* (Rome, 1673), xv, 'relatio Romanae Curiae', disc. xxxiv, par. 1, 'In causis et negotiis cameralibus, nullam habet jurisdictionem vel participationem'.

[3] The appointment of Bartholomeo Dellante as Vice-Auditor of the Chamber, made by the Vice-Chamberlain, is in Div. Cam. 8, fol. 198, dated 31 July 1424. Under Eugenius IV the Auditor was appointed by the Pope; cf. Gottlob, 128, giving the form of appointment, and *Calendar of Entries in the Papal Registers relating to Great Britain and Ireland*, viii (1909), 344, where the Pope refers to Lewis de Garsiis as 'officium Auditoriatus Curie Camere apostolice causarum de mandato nostro regenti'. Other Auditors of the Chamber under Martin V include Domenico of San Geminiano (docs. 13, 14 below), Pantaleone de Bredis (doc. 10 below) and, in April 1426, Giuliano Cesarini (*Calendar of Entries*, vii, 16, 34).

[4] Doc. 10 below.

[5] De Luca, *Theatrum*, xv, 'de iudiciis', and 'relatio Romanae Curiae', disc. xxxiv, par. 31, 'Cum autem sit iudex ordinarius, idcirco eius iurisdictio, durat etiam sede papali vacante, in qua cessat iurisdictio omnium aliorum tribunalium'. Cf. Durandus, *Speculum Iuris*, 'ordinarius', lib. 1, c. 1, 'Item ordinarius est, cui causarum universitas est commissa . . . Pari etiam ratione camerarius domini papae, vice-cancellarius, auditor contradictarum, et auditor camerae, ordinarii sunt . . .'; Hostiensis, *Summa Aurea* (Lugduni, 1568), fol. 76v.

[6] De Luca, *Theatrum*, xv, 'relatio Romanae Curiae', disc. xxxiv, par. 11, 'Appellatur quoque ad eum ab ordinariis, omisso medio, eo modo quo ad ipsum Papam'.

[7] Ibid.

Vice-Chamberlain himself, or before the Auditor of the Chamber; laymen who were followers of the Roman Court could be cited only in the court of the Marshal of the Roman Court.[1] The Auditor of the Chamber was obliged to sit twice a week to hear such cases of first instance. His notaries had to keep a record of the names of the criminals and the charges against them, and the money from their condemnations was to be kept under his personal custody, and paid by him into the Apostolic Chamber.

Third, the Auditor of the Chamber was a judge of appeal for civil and criminal cases arising in the Papal State.[2] At what date he assumed this jurisdiction is uncertain. During the early Avignonese period, special judges of appeal were occasionally appointed to go to Italy to hear cases from the Papal State.[3] Later in the century both the Auditor of the Chamber and the Auditors of the Rota heard such cases, but no evidence has been published which delineates the respective functions of the two courts.[4]

§ 2. The Rota had not, before this period, dealt with cases from the Papal State, but had confined itself to purely ecclesiastical matters.[5] Auditors of the Sacred Palace had been appointed to hear judicial cases since early in the thirteenth century, and early in the following century they had been organised as a college, and had taken on the name of the Rota. Each Auditor had a general commission from the Pope to hear and terminate the cases brought before him, but he also received a special commission to hear each particular case which was assigned to him. It is not therefore clear whether the jurisdiction exercised by the Auditors was 'ordinary' or 'delegated', and the question has been much ventilated among canonists, from Durandus the Speculator to those of the present day. The best opinion appears to be that their jurisdiction was in the later Middle Ages ordinary, but the act of giving judgement may have been one of delegated jurisdiction.[6]

In the sixteenth century and later there was certainly an appeal, in many civil cases from the Papal State, from the court of the Auditor of the Chamber to the Rota.[7] The situation in the fourteenth and fifteenth centuries is far from clear,

---

[1] Doc. 12 below. Cf. de Luca, 'relatio Romanae Curiae', disc. xxxiv, par. 3, and Theiner, iii, no. 30, p. 78, the agreement of Boniface IX with the Roman Commune. 'Item quod Cortesani tam clerici quam layci, et clerici Romani non trahantur nisi ad legitimum forum eorum, videlicet clerici Cortesani coram Auditore Camere, layci Corthesani coram Marescallo dicti domini Pape, et Romani clerici coram Vicario dicti domini Pape'.

[2] De Luca, loc. cit.; Grosse-Wietfeld, 143 f.; Gottlob, 128, the appointment of the Auditor of the Chamber, referring to cases 'que sive per appellationem interjectam a gravaminibus vel sententiis definitivis in terris eidem ecclesie immediate subiectis aut alias ad Sedem Apostolicam delate sint'.

[3] Cf. Samaran and Mollat, doc. 2, p. 203, and the instances quoted by F. Egon Schneider, *Die Römische Rota. Nach geltendem Recht auf geschichtlicher Grundlage*, i (1914), 61–71.

[4] Schneider, 71; Göller, article cited above, in *AKKR*, xciv (1914).

[5] Schneider, 63. For the Rota in general, see also Grosse-Wietfeld, 163 f., and E. Cerchiari, *Capellani papae et apostolicae sedis, auditores causarum sacri palatii apostolici seu sacra Romana Rota ab origine usque ad diem 20 Septembris 1870* (1921).

[6] Schneider, 12 f., 81 f.; Cerchiari, 41–50; Grosse-Wietfeld, who conciliates the opposing views, 169–78.

[7] Grosse-Wietfeld, 164 f.

but it is almost certain that such an appeal normally lay. In the last decade of the fourteenth century there were complaints that the Auditors of the Chamber were trying to try in their court appeals made to the Pope.[1] It is highly unlikely that the Pope would have heard such appeals in person, and the probability is that he would have committed them to an Auditor of the Rota.

This probability is strengthened by a case of Martin V's pontificate. In 1421 Jacopo Orsini, Count of Tagliacozzo, brought a suit against Orso Orsini of Monte Rotondo for the recovery of the *castrum* of Mentana, in the Roman District.[2] The suit was brought in appeal before Tomasso de Virago, judge of appeals of the Capitoline Court,[3] but Orso Orsini then objected to the person of the judge, and petitioned the Pope for it to be given to another judge; the petition was granted, and before any sentence had been passed in the Capitoline Court the Pope transferred the case to the Auditor of the Apostolic Chamber, Domenico of San Geminiano, who proceeded to hear it and to give sentence and costs against Orso Orsini. Orso Orsini thereupon petitioned the Pope that he might be allowed a further appeal on the ground that only one appeal had taken place, and not the two which were allowed by law. He therefore asked that the case might be committed to an Auditor of the Apostolic Palace, qualifying his petition by the clause that he was content that the new judge should first of all decide whether or not a fresh appeal lay. The form in which his petition was made corresponds closely to the *commissio* of later centuries, by which a suppliant asked for his case to be heard in appeal.[4] Where the principal doubt lay, as to whether or not an appeal from the Auditor was permissible, is not stated, but probably the difficulty was that the case had already been through two courts of appeal, although sentence had been passed only in one of them.

The Pope granted Orso Orsini's petition, and appointed Cunczo de Zuola, Auditor of the Rota, to review the case as was petitioned.[5] The case had thus passed in appeal from the court of the Auditor of the Chamber to that of an Auditor of the Rota. There the case reached deadlock on a procedural point; Jacopo Orsini failed to appear at the proper time before Master Cunczo, and was condemned for contumacy. As a result, Master Cunczo issued an inhibition against the execution of the sentence passed by Domenico of San Geminiano being given in the Capitoline Court, where Jacopo Orsini had applied to the collateral judges for execution, and was about to obtain it. At this stage Jacopo Orsini in his turn petitioned the Pope, this time raising another important legal point. He urged in his own favour the statutes of the City of Rome, which forbid any further appeal from the sentence

---

[1] See the document printed by Mollat, *RHE*, xxxii (1936), 921.

[2] The documents in this case were catalogued (not always accurately) by C. de Cupis, 'Regesto degli Orsini e dei Conti Anguillara', *BDA*, 3rd ser., i, fasc. 1, 2 (1910). Two petitions which give an account of the earlier stages of the case are printed below, doc. 14.

[3] Rome, Archivio Capitolino, Archivio di Casa Orsini, II.A.XII. 39.

[4] Cf. Grosse-Wietfeld, 96 and n. These petitions were later heard in the Chancery (ibid.). It is interesting that Orsini's petition was conceded in the form 'de mandato d.n. pape audiat . . .' (doc. 14 below), and not in the forms 'fiat' or 'concessum' used for petitions in the matter of benefices.

[5] Doc. 14 below.

of the judge of appeals of the Capitoline Court.[1] Arguing that the Pope must wish the statutes of the City to be observed, he deduced that the Pope must have therefore appointed Domenico of San Geminiano to sit, not as a higher judge of appeal, but as though he were a judge of appeals in the Capitoline Court. For, as he justly observed, to grant further appeals from the judge of appeals of the City was to go against the intention of the statutes by enabling cases to be dragged out unduly.

This appeal to the liberties of Rome corresponded to the agreement of Alexander V with the Roman Commune, and seems to have found favour with the Pope.[2] He granted Orsini's petition, and ordered that the collateral judges of the Capitoline Court, assisted by the 'assectamentum', do justice in the case:[3] they were given power also to inhibit Master Cunczo from interfering any further in the matter. The decision seems to go against the spirit of the *Constitutiones Egidiane*, which insist so wholeheartedly on the papal monopoly of appellate jurisdiction, and it shows how far were the judicial privileges of Rome from falling into disuse or contempt.

When the collateral judges of the Capitoline Court came to hear the case, they naturally accepted the version most favourable to the liberties of their court, and referred to Domenico of San Geminiano as a 'commissioner delegated by the Pope in place of the judge of appeals of the Roman people'.[4] Fairly certainly, they conferred this title on him quite gratuitously, and in fact he had probably judged the case merely by virtue of a papal commission, without mention of the Capitoline Court.

The Rota could also under certain circumstances act as a court of first instance for cases from the Papal State; one such circumstance was the request of the parties to the case. Thus in 1421 there was a dispute between Poncello Orsini and Giovanni di Vico, the Prefect of Rome, over the *castrum* of Trevignano, in the Roman District. At the instance of Poncello Orsini the Pope commissioned Giovanni de Fabrica, Auditor of the Rota, to hear and decide the case.[5] The commission is of the usual

---

[1] Ibid. Cf. *Statuti della città di Roma*, 'A iudicis autem appellationis sententia nullus audiatur appellans'. For the collateral judges, ibid. 213, lxxvi.

[2] Theiner, iii, no. 109, p. 172. 'Item quod in causis appellacionum Romanorum et districtualium dicte Urbis iudicialiter, aut per modum compromissi terminatis et terminandis, capitaneus et iudex appellacionum et nullitatum prefati populi, qui erit pro tempore, cognoscere et terminare habeat secundum dictorum exigenciam statutorum, et quod ab ipso ac eius declaracione nulli liceat appellare.' Cf. also *Statuti della città di Roma*, 38; Luca Peto, *De iudiciaria formula Capitolini fori* (Rome, 1610), 12, 'Hinc dicebam alias in facta contingentia, quod advena quidam Romam incolens, qui coram Auditore Camerae conventus causam contra se motam vigore privilegiorum Rom. Pon. concessorum in foro Capitolino reassumi fecerat, iam se incolam declaverat, adeo ut iterum in alia causa reus in dicto Capitolino foro conventus forum declinare non possit ex praedictis'. Cf. also 15, 32, ibid.

[3] Doc. 14 below. The *assectamentum* was the joint sitting of the six ordinary judges of the city, *Statuti della città di Roma*, lxxvii.

[4] Archivio Capitolino, Arch. Orsini, II.A.XIII, nos. 11 and 12, 'Dominicus de sancto Geminiano decretorum doctor s.d.n. pape capellanus, ipsiusque et eius camerarii ac curie causarum camere apostolice auditor generalis, iudex commissarius et delegatus cause et partibus infrascriptis et predictis, inter dictas partes loco iudicis appellationum, et tamquam iudex appellationum populi romani, quo ad causam istam per s.d.n. papam deputatus, legitime processu precedente, diffinitivam tulit sentenciam . . .'

[5] Reg. Vat. 354, fol. 286. Cf. De Cupis, in *BDA*, 3rd ser., i, fasc. 1, (1910), 69, 74-6. For Giovanni de Fabrica see Cerchiari, ii, 46, and iii, 119-20.

type given to cases assigned to the Rota—'tibi . . . audiendam commisimus et fine debito terminandam'. The judge was also enjoined that if, as was possible, neither party had any rights to the *castrum*, and this belonged fully to the Roman See, then he was to concede it to Giovanni di Vico as a noble fee.

Giovanni de Fabrica found in favour of Poncello Orsini, and awarded him the sentence and costs. Further appeal to the Pope followed, and another expedient was adopted, typical of the elasticity of the justice of the Roman Court, and of the favour which it showed to prolonged litigation. The case was revived and assigned to a commission of two Cardinals, the Cardinal of Santa Croce and the Cardinal of Venice, who upheld the sentence in favour of Poncello Orsini.[1]

§ 3. There is no evidence that the Apostolic Chamber concerned itself with the State of the Church when it sat in its entirety as a court of justice; such sittings [2] seem to have been concerned with entirely ecclesiastical matters. Nor is there evidence that the Chamberlain frequently exercised the jurisdiction of first instance and appeal which he certainly still possessed. When Terni and Rieti, reviving a case once argued by Cicero, disputed the channel of the river Velino and the artificial waterfalls of Le Mármore, the Pope commissioned the Vice-Chamberlain to hear the case as a specially appointed judge and commissioner, thus granting him a delegated jurisdiction instead of the ordinary jurisdiction which he also possessed.[3]

The Chamberlain used his judicial powers, not so much as a judge of first instance or appeal, as to quash or commit for retrial sentences passed by all manner of judges in the State of the Church. Thus, after the rebellion of Viterbo in 1430, the Judge-General of the Patrimony of St. Peter in Tuscia imposed a fine of 1,000 florins on Ugone Albizzi, a Florentine merchant trading in Viterbo, for his complicity in the rebellion. The Vice-Chamberlain later declared himself convinced of Albizzi's innocence, and quashed the sentence.[4] In several cases the Chamberlain was moved to take action by petitions which had been made to the Pope. Thus, a case was returned to the *capitaneus* of Todi for retrial, on account of his having first decided it by the use of torture, and then having refused to hear certain witnesses.[5] Another case, of theft, was returned to the priors of Rieti for retrial on similar grounds again as the result of a petition to the Pope.[6] The criminal judge of the Deputy-Governor of Spoleto was reported to the Vice-Chamberlain to have condemned certain persons for conspiracy without paying due regard to the correct legal forms. The Vice-Chamberlain accordingly ordered the succeeding Governor to retry the case.[7]

The interference of the Chamberlain in the justice administered by the Senator and courts of Rome was manifold; the Vice-Chamberlain appears to have exercised a paternalist and despotic authority, the prototype of that later exercised by the Vice-Chamberlains as Governors of Rome. A typical example is the case of the

---

[1] De Cupis, loc. cit., quoting documents in the Archivio Orsini.
[2] For such sittings, see *Bullarium Romanum*, v, 76; Gottlob, 117–8.
[3] Div. Cam. 9, fol. 298, 8 October 1426.
[4] Div. Cam. 13, fol. 84.
[5] Div. Cam. 9, fol. 214.
[6] Div. Cam. 13, fol. 142v.
[7] Div. Cam. 8, fol. 248.

Pisan merchant Jacopo Buccha, who was imprisoned in the Chancery of the Capitoline Court on account of a debt he had contracted to an ecclesiastic of the Roman Court. On 27 April 1423 the Vice-Chamberlain wrote to the Senator that Buccha had appealed to the Pope, saying that he was owed far larger sums than those he owed to the Dean of Digne. The Senator was therefore ordered to collect these debts and then to release the prisoner 'statutis et consuetudinibus urbis et aliis quibuscumque presentibus quomodolibet contrafacientibus non obstantibus'.[1] On 11 May, however, it was reported to the Vice-Chamberlain that the merchant had been 'almost released' from prison; this was not the Pope's intention, and accordingly the Senator is ordered to have the prisoner returned to chains, so that he shall not lose his intentions of paying the debt.[2] Finally the promised assets failed to materialise, and a further order to release Buccha from chains was cancelled.[3] Another typical interference was that on behalf of Paolo Jacopo of Trastevere, who was kept for a year in the Capitoline prison for a debt of 40 pence, 'ex quo ut dicitur quod blasfemaverit et deo maledixerit'. The Senator was therefore told to arrange a composition so that the man could be released.[4]

The Chamberlain had a lively eye on the monies to be had from compositions, and instructions to the Senator on this subject are numerous. On one occasion a case about the abduction of a twelve-year-old girl which was in progress in the Capitoline Court was stopped by the Vice-Chamberlain, and the Senator and judges were ordered to accept a composition of 40 pence from the guilty party, and to close the case.[5] On another occasion a judicial enquiry made by the *judex maleficiorum* was declared by the Vice-Chamberlain to be calumnious, and the Vice-Senator was ordered to have it stopped.[6]

This anxiety to exact the maximum profit from the courts by obtaining compositions for unpaid fines resulted in the appointment of commissioners, who were sent to various provinces of the Papal State with authority to collect the profits of justice, and to review sentences and condemnations. Such a commission was given to Angelo of Todi, a notary of the Chamber, in 1430, when he was sent to the Duchy of Spoleto and the districts of Perugia and Todi.[7]

IV. *The Papal Armies*

§ 1. With the exception of the local levies which were raised in time of emergency by the provincial Rector or Treasurer, all the main armed forces of the Papal State were Italian mercenaries, engaged, paid and supervised by the Apostolic Chamber. Foreign mercenaries were no longer employed, or hardly so; the days of the great Companies were over.

The mercenaries were engaged under agreements (*firme*) which usually ran for

---

[1] Div. Cam. 7, fol. 198.   [2] Div. Cam. 7, fol. 211.   [3] Ibid. fols. 224, 236.
[4] Ibid. fol. 244.   [5] Ibid. fol. 253.
[6] Ibid. fol. 25v (21 April 1422), concerning an inquisition into a fire in the house of Antonio Marcellini, in the region of Parione.
[7] Div. Cam. 13, fols. 30v, 31v.

L

periods of between six and eighteen months; the eight year *firma* of Tartaglia was exceptional.[1] Salaries were paid monthly, at the end of each month, but at the beginning of a *firma* it was usual for the Chamber to pay a *prestancia*, an advance of pay, for a considerable sum.[2] The currency in which payments were made was invariably *floreni auri de camera*.[3] The act embodying the *firma* was usually made out in the Chamber by the notaries of the Treasurer.

The unit in which troops were organised had since the sixties of the fourteenth century been the lance (*lancea*), which consisted of a heavily mounted 'corporal', of his attendant man-at-arms (*saccomanus, familiaris*), and of a boy servant (*ragazonus*), the last being mounted only on a nag (*ronzinus*) instead of a war horse.[4] It was usual to place ten lances under the command of a 'constable'.[5] Unlike the practice of the preceding century, when the Chamber sometimes undertook this responsibility, the mercenary had to furnish and replace his own horses.[6] Thus the heaviest capital outlay of an army, its war horses, was laid on the shoulders of the mercenary.

The size of the mercenary bands engaged varied from small troops of 50 footmen or 20 lances to the forces of about 1,500 men (400 lances and 200 foot) enlisted under Angelo della Pergola or Jacopo Caldora.[7] It has to be remembered that the scale of war at this time was extremely small, and that two or three thousand men were reckoned to be a sizeable army.[8]

---

[1] Div. Cam. 14, fol. 81, dated 29 September 1421. This was the third *firma* of Tartaglia, the previous ones being of September 1419 (Theiner, iii, no. 172, p. 245) and September 1420 (Div. Cam. 14, fol. 53). But Tartaglia's last *firma* was cut short in 1422 by his arrest and execution.

[2] E.g. the 2,000 florins paid to Tartaglia as *prestancia*, Theiner, loc. cit.

[3] This was the standard currency of the Apostolic Chamber. For its value and use see Martinori, *Annali della Zecca di Roma: Martino V: Eugenio IV* (1918), 16, 29; Garampi, *Saggi di osservazioni sul valore delle antiche monete pontificie* (first part, printed but never published, copy in the Vatican Library), 24 f. Garampi observes that in the fourteenth century there was no distinction between the papal and the cameral florins (see the *capitula* of the mint of Avignon of 1393, printed by him, doc. 18, p. 65), but that in the fifteenth century, although of the same purity as papal or Roman florins (24 carats), the cameral florin was of a different weight. He estimates its weight in the fifteenth century as 69·12 grains, to the 72 grains of the papal florins or ducats. The value of the cameral florin was usually given in *bolognini*, e.g. IE 387, fol. 66 (June 1429), florenos 200 ad rationem bolendinorum antiquorum trigintanovem, facientes florenos auri de camera 192. Other quotations for the cameral florins are 40 bon. (ibid.), 40 bon. (IE 389, fols. 16v, 22); 4 libr. bon. (ibid., fol. 8v). The mint of Rome was supervised by the Apostolic Chamber; see the *capitula* under Eugenius IV, printed by Martinori, 37 f. See also Reg. Vat. 349, fol. 161. Paolo Silvestri Bucca of Pisa was on 15 July 1421 appointed Governor, Official and President of the mint (*sicla*) of Rome, for the term of the Pope's good pleasure. 'Volentes quod omnia ordinamenta que circa dictam siclam per dilectos filios gentes apostolice camere facta sint, et quod inposterum dicto beneplacito durante per eosdem contigerit fieri adimpleas totaliter' (ibid.). From 1425-7 the office was held by Domenico Gherardini of Florence (Reg. Vat. 355, fol. 257), and by the *superstans* Petro Cecchi Pauli civis romanus (Div. Cam. 9, fol. 15v).

[4] See Orsini's *condotta* of 1407, Theiner, iii, no. 100, p. 188. See also, in general; K. H. Schäfer, *Deutsche Ritter und Edelknechte in Italien während des 14. Jahrhunderts*, i (1911), 44-57; Andrea da Mosto, 'Ordinamenti militari delle soldatesche dello Stato Romano dal 1430 al 1470', *QF*, v (1903); E. Ricotti, *Storia delle compagnie di ventura in Italia* (various editions); G. Canestrini, *Documenti per servire alla storia della milizia italiana dal XIII. sec. al XVI.* (*ASI*, 1st ser., xv, 1851); Gottlob, *Aus der Camera apostolica*, 123-7. D. P. Waley's 'Papal Armies in the Thirteenth Century', *EHR*, lxxii (1957) appeared too late to be used by me.   [5] Schäfer, ii, 53.   [6] Schäfer, i, 57 f.

[7] Div. Cam. 14, fol. 68, 4 July 1421; ibid. fol. 85, 6 August 1428.

[8] Cf. Piero Pieri, *Il Rinascimento e la crisi militare italiana* (1952), 258-69.

§ 2. Payment was normally reckoned as a fixed monthly sum for each lance and each footman (*pagha*), with an additional 'provision' for the mercenary captain, the last being usually reckoned at so much monthly per lance, but sometimes expressed as a monthly or yearly lump payment. Where a mercenary force was liable to be moved from one region to another, a scale of pay was often given which allowed for the varying cost of living in each region. Thus Aloysio de Verme was allowed ten florins a lance monthly in Rome, the Duchy of Spoleto, the Patrimony of St. Peter in Tuscia, the lands of special commission, Campania and Maritima, and the March of Ancona. This was to be increased to eleven florins a month in Romagna, and to twelve in Bologna.[1] His 'provisio' of one florin a lance remained constant. Similarly, Carlo Malatesta was given eleven florins a lance, with a florin of provision, while he was in Bologna or Romagna, and ten florins and one of provision while serving in the rest of the Papal State or in the Kingdom of Naples.[2] The normal monthly pay offered by the Apostolic Chamber for each lance (excluding the provision of the captain, and outside Romagna) was ten florins for the first half of Martin V's pontificate, and nine florins for the second half—that is, from about 1425. The normal monthly pay of a foot soldier was three florins, during the whole period.[3]

The decline of mercenary salaries during Martin's pontificate corresponds to a steady fall which had been going on since the fourteenth century. In the wars of John XXII a heavily armed horseman (*armiger*) had been paid eight florins, in those of Albornoz six or seven florins; in 1371 a lance of three horsemen was paid eighteen florins.[4] Comparison between earlier and later figures is difficult, since the lance comprised three distinctly different soldiers, one heavily armed and mounted on a war horse, one less well mounted, and one a page on a baggage horse. A *ronzinus* in the mid-fourteenth century was paid one or two florins. In 1371, if the pay for the *ragazonus* on his nag is reckoned at three or four florins, then fourteen florins remain for the other two horsemen, a sum equal to that paid much earlier in the century. But early in the fifteenth century the pay of a lance dropped steeply. In 1407 Paolo Orsini was paid only twelve florins a lance;[5] the same rate was paid to Sforza in 1411,[6] to Guid'Antonio of Montefeltro in 1412,[7] and to Braccio when he was engaged by the papal governor of Bologna in 1415.[8] The final drop to nine florins a lance in 1425–1430 means that in a little over a half a century the average pay of a mercenary soldier had been halved, and in the half century following the death of Martin V the pay of the soldiery continued to decline even further.[9] Even the personal provision of the captain, which in the fourteenth century had sometimes been an

---

[1] Div. Cam. 14, fol. 71.   [2] Ibid. fol. 76.

[3] Most of the large forces engaged by the Pope for the war in the Kingdom in 1421–2 were paid ten florins a lance and three florins a footman, Div. Cam. 14, fols. 3–85 and Florence, Biblioteca Nazionale, xix, 82 passim. But all the *firme* from that of Guid'Antonio of Montefeltro onwards (24 March 1425, Div. Cam. 15, fol. 27) are for 9 florins a lance.

[4] Schäfer, i, 43–53; ii, 63.   [5] Theiner, iii, no. 100, p. 160.

[6] Cod. Vat. Barb. lat. 2668, fol. 32.

[7] Theiner, iii, no. 128, p. 187; Cod. Barb. lat. 2668, fol. 40.

[8] Cod. Barb. lat. 2668 A.   [9] Da Mosto, *QF*, v (1905), 26 f.

enormous sum,[1] had by the fifteenth been scaled down to the modest standard rate of one florin per lance. Further, in the later period the mercenary had always to buy and replace his own horses. Between John XXII and Martin V the cost of mercenary warfare had been almost halved, and, as the Popes made war entirely through mercenaries, the fact cannot be of small importance for the history of the Papal State.

The sources from which the mercenaries were paid depended upon the circumstances in which the Apostolic Chamber found itself at the time. If ready money was scarce, assignments would be made on the tallage of the papal provinces.[2] The mercenary might collect his tallage direct from the towns concerned, a system much open to abuse. He was instructed that if towns defaulted in their payments he might 'curri damnificare et predari' in the offending towns, but that he must hand over any booty he took there to the Pope's representatives. It is hard to imagine that this last clause was observed, and there is no doubt but that immense misery was caused by this virtual licence to plunder. A better system was that observed with the tallage of the Patrimony of St. Peter in Tuscia in 1420–1422, which was collected by a special papal commissioner, who then distributed the money to the various mercenaries who had assignments.[3] The Chamber might try to protect itself, as it did with Angelo della Pergola, by stipulating that the captain might not complain of non-payment of his stipend until it was at least two and a half months in arrear, and that he might not occupy any towns in default of payment.[4] But these provisions did not prevent the disgruntled Angelo from seizing Castel San Pietro in the district of Bologna, from dissatisfaction at his unpaid arrears.[5]

In better times mercenaries were paid, either by the Apostolic Chamber direct, or by assignments from the various provincial treasuries.[6] There is no record of tallage being assigned to mercenaries in the Papal State between Braccio's last *firma* of 1423 and Martin V's death. This represents great advance in political and financial stability, and this overcoming of the chaotic arrangements of the Schism is one of the most impressive of Martin V's administrative successes. It was carried out not by cutting down military expenses, but by strengthening papal finances; the war of Bologna of 1428–1430 cost no less than the war in the Kingdom of 1421, or the wars of Martin V's predecessors.

[1] Schäfer, i, 54.

[2] Examples are the *firme* of Angelo della Pergola in 1420 (Div. Cam. 14, fol. 3) and of Braccio in the same year.

[3] Arch. Cam. pt. i, Tes. Prov., Patrimonio, B. 1, vol. 1a. The Commissioner was Stefano de Branchiis of Gubbio, who raised something over 11,500 florins in two years to pay to mercenaries from this source (ibid. fol. 64v). The mercenaries concerned included Tartaglia, Braccio and Aloysio de Verme.

[4] Div. Cam. 14, fol. 3; ibid. fol. 68.

[5] Reg. Vat. 353, fol. 201v, 3 July 1421. He returned the *castrum* later in the same month (ibid. fol. 209), but seized it again in August (Reg. Vat. 353, fol. 257). All this was in spite of the loan of 8,000 florins raised in Bologna to pay his stipend (Reg. Vat. 353, fol. 181v, 8 May 1421).

[6] Mercenaries stationed in a particular province were naturally paid as far as possible from the revenues of that province, e.g. Aloysio di San Severino by Perugia, Arch. Cam. pt. i, Tes. Prov., Perugia, B. 1, vol. 1a, fol. 125, or Ludovico Colonna by the Treasury of the March, ibid. Marca, B. 1, vol. 3, fol. 105. Examples are innumerable; the salary of mercenaries was one of the ordinary expenses of the province.

The pay of the mercenaries, already so much lower than in the previous century, was pared down further by certain innovations of detail, all of them unfavourable to the mercenary. The custom of paying a double month's pay when mercenaries took a town or won a battle, formerly universal, was often in the fifteenth century expressly renounced in the articles of the *firma*.[1] And further, in Martin V's time the Apostolic Chamber kept back considerable percentages of the mercenary's pay as a kind of commission, called *retentiones*, which amounted to between two and four percent of the gross salary.[2]

§ 3. The discipline of mercenary forces was provided for in the *firma*. From the point of view of the Chamber, one of the most important of such provisions was that at ten days' notice the forces of the mercenaries should be available for review (*mostra*) by agents of the Chamber. As soon as the *firma* began, the names of all the soldiers engaged were taken and given to the Chamber, and even horses were registered there. Only by a special arrangement could a mercenary captain be allowed to replace dead men or horses without notifying the Chamber.[3] The inspections provided for in the *firma* frequently took place, and money penalties were imposed on mercenaries whose troops did not correspond with those enrolled.[4]

Other disciplinary provisions in the *firma* forbade the mercenary to spoil papal territory or subjects, enjoined him to obey papal Rectors and Commissioners, and to hand over towns and districts conquered to the government of the papal representatives. He administered discipline to his own troops, except in the presence of the Pope's nephews or Legate, or of some other important dignitary.

The number of mercenaries employed by the Chamber depended entirely upon the political situation, although it was recognised that some forces must always be held in the provinces, and there was a 'condotta of the March'. But times were never normal; even more than most medieval states, the Papal State was in a condition of permanent crisis. The two most serious wars of the pontificate were the war in the Kingdom in 1421/2 and the war of Bologna in 1428/9. If the maximum number of

---

[1] Theiner, iii, nos. 100, 172, pp. 161, 247; Div. Cam. 14, fol. 4 (*firma* of Angelo della Pergola). Cf. Schäfer, i, 54.

[2] Arch. Cam. pt. i, Tes. Prov., Perugia, B. 2, vol. 2b, fol. 28, 'Die undecima Aprilis magistro capitano Loysio de Sancto Severino florenos triamilia trecentos sexaginta. Solvi de mandato s.d.n. quando missus fuit Bononiam; habui litteras de dando 3,400 florenos. Dedi 3,360, et 140 retinui pro camera apostolica, ad rationem quattuor pro centenario'. Ibid., B. 2, vol. 5, fol. 99, where the provincial Treasurer is ordered to pay Michelotto's salary for his *condotta*, 'cum rettentionibus consuetis'. Cf. Theiner, iii, no. 198, p. 269, 'circa retentiones, que de more fiunt, observabitur illud, quod prefatus dominus noster declarabit' (*condotta* of Angelo de Trisacho for the defence of the Apostolic Palace). See also IE 388, fol. 50v, 'E quisti sono per le retentione de fiorini dui per cento per le honoranze de la Camera Apostolica' (accounts of the war of Bologna).

[3] Div. Cam. 14, fol. 34, Braccio's *condotta* of 27 March 1420.

[4] Ibid. fol. 98v, 'Et scribentur omnes, cum nominibus et cognominibus atque locis unde sunt oriundi, preter pagos, quos tamen caporales predicti semper secum habere debeant et tenere. Equi vero et roncini more solito bullabuntur'. Cf. the penalties shown in IE 388, fol. 47, against various mercenaries, 'per mostre non facte et paghe non tenute'. In 1430 the commissioners of the Chamber, Baldinotto of Sarzana and Angelo of Todi, were instructed to fine mercenaries manning the papal fortresses 2½ florins for each man missing (Div. Cam. 13, fols. 31v, 107).

mercenaries employed at any one point in either of these years is taken, then in 1421/2 the Papacy was employing (excluding the *condotta* of Braccio, who was in fact an enemy) about 3,700 horse and 400 foot, at an annual cost of about 170,000 florins. In 1428/9 the equivalent number was about 3,000 horse and 1,100 foot, at an annual cost of about 160,000 florins.[1] The uncertain completeness of the sources, however, makes these figures extremely tentative.

Martin V engaged his own military galleys, largely to protect the ships bringing supplies to Rome,[2] and appointed 'commissioners' to command them;[3] and, although there is no direct evidence to prove this, he probably maintained a small papal fleet, as had Boniface IX and John XXIII.[4]

Martin V certainly had his *condottieri* far more strictly under control than most of his predecessors during the Schism, and he achieved this mainly by the firmness of his character and the soundness of his finances. Nor was the help he had from brothers and nephews unimportant; the Colonna accepted *condotte* from the Church, and also played an important part as the Pope's personal representatives in the field. Martin V's mercenaries were in consequence not allowed to grow into great war lords, or to obtain vast territorial concessions in lieu of the cash which the Chamber was unable to pay them. Braccio, the last and greatest of the war lords of the Schism, was opposed bitterly when he tried to treat Martin V as if he were Gregory XII, and he finally failed to prevail against a Pope implacably and bitterly determined to assert all the temporal rights of the Holy See.

[1] Calculated after Div. Cam. 14, 15; IE 388; Florence, Biblioteca Nazionale, xix, 82. Cf. Fink, *QF*, xxiii (1931/2), 203.

[2] Gottlob, 125–6. One galley cost the Chamber 650 ducats a month.

[3] Theiner, iii, no. 233, p. 286.   [4] Ibid. nos. 47, 123, pp. 95, 184.

CHAPTER V

THE COMMUNE AND THE VICARIATE

I. *The Signoria of the Church*

THE decadence and instability of the Italian commune in the fifteenth century need no illustration : all that was most liberal in the constitution of the Italian city state had by this time been either suffocated by the oligarchy or cut out violently by the *signori*. At the beginning of the fourteenth century the majority of the communes in the State of the Church were free, in the sense that they elected their own officials and governed themselves according to their own statutes.[1] A century later this was true only of a handful of the same communes : where the tyrant or baron had not seized power, the Church almost invariably appointed the *podestà*, and often many of the other officials.[2] The communal statutes continued to have force only with the authority of the *signore* or the Church.

But, even where the tyrant had not prevailed, the papal power was by no means the sole beneficiary of the decline of the free commune. The oligarchic element, always strong in communal government, had now become its dominating principle. Those cities in the State of the Church which were not ruled by tyrants were in practice ruled by a few powerful families. The 'popular' and 'oligarch' programmes which such families claimed to represent had long since lost all their real content, and were only a slight camouflage placed over the simple struggle for power between contending families. The factions of Melcorini and Muffati in Orvieto, of Raspanti and Beccherini in Perugia, of Canetoli and Zambeccari in Bologna, were none of them anything but the instruments of this struggle for power. And power for such families was certainly to be had : although the Church had greatly increased her control of the communes she had by no means gathered all the reins of power into her hands. Local particularism was still immensely fierce and extremely effective, and the Church had to tread very carefully.

The communes and *castra* of the Papal State were classed by the papal lawyers as either *mediate* or *immediate subjecte*.[3] In the first class were all places conceded

---

[1] G. Ermini, *La libertà comunale nello Stato della Chiesa*, first part in *ASR*, xlix (1926), and second part, *L'amministrazione della giustizia*, published separately, Rome, 1927. Idem, 'Caratteri della sovranità temporale dei papi nei secoli XIII e XIV', *ZSSRG*, Kanon. Abt., xxvii (1938); idem, 'I rettori provinciali dello Stato della Chiesa da Innocenzo III all' Albornoz', *RSDI*, iv (1931); G. Falco, 'I comuni della Campagna e della Marittima nel Medio Evo', *ASR*, xlii, xlvii–xlix (1919 f.); U. Aloisi, 'Sulla formazione storica del liber constitutionum sancte matris ecclesie', *AMSM*, n.s., i–v (1904–8); S. Sugenheim, *Geschichte der Entstehung und Ausbildung des Kirchenstaates* (1854), 180–212. Sugenheim tends to minimize the independence of the communes, but there is no doubt but that it was very considerable.

[2] For appointments of *podestà* under Martin V, see above, p. 124, n. 6.

[3] See Ermini, 'Caratteri della sovranità temporale', 317. Cf. Theiner, iii, no. 238, p. 297, where

either in vicariate or in fee. All other places were *immediate subjecte*, and were considered as under the direct rule of the Church, even when, as in Bologna, Perugia and some other cities, the relations of the Papacy and the commune were controlled by agreement. The part played by papal power in the cities immediately subject varied greatly, and depended on the economic and military strength of the city concerned, on the condition of its civil liberties, and on its geographic position. In many of the lesser cities of Lazio and Umbria—Rieti, Todi, Viterbo, Spoleto—accessible to Rome, accustomed by now to despotic rule, and too small to defy the central power single-handed, the Papacy behaved more or less as absolute *signore*. There were rebellions, but they were easily suppressed. But the two great cities of Bologna and Perugia were another matter. Rich, powerful, still acutely conscious of their civic independence, in spite of the despotisms they had endured in the recent past, they were coaxed by their papal Legate and Governor as much as they were ruled. Both enjoyed certain geographic advantages against the Papacy : Perugia was a natural fortress of considerable strength, Bologna was approachable only from Romagna, and was liable to be suborned and supported by any of the Italian powers bordering on the Emilian plain. In Orvieto and Ancona, lesser cities, but still powerful and rich, local interests and families had to be jockeyed with care.

Where she could, the Church acted in a very similar fashion to the tyrant, the *signore*, preserving the formal pattern of government of the commune, and ruling on the whole according to the statutes, but perverting and overriding them in the two most essential matters of the election of officials and the administration of finance. But the Church, even where she stepped into the shoes of some expelled *signori*, lacked many of his advantages. The *signore* usually had all his soldiery concentrated in or near the city which he ruled, and he did not suffer from the papal problem of policing a huge area with a tiny army. His soldiers were bound to him by personal loyalty and interest, and were always mobilised : he did not have painfully to raise new forces every time a serious rebellion occurred. For the Papacy, a rebellion such as that of Spoleto or Viterbo could be dealt with by a small punitive expedition; but the rebellion of such a town as Bologna or Perugia meant an immense effort to raise arms and money—Bologna, indeed, was too hard a nut for the papal forces to crack.

The *signore* often had his own roots in the city he ruled, and his own personal faction there : where this was so he enjoyed advantages denied to the Church, which was essentially an extraneous power, appointing 'foreign' officials and sending 'foreign' soldiers. And not only was the Church extraneous to each city, but also to the land as a whole. By the very nature of the Papal State, its inhabitants could have no real *pietas* or patriotism towards it. Essentially it was a financial and political convenience attached to the main ecclesiastical machine, and it was quite unable to take on any of those characteristics of the national state which were being

---

Castrum Griptarum (near Montefiascone) is declared to be immediately subject to the Holy See. Miss C. M. Ady, *The Bentivoglio of Bologna* (1937), 13, 39, seems to give this phrase a more sinister significance than the proper legal connotation allows.

cultivated by the Visconti *signoria* in the north of the peninsula. Its rule was preferred by many to that of the *signori*, but this feeling was one of local particularism rather than of regional solidarity; its subjects loved the Church for its weakness, and not for its strength.

II. *The Greater Communes: Rome, Perugia and Bologna*

§ 1. Rome, whose fortunes were inextricably linked with those of the Popes, had a long history of increasing and diminishing independence in her relations with the Holy See. The main victory of the papal *signoria* over the liberties of the Roman commune had been won almost a century before, in the pontificates of John XXII and Benedict XII.[1] The vicissitudes of the Papacy had allowed Roman particularism to assert itself many times since that date; notoriously under Cola di Rienzo, and during the ascendancy of the *banderesi*.[2] But the return of the Popes to Italy decisively sealed the fate of the Roman commune, and the treaty of the Romans with Boniface IX [3] laid down the pattern of the papal domination of the city.

The whereabouts of the supreme government of Rome at this period is extraordinarily difficult to determine. In theory, the City was governed by the Senator, according to the statutes, under the Pope. In practice the Vice-Chamberlain, without holding any special mandate for the purpose, was the effective Governor of Rome; his registers are full of detailed orders for the police and administration of the City, directed to the Senator and all manner of communal officials. But the formula in which all his letters were written was 'by the authority of the Chamberlain's office *and also* by order of the lord Pope, specially given to us by word of mouth',[4] and the authority of the Vice-Chamberlain is thus cloaked behind the authority of the Pope. Later, under Eugenius IV, the Vice-Chamberlain became the titular Governor of Rome.[5] Later still the office of Vice-Chamberlain became quite distinct from that of the Chamberlain, and instead of being 'regens' or 'locumtenens' in the office of the Chamberlain, as in the time of Martin V, the Vice-Chamberlain became a quite separate officer, whose main duty was as Governor of Rome. He then was assigned full criminal jurisdiction in the City, supervision of the civil jurisdiction being left to the Auditor of the Apostolic Chamber (who from the end of the fifteenth century was quite cut off from the Chamberlain and the Chamber). Later authors considered that the Vice-Chamberlain had inherited many of the functions of the early medieval *prefectus urbis*, which had ceased to function at the time of the

---

[1] A. de Boüard, *Le régime politique et les institutions de Rome au Moyen-Age, 1252–1347* (1920), 66 f.; G. Mollat, *Les Papes d'Avignon* (1949), 239 f.

[2] A. Natale, 'Le felice società dei balestrieri e dei pavesati a Roma e il governo dei banderesi dal 1358 al 1408', *ASR*, lxii (1939).

[3] Theiner, iii, no. 30, p. 78. See also the treaty with Innocent VII, ibid. no. 71, p. 131, and that with Alexander V, ibid. no. 109, p. 172.

[4] Many examples are in the appendix of documents below; others are in the appendix to Malatesta, *Statuti delle gabelle di Roma*.

[5] Theiner, iii, no. 279, p. 336, Giuliano de' Ricci, Archbishop of Pisa and Apostolic Vice-Chamberlain (see Gottlob, *Aus der Camera apostolica*, 269) is appointed Governor of Rome. Cf. Gottlob, 94–5, and G. Moroni, *Dizionario di erudizione storico-ecclesiastica da S. Pietro sino ai nostri giorni*, vol. xxxii.

feudalisation of the office in the family of the Prefects of Vico.[1]   But although this may be true in practice, it has no juridical significance; the authority of the Vice-Chamberlain stemmed essentially from the position of the Chamberlain as the chief authority of the State of the Church, and so far as his authority resembled that of the Prefect, it was merely authority which he had usurped from the Senator, and which had fallen into the hands of the latter during the thirteenth and fourteenth centuries.

That under Martin V the Vice-Chamberlain was the effective Governor of Rome is made even more probable by the appointment of a Vicar-General in temporals of Rome, Ardicino della Porta, when Martin V left the City to summer in the Alban Hills in 1429 and his Vice-Chamberlain left with him.[2]   The appointment was probably made because the rebellion in Bologna ('propter presentem temporum gravitatem') caused the Pope to require the Vice-Chamberlain to accompany him, contrary to the usual practice.

The Pope also appointed a Vicar in spirituals for the City, as he had done since the early thirteenth century.[3]   Besides carrying out the general supervision of the Roman clergy, he also was the judge ordinary of civil and criminal cases involving clergy, or laity and clergy, but not clergy who were courtiers of the Roman Court, the last going to the court of the Auditor of the Chamber.[4]   The Pope was, in his own dominions, just as sensitive to abuses of privilege of clergy as any other European sovereign, and the Vicar in spirituals was told that clerks in minor orders who went about without the habit or tonsure, or exercised an artisan profession, were liable to the justice of the Senator and not to that of the Vicar in spirituals.[5]

§ 2.   The control of the Papacy over the main officers of the commune of Rome was nothing less than rigid; the Pope appointed and supervised them all.   According to the agreements of Boniface IX and subsequent Popes, Martin V named the Senator of Rome, usually for a term of six months,[6] and also the *conservatores camere*, the officers in charge of the *camera urbis*, who had powers almost equal to those of the Senator, and substituted for him in his absence.[7]   The Senator had in the fourteenth century named his own judges, but since the convention of Innocent VII

---

[1] Cf. Calisse, 'I prefetti di Vico', *ASR*, x (1887).

[2] Reg. Vat. 351, fol. 126v.   'Cum itaque propter presentem temporum gravitatem et pestilenciam imminentem nec immerito formidandam, cum curia nostra ad partes Campanie transferire de proximo intendimus . . .' he is appointed Vicar-General in temporals at the Pope's good pleasure, giving him full power of government, and of judging civil and criminal cases, 'cum mero et mixto imperio et gladii potestate'.   The Vice-Chamberlain went into the Campagna with the Pope; a document initiated by him is dated Ferentino, 12 August 1429 (Div. Cam. 12, fol. 287).

[3] K. Eubel, 'Series Vicariorum Urbis a. 1200–1558', *RQ*, viii (1894).

[4] Theiner, iii, no. 30, p. 78, and doc. 12 below.

[5] Div. Cam. 13, fol. 13, to the Bishop of Lucca, Vicar in spirituals, telling him that the 'clericos in minoribus ordinibus constitutos, non incendentes in habitu et tonsura', or plying a mechanic art, are not to enjoy the privileges conceded by canon law to the clergy (15 February 1430).

[6] Theiner, iii, no. 30, p. 78; A. Salimei, *Senatori e Statuti di Roma nel medio evo* (1935), 164 f.   For the office of Senator see de Boüard, 134 f., and Re, *Statuti della città di Roma*, lxxii f.

[7] Natale, 'La felice società', 20; Re, *Statuti della città di Roma*, 202; Salimei, loc. cit.   Their powers were analogous to those of the *Riformatori* of the fourteenth century, and to whom recourse was again had in 1416.

with the Roman people, the appointment of the most important,[1] the judge of appeals, had belonged to the Pope. This appointment was now, under Martin V, made by the Vice-Chamberlain.[2]

The *syndicus generalis*, whose duty it was to audit the accounts and supervise the administration of the Senator and all the communal officials, was also appointed by the Pope.[3] It is also evident that this important office was closely supervised by the Vice-Chamberlain. When Giovanni Beccaliti, at the end of his term of office as Senator, was inconvenienced by the delay in auditing his accounts, the Vice-Chamberlain ordered the Conservators to see that the audit was expedited, and if necessary to carry it out themselves—the last was a proceeding completely at variance with the statutes.[4] In the imposition of sentences and making of compositions the Vice-Chamberlain took a particular interest. The Senator and Conservators were instructed to increase or reduce the penalties imposed for crimes,[5] although the faculty of making compositions was assigned by the statutes to the Conservators alone.[6] The Conservators were also ordered, that as so many people had fled the City on account of the penalties imposed on them by the Capitoline Court, they were to be allowed to return to the City and to make compositions for their offences with the Syndic-General and the Treasurer of the City.[7]

The Vice-Chamberlain also freely appointed officials who were given special police powers to impose peace in the bloodthirsty quarrels of the Roman citizens. In 1423 the Conservators were told to choose four nobles, who were then to enlist a sufficient number of *banderesi* to assist them in policing the City.[8] In the same year, and again in the following year, other commissioners were appointed to compromise and arbitrate in the quarrels which were perturbing the peace of the City.[9]

Martin V enjoys a quite undeserved reputation among historians as a friend to the liberties of Rome, mainly because he commissioned Nicolò Signorili to write the 'de iuribus et excellentiis urbis Romae'.[10] This work is in fact very little concerned with

[1] Theiner, iii, no. 71, p. 131.

[2] Div. Cam. 6, fol. 265v, appointment of Thoma de Virago (31 October 1420).

[3] E.g. Matheo de Patearinis, 7 February 1423, Reg. Vat. 349, fol. 257.

[4] Div. Cam. 6, fol. 244v (20 November 1420). Cf. *Statuti della città di Roma*, 216-7.

[5] E.g. Div. Cam. 7, fols. 248, 250v, 253.   [6] *Statuti della città di Roma*, 273.

[7] Div. Cam. 7, fol. 280, 13 August 1423.

[8] Div. Cam. 7, fol. 245. 'Committimus et mandamus quatenus pro defensione atque conservatione pacis et tranquilitatis et boni status dicte urbis, quatuor nobiles cives romanos qui vobis ad hec ydoneos videbuntur quamtocius eligatis, et ordinetis quod de aliquibis balistariis civibus et incolis romanis ad hoc ydoneis et expertis usque ad aliquem certum et sufficientem numerum de quo vobis videbitur, et qui ad defensionem et conservationem dicte urbis et status presentis in necessitatibus et cuiuslibet occurrentibus parati existant se diligenter informent, eorumque balistariorum nomines in scriptis redigant, ac sanctissimo domino nostro pape reportent' (23 June 1423).

[9] Div. Cam. 8, fol. 50. They were Jacopo Lelli de Cinchiis, Saba Colucie and Giovanni Stefani. Their re-appointment for 1424, ibid. fol. 144v. They had certain minor judicial powers, and were given no salary.

[10] L. von Pastor, *Geschichte der Päpste* (8/9 edn., 1926), 236-237. 'Martin V. liess die kommunale Verfassung seiner Vaterstadt völlig unangetastet'; O. Tommasini, 'Il Registro degli Officiali del Comune di Roma esemplato dallo scribasebato Marco Guidi', *ARAcLinc*, Classe di scienze morali, storiche e filologiche, 4th ser., iii (1887), 181, 'A romani che avevano prima durato l'oppressione ecclesiastica favorita dagli Orsini, la prudenza del pontefice colonnese seppe quasi di libertà'.

the communal liberties of Rome,[1] and Martin V was no kinder to those liberties than any other Pope.   He appointed all the officials of the City, including those for whom the statutes prescribed election every three months under the system of *imbussulatio*, which thus became extinct.   Every three months a list of all the officials to be appointed for the next three-monthly period was sent to the Conservators by the Pope.[2]   It is very probable that the extinction of the *imbussulatio* for these offices dates from the time of Gregory XII,[3] and a casual reference in the treaty of Alexander V with the Roman commune suggests that the same practice obtained during his pontificate.[4]   Eugenius IV therefore only spoke truth when he issued such appointments in 1432 'ut est moris'.[5]

The Pope also appointed such officials as the *magister viarum et stratarum* [6] and *custos murorum*,[7] besides the officials for collecting indirect taxes who are described

---

[1] It is in two parts, one mainly concerned with the antiquities of Rome, and the other with its churches.   I have used the Vatican MS., Vat. lat. 3536.   See, however, the passage about the regions quoted by Tommasini, 197, n.

[2] The plan of the appointments for a whole year for 1447 is printed by Tommasini, 197 f., arranged under the regions of the city, with the list of offices assigned to the inhabitants of each region, entered beside their names.   For the period of Martin V documents of a similar type have provided exactly the same information.   Vatican Archives, Fondo Borghese, Serie 4, 60 (a sixteenth-century transcript) gives the papal letters appointing the officials of the City, from December 1424 to March 1430.   The officials were appointed for three-monthly periods (cf. *Statuti della città di Roma*, 217–22), e.g. (fol. 2 of MS. quoted) 'Conservatoribus camerae almae urbis.   Ad salutarem regimen huius nostrae almae urbis prae ceteris sollicitis studiis intendentes, significamus devotioni vestrae per presentes officiales quos deputavimus in ea, quemadmodum in cedula presentibus interclusa subscripta manu venerabilis fratris Pauli episcopi Ebroicensis secretarii nostri descripta sunt.   Volumus autem quod prefatae officiales antequam officia incipiant exercere present in manibus nostris ut moris est juramentum.   Datum Romae apud sanctus Petrum apostolos (sic), III kalendas Januarii pontificatus nostri anno octavo.' Follows the list of officials, with the names of those appointed.   The offices concerned are largely as in Tommasini, 197 f., *Statuti della città di Roma*, 217–22, and Theiner, iii, no. 109, p. 172, i.e. Conservatores, Cancellarius, sindaci populi, scribasenatus, notarius conservatorum, prothonotarius, notarius camerae, marescalli, notarius marescallorum, scriptores camerae, scriptores gabelli, notarius actorum pendentium, notarius appellationum, sindaci officialium, notarius sindaci, camerarius ripae, notarius ripae, and finally the 13 and 26 boni viri ac comestabili for each region of the City (called in Tommasini's list the 'capitanei regionis').   Some of these offices were, however, on occasion conferred separately and not in this omnibus fashion, and for periods longer than for three months, e.g. marshal of the Capitoline court (Div. Cam. 7, fol. 40, 10 May 1422); scribasenatus (Tommasini, 174 f.); chancellor (Theiner, iii, no. 205, p. 272).

[3] Tommasini, 178 f.

[4] Theiner, iii, no. 109, p. 172, where the fact that these officials were appointed by the Pope seems to be referred to incidentally, 'Item quod in ipsa Urbe sint et omni tempore conserventur omnes et singuli officiales esse in eadem Urbe hactenus consueti, qui de tempore in tempus perpetuis futuris temporibus per nos vel successores nostros prefatos, seu per apostolice sedis legatos aut vicarios generales in prefata Urbe pro nobis et eadem ecclesia, successoribus nostris deputatos seu deputandos nominari et eligi debeant, ante inicium officiorum ipsorum in nostris, successorum, legati seu vicarii predictorum vel camerarii nostri manibus de eorum officiis bene et fideliter, et alias fidelitatis solitum iuramentum in forma debita prestare debentes, videlicet unus senator forensis . . . et omnes alii etiam officiales consueti . . .'

[5] Pace Tommasini, 182, who represents Eugenius IV as an innovator in these matters.

[6] Theiner, iii, no. 231.   Cf. E. Re, 'Maestri di Strada', *ASR*, xliii (1920) C. Scaccia Scarafoni, 'L'antico statuto dei "magistri stratarum" e altri documenti relativi a quella magistratura', *ASR*, l (1927).

[7] Reg. Vat. 350, fol. 306v.   The appointment is of Antonio Craffi, who is confirmed in the office, which he is said to have held under previous Popes.

below.   He also laid down the salaries of the officials of Rome, in a schedule drawn up by the Vice-Chamberlain.[1]

§ 3.   The interference of the Pope and the Vice-Chamberlain in the justice of the Capitoline Court has already been discussed.[2]   Processes could be interfered with at any stage, or stopped at the will of the Vice-Chamberlain.   The power of grace lay with the Pope, above the Senator, to whom it is alone accorded in the statutes : papal absolution given to a commune for its offences applied equally to offences for which it had been sentenced in the Capitoline Court.[3]   The Senator or Vice-Senator was given certain additional judicial powers by the Pope or the Vice-Chamberlain *statutis urbis non obstantibus*, to impose heavier penalties than those laid down in the statutes for fighting and brawling,[4] or to judge all civil and criminal cases, or commit them to whom he pleased for argument.[5]   The Vice-Chamberlain was also extremely energetic in combating the invasions of the Capitoline Court on the criminal jurisdiction of the Apostolic Chamber over the courtiers of the Roman Court; a whole series of documents, some of which threaten the Senator with excommunication, testify to his vigilance.[6]

No Vice-Chamberlain went so far under Martin V as the Chamberlain Ludovico Scarampi under Eugenius IV.   Scarampi instituted a 'visitation of the Campidoglio', by which the Chamberlain sat once a week on the Capitol and, hearing all manner of cases against the officials of the City, settled them without possibility of appeal.[7]   The liberties of the City could hardly have been flouted more despotically than this.

§ 4.   In the late thirteenth century the commune of Rome, with the help of the Angevin Senator, had dispossessed the Pope from the control of communal finances.[8]

[1] Div. Cam. 6, fol. 265v, 1 November 1420.   This *tabula* of salaries is referred to in the agreement of the commune with Alexander V, Theiner, iii, no. 109, p. 172.   See also the list of salaries printed by Tomassetti, 'Del sale e focatico del comune di Roma nel medio evo', *ASR*, xx (1897), 357-9.

[2] See p. 150 above.

[3] Reg. Vat. 354, fol. 87, telling Marino that its absolution extended to all crimes of which it stood accused in the Capitoline Court (1 February 1426).

[4] Ibid. fol. 126v, to Nicola Magni (here 'Mandi') of Anagni (20 March 1422).

[5] Reg. Vat. 354, fol. 244 (19 June 1423), to the Senator Mastino de Burgo (cf. Salimei, p. 169), '. . . nobilitati tue audiendi examinandi discutiendi per te vel alium seu alios quoscumque tamen seu causas civiles et criminales inter personas seculares quascumque prefate urbis et districtus emergentes earumque argumentionem et discussionem alio vel aliis communiter vel divisim prout tibi videbitur committendi, et ad te cum placuerit revocandi, necnon de omnibus delictis tam preteritis quam futuris tam per accusationem tam per viam inquisitionis procedendi cognoscendi condemnandi et absolvendi tenore presencium plenam concedimus facultatem . . .'   Other extensive powers in criminal cases, giving the Senator power to punish and prorogue and fix terms, not according to the Statutes, but as seems best to him, in Div. Cam. 9, fol. 162 (15 November 1425), given by the Vice-Chamberlain to the Senator Valerio de Luschis of Vicenza.

[6] See p. 153 above, doc. 12 below; other instances, all of the same type, are in Div. Cam. 6, fol. 267; Div. Cam. 8, fol. 7v; ibid. fol. 15v, to the Senator, Mastino Roberto, 'Mandamus quatenus Michaelem de Pisis curtesanum, quem, ut accepimus, detinetis, ratione certorum excessuum per eum, ut asseritur, commissorum, in cancellaria curie Capitolii carceratum, ad venerabilem et circumspectum virum dominum Nicolaum de Mercatello decretorum doctorem, apostolice camere clericum, et domini auditoris nostri et curie camere apostolice generalis auditoris locumtenentem, una cum omnibus informationibus quas habetis, receptis presentibus remitatis' (28 September 1423).   [7] Tommasini, 'Il Registro', 183.

[8] De Boüard, 170 f.; S. Malatesta, *Statuti delle gabelle di Roma* (1885), 23 f.

For over a century this advantage was maintained, but under Boniface IX the commune began to retreat in this field, and the treaty of the commune with Alexander V finally reversed the process, and fully restored control to the Pope.[1] In practice, the papal Vice-Chamberlain controlled the entire finances of the City, issuing orders to the financial officers of the commune exactly as he saw fit.

The finances of the commune were administered by the *conservatores camere urbis*, the *camerarius urbis* and the *thesaurarius urbis*. All were appointed by the Pope,[2] but the last was more properly a papal than a communal official. The income of the commune was paid in part to the *camera urbis*, and in part direct to the *thesaurarius urbis*. The *camera urbis* received the profits of justice, some of the salt and focage taxes, and the complex of customs duties and taxes on the sale of goods later known as the 'dogane di S. Eustachio', and 'de la grassa'.[3] The *camera urbis* was served by a *depositarius urbis*, quite different and distinct from the Apostolic Depositary who served the Chamber.

But in spite of its seemingly autonomous organisation, the *camera urbis* enjoyed no real autonomy, and there were no sources of income which could be called 'communal' as distinct from 'papal'.[4] Not only did the *camera urbis* pay a great part of its revenues to the *thesaurarius urbis*—which amounts to paying them to the Apostolic Chamber—but Conservators, the Chamberlain of the City and the Depositary of the City were all freely ordered by the Apostolic Chamberlain to make such payments as he saw fit.[5]

The Treasurer of the City, nominated by the Pope,[6] made payments only at the mandate of the Vice-Chamberlain, which was issued to him in the same form as the mandate to the Apostolic Treasurer. Under such mandates all the officials of the City and castellans of the Roman District were paid,[7] and payments and assignments

---

[1] Theiner, iii, no. 109, p. 172, 'Item quod omnes introitus dicte camere Urbis, qui pervenerunt seu pervenient ad manus Camerarii eiusdem camere vel ad quodvis alios, solvi et assignari debeant depositario apostolice Camere per nos aut successores nostros prefatos in dicta Urbe deputando.' Cf. Malatesta, 62 f., and Gottlob, *Aus der Camera apostolica*, 101 f.

[2] For the Treasurer, see the appointment in Theiner, iii, no. 176, p. 251. Johannes de Astallis was a Roman banker who remained in office as Treasurer of Rome for the whole of Martin's pontificate.

[3] Cf. Arch. Cam. pt. i, Camera di Roma, B. 84, vol. 342, described below, p. 208. The income in this book is from condemnations in the Capitoline court, from some isolated payments of the salt and focage tax, and from the gabelle of Sant' Angelo, *pannorum, plani, vini ad grossum, lani lactis et casei, lignamini, culturiorum, salsuminis et mercarie, pelliparie, guarnellorum, spitarie, camigliani*. These correspond, in general, with the later books described by Malatesta, *Statuti delle gabelle di Roma*, 72–84. Cf. also *ASR*, 1 (1927), 349. The *exitus* part of this volume of 1421–5 shows the payment of many thousands of florins to the Treasurer, Johannes de Astallis.

[4] Pace S. Malatesta, *Statuti delle gabelle di Roma*, 65, 'Conservò peraltro il comune la facoltà di potere liberamente disporre dei redditi puramente comunali . . .'

[5] See the mandates to Petro Zuliani (or Juliani), the Chamberlain of the City, in *Statuti delle gabelle di Roma*, doc. 11, p. 138, and in Arch. Cam. pt. i, vol. 826, fol. 3. Ibid. vol. 825, fol. 52 (14 September 1427), mandate of the Apostolic Vice-Chamberlain to the Conservators, telling them to spend 63 florins of the money of the *camera urbis* on repairing the palace of S. Lorenzo in Lucina, 'quos in vestris computis seu thesaurarii dicte camere admittemus'; ibid. vol. 826, passim, where the Depositary of the City, Francesco Altobianchi de Albertis, is ordered to make various payments to Antonio Colonna, 'ad stipendia Romani populi militantium' (cf. also vol. 825, fol. 145).

[6] Theiner, iii, no. 176, p. 251.

[7] See the documents printed by Malatesta, *Statuti delle gabelle di Roma*, 137–8, and doc. 8 below.

of all descriptions were freely made at the convenience of the Apostolic Chamber.[1] The Treasurer of the City had his accounts audited in the Apostolic Chamber, by two officers of the Chamber and a Roman citizen, in the same form as that in use for the audits of provincial Treasurers.[2] He paid his monies to the Depositary of the Apostolic Chamber,[3] and not, normally, to the Depositary of the Chamber of the City. He was thus in all essentials an official of the Chamber, and not of the commune.

The Vice-Chamberlain also controlled the detailed administration of the indirect taxes of Rome. The main officer in charge of the imposition of these taxes, the *gabelle*, which fell on all goods imported into the City or exported from it, calculated according to their value, was the *gabellarius generalis* or *major*, who was appointed by the Pope, usually for a term of six months.[4] The Vice-Chamberlain appointed Roman citizens to examine (*sindicare*) his accounts and actions, the Conservators being ordered to admit them to this office and administer them the oath.[5] The *gabellarius* had judicial powers to proceed against breaches of the gabelle,[6] and on one occasion the Conservators were ordered to remit to him, as *iudex in negotiis gabellarum urbis*, a case in which Tivoli was accused of refusing to pay certain customs duties on meat, wool, cheese and sheep.[7] He was a salaried official, paid by the *camera urbis*.[8]

There was also the *gabellarius* of the Ripa and Ripetta, who imposed customs duties on goods entering and leaving Rome by the river,[9] but he does not appear to have been a salaried official.[10] He had, however, a *camerarius Ripe et Ripette* who

---

[1] E.g. the assignment of 250 florins a month which he was to pay to Oddo de Poccia, for the latter to use for the private purposes of the Pope, Reg. Vat. 354, fol. 137v, 'Magistro Oddoni subdiaconi nostro . . . Cum a tempore nostri primi adventus ad almam urbem, videlicet anno domini millesimo quadragentesimo vicesimo pontificatus nostri anno tercio, ex certis causis et expensis fiendis ex commissione nostra dilectus filius nobilis vir Johannes de Astallis camere prefate urbis thesaurarius, de pecuniis dicte camere ad manus suas proventis, singulis mensibus a kalendis novembris tunc futuris, continuo tibi ducentos et quinquaginta florenos auri, et usque in presentem diem summam quinquemilium septingentorum quinquaginta florenorum similium, ad quam dictum inter lapsum temporis ascendit . . .' goes on to give Oddo Poccia a quittance for this amount. Cf. *JEccH*, iv (1953), 66–7. The quittance given to Giovanni de Astallis for the same payments, in Reg. Vat. 354, fol. 138. Cf. Reg. Vat. 355, fols. 89, 89v, where the total drawn from the *camera urbis* by Oddo Poccia between 1 November 1420 and 1 July 1424 is said to amount to 11,000 florins. For other payments made by Giovanni de Astallis, see the series of quittances in Reg. Vat. 354, fol. 231–2, where among many other payments is mentioned one of 16,185 florins, to the mercenary Donato de Lavello. See also the 'Introitus et exitus camere urbis' (IE 381), which includes all manner of like payments, and further, Malatesta, *Statuti delle gabelle di Roma*, doc. 23, p. 146.

[2] *Statuti delle gabelle di Roma*, 69, and doc. 24, p. 147.

[3] IE 386, fols. 79v, 84, 88, payments to Antonio de Piscia.

[4] *Statuti delle gabelle di Roma*, 43 f. and docs. 5–7, pp. 134–6.

[5] Ibid. docs. 8–9, pp. 136–7.   [6] Ibid. 112–13.

[7] Div. Cam. 8, fol. 219, 20 October 1424. The Conservators had previously been told to appoint a Doctor of laws to judge this case (ibid. fol. 167v, 20 May 1424), but they evidently had not done so; or else their choice had not been accepted.

[8] Arch. Cam. pt. i, vol. 825, fols. 29, 40v, 119, 142, records mandates for the payment of his salary.

[9] *Statuti delle gabelle di Roma*, 66; P. Fedele, 'Contributo alla storia economica del comune di Roma nel medio evo', in *Raccolta di scritti storici in onore del Prof. Giacinto Romano nel suo xxv° anno d'insegnamento* (Pavia, 1907).

[10] He does not appear in the list in Tomassetti, *ASR*, xx (1897), 358, nor in Div. Cam. 6, fol. 265v. Cf. *Statuti delle gabelle di Roma*, 57–8. His position is not at all clear, as he did not buy the farm of the

was salaried,[1] and who made payments from the *camera Ripe et Ripette* at the mandate of the Vice-Chamberlain.[2]　The profits drawn from this office were considerable; at least 16,000 Roman florins were assigned from it in ten months of 1429/30, and under Sixtus IV they were reckoned at 10,000 florins a year.[3]

Some of the gabelles, such as the gabelle of wine, were put out to farm through the Conservators, sometimes being sold at the instruction of the Vice-Chamberlain.[4]

The *dogana pecudum* of Rome has already been discussed above.　It was attached to the gabelle of meat, cheese, wool and milk, the whole being sold every year to a farmer, and known as 'lo gruosso'.　It was sold by orders of the Vice-Chamberlain, at a price named by him.[5]

The *dogana salis* was also put out to farm.[6]　The *doganerius* was assisted by a *guardianus*, *notarius* and *mensuratores*.[7]　The exact line of distinction between the *doganerius salis* and the *sale e focatico* exacted by the Conservators in the Roman District and paid into the *camera urbis* is not clear, but it is probable that the *doganerius* imposed the salt monopoly in Rome itself, and the Conservators that of the District.　The question is probably bound up with the distinction between a *salaria maior* and a *salaria minor*.[8]

The Vice-Chamberlain gave licences to sell salt (*tracta salis*);[9] the Pope freely gave exemptions from the payment of salt and focage;[10] the Vice-Chamberlain gave various temporary remissions [11] and controlled its imposition by the commissioners.[12]

The actual salt pans at Ostia seem to have been controlled by officials of the

---

gabelle.　I have not been able to examine the account books of his office in the Archivio di Stato, nor did I see the statutes of the Ripa and Ripetta in the Archivio Capitolino (cf. *Statuti delle gabelle di Roma*, 59).

[1] *Statuti delle gabelle di Roma*, 57–9, and Tomassetti, loc. cit.　Cf. Arch. Cam. pt. i, vol. 825, salary of 36 florins to be paid to Antonio Lucii de Tuscanella, Chamberlain of the Ripa and Ripetta; Reg. Vat. 349, fol. 22, appointment of Lorenzo de Ficotiis to this office (23 February 1420).

[2] E.g. a series of payments to the Bishop of Tivoli, from November 1429 to August 1430, for the private purposes of the Pope, Arch. Cam. pt. i, vol. 825, fol. 122v (2,000 florins *ad rationem 47 solidos ad florenum*); fol. 126 (3,000 florins *ad rat. 57 sol.: 1 flor.*); fol. 136 (1,000 florins *ad rat. 47 sol.*); fol. 141 (4,000 *florenos currentes ad rat. 47 sol.*); fol. 142v (3,000 florins); fol. 143v (3,000 florins).

[3] See *ASR*, 1 (1927), 349, and preceding note.

[4] E.g. Div. Cam. 7, fol. 289 (23 August 1423), the Conservators are ordered to make Romano Cecchi Dei the *gabellarius vini*, for a year, for the price of 1,000 florins.

[5] See doc. 33, p. 152, in *Statuti delle gabelle di Roma*, where Jacopo Orsini of Tagliacozzo pays 6,500 Roman florins for a half share in 'lo gruosso' for a year.　In 1423 the whole *dogana* was sold for a year for 10,500 florins, to Antonio Colonna, see p. 119 above, n. 3.

[6] See p. 145 above.

[7] Tomassetti, 'Sale e focatico del comune di Roma nel medio evo', *ASR*, xx (1897).

[8] See the list of officials in Tomassetti, article cited above, p. 358—'guardianus salarie maioris', 'dohanerius salarie minoris'.　The latter was a minor post, paid 2 florins a month.　Nor has anyone shed light on the distinction between salt 'a grosso' and 'a minuto' (*ASR*, 1, 1927, 349).

[9] Div. Cam. 6, fol. 239, Simeone Giovanni Fate is licenced to take 70 *rubbra* of salt from the *salaria urbis*, and sell it where he pleases.

[10] E.g. F. Contelori, *Genealogia Familiae Comitum Romanorum* (1650), 22; idem, *Vita Martini V*, 55.

[11] E.g. Nazzano is remitted salt and focage tax for two years (Div. Cam. 6, fol. 261, 5 December 1420, marked 'gratis pro Alto de Comite'); Sambucco is remitted its arrears of the same tax (Div. Cam. 7, fol. 247, 1 July 1423); so also are Fiano and Civitella (ibid. fol. 276, 11 August 1423).

[12] Div. Cam. 6, fol. 255v, the Conservators are ordered not to attempt to impose the tax of salt and focage on Gallese, as this had not before been customary, 29 November 1420.

Roman commune, known as the *syndici salinarum urbis*,[1] who sold salt to the Conservators, and were charged with repairing damages to the *salina*, but their relation to the *doganerius salis* is obscure.

§ 5. The Popes took the view that the statutes of Rome, just as much as the statutes of other cities, required their approval and confirmation, and could be set aside or changed by their authority.[2]   Martin V specifically ordered that two clauses of the statutes relating to criminal law be cancelled,[3] and also ordered that a tariff of salaries for the notaries be inserted into the statutes.[4]   The statutes of the various offices such as that of the gabelle were also altered at will,[5] not only by the Pope, but by the Vice-Chamberlain.[6]

It would be impossible to calculate the profits which the Apostolic Chamber drew from the City of Rome at this period without a far longer and more detailed study of the account books than I have been able to give.   The monies handled by the Treasurer, Johannes de Astallis, in the two years ending 31 December 1424, totalled 205,927 Roman florins 31 sol. 3 den., at the rate of 47 sol. = 1 florin.   This gives a gross annual income of a little over 100,000 florins.[7]   But it is far from including all the revenues of Rome; it excludes those of the Ripa and Ripetta, and may exclude those of other offices, particularly the *salaria*.

There is no trace of the slightest resistance to papal authority in Rome in Martin V's time, and no doubt his strong rule there, after the lean and disorderly period of the Schism, met with nothing but praise and gratitude.[8]   The thoroughness with which the Apostolic Chamber controlled the government of the commune is impressive : the organisation of the commune had been transformed into a unit of authoritarian papal rule.   The communal spirit may indeed have still lived on as an attractive memory of a recently buried past, but it is difficult to think that the conspiracy of Stefano Porcari, twenty-five years later, has any significance except as an isolated incident.

§ 6.   The political climate of Perugia was very different from that of Rome.   To begin, the direct subjection of the City to the Holy See was a comparatively recent event.   Perugia had been under the 'protection' of the Popes since the time of Innocent III,[9] but only at the end of the fourteenth century did the Popes manage to turn this 'protection' into a direct domination.[10]   In 1392 the city made a full

---

[1] Arch. Cam. pt. i, vol. 825, fols. 1–2 (1 June 1426).
[2] Re, *Statuti della città di Roma*, cii f.
[3] Theiner, iii, no. 230, p. 289.
[4] Re, *Statuti della città di Roma*, civ.
[5] A 'reform' of Martin V is quoted by Malatesta, *Statuti delle gabelle di Roma*, 70.
[6] Malatesta, 70, 116, printing a 'reform' of Martin V's Vice-Chamberlain, Oddo Poccia.
[7] IE 381, fols. 179–180v.
[8] Cf. Pastor, *History of the Popes*, i, 222–3.
[9] Potthast, *Regesta Pontificum Romanorum*, i (1874), no. 381.
[10] O. Scalvanti, 'Considerazioni sul primo libro degli statuti perugini', *BSU*, i (1895); idem, 'Un opinione di Bartolo sulla libertà perugina', *BSU*, ii (1896).

M

and voluntary submission to the Holy See.[1]   The city was at this period sometimes ruled by Legates and sometimes granted in vicariate to the commune, but in principle it was regarded as being directly subject to the Holy See.   Its relations with the Papacy were broken for a long period by the *signorie* of Ladislas at Perugia and of Braccio di Montone, but after the battle of Aquila in 1424 the city returned finally to papal government.

The conditions of the return of Perugia to papal obedience were set out fully in an agreement between the Pope and the commune.[2]   Although 'full rule' of the city was conceded in the agreement to the Pope, the other conditions are such as to save a very considerable degree of self-government for the city.   The Legate whom the Pope shall appoint shall be 'confidata et grata' to the city, and in matters concerning the government of the city ('de occurentibus in Communi') he is to consult with the Priors and Chamberlains.   The Pope appointed the *podestà*, but the remainder of the officials of the city are to be elected by extraction from the bags, according to the statutes, only with the consent of the Legate.   The taxes are not to be immoderately increased beyond what they were in the last period of direct rule by the Church.

This agreement in some respects comes close to an arrangement for the joint rule of the city by the communal officials and the Legate, although the last word is certainly reserved to the Pope and his officials.   The agreement also allows the commune to send ambassadors to the Pope when it wishes, and this was much practised, so much that in many matters the Legate was passed by, and he could become a mere agent for carrying out the decisions agreed by the commune with the Pope.[3]   But with such loosely defined powers given to both Legate and commune, it is evident that the importance of the Legate depended on his person, and it is not surprising that while Pietro Donato was little more than a lay figure, Domenico Capranica did not allow his powers to be thus circumvented.[4]

The principal officers of the commune were the priors, who were elected every six months, and the chamberlains of the major arts.   Together they formed the main council of the commune, although several other councils in fact existed.[5]   The

---

[1] Theiner, iii, no. 23, p. 71, 'civitatem . . . summiserint eidem domino nostro pape, et eundem in generalem dominum, Rectorem, gubernatorem et administratorem recognoverint, et assumpserint cum mero et mixto imperio et omnimoda iurisdictione, regimine, gubernacione, et administracione . . .' This document is overlooked by Scalvanti.

[2] Printed by Fumi, *Inventario e Spoglio dei Registri della Tesoreria Apostolica di Perugia e Umbria*, xxx f.

[3] Cf. K. A. Fink, 'Dominicus Capranica als Legat in Perugia', *RQ*, xxxix (1931), 274–5, 'bei der mit Recht durchaus selbständigen und stark von zentralischen Tendenzen geleiteten Politik des Papstes die Legaten weniger aus einiger Initiative vorgehen konnten, als das vielmehr eine ihrer Hauptaufgaben darin bestand, die durch direkte Verhandlungen zwischen der Kommune und der Kurie herbeigeführten päpstlichen Erlasse zur Durchführung zu bringen'.

[4] When the mob gained control in Perugia in 1430 during the incident of Agnolo di Pascuccio (p. 174 below) the Governor Donato, at the height of the tumult, threatened the Priors that he would 'ride off' from the city (Graziani, 339, n.).   Such conduct is unthinkable of Capranica.

[5] When the papal embassy came to discuss the submission of the commune in 1424, 'Adì primo de luglio in sabato intraro in offizio li Priori nuovi, et subito fecero chiamare li Camerlenghi per la sera, et lì el detto Carlo expuse la inbasciata per parte del Papa'.   Cf. V. Alfieri, 'L'amministrazione economica dell'antico comune di Perugia', *BSU*, ii (1896), 397 f.

podestà was appointed by the Pope, and was in effect a papal official, as is made quite clear by Domenico Capranica's correspondence.[1]

An energetic Legate or Governor was able to intervene even in the details of communal administration. Domenico Capranica frequently appointed the officials of the commune : he issued letters of appointment for the *sindaco maggiore*; for the judge of appeal; for the criminal judge (*officialis damnorum datorum*),[2] for the officials of the *abundanzia*,[3] for the depositary of the Chamber of the *conservatores monete*.[4] It is probable that some, perhaps all, of these appointments were merely confirmations of elections already made *de sacculo* according to the statutes of the commune : this is expressly stated for the appointment of the *podestà* of Fossato, one of the villages subject to Perugia,[5] and it is almost certainly true of the appointment of the captains of the *contado*, who were 'appointed' by the Governor in September 1430,[6] but since 1429 had, with the approval of the Pope, been extracted *de sachecto*.[7] But even if the Governor merely confirmed the appointments of the commune, he at least showed that he did not intend to treat as an empty formula the clause of the agreement of 1424 that officials be elected 'de consensu Legati'.

§ 7. The complexity and delicacy of the division of power in Perugia is shown to the full in the financial administration of the commune. Even before the advent of the Church, this was far from simple.[8] The main revenues of the city were divided between two 'chambers' or principal sets of officials, the chamber of the *conservatores monete*, and that of the *massari*. To each of these chambers were assigned a particular class of revenues and particular duties of expenditure. Communal monies were also collected and expended by the officials for the supply and control of corn (*officiales abundantie et campionis bladi*). Upon these officials the Pope now imposed an Apostolic Treasurer, who supervised the entire financial organisation of the commune.[9]

The tributary basis of the agreement of 1424 was that when all the expenses of the commune of Perugia had been paid, including the salaries of the Legate and Treasurer, the Pope should take annually 12,000 florins.[10] It is clear that the Pope took not only this sum, but also any further credit balance above it, since in 1427 the city asked in vain for 2,000 florins a year to be directed to repairing the walls, in spite of the fact that the profits of the city had been exceeding the amount of

---

[1] See, for example, docs. 18, 20, 21 below.
[2] Div. Cam. 12, fol. 7v.
[3] Ibid. fol. 51v.
[4] Ibid. fol. 57v.
[5] Ibid. fol. 31v.
[6] Ibid. fol. 24v.

[7] F. Briganti, *Città Dominanti e Comuni Minori nel Medio Evo* (1906), 131, 143. I have not been able to consult Giustiniano degli Azzi-Vitelleschi, *I Capitani del Contado nel Comune di Perugia* (1897).

[8] V. Alfieri, 'L'amministrazione economica dell'antico comune di Perugia', *BSU*, ii (1896).

[9] He was also Treasurer for the entire area governed for the Pope from Perugia, an area which went far outside the bounds of communal territories.

[10] Fumi, *Inventario e Spoglio*, lvii, 'solutis provisionibus et expensis pro d. legato et Thesaurario prefatus d. noster habeat annuatim duodecim mille (sic) flor. auri de Camera'. This agreement was subsequent to that of July 1424, see p. 173 below.

12,000 florins named in 1424.[1]   Under Martin V the Papacy was therefore in complete control of the finances of the city.   Eugenius IV however, seems to have reduced his share of the profits of the city to 8,000 florins a year, called a 'subsidy'.[2] The gross, as opposed to the net income of the city, was about 35,000 florins a year.[3]

The accounts of the Apostolic Treasurer of Perugia do not include the complete accounts of the city, but are a kind of cash account, showing the cash paid to the Treasurer, and his expenditure, combined with a sort of summary of the accounts of the *conservatores* and *massarii*.[4]   Orders for payments to be made (*bollecte*) were issued by the Legate or Governor, addressed to both the Apostolic Treasurer and either the *conservatores monete* or the *massarii*, according to the nature of the payment.[5]   Payments could also be made by the Treasurer on his own authority,[6] and probably by the *conservatores* and *massarii* on theirs.

The system of joint government is reflected also in the public instructions or *bandi* which were issued, for financial matters, in the name of the Treasurer and the *conservatores monete*, and for other matters, in the name of the Governor or his officials and the priors.[7]

The imposition of taxes in Perugia was usually negotiated direct between the Pope and the commune; the Legate or Governor was concerned more with the administration of taxes than with their imposition.   By the end of 1424 the Pope demanded

[1] Graziani, *Cronaca di Perugia in ASI*, 1st ser., xvi, pt. 1 (1850), 343 n., 'considerate tucte le conditione fuoro poste ne la prima concessione sieno verificate e per lo passato e al presente, cioè oltra li xij milia fiorini l'anno, come nella dicta concessione se contiene, ma eziando n'avanza alcuno migliaio di fiorini più l'anno'.

[2] Cf. A. Fabretti, *Documenti di Storia Perugina*, i (1887), no. 6, p. 16.   This 8,000 florins included money paid by the chamber of Perugia to papal mercenaries.

[3] Arch. Cam. pt. i, Tes. Prov., Perugia, B. 1, vol. 1 b, fol. 127v (1424/5).   The *introitus* reckoned in cameral florins was 34,920 florins 15 sol. 9 den., the *exitus* 33,720 florins 28 sol. 6 den.   Fumi, *Inventario e Spoglio*, 18 gives the *exitus* in florins of Perugia instead of in cameral florins.

[4] E.g. Arch. Cam. pt. i, Tes. Prov., Perugia, B. 2, vol. 1, fol. 69, 'El conservadorato presente de Tancredo dei Raniere hebbe per le mano de Francesco de Lippo fancello del dicto conservadorato dal sopradicto conservadorato de Saracino de Rustico per le mano de Paolo de Bartolomeo, fancello del dicto conservadorato de Saracino, fiorini doicentoquarantotto, et sol' cinquanta et mezo de camera ad sol. 80 per fiorino, li quale sommano più l'antrata del dicto conservadorato de Saracino che la sua uscita, et liquali volse messer Giovanni thesaurarie sopradicto cogliesse per darli a monsignore lo governatore, et cosi li fuorono dati' [in margin, 'Pone ad introitum et videantur soluta'].   A 'fancello' was a minor financial official, an assistant : cf. Pellini, *Dell'Historia di Perugia*, ii, 376; Fumi, *Inventario e Spoglio*, lvii.   F. Edler, *Glossary of medieval terms of business (Italian series 1200–1600)*, 115, is to be augmented in this sense.

[5] E.g. Arch. Cam. loc. cit. B. 2, vol. 7, fol. 2v, 'P[etrus] episcopus venetiarum et Perusii etc. gubernator.   Mandamus vobis domino Johanni de Cafarellis de urbe Perusii etc. thesaurario, et conservatoribus monete camere Perusii, quatenus de pecuniis dicte camere dari et solvi faciatis venerabili viri domino fratri Thome Damiano de Venetiis abbati de Pola camerario nostro . . . florenos quinque ad rationem xxxviiii bol' pro floreno, videlicet florenos v. Datum Perusi' die xxi August 1426. P. Venetiarum.' Div. Cam. 12, fol. 119, 'Dominicus etc.   Mandamus vobis venerabili viro domino Nicolao de Valle apostolice camere clerico, Perusii etc. thesaurario, et conservatoribus monete camere perusine, quatenus de pecuniis dicte camere per vestrum depositarium et fancellum dari et solvi faciatis infrascriptis hominibus et personis infrascriptas florenorum et pecuniarum quantitates eis debitas infrascriptis de causis, videlicet . . .'

[6] Arch. Cam. loc. cit. B. 2, vol. 7, fol. 40, *bullecte* issued by the Treasurer to the Depositary or *fancello*, telling him to pay various sums.

[7] Graziani, 307, 'se bandì a doi trombi per parte del Tesauriere e dei Conservatore delle monete . . .'; ibid. 331, 'se fece bando per parte dello auditore de Monsignore e delli Priori . . .'

that Perugia support the expenses of 100 lances for the defence of the provinces.[1] The demand led to an embassy being despatched to Rome under Francesco de' Coppoli, and to an important and detailed agreement with the Pope about the finances of the commune.[2] The agreement settled the imposition of an extraordinary tax, or subsidy, of a type familiar in the city as a means of extraordinary taxation,[3] and fixed the minimum amount which the Pope was to draw from the city, estimated at 12,000 florins. Other clauses concerned the abolition or reduction of certain minor taxes, on measures, grain and salt, to offset the burden of the subsidy; also the reduction of the salary of the *podestà*, and the disposal of the goods of rebels. The Pope then wrote to Cardinal Antonio Corrario, Vicar-General of the city, instructing him to approve the subsidy, which was to be imposed by the ten priors and ten chamberlains of the arts, and to carry out other clauses of the agreement in conjunction with the priors and chamberlains. This was duly done, and in March 1425 the subsidy was imposed.[4] It was raised annually, and in 1428 a Perugian embassy asked the Pope to reduce it by a half. But with the war in Bologna in progress there was little hope of this, and the request was refused.[5]

The administration of the subsidy was closely watched by the Governor. Thus in 1430 it was found that some inhabitants of the *contado* were evading taxation (which was higher in the *contado* than in the city) by having their assessments for the *catastro* entered in the books of the *armario* of the city, instead of those for the *contado*. The Governor, Domenico Capranica, therefore issued a decree that this abuse be rectified, adding that anyone who felt himself injured by the change could appeal to the *syndicus major* of the city.[6] No doubt he acted with the advice of the priors, but it is significant that the order was issued in his name.

It was evidently not easy for the Governor to interfere with a free hand in the financial practice of the city. Capranica as Governor granted several privileges to various persons, authorising them to export grain from the city. This was an infringement of the jurisdiction of the officials of the *abundanzia*, and indeed, Capranica himself, in letters issued at the same period, ordered the captains of the *contado* and the officials of the *abundanzia* to forbid all such exports, on account of an anticipated scarcity.[7] When the priors complained to him of the privileges he himself had issued, he was compelled to be extremely apologetic,[8] and without any delay to have all of them cancelled.[9]

---

[1] Pellini, *Dell'Historia di Perugia*, ii, 286-7.   [2] Documents in Fumi, *Inventario e Spoglio*, liii-lix.

[3] Alfieri, in *BSU*, ii (1896), 462-7; Fabretti, *Documenti di Storia Perugina*, ii (1892), 68-94.

[4] Graziani, 308, 'per lo abisognio e sussidio caritativo el fuoco (ma non disse fuoco) : disse, come che ditto è, per sussidio al modo usato'. For the execution of the other clauses of the agreement, see Graziani, 307.   [5] Graziani, 342-3 and n.   [6] Div. Cam. 12, fol. 19v, 7 September 1430.

[7] Ibid. fol. 6 (19 July 1430); ibid. fol. 51v (18 December 1430).

[8] Ibid. fol. 45. 'Habuimus litteram vestram multum querelam de bulletinis quas fecimus. Et prima facie, visa littera, dubii fuimus ne forsan cancellarius noster errorem commissise, et illico queri fecimus in registro nostro. Quo viso, non indetur nobis sic insulse egisse, si tria aut quatuor bulletina tempore nostro concessimus . . . Quatenus ad revocationem illorum cogitare volumus, et sapientis habere consilium, si de iure revocari debent' (25 November 1430). Ibid. fol. 45v, 'Et siamo certi, come voy sapeti, che la mazor parte di noy e mal contenta quando fosse fatto cosa alchuna che non fosse honore ali officiali de nostra santità' (28 November 1430).

[9] Letter of 29 November 1430 to the *podestà*, telling him to cancel all such privileges which were granted *in fraudem* (ibid. fol. 45v).

§ 8. The administration of justice in Perugia was dealt with pretty fully in the agreement of 1424. On the vexed question of appeals, the commune held its ground with much success.[1] It was agreed that civil and criminal appeals of first and second instance (i.e. all appeals) should not go outside Perugia, but that they might be heard in the Vicar's or Legate's Court, where procedure would be according to the statutes of Perugia. The Vicar or Governor therefore appointed his own Auditor of appeals,[2] and also named the judge of appeals of the commune.[3] It was nevertheless a victory for the Perugians that they had kept out the jurisdiction of the Roman Court, and they continued to hold this position until the time of Pius II.[4] The *collegium doctorum*, which later heard appeals for cases involving sums of less than 100 ducats, had not at this time begun to do so.[5]

In practice, conflicts of jurisdiction between Governor and commune could be serious and stormy. In 1430 the exiles who had been captured in an attempt to surprise Monte Fontagiano were being held by the *podestà* to await trial. One of them, Agnolo di Pascuccio, was a monk, and the Pope ordered that he be sent to Rome.[6] The Governor, Pierdonato Bishop of Padua, told the priors this, and they called a general council in the commune which rapidly turned itself into a mob. The prison was broken open and Agnolo di Pascuccio seized, and after some fruitless negotiation with the Governor, the priors had the monk hanged on the spot. It is significant that as a result of these events no one was punished, but the Governor was shortly afterwards recalled.

Nor did Pierdonato's successor, Domenico Capranica, have a very much more peaceful passage. One Pietro Filippo, a notable of the city and a prior in the later part of 1430, quarrelled with his fellow priors over the nomination of a notary, which had been made in his absence and against his will.[7] For the disorder which he caused, and for certain seditious remarks which he made against the Governor, Capranica had him arrested by the *podestà*, and at first expressed his intention of having him tried by the *consiglio di Savio*, a tribunal of the commune.[8] But, probably on learning the unfriendly disposition of the priors towards him in this case, Capranica changed his plan, and determined to have Pietro Filippo tried by the *podestà*, setting aside for this purpose the statute of the city which forbade the *podestà* to try any of the priors who were in office at the same time.[9] Finally, the intercession of the priors procured Pietro Filippo's release.[10]

Capranica accused Pietro Filippo of attempting to set himself up as a tyrant in the

---

[1] Fumi, *Inventario e Spoglio*, xlii–iii. Cf. Scalvanti, *BSU*, i (1895), 328–31.

[2] The first one (appointed in 1424) was the Bishop of Emona (Fumi, *Inventario e Spoglio*, 9).

[3] Div. Cam. 12, fol. 7v, 28 July 1430. This is in spite of the request of the commune that he be appointed according to the statutes, to which the Pope replied 'super facto appellationum provideat Legatus' (Fumi, *Inventario e Spoglio*, xxxix).

[4] Scalvanti, *BSU*, i (1895), 330.   [5] Ibid. p. 331.

[6] Graziani, 337–40; Pellini, ii, 315–16.

[7] Fink, 'Dominicus Capranica als Legat in Perugia', *RQ*, xxxix (1931), 275–7, and docs. 17–21 below.

[8] Docs. 17–19, and doc. 20, 'nec eum intendimus ab aliis quam a perusinis, et legibus et doctoribus condempnari'.

[9] Doc. 21.   [10] Fink, 'Dominicus Capranica', 277, n.

city,[1] but there can have been little truth in the charge. Pietro Filippo was not a potentate on his account, but a follower of Malatesta Baglioni, who was at that moment, with the assistance of papal favour, inflating his family to the power which would, two generations later, enable it to seize the virtual *signoria* of the city. The incident seems to show that a determined Governor could override the judicial processes of the commune without much difficulty. But it also shows that, in spite of his declared antipathy towards the stiffnecked *grandi* who were reaching out for absolute power in the commune, Capranica had to humour and tolerate them. The Baglioni had been prominent in the restoration of the city to the Church, and the Pope had duly rewarded them.[2] Like the Gatti of Viterbo and the Monaldeschi of Orvieto, besides being powerful citizens of the city, they were also powerful *signorotti* in their own right, with their own feudal holdings and vicariates. It was on such foundations that the *signorie* of the fifteenth century were built.

The *podestà*, being virtually a papal official, had to conduct his judicial proceedings according to the will of the Governor or Legate, initiating or suspending them as he was ordered.[3]

§ 9. The *contado* of Perugia was governed by 'captains', a new office instituted in 1428. In that year the priors issued, with the consent and approval of the Governor, a set of statutes laying down the duties of the office.[4] The captains were appointed for a six-monthly term, and they had general duties of policing and governing the *contado*, including the duty of collecting the subsidy, or hearth tax. Their oath of allegiance was made to the Pope, and references to the Governor or Legate, and the 'Apostolic Chamber of Perugia', are frequent in the statutes. A year later a new set of statutes was issued, being the same as the first set, but with many additions of administrative detail,[5] and issued by the Governor instead of by the priors. All the ordinances are changed by the Governor into the first person, and instead of being a document of the commune, the statutes are thus cast into the form of a decree issued by papal authority. But it is much to be doubted if the practical effect was any different. This second version of the statutes states that the Pope has instructed the Governor to nominate the captains, and the first nominations are incorporated into its text.[6] Capranica also named the captains,[7] but it is quite probable that this 'nomination' was in fact merely a confirmation of elections already made by the commune. Such elections *de sachecto* were certainly being made for the captains of

---

[1] Doc. 19.

[2] Malatesta Baglioni was given Cannara in vicariate (Reg. Vat. 356, fol. 20) and a pension of 400 florins a year (ibid. fol. 23v). He and his brother Nello were also made Governors of Spello, at the Pope's good pleasure (ibid. fol. 11). Spello was granted in 1425, Cannara in 1427.

[3] E.g. Div. Cam. 12, fol. 11v, ' volumus et contentamus quod condemnationem Massii Jacobi de Perusio per totum mensem Augusti supersedeatis . . .'; ibid. fol. 25v, the *podestà* is on no account to proceed against Master Luca; ibid. fol. 29v, 'Nolumus ut contra dominam Katarinam procedeatis, nisi aliud in mandatis habueretis, aliquo maleficio non obstante'.

[4] Fabretti, *Documenti di storia Perugina*, i, 122.

[5] Ibid. p. 152.

[6] Ibid. See also the brief of September 1429 in Briganti, *Città dominanti e comuni minori*, 131.

[7] See p. 171 above.

the *contado* in May 1431, and the commune did not lose the right of making them until 1462.[1] The Governor also carried out the review of the captains, with their notaries and soldiers, at the beginning of their term of office.[2]

The statutes of 1428/9 were thus launched under the aegis of the Papacy, as was the office which they introduced, and in spite of the larger part assigned by them to the commune, there is little doubt that from the beginning the 'captains' were a powerful aid to the papal Governors in seizing control of the administration of the *contado*.

§ 10.   Bologna had a longer history of subjection to the Holy See than Perugia,[3] but the former commune was the richer, the more populous, and the less accessible from Rome, and its spirit of independence was not merely strong, but fierce. Bologna rendered obedience to Martin V most unwillingly, twice revolted against him, and was still in a state of virtual revolt at the time of his death.

The conditions of papal government in Bologna were controlled by a series of agreements between the Pope and the commune—the first of 1419,[4] the second of 1420 and the third of 1429.[5] The text of the second of these agreements is lost. As I have not been able to use the archives of Bologna, nor to find very much relevant material in Rome,[6] I have been unable to throw any light on many important aspects of papal government there.

The first agreement of Martin V with Bologna in 1419 was in all but name a concession of the vicariate to the commune. The withholding of the title of vicariate was nevertheless extremely important, and had been one of the hardest fought points of the negotiations : there was a great distance between the cities *mediate* and *immediate subjecte*. Where the commune held the vicariate the Apostolic Legate had little more than an empty title, as the later history of Bologna was to demonstrate clearly. But the agreement of 1419 still contained some important concessions on the part of the Papacy, and the despotic government of the city by John XXIII was evidently not to be repeated. Not only were the officials of the commune, save for the *podestà*, to be elected according to the statutes, but the finances of the commune were to remain in the hands of the commune, the Pope being satisfied with an annual tribute. The *podestà* was selected by the Pope from three candidates of the commune, and this only while he was within a hundred leagues of the city : when the Pope was in Rome the selection of the *podestà* fell to the Bishop of Bologna.

---

[1] Briganti, 143, 146–7.

[2] Div. Cam. 12, fol. 26, 1 October 1430. Cf. Fabretti, i, 158, a record is to be made of this muster, 'Et che le decte [a] pontature incontenente retornato che sirà sia tenuto notificare in scripto a la Cancellaria nostra'.

[3] For the first papal *signoria* there, see L. Ciaccio, 'Il Cardinal Legato Bertrando del Poggetto in Bologna, 1327–1334', *AMDR*, 3rd ser., xxiii (1905).

[4] Theiner, iii, no. 166, p. 236; see also the earlier versions of the bull in Zaoli, *Libertas Bononie e Papa Martino V*, 59 n.

[5] Extracts are printed by Fink, 'Martin V. und Bologna', *QF*, xxiii (1931/2), 213 f.

[6] The earliest volume belonging to the papal Treasurers of Bologna to be preserved in the Archivio di Stato at Rome is Arch. Cam. pt. i, Tes. Prov., Bologna, B. 1, vol. 1, the accounts for 1432. The other volumes in the same *busta* are for 1468, 1477, 1543 and dates after 1554. See now, however, Orlandelli, 'Note di storia economica sulla signoria dei Bentivoglio', *AMDR*, n.s., iii (1953).

The terms obtained by the commune after its rebellion of 1420, when the peace of Florence had been signed and Braccio had become a papal *condottiere*, were certainly far less favourable than those of the previous year. All that the chronicles relate of these terms is that the ancients and *gonfalonieri* were to be elected in the usual way, that all the offices remained in the hands of the citizens save for those of the Treasurer and of the *bollete*, and that the Pope undertook not to build any fortress in Bologna.[1] But more can be inferred from the papal practice between 1420–1428. It is evident that the concession of the government of the city to the commune had been forfeited by the rebellion, and that the city was now to be directly governed in the same manner as Perugia and the other communes directly subject. A Legate was at once appointed, and the *podestà*, instead of being selected from the candidates of the commune, was appointed directly by the Pope.[2] The tribute payable to the Pope lapsed; the whole finances of the city returned to papal control, and an Apostolic Treasurer was appointed to administer them.[3]

§ 11. As at Perugia, the Pope left the financial machine of the commune virtually untouched, and the duty of the Apostolic Treasurer was to supervise the operation of the various offices, and control payments. The office of Treasurer, however, was one which already existed in the communal administration. The Treasurer of Bologna was a Florentine merchant instead of an official of the Chamber, but this may be explained by the loans which the Florentines made to the papal organisation in Bologna.[4] The financial offices of the commune were preserved, even to the 'defensores havere' of the former popular régime.[5] The Pope also appointed the *capitanei montanearum*, who were among the most important financial officials of the commune.[6] The book-keeping arrangements made can only be guessed at, but it is probable that they were virtually the same as at Perugia, that is, that the

---

[1] *Corp. Chron. Bonon.*, iii, 566. Cf. Zaoli, 116.

[2] Reg. Vat. 349, fol. 137v, contains the appointment of Antonio Alexandri de Alexandris of Florence, for the term beginning 1 May 1421. There is no mention of any rights of the commune in his nomination.

[3] See next note.

[4] Petro Bartolomeo de Borromeis de Sancto Miniato, a Florentine, was appointed Treasurer on 4 August 1420 (Reg. Vat. 349, fol. 63; Div. Cam. 3, fol. 74). At the same time he lent the Apostolic Chamber 10,000 florins, on the understanding that after a lapse of a year he could recover them from the revenues of Bologna (Reg. Vat. 354, fol. 43). But in fact he had not recovered his money before his supersession, in August 1422 (Reg. Vat. 349, fol. 230). Cf. *Commissioni*, ii, 119, 'Pensiamo che voi sappiate, come noi prestamo allo Legato vecchio di Bologna fiorini 10,000 di camera, per pagare soldati et altre spese necessarie per la salvezza di Bologna . . .' but the Legate (Condulmer) refused to repay more than 4,000 florins. Petro Borromei was at the beginning of his office supervised by a second papal Treasurer of Bologna, the cameral clerk Paolo de Caputgrassis of Sulmona. The latter was appointed on 25 August 1420, with the proviso, 'Volumus autem quod de pecuniis ex introitibus camere Bononien', quas ad manus dicti Petri [de Borromeis] tamquam thesaurarii seu depositarii venire contingent, cum illas solvere contingerit, tu habito primo mandato a dilecto filio Alfonso Sancti Eustacii diacono cardinali ibidem apostolice sedis legato, prefato legato eidem Petro litteras seu bullectas solutionis fiendarum facias et decernas, qui Petrus in huiusmodi faciendi solutionibus tibi pareat et intendat, nec aliter solvere valeat quoquemodo . . .' (Reg. Vat. 349, fol. 79v). Another Florentine, Giovanni de Corbitiis, was appointed Treasurer of Bologna in 1429 (Reg. Vat. 351, fol. 142v).

[5] See Zaoli, 23 n. Martin V approved the appointment of such officers in 1423, but declined to pay them (Reg. Vat. 354, fol. 269).

[6] Theiner, iii, no. 241, p. 298, 15 November 1427.

Apostolic Treasurer recorded only in summary the transactions of the financial offices of the commune, but that he was fully responsible for the eventual disposal of the monies.[1]

The Church was compelled to honour the obligation of the popular régime which had preceded it in Bologna. The Pope attempted to cancel the repayments of the loans raised by the popular régime,[2] but at the instance of the ambassadors of the commune he reversed this decision, and ordered that when the ordinary expenses of the commune (reckoned at 6,080 ducats a month *ad rationem* 40 *bol.* = 1 *ducato*) had been paid, 500 *lib. bonen* per month were to be devoted to repaying the loan.[3] The original loan was of 94,000 *lib. bonen* at interest of ten per cent, afterwards reduced to six.[4]

The agreement which closed the revolt of 1428/9 preserved these financial arrangements,[5] and the Pope continued to appoint the Treasurer of the city.[6] But he also promised to appoint a second holder of each of the offices of Treasurer, of the *bollete* (orders for payments to be made) and of the *capitaneus montanearum*, this second official in each case to be a Bolognese citizen.[7]

Papal interference in the government of the *contado* of Bologna was far less than at Perugia. The Pope named the *podestà* and castellans of one or two strongpoints such as S. Giovanni in Persiceto, but the organisation of the 'vicars' who ruled the *contado* continued to fall to the commune.[8]

§ 12. The most characteristic and important of the constitutional innovations of Bologna in the late fourteenth century was that of the sixteen *Riformatori dello stato della libertà*. These officers were of an essentially revolutionary nature; they were elected by the Council of Six Hundred for a year instead of for the two months' term of the *anziani*, and they had the widest possible powers of legislation and government.[9] The office of the *riformatori* represents a considerable step away from the free commune towards the *signoria*, and the *riformatori* at Bologna may be compared with the equally revolutionary office of the *balestieri* at Rome.

The essential weakness of Martin V and Eugenius IV at Bologna was their failure to suppress the *riformatori*. Elected at the time of the popular régime of 1416–1419, and again for the rebellion of 1420, they were not granted a place in the government of Bologna in the treaties of 1419 and 1420. They thus disappear until the revolu-

---

[1] This is evident from an examination of the accounts for 1432, in the volume quoted above, p. 176.

[2] Reg. Vat. 353, fol. 131v, 8 March 1421.

[3] Ibid. fols. 180, 181, 8 May 1421.

[4] For such loans see G. B. Salvioni, 'Sul valore della lira bolognese', *AMDR*, 3rd ser., xix (1901), 387–8.

[5] Fink, 'Martin V. und Bologna', *QF*, xxiii (1931/2), 213.

[6] Domenico, Abbot of Savino, was appointed Treasurer on 18 January 1430, Reg. Vat. 351, fol. 143.

[7] Fink, 'Martin V. und Bologna', 215.

[8] Bosdari, *AMDR*, 4th ser., iv (1914), 137–8; A. Palmieri, 'Gli antichi Vicariati nell'Appennino Bolognese', ibid. 3rd ser., xx (1902).

[9] O. Bosdari, 'Il comune di Bologna alla fine del secolo XIV', *AMDR*; 4th ser., iv (1914), 126 f.; M. Longhi, 'Nicolò Piccinino in Bologna', ibid. 3rd ser., xxiv (1906), 198 f.; C. M. Ady, *The Bentivoglio of Bologna*, 5.

tion of 1428, when the leading members of the faction of Canetoli and Zambeccari were at once elected as *riformatori*. In the peace of 1429 the existing *riformatori* were confirmed in their office, and given powers to elect their own successors,[1] and a similar clause was granted by Eugenius IV in 1433.[2] These concessions amount to nothing less than the absolution of the faction which had controlled the revolt, and the prolongation of its revolutionary powers. Such concessions placed the papal Legate in an impossible position, and the rapid erosion of papal power in Bologna in the middle of the fifteenth century is far from surprising. But it would almost certainly be a mistake to suppose that these concessions were granted in ignorance of their probable effect. Martin V confirmed the *riformatori* because, on the one hand, the only practical way to rule the great cities was to humour their great families, and, on the other, he had to accept from the commune the best terms he could get. Knowing that this way might easily lead to the *signoria* of some great family, he was nevertheless powerless to prevent it. Of all the cities in the Papal State, Bologna was the plum. It was far richer and more populous than Perugia, perhaps also than Rome.[3] Such riches made the successful revolt of the city possible; they also made the Roman Court consider it better to accept a reduced sovereignty over the city rather than risk losing it altogether.

III. *The Other Communes of the Papal State*

§ 1. There was no uniformity in the treatment of the communes by the Popes: papal government lay heavily upon some areas and lightly upon others. In the March of Ancona the variations of independence from one commune to another are particularly striking.

The richest and most independent of the communes of the March was Ancona.[4] The maritime city had a long tradition of commercial and cultural links with cities outside the March, particularly Venice—which was nevertheless its most feared rival—and Bologna. The commune of Ancona elected all its own officials, and its relations with the Legate of the March were mainly tributary. The *anziani* described themselves as councillors of the Legate of the March,[5] and they had to accede to certain judicial encroachments of the Church, particularly in appeals,[6] and in the exemption of clerks from the communal imposts.[7] One of the most powerful families

---

[1] Fink, 'Martin V. und Bologna', 214–5.   [2] Theiner, iii, no. 266, p. 316.

[3] Cf. K. Beloch, *Bevölkerungsgeschichte Italiens*, ii (1939), 70, 90 ff. The gross annual income of Perugia was about 35,000 florins (p. 172 above). That of Rome was probably upwards of 130,000 florins, but the figure is a very dubious one (p. 169 above). The gross annual income of Bologna was reckoned at 125,000 florins in 1404 (Theiner, iii, no. 74, p. 140), and in fact amounted to about 140,000 florins in 1432 (Arch. Cam. pt. i, Tes. Prov., Bologna, B. 1, vol. 1, calculated after the monthly totals).

[4] Cf. Guiraud, *L'Etat Pontifical*, 208–10.   [5] Ancona, Atti Consigliari, vol. 30, fol. 4.

[6] See p. 127 above, n. 1.

[7] Ancona, Atti Consigliari, vol. 30, fol. 41. The ancients, 'auditis querelis eisdem dominis factis pro parte cleri dicte civitatis, conquerentis de datiariis datii vini portarum dicte civitatis, recusantibus eidem clero observare constitutionem factam in publico parlamento provincie per dominum legatum, de exemptione dicti cleri . . .' therefore sent for the official in charge of the wine customs, the *datiarius vini*, and told him to observe the Legate's constitution.

of Ancona, the Ferretti, was involved in a bitter quarrel with the Legate Condulmer, over some matter now unknown, but succeeded in appealing over the Legate's head to the Pope,[1] who committed the case to a commission of cardinals, and as a result of their decision, quashed the case against Francesco Ferretti and ordered his release.[2] Francesco Ferretti was nevertheless forbidden to enter Ancona without special licence, and when the commune admitted him within the walls in 1423 the Pope threatened the city with an interdict if they would not expel him;[3] the act appears to have been accompanied by a rebellion, or something approaching one.[4] But evidently the rebellion fizzled out, for no more is heard of it, and for the remainder of the pontificate the state of Ancona was quiet.[5]

Although the financial administration of Ancona was in principle free, the weight of papal taxes was such as to leave the commune very little freedom in spending its money. When the salaries of officials had been paid, half the ordinary income was spent, and the remaining half went as tallage, *census* and *affitti*, mainly the first. In 1421 Ancona paid 3,484 ducats to the Church, representing more than 54% of the total expenditure of the commune.[6] In many years the ordinary income would not meet expenses, and forced loans were a permanent feature of communal finances.[7]

A second city of a certain prosperity and independence was Macerata. The commune elected its own officials, including its own *podestà*, and continued to make good certain important privileges, such as that of exemption of its officials from undergoing audit (*sindacatio*) in the rectoral court.[8] As a frequent seat of the Legate or Rector of the March, it gained economically, but must have lost a certain measure of independence. Like Ancona, it paid a very high proportion of its revenue in tallage, and was often hard put to balance its budget.[9]

Equally independent, and, to judge by its assessment for tallage, richer than

---

[1] Reg. Vat. 353, fol. 107; Condulmer is ordered to free Angelo Ferretti and his brother, and to give them a safeconduct (13 January 1420).

[2] Ibid. fol. 137v (6 April 1421). 'Nuper siquidem cum dictus miles super quibusdam pretensis excessibus criminibus et delictis per eum et suos contra nos et Romanam ecclesiam perpetratis, ab eius emulis in partibus indigne diffamatus fuisset . . .'; the case was committed to Jean de Broniac the Vice-Chancellor, Francesco Lando the Cardinal of S. Croce, and Cardinal Raynaldo Brancaccio, of the title of S. Vito in Macello. Cf. A. Peruzzi, *Storia d'Ancona dalla sua fondazione*, ii (1835), 247 f.

[3] Reg. Vat. 354, fol. 292v, 12 December 1423.

[4] *Commissioni*, i, 569, 'che uno ser Ioanni dalla Roccacontrada [this was Braccio's chancellor] era andato ad Ancona a confortàgli che si tenessono, e non temessino, però che subito il signor Braccio gli verebbe a soccorrere, ec. : e, come voi sapete, essi si sono rubellati, e fatti e Dodici della balìa' (14 November 1423).

[5] Francesco Ferretti was again imprisoned as a result of this rebellion, and was not freed until March 1427, Ancona, Atti Consigliari, vol. 31, fol. 21. Another of the Ferretti, Felice, secured the quashing, in 1429, of the processes brought against him both by Condulmer and by Pietro Emigli (Reg. Vat. 356, fol. 32, 19 August 1429).

[6] Remo Roia, 'L'amministrazione finanziaria del comune d'Ancona nel secolo XV', *AMSM*, 4th ser., i (1924), 144–5, 207.

[7] Roia, passim; Atti Consigliari, vol. 31, fol. 21 f.

[8] See p. 126 above.

[9] E.g. Riformanze, vol. 12, fol. 40, on 3 June 1421 the commune is unable to repair the Legate's palace against his arrival, 'cum non sit pecunia in communi'; ibid. fol. 132v, the commune borrows money from the Marshal of the March.

Macerata, was Recanati.[1] The city was sufficiently free to form alliances with powers outside the Papal State, and in 1422 it accepted the protection of Venice against Ancona, being guaranteed against the aggression of Ancona at sea.[2]

With this short list, the tale of the important free communes of the March is exhausted.[3] The minor communes were also tenacious of their institutions and independence,[4] but they were irresistibly drawn into the orbit, either of the Church, or of the neighbouring *signori*, and in any event, their *podestà* was often appointed by the Church. There remains to be discussed a number of more or less important cities recovered by Martin V from their tyrants, and restored to the direct government of the Church. On these cities, of which the most important was Ascoli Piceno, the hand of the Church fell with some weight. The capitulations of Ascoli with the Governor of the March in 1426 [5] cannot be compared with the terms given to Perugia and Bologna. The Governor reserved the right to appoint a *podestà*, and refused every demand which conflicted in any way with the direct government of the Church. A Governor was appointed for the city,[6] and a papal Treasurer, and the communal finances were then directly administered by the Church, as they were at Perugia. The *depositarii*, the communal officials at the head of the financial administration, were appointed by the Governor. Although Ascoli continued to pay tallage, this became more or less a piece of internal book-keeping, involving no more than the transfer of the money from the papal Treasurer of Ascoli to the papal Treasurer of the March.[7] In the capitulations of 1426 only minor concessions were made to the demands of the commune, such as that debts contracted by the previous régime were to be honoured, and that the city was not to be deprived of its *contado*.

All that has been said of Ascoli is equally true of Fermo which came under the direct rule of the Church in very similar circumstances. The Pope refused to destroy the fortress of the city, just as the Governor had refused to do so at Ascoli. The revenues of the city were to be administered directly by the Church, as at Ascoli, and requests for a reduction of papal taxes, and especially that taxes be not exacted to repair the hated fortress of the Migliorati, the Girfalcon, met with a brusque refusal.[8] Taxation remained at the same level as under the Migliorati, and it was

[1] Arm. 33, vol. 11, fol. 6, Macerata paid 700 florins and Recanati 1,450 (cf. Guiraud, *L'Etat Pontifical*, 206–7).

[2] L. Zdekauer, 'L'Archivio del comune di Recanati ed il recente suo riordinamento', *Le Marche*, v (1905), 26–7.

[3] Guiraud, *L'Etat Pontifical*, 211, errs in citing Ascoli and Cingoli as free communes.

[4] Cf. A. Menchetti, *Storia di un comune rurale della Marca Anconitana, Montalbodo oggi Ostra* (1913–37).

[5] Doc. 23 below.

[6] Matteo del Carreto, Abbot of Subiaco, was appointed *locumtenens* on 10 November 1426, Reg. Vat. 350, fol. 272.

[7] Arch. Cam. pt. i, Tes. Prov., Ascoli, B. 1, vol. 1, fol. 102, 'dominus thesaurarius retinuit penes se de introytibus camere civitatis Esculi pro ultima sextaria tallearum anni proxime preteriti, quos posuit ad introytum thesaurarie Marchie, computatis capitibus solidorum et quietantia, ducatos 504, bon. 20'.

[8] *Cronache della città di Fermo*, 59, and 61, 'Infacto vero introitus et exitus, Dominus Noster volebat introitus pro ipso, et similiter facere expensas; sed volebat quod solverentur talie quolibet anno et gabelle solverentur prout erat tempore domini Ludovici, excepto quod volebat quod solverent grani et vini ad portas et hoc Dei gratia.' Cf. Fermo, Archivio Priorale, no. 471, copy of a brief to the Treasurer

evident that in this respect the city had gained nothing by the change of régime.   In 1429 the Bishop of Teramo was sent to govern both Ascoli and Fermo.[1]

At San Severino, which was recovered from the Smeducci in 1426, Nicolò de Acziapaziis was appointed *locumtenens* for the Church,[2] and the arrangements for government were probably the same as at Ascoli and Fermo.   At Iesi and Cingoli the Church was content merely to appoint the *podestà*; no doubt they were too poor to support the expenses of a Governor.[3]

§ 2.   The province of Romagna can be dealt with shortly, as this homeland of tyrants gives little room for discussion.   Forlì and Imola were ruled by a papal Governor, with his own Treasurer at Forlì,[4] and without doubt the Church ruled them with little more regard for communal liberties than had the Ordelaffi or Alidosi.   When the commune of Forlì sent ambassadors to the Pope in 1430, their demands were that the proceeds of condemnations should go to the commune to repair the sea-walls, that certain taxes be relaxed, and that the officials of the city (save for the *podestà*) be citizens of Forlì.[5]   The Pope received the embassy kindly, granted the commune half the proceeds of condemnations, and conceded most of the other requests.   But the requests were modest in the extreme.   In the rest of the province, outside Bologna, the tyrants were supreme.

The appointment of a Governor or Rector to rule the cities directly subject to the Holy See was far from being an innovation, and the practice was, indeed, many centuries old.   But while in the thirteenth century the existence of a papal Rector was compatible with a high degree of communal independence,[6] under Albornoz the Rector came to inherit or to assume the powers of *signore*, and to deal with communal

---

of the March.   'Fuerunt ad nos oratores civitatis nostre Firman' duo, petentes primum quod declarari faceremus ut dicta civitas bene gubernetur, et, prout alias nobis supplicaverunt, debitum camere nostre iuxta qualitatem temporis facere possit, cum dicta camera insupportabilibus [*supply* oneribus] subiciatur, secundum ad quod certas pecunias expositas per te et thesaurarium nostrum tam pro tuitione Girfalchi quam civitatis, necnon pro talleis decimam quintam (sic) mensium, de quibus partitis solutum remictere digneremur.   Quibus prime petitioni respondimus quod gabelle ponantur prout erant tempore novitatis quam fecerunt, reducendo se ad nos et sanctam matrem ecclesiam.   Et quod dativa quattuor milium florenorum vel circha que dicto tempore exigebatur pro talleis et cetera ponantur.   Preterea quod assectamenta comitatus, que dicuntur ascendere ad summam similem vel quasi, que solvuntur per comitativos pro expensis ordinariis et aliis oneribus dicte civitatis, etiam continuo exigantur.   Nihil imponendo vel exigendo de cassectis, que omnia una cum aliis introitibus, si qui sint, exigantur, et de eis solvatur pro expensis dicte civitatis, et Girfalchi, et tallearum, per deputandos a nobis . . . [the rest is too damaged to be legible] . . . Datum Rome . . . die xxiiii Novembris pontificatus nostri anno tertiodecimo.'

[1] *Cronache della città di Fermo*, 61.   The Deputy of the March became Governor in his stead on 8 October 1430, Reg. Vat. 351, fol. 160v.

[2] Reg. Vat. 350, fol. 276, 29 December 1426.

[3] See the tallage recorded by Guiraud, *L'Etat Pontifical*, 206–7.   San Severino was assessed at 1,400 florins, Iesi at 800, Cingoli at 850.

[4] See p. 99 above.   There is frequent mention of the Chamber of Forlì in IE 388, the accounts kept for the war of Bologna.

[5] Giovanni di M° Pedrino, *Cronica*, 249–51.

[6] O. Vehse, 'Benevent als Territorium des Kirchenstaates bis zum Beginn der Avignonesischen Epoch', *QF*, xxii–iii (1930/2); idem, 'Benevent und die Kurie unter Nicolaus IV', *QF*, xx (1928/9).

institutions as he would.[1]   The office of Governor or Rector was thus the instrument by which the Church imposed her *signoria* over the larger cities, in the particular juridical sense which the word *signoria* held in the Renaissance period, and it is significant that, save in the few cities in the March which have just been discussed, Martin V appointed a Governor or Rector in every important city which was directly subject to the Holy See.

§ 3.   In the Patrimony of St. Peter in Tuscia the Church carried out the same policy of making herself *signore* in the cities, at the same time favouring and working almost in co-operation with the dominant families and factions.   The capital of the Patrimony and residence of the Rector of the province was normally at Viterbo. Here there was consequently no need to appoint a Rector, once the rule of the Church was firmly established.[2]   The Church appointed not only the *podestà* of Viterbo, but also the other main administrative and financial officers.[3]   The Gatti of Viterbo were much favoured by Martin V, as they had been by John XXIII,[4] and the Pope directly intervened to protect them from their enemies in the city.[5] To favour one faction, however, always exposed the Papacy to the enmity of another, and the favour shown to the Gatti resulted in two minor rebellions, or rather 'tumults', little more than riots, instigated by the opposing faction of Maganzesi. The first was due to the refusal of the Rector of the province to put into effect certain anti-semitic measures demanded by the populace, the second was a simple battle between the two factions.   But neither disturbance appears to have given the Pope cause for much more than annoyance : the first, in 1428, was solved by sending Iacopo Bishop of Teramo to pacify the city, and the second by a general pacification and by the re-entry of the exiles into the city.[6]

The history of Orvieto in the same period is not dissimilar.   A Governor or later a *locumtenens et potestas* was appointed there,[7] and the Monaldeschi, the former *signori* of the city, were given lands, privileges and a marriage alliance with the Colonna.[8]

---

[1] Cf. Ermini, 'La libertà comunale nello Stato della Chiesa', *ASR*, xlix (1926), 35–48, and pt. ii of the same study, 'L'amministrazione della giustizia' (1927), 56–7.

[2] While Braccio was ruling unchecked in the Patrimony in 1419, Francesco Pizzolpassi was appointed as Vice-Rector of the city (Reg. Vat. 352, fol. 242v, 27 March 1419).   From 1420 the Church merely appointed the *podestà*, e.g. Reg. Vat. 348, fol. 205.

[3] E.g. the *gabellarius generalis* (Theiner, iii, no. 179, p. 254) and the *officialis custodie damnorum datorum* (Reg. Vat. 348, fol. 204v, 1 February 1420).

[4] Celleno was regranted to Giovanni and Petruccio Gatti by Martin V (Reg. Vat. 348, fol. 193, 12 December 1419), as it had been by John XXIII (Silvestrelli, *Città Castelli e Terre della regione Romana*, 772).   The Gatti had held the place since 1375 ; it had originally been part of the *contado* of Viterbo, see Guiraud, *L'Etat Pontifical*, 147–8.

[5] See the brief exonerating them from their calumniators, of 22 March 1425, in C. Pinzi, *Storia della città di Viterbo*, iii (1899), 556.

[6] Pinzi, iii, 556–63 ; Signorelli, *Viterbo nella storia della Chiesa*, ii, 59–60.

[7] Agapito Colonna was *locumtenens et potestas* there in 1421 (Reg. Vat. 349, fol. 151v, 5th May) ; Giovanni de Rayneriis held the same office in the same year (Reg. Vat. 353, fol. 281, 28 November) ; Giovanni de Tomariis, auditor of the Rota, was made *locumtenens* in Orvieto and Todi in 1426 (Reg. Vat. 350, fol. 260v, 11 July).   Cf. G. Pardi, 'Serie dei supremi magistrati e reggitori di Orvieto', *BSU*, i (1895), 408 f.

[8] See p. 64 above, and cf. D. Waley, *Mediaeval Orvieto*, 126 f.

The Pope disposed of the communal revenues to the extent that he could grant the gabelle of meat for five years as a gift,[1] but it is probable that the city nevertheless administered its own finances.   In 1430 the *podestà* of Orvieto was killed in a riot, probably with the connivance of the *conservatores*; Martin V thereupon sent the cameral clerk Giovanni of Rieti as Commissioner, with powers to reform the city and appoint the officers of the commune.   There was no question of rebellion, and long before the Commissioner arrived the *conservatores* were considering, with every expression of devotion to papal rule, the means of better ordering the city.   The cause of the attack on the *podestà* seems to have been his Roman origins, and the incident reveals not the slightest instability in the papal hold over the city.[2]

In the rest of the Patrimony the supervision of the Papacy over communal government seems to have been no less close.[3]   In Corneto the Pope appointed not only the *podestà*, but the Treasurer [4] and Chancellor,[5] and disposed freely of communal revenues.

§ 3.   In Umbria the *signoria* of the Church was imposed in the same manner as elsewhere.   There were no communes with a considerable degree of independence besides Perugia, and Governors or *podestà* were appointed by the Church in all towns of any importance—in Spoleto, Narni, Terni, Todi, Amelia, Rieti there were papal Governors, *locumtenentes*, or *podestà*, sometimes of a single city, sometimes of a group of cities.[6]   In this area the Pope appointed not only the *podestà*, but other communal officials, as he did in the Patrimony.[7]   These cities were not always easy to rule, and either by rebellion against the Church or by the ceaseless feuds they pursued among themselves,[8] they gave the Pope a considerable amount of trouble.   But the territory was nevertheless firmly under the hand of the Church : there were few barons in the area, and, after the expulsion of the Alfani from Rieti,[1] no *signori*. The brutally firm treatment of the ambassadors of Rieti, when the city submitted to the Church in 1425, shows clearly that essential communal liberties in this region were practically dead.[9]

---

[1] Fumi, *Codice diplomatico della città di Orvieto*, no. 734, p. 677.   [2] Ibid. 683–8.

[3] Cf. Guiraud, *L'Etat Pontifical*, 142 f.

[4] Salvatore Mattei, a Florentine, had lent 2,000 florins to the Apostolic Chamber under John XXIII, and had been made Treasurer of Corneto, with authority to recoup 250 florins of the debt every year from the revenues of the city.   This appointment was confirmed by Martin V (Reg. Vat. 348, fol. 95v, 29 November 1418).

[5] Reg. Vat. 348, fol. 204 (5 January 1420).

[6] Narni, Terni and Amelia were ruled by a single Rector until 1424 (Reg. Vat. 349, fols. 39, 204; Reg. Vat. 350, fols. 8v, 24), but after the end of the struggle with Braccio the Pope contented himself with appointing the *podestà*.   Cf. Guiraud, *L'Etat Pontifical*, 165–6.   Todi was ruled by a *locumtenens* (e.g. by Antonio, Bishop of Montefiascone, appointed 7 October 1428, Reg. Vat. 351, fol. 69).   Rieti was ruled by a commissioner in temporals (Reg. Vat. 351, fol. 142, appointment of 1 January 1430).

[7] E.g. Theiner, iii, no. 191, p. 263, appointment of the *gabellarius* of Narni.

[8] See Guiraud, 96–7, 165–8 and 188–90, for the feud of Norcia with Spoleto.   Norcia was a particularly aggressive commune, enjoying as it did the protection of the mountains.   Narni was called to answer before the Vice-Chamberlain for its aggression against the *castrum* of San Gemini in 1430, Div. Cam. 13, fol. 19.

[9] Nor did Rieti secure much better terms from Eugenius IV; see Michaeli, *Memorie storiche della città di Rieti*, iii, 330–34 (wrongly headed 1427, instead of 1431).

§ 4. In Umbria, the Patrimony and the March one common phenomenon is visible, the subjection of the *contado* of the larger cities to the dominating commune, a process which has been called 'comitatinanza', from its relation to the juridical unit of the *comitatus*. The Papacy implicitly recognised this juridical concept, and most of the documents concerning the cities which it issued talk of the *civitas et comitatus*. There is little trace of the central powers trying to stop the domination of the cities over their *contado*, and the measures taken in this direction against Orvieto in 1418/9 are exceptional. Thus in 1420 the Pope, in the capitulations made by Orvieto on its return to the direct government of the Church, granted that all inhabitants of the *contado* and district be under the direct jurisdiction of Orvieto.[1] The idea of the *comitatus* was firmly embedded in the papal chancery and Chamber, and where cities were ruled directly for the Church the *comitatus* continued to be united to the city and subject to it. This is in spite of the attempts of the Papacy in the thirteenth and fourteenth centuries to suppress the domination of the cities over the *comitatus*. It is probable that the Papacy gave way in this conflict for the same reason that it had given way in the struggle to obtain *merum et mixtum imperium*—that having obtained the reality of seignorial power over the cities by means of a papal Rector or *podestà*, the Papacy could afford to concede to the cities the rights of mere and mixed empire, or domination over the *contado*, knowing that the city could always be called to book in a papal court if it misused these rights. Thus when Fermo was being governed by a papal Rector in 1399, the papal Treasurer listed 37 *castra* which were subject to the commune of Fermo and paid *affitti* through the commune.[2] That the *comitatus* was the decisive legal factor recognised by the Papacy is clearly shown by the terms of the submission of Ascoli in 1426. The request of the commune that the parts of the *contado* which the Church had subtracted from the jurisdiction of the commune be restored, was granted by the Governor only for those *castra* which formed part of the *comitatus*.[3]

To maintain or extend this subjection of the *contado* was one of the main concerns of most of the larger communes. The subject is too large to be developed here, but it may be noticed that in 1424 the commune of Spoleto was still receiving acts of submission from its subject communes, of a kind familiar in Umbria throughout the Middle Ages.[4] The taxes owed by a commune for its whole subject area were

---

[1] Valentini, *BSU*, xxvi (1923), 103–4. For earlier and later requests of this kind by Orvieto, and for the relation of the city to the countryside in general, see Waley, *Mediaeval Orvieto*, 149–51, and G. de Vergottini, 'Il Papato e la comitatinanza nello stato della chiesa', *AMDR*, n.s., iii (1953), especially at pp. 157 f.

[2] Arch. Cam. pt. i, Tes. prov., Fermo, B. 1, vol. 1.

[3] Doc. 23 below. 'Item quod omnia et singula castra communitates et universitates hactenus possessa et possesse per comunem Esculi vel gubernatores eius, que actenus reverse essent ad manus officialium ecclesie romane et separate a comitatu et districtu Esculi, restituantur sub iurisdictione comunis et populi civitatis Esculi'. 'Concessum de castris qui sunt de comitatu. P. gubernator.'

[4] Spoleto, Archivio Storico del comune, no. 352. Original parchment, recording the submission of the commune of Roccafranca ('Aquefrancha') to the commune of Spoleto, dated 27 September 1424. They agree to accept and pay the *podestà* appointed by Spoleto, promise to recognise no other lord, tyrant or baron, and to pay the customary hearth tax of '26 den. pro quolibet foculari'. Similar submissions to the commune of Perugia, of an earlier date, may be seen in plenty in the documents published by Ansidei, 'I codici delle Sommissioni al Comune di Perugia', *BSU*, i–vi (1895–1900).

N

collected in detail by the city from the minor communes and *castra*, and passed into the main communal finances. Thus, Ancona paid a large tallage to the Church, for itself and its *comitatus*, and collected an equivalent tax known as the *tallia* from the communes of the *contado*.[1]

§ 5. In Campania and Maritima the free commune was as moribund as in Umbria, and, indeed, even nearer dissolution.[2] But there was a powerful baronage which exercised great power over the communes of the province, even where they were in theory directly subject to the Holy See. A very large number of the communes were granted to these Roman baronial families, either in vicariate or in fee.[3] Only Velletri seems to have been under the effective protection and direct government of the Holy See.[4] The nepotism of Martin V had more direct consequences in this province than any other, by reason of the extra grants and favours given to the Colonna there, and by their evident abuse. When Agapito Colonna was appointed Governor of Maritima in 1423 he acted oppressively and tyranically, and was removed from the office by his angry relative within three or four months. Terracina, which was directly subject to the Holy See, had to seek a pardon from the Pope for the assistance which it gave to Agapito.[5] When his own house could show such lawlessness, it is scarcely surprising that the other feudal barons of Campania were difficult to control, and that the Caetani and Conti were able, in 1424, to indulge in open warfare, while the Pope preserved an undignified neutrality,[6] or that the Savelli and Annibaldi were able to conduct a quarrel which ended with the murder of Savello Savelli by Paluzio Annibaldi.[7] In such circumstances the communes of Campania and Maritima could expect neither independence nor prosperity.

IV. *The Apostolic Vicariate*

§ 1. It is as well to remember that, however effective papal government may have been in the lands *immediate subjecte*, a very large part of the papal lands was virtually subtracted from the rule of Rectors or Legates by being granted as apostolic

---

[1] Ancona, Atti Consigliari, vol. 30, fol. 4, 'Item le talghe del contado non mettendo le castella guaste, in summa duc' 600 l'anno'.

[2] G. Falco, 'I comuni della Campagna e della Marittima nel Medio Evo', *ASR*, xlix (1926), 282–4.

[3] Guiraud, 47–75; 81–3.

[4] See the quotations from the MS. of Ascanio Landi in A. Borgia, *Istoria della Chiesa, e Città di Velletri* (Nocera, 1723), 350–1.

[5] Dominico Antonio Contatore, *De historia Terracinensi* (Rome, 1706), 112–13. This bull, dated 4 June 1423, is also in Reg. Vat. 354, fol. 240. I have been unable to identify this Agapito Colonna, who does not figure in the genealogies of Galletti (Guiraud, *L'Etat Pontifical*, 50), Coppi (*Memorie Colonnesi*) or of Prince Prospero Colonna (*I Colonna dalle origini all'inizio del secolo XIX*, Rome, 1927). He is certainly not the former head of the house of Genazzano, father of Martin V. He may be a bastard son of the same branch.

[6] Reg. Vat. 355, fol. 122. Officials of the Church are instructed to admit subjects of either side to sanctuary within the cities of the Church, 1 December 1424. Cf. *Commissioni*, ii, 303.

[7] Lanciani, 'Il patrimonio della famiglia Colonna', *ASR*, xx (1897), 401; Tomassetti, *La Campagna Romana*, iv, 479–81.

vicariates.[1] From the mid-fourteenth century the Church had by these grants conceded legal status to the independent states of the various *signori*—for the existence of these states was a fact with which she had come to terms—while preserving as much as she could of papal sovereignty and jurisdiction. She had also, on occasion, granted the vicariate to the commune, but under Martin V this occurred only with Città di Castello, and that only in the two years preceding Braccio's seizure of the city in 1422; when Città di Castello returned to the Holy See in 1427 it was ruled by a papal governor.

If the actual effect of the grant of a vicariate had corresponded fully with the text of the grant, the Popes would not have sacrificed overmuch of their sovereignty thereby. It is true that the area granted was removed from direct papal government; the vicar was granted *merum et mixtum imperium et omnimoda iurisdictio temporalis*, was given power to collect and enjoy the revenues due to the Church in the area, and was empowered to appoint and remove officials and *podestà*, who were to have authority to hear and decide the cases brought before them.[2] But against this were set many important reservations. At the time the vicariate is granted, the lands concerned are said to be the immediate property of the Holy See. It is granted for a fixed time, which under Martin V was usually for three years, in conformity with a decree of the Council of Constance.[3] The alienation of rights or lands is forbidden to the vicar, as to all other papal officials. At the end of the term of his vicariate, the vicar is held to return the lands to the Apostolic See or its representatives.[4] All statutes tending against ecclesiastical liberties are to be cancelled by the vicar. An annual *census*, usually of very formidable proportions, has to be paid to the Apostolic Chamber, and, in some grants at least, non-payment of *census* entails loss of the vicariate.[5] There are also important restrictions on the taxes which the vicar might demand, and on the jurisdiction of the vicar's officials in appeal. Other qualifications, such as the obligation to display the arms of the Church, emphasise the continued sovereignty of the Popes.

But the gap between the theory and the practice of the apostolic vicariate was very wide. By these grants the Popes endorsed the title of rulers who were declaredly tyrants—*domini, signori*—and, inevitably, what these rulers did within their own domains could not in fact be called in question by any papal official. In practice, most of the clauses designed to save the sovereignty of the Church were only

---

[1] See P. J. Jones, 'The Vicariate of the Malatesta of Rimini', *EHR*, lxvii (1952). I have also been able to consult the unpublished thesis from which this chapter was taken. See also G. de Vergottini, 'Note per la storia del vicariato apostolico durante il secolo XIV', in *Studi in onore di C. Calisse* (1940), iii; idem, 'Ricerche sulle origini del vicariato apostolico', in *Studi in onore di E. Besta*, (1938), ii.

[2] Jones, in article cited above, and cf. Theiner, iii, nos. 7, 8, 13, 25, 157, 158, 171. My analysis is based mainly on no. 157, p. 224.

[3] Jones, 328 n.

[4] See the oath taken by Braccio, printed by Valentini, 'Lo Stato di Braccio', 227. 'Finita quoque gubernatione praedicta, civitatem, comitatum, territorium districtumque predicta, cum iuribus et pertinentiis ipsorum, restituam et reducam ad ius et proprietatem Domini nostri'.

[5] E.g. in the grant of Rimini to the Malatesta, Theiner, iii, no. 13, p. 28. It was on this account that Martin V declared the lands forfeit in 1428/9. See also Theiner, iii, no. 7, p. 16.

occasionally honoured, and some of them never. Whether the vicariate operated satisfactorily or not depended entirely on the reigning Pope, on his political prestige and his military power. The existence of the apostolic vicariate was not really compatible with good and strong government, and it is the essence of Martin V's policy that he realised to the full that no *signore* could be more than a temporary friend to the Church, and that all were in the end her enemies.

§ 2.   Nevertheless, the financial relations of the Church with the *signori* were not always entirely to the advantage of the latter.   Although the vicar was given the faculty to collect all revenues due to the Church, and in some cases was promised that he would not be taxed in any way not mentioned in the concession of vicariate (unless the extra tax fell on the whole province),[1] he could nevertheless be liable for several taxes.   In some cases the *fumantaria*, or hearth tax peculiar to Romagna, was specifically said to be payable,[2] although the amount of this tax was exiguous. The equivalent of the hearth tax in the March of Ancona was the *census* and *affictus*,[3] which were due from some or most of the cities, and continued to be payable by their apostolic vicars.[4]

An important liability of the apostolic vicars of the March of Ancona was for the *tallia militum*.   There were some exemptions accorded from this rule, notably that of the Malatesta for Fano, Pesaro and Fossombrone, and of the Montefeltro for Urbino and their other lands.[5]   But in general the apostolic vicars paid tallage,

---

[1] Theiner, iii, no. 157, p. 224.   [2] Ibid. and Jones, 'The Vicariate', 344-5.

[3] See p. 117 above.   In Reg. Vat. 352, fols. 205, 207v, Giovanni de Secca of the diocese of Gubbio is conceded the 'census et affictus aut fumantaria' in San Marino, Monte Nuovo, Marino and Cagli, all of which are in the March. (8 July and 22 December 1418.)

[4] Arm. 33, vol. 11, fols. 7-8; Jones, loc. cit.   Osimo, which was held by Pandolfo Malatesta, was assessed for tallage and *affictus*, but not for *census*, in the list in Arm. 33.   Most of the possessions of the Varano of Camerino were assessed for *census* or *affictus*, and this is mentioned where they make a lump payment to the Chamber, e.g. that recorded in IE 379, fol. 11v; Div. Cam. 4, fol. 214.

[5] In the list of 'tallie Marchie Anconitane' in Arm. 33, vol. 11, fols. 6v-7, it is noticeable that the following towns appear out of alphabetical order, under the separate heading of 'T'o' (? 'tercio', which would be strange, as it is the second list) :

Castra et comitatus quondam Fani	florenos MCXXV
Calvum	C
	VIII
Fanum	C
	MII
Forosinfronium	C
	VII
Pensaurum	M
Urbinum	C
	MVI
Tolentinum	C
	VI
Sanctus Genisius	C
	VI

For the exemption of the Malatesta from tallage, see Jones, 346; for that of the Count of Montefeltro, see above, p. 114.   But the presence of Tolentino and San Ginesio in this list is puzzling; I have no other record of their exemption from tallage, which was due from all the other lands of the Varano.   Similarly, some other lands of the Malatesta paid tallage, e.g. Osimo.

either to the Rector of the province, or direct to the Apostolic Chamber.   The *signori* collected the tallage from their own subjects and passed on the money to the Apostolic Chamber,[1] as they did also for the *census* and *affictus*.   No doubt, where the Pope conceded the vicar an exemption from tallage, this did not stop the latter from continuing to exact the tallage from his subjects, and to pocket it as profit.

The most important financial burden of the vicariate was the *census vicariatus* This was never low, although the tendency in the century following Albornoz seems to have been to reduce it.[2]   Nevertheless, it seems to have absorbed up to half the profits of the *signoria* [3]—if it was paid.   It is evident that when the Papacy was weak or divided, as it was during the last part of the Schism, the *signori* would not dream of paying their *census*.   A careful examination of the records seems to show that even a strong Pope could not exact regular payment from his vicars.

Payment of *census* in the early years of Martin V's pontificate is difficult to assess, since the Papal State was disordered by the war with Braccio; some vicars were in alliance with Braccio, and though there are numerous assignments made on the *census* of other vicars, there is no way of telling whether or not these were honoured. After 1424 the Papal State was reduced to order and the *census* of vicars tended to be paid in cash rather than assigned to mercenaries.   The Malatesta of Rimini owed the immense sum of 8,000 florins a year, the largest of all the assessments of *census*. Only 5,000 florins seems to have been paid by them between 1427 and 1429.[4]   The Malatesta of Pesaro paid 8,650 florins between August 1424 and June 1430;[5] they owed 1,000 a year.[6]   The Manfredi paid no *census* between 1420 and 1425, and Florence, to protect her *condottiere* from papal sanctions, was obliged to pay the arrears on Manfredi's behalf.[7]   From this date, the Manfredi paid their *census* of 1,000 florins a year with regularity.[8]   The Montefeltro appear to have been assiduous in paying their annual 1,300 florins.[9]   There is no record of the Polenta of Ravenna

---

[1] As did the Varano for Amandola.   Cf. P. Ferranti, *Memorie storiche della città di Amandola*, pt. i (1891), 177.

[2] E.g. the *census* of Ferrara was reduced from 10,000 florins to 8,000 by Boniface IX, and then to 6,000 by John XXIII (Theiner, iii, no. 7, p. 16; Reg. Vat. 342, fol. 125v, dated 7 December 1410), and finally to 5,000, of which 1,000 were repayable to the Este in the form of a pension, by Martin V (Reg. Vat. 356, fol. 15).   The brothers Migliorati had a *census* of 3,000 ducats imposed on them for Fermo by John XXIII (Reg. Vat. 341, fol. 34), but they paid only 1,000 florins to Martin V (Reg. Vat. 348, fol. 138v, 1 August 1419).   For the reductions accorded the Malatesta, see below.

[3] When the Venetians occupied Faenza in 1503 they estimated that the Manfredi, who had paid 1,000 ducats a year to the Apostolic Chamber, drew a gross income of 7,575 ducats from the city, of which 2,868 were net (M. Brosch, *Geschichte des Kirchenstaates*, i, 8).

[4] IE 385, fol. 111v; IE 389, fol. 7.   The *census* was reduced from ten to eight thousand florins on 1 November 1421 (Reg. Vat. 353, fol. 266v).   Jones, 'The Vicariate', 347–8, errs in putting it at 6,000 florins.

[5] IE 382, 383, 385, 387, 389 *passim*.   500 florins were remitted in 1426, IE 383, fols. 77, 91v.

[6] The *census* for Pesaro, Fossombrone and Castel Gagliardo was reduced from 1,600 florins to 1,000 on 3 April 1426, Reg. Vat. 355, fol. 261v.   Cf. Theiner, iii, no. 163, p. 234.

[7] *Commissioni*, ii, 445, 460–1, 466, 517; C. Monzani, 'Di Leonardo Bruni Aretino', *ASI*, 2nd ser., v, pt. 2 (1857), 30, 32–3.   Florence paid the Pope 4,000 florins on this account on 2 August 1426, Reg. Vat. 355, fol. 289.

[8] IE 385, fols. 97, 112; IE 389, fols. 6v, 59v.   The vicariate was re-granted to them for five years, at a *census* of 1,000 florins a year, on 28 October 1428, Reg. Vat. 351, fol. 74v.

[9] IE 387, fols. 34v, 65v; IE 389, fol. 61.

paying their *census* of 1,000 florins into the Chamber after 1424,[1] but it is not impossible that they paid the money to the Legate of Bologna. The Trinci of Foligno were faithful creditors; after Braccio's death and the end of their own rebellion, they settled a debt of no less than 8,000 florins with the Chamber, and for the rest of the pontificate they paid an annual *census* of 1,000 florins without default.[2] The position of the Varano of Camerino was peculiar in that they were not the *signori* of Camerino, but merely exercised a pre-eminence over the city which was recognised by the Pope. They therefore paid nothing for Camerino, and held in vicariate only a group of minor lands, whose aggregate *census* for the vicariate was 845 florins.[3] They also held Tolentino and San Ginesio as a noble fee, a concession first made by Boniface IX, and repeated by Martin V, first for twelve years,[4] and then perpetually.[5] The *census* for this fee was 300 florins annually, and the total of 1,145 florins which they thus owed was paid faithfully every year.[6] The Este of Ferrara also seem to have paid rather irregularly their *census* of 4,000 florins, but the incomplete state of the records makes it hard to be certain when payments were missed.[7] The Chiavelli, the *signorotti* of Fabriano, paid their *census* of 400 florins to the Rector of the March:[8] they appear to have been fairly assiduous in its payment.[9]

In 1423 the Chamber received 3,300 florins in cash from such vicars, and assigned 7,485 florins; there is no means of knowing how many of these assignments were paid. In 1428, out of a total of about 19,000 florins due annually from apostolic vicars, the Pope received about 8,160; in 1429 about 11,160.[10] If at its strongest the Papacy could collect only a little more than half the debts owed it by its vicars, the system can hardly be said to have functioned well.

---

[1] IE 382, fol. 60. The vicariate is in Reg. Vat. 348, fol. 109v, reproducing and confirming a bull of Boniface IX.

[2] On 30 March 1425, 5,000 florins were paid as part of the debt of 8,000 florins, IE 382, fols. 84, 180 (cf. *Commissioni*, ii, 282). For later payments, IE 383, 385, 387, 389 passim.

[3] See pp. 47–8 above. The lands held by the Varano in vicariate are listed by Guiraud, *L'Etat Pontifical*, 199, but with an error (Belforte del Chiente paid 50 florins and not 10) and an omission (Morrovalle, *Murrum*, which was lumped together with Appignano and Montefortino). See Reg. Vat. 348, fol. 66; Reg. Vat. 349, fols. 22v, 68; Reg. Vat. 351, fol. 52v; Reg. Vat. 355, fol. 102.

[4] Reg. Vat. 348, fol. 60v.

[5] Reg. Vat. 355, fol. 108, 25 October 1424.

[6] For the period October 1424–June 1430, the payments are recorded in IE 382, 385, 387, 389 passim.

[7] From 1421–6 this *census* was collected by the Legate of Bologna (Reg. Vat. 353, fol. 255), and there is consequently no means of checking the payments. In 1426 a payment of 3,000 florins was accepted to cover all arrears up to June 1427, and it was agreed that the Marquis should be liable for a *census* of 5,000 florins, but should be given a pension of 1,000 florins, which thus reduces the effective *census* to 4,000 florins (Theiner, iii, no. 236; Reg. Vat. 356, fol. 15). 4,000 florins were paid in the year 1427/8 (IE 385, fol. 93v; Reg. Vat. 356, fol. 24v), but only 2,000 are recorded for 1428/9 (IE 387, fol. 66). Part of the Introitus for this period is missing. There is no record of payments in 1429/30. For 1435, 1437, see Guiraud, *L'Etat Pontifical*, 226.

[8] Reg. Vat. 354, fol. 93, tells the Treasurer of the March to assign the census of Tomasso [Chiavelli] of Fabriano (so also Reg. Vat. 353, fol. 183). See also Guiraud, 198, who quotes 300 florins as the amount of *census* due in 1434.

[9] For 1429/30, payments are recorded in IE 387, fol. 44v, IE 389, fols. 18v, 19, 59. The arrangement to pay through the Treasurer of the March had evidently by this time lapsed.

[10] Sources as in preceding notes.

§ 3. The obligation to do military service for the Papacy, common in fourteenth-century grants of the vicariate, seems to have tended to drop out in the fifteenth century, as the *signori* all became more and more dependent upon their profession of arms.[1] But the vicar was nevertheless *homo ecclesie*, a quasi-feudal officer,[2] and he could always be called on by the Church for help in time of need. Thus Ludovico Migliorati, without holding a *condotta* of the Pope, gave a great deal of military help to the Rector of the March, and the Marquis of Este was more than once asked for military aid by the Pope.[3] It does not seem as though Guid'Antonio of Montefeltro held a papal *condotta* during the war of 1418/9.

The majority of vicariates conceded by Martin V were for a term of three years. There were, however, some notable exceptions to this rule. The vicariate of the Polenta of Ravenna was given in the same form as by Boniface IX, which was a term of ten years.[4] Carlo Malatesta, brother of Malatesta of Pesaro, was appointed vicar in Senigaglia for his life and that of his sons, in 1430;[5] just as the Malatesta had previously held their vicariates for two generations.[6] The vicariate of the Alidosi, having already been granted for three years in 1418, was at the same time extended *ad beneplacitum*,[7] and so was that of the Ordelaffi.[8] But a concession *ad beneplacitum* was a poor privilege; what the *signori* wanted was an hereditary concession which would turn the vicariate—virtually—into a fee.

It is more than doubtful whether the Popes managed to save their jurisdiction in cases of appeal from the encroachments of the apostolic vicars. For a citizen subject to some such tyrant as Corrado Trinci or Ludovico Migliorati to appeal from the court of his *signore* to that of the Pope or Rector was certainly impractical, and although the papal reservation of cases of appeal was always carefully worded, it is practically certain that it never took effect,[9] save in the case of very minor *signorotti*.

It is probable that the clause obliging the vicar to have his officials take an oath of loyalty to the Pope every six months was equally impossible to enforce.[10]

Beyond the legal framework of the vicariates there was certainly a concept of the apostolic vicar as *homo ecclesie*, as a man who had taken an oath of loyalty to the Apostolic See.[11] From this it became in principle necessary for an apostolic vicar to

[1] Jones, 'The Vicariate', 342–3. The Alidosi and Ordelaffi were not specifically held to do military service (Theiner, iii, nos. 157, 158), but it is noticeable that such lesser *signorotti* as the Orsini were (ibid. no. 171, p. 242). [2] Cf. Jones, 325–6.

[3] E.g. against the rebellious mercenary, Angelo della Pergola, Reg. Vat. 353, fol. 257, 28 August 1421.

[4] Reg. Vat. 348, fol. 109v, 29 January 1419. The bull of Boniface IX is in Fantuzzi, *Monumenti Ravennati de' secoli di mezzo*, iii, no. cxxiv, p. 235.

[5] Reg. Vat. 351, fol. 166, 16 September 1430. [6] Jones, 329–30.

[7] Reg. Vat. 352, fol. 294. [8] Reg. Vat. 348, fol. 96v, 28 November 1418.

[9] Cf. Jones, 336. The reservation in the vicariate of the Migliorati is particularly explicit 'causas in (sic) omnium et singularum appellationum et etiam nullitatum quarumlibet, tam criminalium quam civilium, nobis et successoribus nostris expresse et specialiter retinemus et etiam reservamus' (Reg. Vat. 348, fol. 138v, dated 1 August 1419). [10] Jones, 334–5.

[11] See Finke, *Acta Concilii Constanciensis*, iv, 202, where Pandolfo Malatesta describes himself to the Venetians as 'homo et vicarius ecclesie'. For the oath, see Jones, 341–2. Cf. also *Corp. Chron. Bonon.*, ii, 565, where the *signori* of Rimini, Forlì, Ravenna, Faenza and Imola—all the tyrants of Romagna—send to the commune of Bologna 'pregando la segnoria de Bologna che a loro dovesse piacere de azetare el papa, avixando che igli erano suoi soldati, sì che per questo, se'l papa li comandasse, non poriano fare de meno de ubedire a lui'.

have the consent of the Pope before he entered a *condotta* for another power. Thus in 1423 Martin V gave his consent to the Malatesta entering the service of Florence; until it was given they had declined to move,[1] and a little later the same consent was given to the Carrara of Ascoli,[2] and the Manfredi of Faenza, whose *census* the Florentines paid in order to obtain the Pope's approval.[3] But how real was Martin's power to stop his vicars going to the service of other powers is somewhat doubtful; it is noticeable that in the same conflict he did not try to forbid the Varano to fight for Florence, but merely advised them to remain neutral.[4] Guid'Antonio of Montefeltro was positively ordered by the Pope to remain neutral,[5] and this order was obeyed, although very probably for reasons of personal policy, and not from any sentiment of obedience. Montefeltro was later authorised to become captain-general of the forces of Venice.[6]

§ 4. The relations of Martin V with his vicars were a matter, not of legal bargaining, but of practical politics. And here Martin's ability cannot but be admired. He was one of the few Popes to overcome the paradox that the Papal State contained the best soldiers in Italy, and yet was one of the weakest of Italian powers. And he achieved this by presenting himself to the *signori* of the Papal State, not so much as a lord as an employer. All the *signori* were for sale, and Martin's financial ability enabled him to buy them, and, on many occasions, to use them against one another. From the moment of his gathering the papal *vicarii* outside the walls of Bologna in 1420, this policy knew nothing but success, and its application reduced the number of *signori* in the Papal State by a good half-dozen. A Papacy which continued this policy consistently for twenty years, without falling into the pits of rebellion and bankruptcy, might well have broken all the *signori* before the century was half through, instead of being exposed to chaotic rebellion for almost a further century. But this is a vain conjecture, for Eugenius IV was forbidden to continue Martin's successes, both by the circumstances in which he found himself, and by his own personality.

---

[1] *Commissioni*, i, 471 and 494, 'le constituzioni della Chiesa non lo consentivano, che sanza licenzia del Papa niuno sottoposto alla Chiesa si potessi accomandare'. This licence was granted, and another to Pandolfo Malatesta, of which Martin later said 'tandem a nobis licentiam non obtinuit, sed extorsit' (Valentini, 'Lo Stato di Braccio', doc. 8, p. 355).

[2] *Commissioni*, ii, 103–4, 329.   [3] Ibid. 445.   [4] The brief in *Commissioni*, ii, 366.

[5] Ibid. 345, 'Quia nonnulli vicarii ecclesie, propter casus in quibus inciderunt, aliquas promissiones et obligationes fecerunt que honestatem forsitan in se minime obtinent . . .' and cf. *Commissioni*, i, 492.

[6] Cod. Vat. Ottob. lat. 3014, fol. 60, and Arm. 39, vol. 7a, fol. 108. 'Francesco Foscari duci venetiarum. Grata et accepta est nobis electio quam tu et comunitas tua fecistis de persona dilecti filii nobilis viri Guidantonii comitis Montisferreti . . . in vestrarum gentium armigerarum capitaneum generalem, sicut nobis per tuas litteras nuntiasti . . . Itaque placet nobis et contenti sumus, ut cum voluerit proficiscatur ad administrandum hoc capitaneus officium, sperantes semper quod in omni casu necessitatis nostre, quo prefate comite indigeremus, ut ipsa ad mandata et servitia nostra rediret, etiam tua nobilitas remaneret bene contenta. Datum etc.' (Fink, 'Politische Korrespondenz', no. 428.)

CONCLUSION

I. *The Place of Martin V in the History of the Papal State*

SEEN against the medieval history of the Papal State, Martin V is a far from un-familiar figure. The Pope of the great baronial family, who lends the support of his relatives to the Papacy and sees that they do not lose thereby, is a frequent enough figure in the thirteenth century and long before : no such Pope greater than Boniface VIII. Nor is there anything novel in Martin V's administration of the Papal State, which was a simple continuation of institutions and policies not notably changed since the time of Albornoz.

There is, however, a particular significance in the era in which Martin V appeared on the scene. He is not only important because he rescued the Papal State from the chaos into which it had fallen during the Schism. The Papacy was at the same moment undergoing a severe economic crisis. The abundant revenues gathered from the universal Church by the Avignonese Popes were many times reduced. The pretensions of temporal princes, the revenues abandoned under the reform decrees at Constance, the further revenues lost under the Concordats, and the general debility of papal power engendered by the Schism, all combined to reduce papal income perhaps to one-third of its former amount.[1] Nor was it likely that the level of the 'spiritual' revenues would ever be restored; on the contrary, they were destined to continue to shrink for over a century.[2] It therefore became vital that the revenues of the State of the Church should expand in order to supply the deficit. The struggle to pacify the Papal State and enjoy its revenues peacefully had been one of the main concèrns of the Popes for some centuries, but it now became more than ever urgent. Failure might expose the Popes to the most extreme claims of the conciliar party, and, since reform in one sense depended on the financial stability of the Roman Court, indefinitely postpone the reform of the Church.

It is doubtful if the anticipated and ideal revenues of the Papal State varied a great deal in the century following Albornoz. What was important was the extent to which these revenues could be collected. In 1426/7 the provincial treasuries, excluding those of Rome and Bologna, sent to Rome a net profit of about 43,500

---

[1] Gottlob, *Aus der Camera apostolica*, 238. The report of the commission of cardinals of 1423, in Haller, *Concilium Basiliense*, 168, referring to the number of clerks in the Apostolic Chamber, says 'Dignetur igitur dominus noster honestiori modo quo poterit horum refrenatam multitudinem restingere et reducere ad antiquum numerum, qui sufficiebat, cum camera in triplo plus habundabat'. The income in the *Introitus et Exitus* volumes for March 1421–February 1422 is 110,237 florins (IE 379). That for 1426/7 is 114,385 cameral florins (see below). That for January–December 1436 is only about 59,000 cameral florins (IE 400).

[2] Gottlob, 179 f. C. Bauer, 'Die Epochen der Papstfinanz', *Historische Zeitschrift*, cxxxviii (1928), although many of the most important parts of this article are little more than conjecture.

cameral florins.[1] To this must be added not less than another 30,000 or 40,000 florins from Rome and Bologna, making a total of something like 80,000 florins. This is not so very far off the estimates of optimum temporal revenue made sixty years before, under Urban V, or sixty years after, under Sixtus IV.[2] The total recorded income in the *Introitus et Exitus* volumes for the same year, 1426/7, is 114,385 cameral florins,[3] of which 22,225 florins were paid to the Chamber from the State of the Church. The total income of the Church was therefore about 170,000 florins, of which about 90,000 florins came from the spiritual power, and about 80,000 from the temporal power. These figures must be treated with much caution,[4] but the proportion of 'spiritual' to 'temporal' revenues here revealed shows clearly what a vital matter the government of the State of the Church had become.

II. *The Consequences of Nepotism*

In the early morning of 20 February 1431 Pope Martin V died of an apoplexy.[5] Two months later Antonio Colonna, the Prince of Salerno, determined to give up to Eugenius IV nothing of the lands and goods he had received from his uncle, entered Rome through Porta San Sebastiano and attempted to seize the city.[6] The Romans failed to rise in his favour, and he was thrown back into the Campagna, while the mob showed its loyalty by looting the Colonna palaces. In spite of the repulse, the episode was ominous for the future of the Papal State, and it heralded a pontificate of bloodshed and chaos, of warfare with the baronial families of the Campagna, of the seizure of great tracts of the Papal State by such adventurers as Francesco Sforza, and of the universal decay of papal rule.[7]

Martin V has been accused of leaving Eugenius IV an evil heritage,[8] and it is

---

[1] This figure is based on the volumes of the *Introitus et Exitus*, and also on the accounts of provincial treasurers in the Archivio di Stato.

[2] A marginal entry in the Avignonese registers for 1368 gives an estimate of probable income as 86,000 florins (Schäfer, *Deutsche Ritter und Edelknechte in Italien*, i, 41). Under Sixtus IV, when the usual estimate ('secondo il comune uso') in use in the Curia was between 118,000 and 123,000 ducats, a new estimate based on the actual account books gave a figure nearer 96,000 ducats (*ASR*, l, 1927, 350, 392, and cf. Gottlob, *Aus der Camera apostolica*, 253–5). It should, however, be noticed that the composition of the temporal income at the two periods was quite different, e.g. in 1426/7 the Pope enjoyed the whole revenue of Bologna, whereas Sixtus IV drew from the city only the 4,000 ducats of the *dazio del vino*.

[3] I must here retract the figure which I gave in *JEccH*, iv (1953), 68. The error is due to my having counted in with the income the various deficits of the Chamber with the Depositary, which were always included in the monthly totals of income and expenditure (see p. 137 above).

[4] Cf. *JEccH*, iv (1953), 68.

[5] Pastor, *Geschichte der Päpste* (3/4 edn., 1901), i, 278. Misprinted 29 February in the English edition, i, 281.

[6] Pastor, *Geschichte*, 283; L. Fumi, 'I Colonna contro Roma nel 1431', *BSU*, i (1895); A. Coppi, 'Documenti storici del medio evo relativi a Roma ed all'Agro Romano', *Dissertazioni della Pontificia Accademia Romana di Archeologia*, 1st ser., xv (1864), 324–5. For Eugenius IV's attempt to recover the treasure of Martin V from Oddo Poccia, see above, p. 137, and *JEccH*, iv, 67.

[7] Cf. Poggio Bracciolini, *Historiae de varietate fortunae* (Paris, 1723), 85, 'Nam quis unquam putasset aureum illud saeculum, quod nobis Martini restituit prudentia, in extremam versum iri perniciem et calamitatem.'

[8] Pastor, *Geschichte*, i, 295. Cf. Von Reumont, *Geschichte der Stadt Rom*, iii, pt. 1 (1868), 65–8; Guiraud, *L'Etat Pontifical*, 50–9.

true that his successor had to pay the price for Martin's nepotism and for the intensely personal character of his rule. Oddo Colonna had behaved, on being elected Pope, as though he had acquired the *signoria* of a great city. In the manner of any Italian tyrant, he had placed all his family in office, and had woven a thick web of family alliances. For a few years, the fortunes of the Colonna became identical with those of the Church. The Pope spent large sums in buying lands for his family, and in placing them in control of the main strategic points of the Campagna and the Roman District; of the long list of lands attributed to the Colonna of Genazzano in the division made by Martin V in 1427, the great majority were acquired during his pontificate. Most of the lands which the family had held before 1417 were made into an inalienable patrimony, held in common, while the rest were shared among the three sons of Lorenzo Colonna.[1] Nor were the Colonna of Riofreddo and Palestrina forgotten; Antonio Colonna, who had rendered good service as a papal mercenary, was rewarded with a respectable patrimony in the Tiber valley,[2] while Ludovico Colonna acquired Bassanello and Stroncone.[3]

The money known to have been spent in purchasing these lands for the Colonna is not less than 135,000 florins; to this must be added payments not recorded, and the lands ceded by the Holy See from those *immediate subjecte*. This is a modest sum when compared with the half-million expended by Boniface VIII for the Caetani,[4] but it is nevertheless not inconsiderable.

The very lavishness of these gifts made it inevitable that Eugenius IV should want to recover them, and that the Colonna should be the rebellious opposition of the next pontificate. But perhaps the deprivation of the services of the Colonna was an even more serious matter for the Church than the addition of their enmity. Nepotism had been as much the means of Martin's policies as it had been their end, and the Colonna had been far from useless in furthering the interests of the Church— or, at least, those of the Papal State. The more Martin was successful in binding the Colonna family into the *signoria* of the Church, the more dangerous was the vacuum in papal policy occasioned by his death. The marriages of the Colonna with the Montefeltro, Trinci, Monaldeschi, Annibaldeschi, Malatesta, which had at first been so many ties of loyalty to the Church for the families concerned, became

---

[1] See endnote at foot of this section.

[2] See G. Presutti, 'I Colonna di Riofreddo', *ASR*, xxxv (1912), 111–22. Particularly important was Calvi in Umbria (*Carbium, Narniensis diocesis*), which was in 1420/1 under the direct rule of the Church (Reg. Vat. 349, fol. 39; ibid. fol. 145v), and then on 14 September 1421 was granted in vicariate to Antonio Colonna of Riofreddo, first for a term of three years (Reg. Vat. 349, fol. 180). It was then granted him for life (Reg. Vat. 351, fol. 13), and finally to Antonio and his sons, Giovanandrea and Giacomo, in common, for the term of their lives (ibid. fol. 90, 1 February 1429; cf. Contelori, *Vita Martini V*, 55, with rather different dates). Soriano was acquired for the Holy See by Martin V in 1420 from the Breton Jean Grammont, for the price of 9,000 florins, and then in 1424 was conceded in fee to Antonio Colonna (Silvestrelli, 693; *Liber Censuum*, ed. Duchesne, ii, 82). Cf. P. Egidi, 'Soriano nel Cimini e l'archivio suo', *ASR*, xxvi (1903), 390, 403–4.

[3] Coppi, *Memorie Colonnesi*, 173; Contelori, *Vita Martini*, 55; Reg. Vat. 349, fol. 287v; Div. Cam. 8, fol. 26v.

[4] F. Baethgen, in *QF*, xx (1928/9), 193. The total spent by Martin V on behalf of his nephews is calculated by Lanciani, 'Il patrimonio', 372, but to his total should be added the price paid for Marino, Soriano and a third of Monterano.

on Martin's death a matter of indifference for the Church, if not a positive danger. Martin's *signoria* in the State of the Church had been as personal as that of any Renaissance tyrant, and his death was therefore a matter of immense moment.

Eugenius IV lacked all the most important personal qualities of his predecessor. Martin V was parsimonious in the extreme; in no other way could he have paid his mercenaries.[1] He was warlike, under an affable exterior,[2] tenacious, cunning, and possessed of a profound knowledge of all the arts and deceits of the Italian *signori*. Such may not have been the qualities of a head of the universal Church, but they were, almost to perfection, the qualities required of the head of an Italian state. Filippo Maria Visconti found Martin V a sympathetic spirit, and a political understanding of much importance resulted. Francesco Condulmer had already, in his legation in Bologna, much offended the Visconti, and after his election to the Papacy he showed himself to be no more subtle or conciliatory than before. His precipitant personality is in strong contrast with the long-drawn, hot-and-cold diplomatic subtleties of Oddo Colonna, which gave years of unhappiness and uncertainty to the Florentine diplomats, and which enmeshed even the wily Visconti.[3]

The disorders of the State of the Church under Eugenius IV are nevertheless so marked that they suggest that Martin V's work there was impermanent, and that perhaps the hand that gave favours to the Colonna more than undid the good which his other hand wrought.[4] This would almost certainly be too harsh a verdict. Martin made chaos into order, and this already outbalances the faults of his family. His determined re-imposition of the old system of temporal government, and his emphasis on all its most centralising aspects, had permanent effects which, if obscured under Eugenius IV, may be plainly observed in the Papal State of the latter half of the century. Few of the families of *signori* which he laid low ever raised their heads to trouble the Church again. Martin V is a less heroic figure than Albornoz; he falls far short in imagination and grandeur of mind. But the policies bequeathed by the great Cardinal never had a more forceful and faithful executant.

---

[1] Cf. *Liber Pontificalis*, ed. Duchesne, ii, 545, 'vero avarissimus fuit : miser in palatio apud Sanctos Apostolos vixit'; ibid., 555, 'Parcus fuit, et qui a supervacuis expensis abhorreret'; and, above all, the happy remark of another Colonna, 'Papa Martino al denaro non ce remedio' (Michaeli, *Memorie storiche della città di Rieti*, iii, 327–8). Cf. also Albizzi's ironical 'sai la natura sua dello spendere volentieri', *Commissioni*, ii, 249.

[2] Cf. Leonardi Bruni, *Rerum suo tempore gestarum commentarius* (Muratori, *RRIISS*, xix, pt. 3, 444), who says that before his election 'vir antea nequaquam sagax existimatus, sed benignus. In Pontificatu tamen ita opinionem de se prius habitus redarguit, ut sagacitas in eo summa, benignitas vero non superflua neque nimia reperiretur.'

[3] Cf. *Liber Pontificalis*, ii, 515, 'Secreti sui abstinentissimus fuit, ita ut perpauci quid facturus esset vix unquam intelligere possent'; *Commissioni*, ii, 162, 'Quello che s'abbia in animo, non può sapere se non solo Iddio', and ibid. ii, 441, 'E anche vi debbe ricordare, che'l signore Malatesta ci disse a Galicano, la natura del Suocero [i.e. the Pope] era, aveva una dolce raccoglienza e una buona dimostrazione di fare; poi si raffredava nella cosa.' This tortuous disposition procured him an undeserved reputation for timidity : ibid. ii, 172, 'noi conosciamo le condizione del santo Padre essere buona, ma non corrente [i.e. not disposed to act]; o forse si potrebbe chiamare troppo timida, se l'onestà il patisse'.

[4] Cf. Guiraud, *L'Etat Pontifical*, who continually emphasises the disorders of the Papal State at this period, perhaps because he consulted the Registers of Eugenius IV, but hardly looked at those of Martin V. It is this which somewhat unbalances his book, which is in many ways admirable.

The Lands of the Colonna of Genazzano

For Martin V's division of the lands of the Colonna of Genazzano, see Guiraud, *L'Etat Pontifical*, 50–5 (the division was in 1427, however, and not in 1428, as said there). The inalienable group of lands common to the whole family was certainly a strategic centre in Campagna (Guiraud, 52), but they were also the oldest of the lands owned by the family. Of this group, only Palliano and Serrone had been acquired during the pontificate of Martin V (Contelori, *Vita Martini V*, 55; Reg. Vat. 356, fols. 8, 11v, 9 September 1425). Palliano and Serrone had belonged immediately to the Holy See, and in 1425 were given to Prospero, Odoardo and Antonio Colonna as a noble fee. Of the other lands made common to the whole family, Genazzano had been with the Colonna since 1292 (Silvestrelli, *Città Castelli e Terre della Regione Romana* [1940], 309); Olevano since 1232 (ibid. 343); Capranica and San Vito since 1252 (ibid. 307, 310); Pisciano—now Pisoniano—since the thirteenth century (ibid. 346); Ceciliano—not Cirigliano, as in Guiraud, 51—since 1373 (Silvestrelli, 369). A third of Cave and Rocca di Papa had belonged to them since 1400, and the last third of these places was bought by them from Mascia Annibaldi in 1425 (Silvestrelli, 305).

Almost all the other lands mentioned in the division of 1427, besides many others, were acquired by the Colonna under Martin V. The following were held in common by Antonio, Prospero and Odoardo Colonna, but are not mentioned in the division : two-thirds of the *castrum* of Scorano in the Tiber valley, both bought from the Conti in 1427, one-third for 1,400 florins (Lanciani, 'Il patrimonio della famiglia Colonna al tempo di Martino V', *ASR*, xx [1897], 422–3; Contelori, *Genealogia familiae Comitum Romanorum* [1650], 22–3; Silvestrelli, 534). Nepi and some associated *castra* were bought in 1427 from Rainaldo Orsini for 30,000 florins (Lanciani, 'Il Patrimonio', 419–21; Silvestrelli, 558; cf. de Cupis in *BDA*, 3rd ser., i [1910], 97). The brothers also bought a two-thirds share in Fusignano (now Focignano, near Ardea) from Giovanni degli Annibaldi in 1427 (Lanciani, 416–7; Silvestrelli, 119). Malafitto, a *castrum* adjoining Genzano, Nemi and Rocca di Papa was bought from Niccolò Savelli in 1428 for 5,600 florins (Lanciani, 424–5; Tomassetti, *La Campagna Romana*, ii, 165; Silvestrelli, 175). Genzano and Nemi were first acquired by Giordano Colonna in fee from the monastery of S. Anastasio alle Tre Fontane in 1423, and then were bought for Antonio, Prospero and Odoardo Colonna for 15,000 florins in 1428, being (at the same time?) conceded to them as a vicariate for the term of three years, and then *ad beneplacitum* (Lanciani, 405–7, 438–44; Silvestrelli, 177, 182; the grant of vicariate is in Cod. Vat. Rossian. 684, fol. 7v, undated, a fifteenth-century copy in a codex from Domenico Capranica's library). All these lands adjoin the ancient possessions of the branch of Genazzano, together making an even more formidable block.

Most of the lands attributed to Antonio Colonna, Prince of Salerno, in the division of 1427, were acquired under Martin V. Morolo was bought for 8,000 florins from Lucrezia Colonna in 1423 (Lanciani, 399–400; Silvestrelli, 154), and the half share in Morolo which was held by the Monastery of S. Maria Nuova was sold back to the Colonna by the monastery on 17 October 1423 (Reg. Vat. 354, fol. 285, wrongly dated 12 October 1422 by Silvestrelli). San Stefano was bought from the Conti in 1423 (Silvestrelli, 53; cf. Reg. Vat. 349, fol. 278). Half the *castrum* of Supino was bought in 1421 from the sons of Francesco Count of Anguillara (Silvestrelli, 149; de Cupis, *BDA*, 1910, 69). Strangolagalli was given by Martin V as Pope in 1421 (Silvestrelli, 56). Guarcino and Collepardo were acquired under Martin V (ibid. 67, 70). Ripi and Castro in Lazio had been acquired in 1410 (ibid. 48). Mugnano, near Orte, was confiscated by the Pope from the rebel Ulisse Orsini in 1424 and given to Antonio Colonna (Silvestrelli, 681). So also was Chia ('Chegia'). The important ports of Nettuno and Astura were exchanged by the Orsini in 1426 for lands in the Kingdom of Naples (Lanciani, 411; cf. *Giornal. Napolitan.*, *RRIISS*, xxi, 1092; Tomassetti, *La Campagna Romana*, ii, 321).

Similarly, the lands attributed to Prospero Colonna in the division of 1427 were for the most part acquired during his uncle's pontificate. Thus the important fortress of Ardea, commanding the roads from Rome to the ports of Nettuno and Anzio, was restored to the monastery of S. Paolo fuori le Mura in 1421. Reg. Vat. 349, fol. 58v, Pietro Palozzi de Fuscis is to receive the place and govern it for the Church. In the same year the monastery agreed to grant Ardea to Giordano Colonna for three years (Div. Cam. 14, fol. 47v; Tomassetti, *La Campagna Romana*, ii, 452), and also in 1421 the monastery agreed to accept other lands in exchange for Ardea, which thus became entirely a possession of the Colonna (Tomassetti, loc. cit. and cf. Silvestrelli, 617). Marino seems to have been transferred to the Colonna as early as 1419 (cf. Contelori, *Vita Martini*, 54); certainly 12,000 florins were paid for it to Cristoforo Caetani in March 1423 (C. Caetani, *Regesta Chartarum*, iv, 32, and cf. Silvestrelli, 207). Rocca di Papa was bought from the Annibaldi in 1425 for 10,000 ducats (Lanciani, 414–5, but 1425 should be read for 1426; Tomassetti, *La Campagna Romana*, iv, 481; Silvestrelli, 203, has the mistaken date). Monte Compatri passed to the Colonna in 1423 as the result of a complicated series of transactions, in which the Colonna were assisted by the Apostolic Chamber (Silvestrelli, 188; Lanciani, 400–05), as did also Molara (ibid.). Frascati was bought by Giordano Colonna from the Lateran Chapter for 10,000 florins in 1422, with the approval of the Pope and of a commission of Cardinals (Lanciani, 386; Tomassetti, 404–05; Silvestrelli, 195). The value of Frascati was then said to be 70 florins a year (ibid.), but it is interesting that Paola Colonna was assigned an annual pension of 550 florins on Frascati in 1437 (Tomassetti, iv, 406; cf. Contelori, 55).

Odoardo Colonna held from Martin V the counties of Alba and Celano, which, although in the Kingdom, were strongly under the influence of the Papacy. He was also assigned by the division of 1427 Fragiano, Civitella (cf. Tomassetti, iii, 321 and *ASR*, vii, 356; de Cupis in *BDA* [1910], 72), Monte della Guardia (bought in 1427, Lanciani, 415), and Monterano, part of which was bought in 1413 (Silvestrelli, 589), and part in 1424, for 2,000 ducats (de Cupis, *BDA* [1910], 93).

THE SOURCES

1. The Apostolic Chamber

IN the Apostolic Chamber were engrossed and registered both correspondence written in the name of the Pope and the strictly cameral correspondence written in the name of the Chamberlain or Vice-Chamberlain.[1] Besides such letters, many other documents were either registered or conserved in the Apostolic Chamber, the whole forming the archive of the Chamber, both in its function of central financial bureau of the Church and of central governmental organ of the Papal State.[2]

Many classes of documents which are today dispersed in various sections of the Vatican Archives and the Roman Archivio di Stato, belonged in the fifteenth century to the Apostolic Chamber, and were preserved in a common deposit.[3] It is convenient to treat the archive of the Apostolic Chamber as it was listed in an inventory of 1440,[4] not only because this treatment corresponds to the original provenance of the documents, but because it also serves, better than do the modern archival classifications, to illustrate the workings of the Chamber. Some documents must be added which do not appear on the list of 1440.

(a) *Papal Letters Registered in the Apostolic Chamber*

These volumes contain the main political correspondence, except that issued in the form of briefs. The letters were initiated either by the secretaries or by the cameral clerks, and were engrossed by the notaries of the Chamber.[5] They were divided into the volumes dealing with the appointments of officials (*libri officiorum*) and those dealing with all other matters (*libri de curia*). Thus the list of 1440 gives 'Registra bullarum de curia sex' (Reg. Vat. 352–6) and 'R. bullarum officiorum

---

[1] See E. von Ottenthal, 'Die Bullenregister Martin V. und Eugen IV.', *MIöG*, Ergbd. i (1885), 484–95; idem, 'Römische Berichte IV : Bemerkungen über päpstliche Kameralregister des 15. Jahrhunderts', *MIöG*, vi (1885); E. Göller, 'Mitteilungen und Untersuchungen über das päpstliche Regester- und Kanzleiwesen im 14. Jahrhundert', *QF*, vi (1904), 298–309; idem, *Repertorium Germanicum*, i (1916), 29*–31*; G. Tellenbach, ibid. ii (1933), 69*–77*. Cf. F. Bock, 'Einführung in das Registerwesen des Avignonesischen Papsttums', *QF*, xxxi (1941), 62–76.

[2] Cf. E. Göller, 'Untersuchungen über das Inventar des Finanzarchivs der Renaissancepäpste (1447–1521)', in *Miscellanea Francesco Ehrle*, iv (1924).

[3] Cf. M. Giusti, 'I registri vaticani e le loro provenienze originale', in *Miscellanea Archivistica Angelo Mercati* (1952), 383 f.; L. M. Baath, 'L'Inventaire de la Chambre Apostolique de 1440', ibid. 136 f. Ottenthal, 'Die Bullenregister', 407–8, solves the same problem in a slightly different manner, rejecting the later classification of the material, and proposing to deal with it according to the papal office in which it was registered, e.g. 'in camera', 'in cancellaria', 'per secretarios'.

[4] Printed, with a commentary, by Baath, 'L'Inventaire'.

[5] Ottenthal, 'Die Bullenregister', 484 f. Reg. Vat. 356 is marked 'regestrum secretum', but in a far later hand, and there was probably no separate class of secret registers (cf. Ottenthal, 417, 440).

quatuor' (Reg. Vat. 348–51). Of the six registers *de curia*, 'liber II de curia' has been lost.[1]

> Reg. Vat. 352.
> See Ottenthal, 'Die Bullenregister', 415, 487–95, 564–7; Giusti, 'I registri vaticani', 419–20.
>
> Reg. Vat. 353.
> Ottenthal, 416, 487–95, 564–7; Giusti, loc. cit.
>
> Reg. Vat. 354.
> Ibid.
>
> Reg. Vat. 355.
> Ibid.
>
> Reg. Vat. 356.
> Fols. 1–26 of this volume are part (or perhaps the whole) of a 'liber de curia', although they were later called a 'regestrum secretum'. The remainder of the volume is a secretary's register, that of Poggio. See Ottenthal, 417–19, 440, 481, 564–7; Giusti, 419–20; K. A. Fink, 'Poggio-Autographen Kurialen Herkunft', in *Miscellanea Archivistica Angelo Mercati*.
>
> Reg. Vat. 348.
> Ottenthal, 414, 564–7; Giusti, loc. cit.
>
> Reg. Vat. 349.
> Ottenthal, 414–15, 564–7; Giusti, loc. cit.
>
> Reg. Vat. 350.
> Ibid.
>
> Reg. Vat. 351.
> Ibid.

I have also used the registers of John XXIII, Reg. Vat. 340–345.

(b) *Letters emanating from the Chamberlain or Vice-Chamberlain*

This is the day-to-day correspondence of the Apostolic Chamber, originated in the Chamber and engrossed and registered by cameral notaries.[2] The volumes in which it was registered were originally called the 'libri diversarum', and the collection has since become known in the Vatican Archives as the 'Diversa Cameralia'.[3]

---

[1] Ottenthal, 'Die Bullenregister', 440. This missing volume still existed in the Curia under Innocent VIII, when an analysis of the vicariates granted by former Popes included several noted from the 'liber II bullarum domini Martini pape V' (Arm. 35, vol. 5, fol. 378; see, for this collection, Guiraud, *L'Etat Pontifical*, 45–6). Ottenthal also suggests (441–2) that a further volume of the registers *de curia* may be missing, for the years XII–XIV of the pontificate. But in spite of the paucity of bulls registered in these years in the existing registers, this is not necessarily so. An immense number of bulls were never registered at all, and the number which were registered in any year seems to have been quite arbitrary.

[2] Von Ottenthal, in *MIöG*, vi (1885); Bååth, 'L'Inventaire de la Chambre Apostolique', 143; Göller, *Repertorium Germanicum*, 33*–35*; U. Berlière, *Inventaire analytique des Diversa Cameralia au point de vue des anciens diocèses de Cambrai, Liège, Thérouanne et Tournai* (1906).

[3] They are preserved in Arm. 29, see Fink, *Das Vatikanische Archiv* (1951), 51–2. I continue to refer to them here as the 'Div. Cam.'

The list of 1440 records 'R. diversarum octo'. Eight volumes still remain, and the 'liber II diversarum', containing letters of January 1421–January 1422, had evidently already been lost by 1440.[1]

Div. Cam. 4. Ann. I–II.
Title, fol. 3. 'Regestrum sive liber diversarum primus inceptus anno primo domini Martini divina providencia pape quinti, in apostolica camera registrata.'

Div. Cam. 5. Ann. II–III.
Title, fol. 3. 'In nomine domini amen. Regestrum diversarum litterarum inceptarum Mantue de mense Januarii MCCCCXVIIII, pontificatus sanctissimi domini nostri domini Martini pape V anno secundo.'

Div. Cam. 6. Ann. III–IV.
Title, fol. 8. 'Regestrum litterarum diversarum tercium inceptum Florencie anno domini millesimoquadringentismo vicesimo, die XXIII mensis Januarii pontificatus sanctissimi domini nostri domini Martini, divina providencia pape quinti, anno tercio.'

Div. Cam. 7. Ann. V–VI.
Has no title.

Div. Cam. 8. Ann. VI–VIII.
Title, fol. 3. 'Regestrum sextum litterarum diversarum Rome inceptum de anno domini millesimo quadringentismo vigesimoquarto, indictione secunda, pontificatus domini nostri Martini, divina providencia pape quinti anno sexto.'

Div. Cam. 9. Ann. VIII–IX.
Has no title.

Div. Cam. 11. Ann. IX–XIII.
No title, but the original cover is bound in with the volume, and bears in a fifteenth century hand the title 'Diversarum octavus'.

Div. Cam. 13. Ann. XIII–XIV.
Has no title.

(c) *The 'Manualia' of Cameral Notaries*

Either the 'quaterni clericorum antiqui—duo' or among the 'sex manualia notariorum camere apostolice' of the list of 1440.[2]

Div. Cam. 3.
Described by Kühne, *Repertorium Germanicum*, iii, 10.*
See also Ottenthal, *MIöG*, vi (1885), 623.

Arm. 34, vol. 4.
Kühne, loc. cit., and A. Mercati, 'Una fonte poco nota per la storia di Gregorio XII', *ASR*, l (1937).

---

[1] It is clear from Professor Sella's chronological index to the *Diversa Cameralia* (MS. in the Vatican Archives), that this is the volume lost. Div. Cam. 6 ends in December 1420; Div. Cam. 7 begins in February 1422.

[2] Bååth, 154, 156. For these *manualia*, see above, p. 135.

(d) '*Regestra Juramentorum Officialium*'

The list of 1440 records two of these volumes,[1] and both seem to have survived.

> Cod. Vat. lat. 8502.
> Described by Von Mitteis, 'Zwei Amtsbücher aus der Kammer Martins V', *MIöG*, Ergbd. vi (1901), 423–39.
> Rome, Archivio di Stato, Archivio Camerale, pt. i, no. 1711.
> Von Mitteis, loc. cit.

(e) '*Regestra Capitulorum Gentium Armigerarum*'

These registers of the *firme* of mercenaries often contain other material which can be lumped under the heading of 'capitula', sometimes financial, such as agreements concerning the *salaria*, and sometimes political, such as John XXIII's agreements with Ladislas. Examples of these volumes from previous pontificates are the *capitula* of Gregory XII (Reg. Vat. 335, fols. 134–205), and those of John XXIII (Cod. Vat. Barb. lat. 2668, 'Liber pactorum et capitulorum inceptus secundo anno domini Johannis XXIII'). The two volumes of *capitula* of Martin V in the list of 1440 still exist.

> Div. Cam. 14. Ann. II–XIII.
> The first part of this volume has no heading, but on fol. 93 there is a title which may refer to the remainder of the volume (fols. 93–114), the folios of this part being gathered separately. 'Registrum capitulorum gentium armigerarum, tam equitum quam peditum, ad stipendia sanctissimi in christo patris et domini nostri domini Martini, divina providencia pape quinti, ac Romane ecclesie et camere apostolice conductarum, inceptum ut sequitur.'
>
> Div. Cam. 15. Ann. VII–XII.
> Title, fol. 11. 'Registrum capitulorum atque pactorum gentium armigerarum, tam equitum quam peditum quam etiam marinariarum (sic) ad stipendium sanctissimi in christo patris et domini nostri domini Martini, divina providencia pape quinti, et Romane ecclesie et camere apostolice conductarum, inceptum sub infrascriptis datalibus et diebus.' Fols. 1–126 refer to the pontificate of Martin V, the rest to that of Eugenius IV.

(f) '*Introitus et Exitus*' *Volumes*

Ten of these volumes existed in 1440 ('R. thesaurarie decem') but it is impossible to tell to what extent they correspond to the present series, which includes several volumes additional to the *Introitus et Exitus* strictly so called. If IE 380, which is an eighteenth-century copy, be excluded, and IE 379 counted as two volumes (since it has the *Introitus* of 1418–1419 bound with the *Introitus et Exitus* of 1421–1423), then the volumes now running from IE 379 to IE 390 still form a series of ten for the pontificate of Martin V,[2] and it may well be that the composition of the series is still the same as in 1440. If this is so, many volumes were even at that date lost. There

---

[1] Bååth, 154. He omits to mention Cod. Vat. lat. 8502.

[2] Cf. Gottlob, *Aus der Camera apostolica*, 31–2. Bååth, 154, makes no attempt to account for the vicissitudes of this series.

were originally three copies of each volume of the *Introitus et Exitus*,[1] and in some cases two or three such copies have survived from a particular year.

I list below only the volumes which strictly belong to the *Introitus et Exitus* of the Apostolic Chamber. IE 381 is an eighteenth-century transcript from IE 382, IE 380 and IE 386 come from the *camera urbis* (see below), and IE 388 is the account of the expenses of the war of Bologna (see immediately below).

> Introitus, May 1418–June 1421.
> IE 379, fols. 1–21v.
>
> Int. et Exit., March 1421–May 1423.
> IE 379, fols. 30–254.
>
> Int. et Exit., June 1423–April 1425.
> IE 382.
>
> Int. et Exit., May 1425–April 1426.
> IE 383.
>
> Int. et Exit., September 1426–June 1428.
> (i) IE 385.
> (ii) IE 384 is the Depositary's copy.
>
> Int. et Exit., July 1428–July 1429.
> (i) IE 387.
> (ii) Arch. Cam. pt. i, Mandati Camerali, vol. 1752 is the Vice-Chamberlain's copy.
> (iii) Arch. Cam. pt. i, Mand. Cam., vol. 1753 is the Depositary's copy.
>
> Int. et Exit., July 1429–June 1430.
> IE 389.
>
> Int. et Exit., October 1431–June 1433 (under Eugenius IV).
> (i) IE 390.
> (ii) IE 391 is the Depositary's copy.
> (iii) IE 393 is the Vice-Chamberlain's copy.

(g) *Records of Payments Made to Mercenaries*

These are volumes kept by the Treasurer or the officials of the Chamber; they appear to have been made up only for particular campaigns, and do not form a regular or uniform system of account books. Two are known for Martin V's pontificate. IE 401, 'liber exitus camere apostolice pro capitaneis et militibus S.R.E.' is a similar volume for 1437/8.

> Florence, Biblioteca Nazionale, xix, 82.
> See Fink, *Martin V. und Aragon*, 73. Title, on cover, 'Liber capitaneorum et aliorum negotiorum camere apostolice'. Fol. 5v, '† MCCCCXX. Hec liber pro capitaneis et aliis feci scribi ego Antonius episcopus Senen', thesaurarius domini pape . . .' (in the autograph of Antonio Casini, the Apostolic Treasurer). The payments noted in the book run from 1420–1423. It was written by the notaries of the Treasurer; fol. 10, 'Et ego Laurentius Domenici de Rotella apostolicus imperiali auctoritate notarius, et nunc notarius et scriba cum prefato domino thesaurario . . .' The volume contains 129 folios.

[1] See p. 137 above.

IE 388.

Title, fol. 6, 'MCCCCXXVIIII°. Al nome del omnipotente dio et de la sua gloriosa madonna sanctissima Maria et de li beati apostoli misser S. Piero et de misser S. Paulo, et de tucta la corte celestiale. Qui in questo libro rosso scrivero tucti li saldi in somma de zaschuna homo d'arme e fante apè, levato dal libro del conto di soldati. Et similmente tucte le intrate pervenute in le mane del nostro reverendissimo monsignore lo Governadore, levate dal dicto libro del conto. Comenzate a di primo de luglio 1429, per la guerra di bologna.' The payments and receipts run from July to October of 1429. The book keeping is double entry, the only example among the papal accounts of this pontificate, and the earliest known among papal documents. The volume contains 119 folios.

(h) *Mandates of the Vice-Chamberlain Addressed to the Apostolic Treasurer*

These are orders made in the name of the Vice-Chamberlain for payments to be made by the Treasurer.[1]

Archivio di Stato, Arch. Cam. pt. i, vol. 824.
This volume contains mandates from May 1418 to May 1421. It has no heading or title. Since Miltenberger used it in 1894 (*MIöG*, xv), fols. 69–97 have been removed. Fols. 190–195 contain cameral letters of February–May 1417.

(j) *Mandates of the Vice-Chamberlain Addressed to the Officials of the City of Rome*

These are orders of a similar kind, for payments to be made by the Treasurer of Rome, by the Chamberlain of the Ripa and Ripetta, by the commissioners of the manufacture of salt, by the Chamberlain of Rome, by the Depositary of Rome, and so on.[2] The distinction between this and the preceding volume is made clear by a letter of the Vice-Chamberlain addressed to the Apostolic Treasurer, telling him to pay 300 florins from the monies of the Chamber to Gaspar de Vignola, the patron of a galley. The entry is cancelled, and there is written in the margin, 'Debet registrari in libro bullectarum camere apostolice. Registratum est in libro bullectarum fo. 149. Io[hannes] cass' hic.' (Arch. Cam. pt. i, vol. 825, fol. 51.) There are, however, mandates in these volumes addressed to the Apostolic Treasurer, telling him to pay various sums *from the monies of the camera urbis* (e.g. vol. 825, fol. 14). The mandates are signed by cameral clerks and notaries, e.g. C. de Lambardis, Johannes de Gallesio, L. Robring, A. de Sarzana, A. de Pisis, L. de Rotella, A. de Pistorio, Ph. de Piscia. The correcting is sometimes by the same hand, sometimes by B. Dellante or B. de Guidalottis.

Archivio di Stato, Arch. Cam. pt. i, vol. 825.
No title. In the original binding, with leather clasps. Contains mandates from June 1426 to September 1430.

Archivio di Stato, Arch. Cam. pt. i, vol. 826.
No title, and bound as the preceding volume; fols. 1–11 contain mandates from October 1430 to January 1431, and the rest of the volume refers to the pontificate of Eugenius IV.

---

[1] See pp. 136–7 above. Cf. Gottlob, 32; Arnold, *Repertorium Germanicum* (1897), xlvi; A. Lodolini, *L'Archivio di Stato in Roma e l'Archivio del Regno d'Italia* (1932), 44 f.

[2] See p. 166 above. A specimen is below, doc. 8.

2. The Secretaries

It is possibly anomalous to talk of a register of briefs under Martin V.[1] The secretaries were personal attendants of the Pope, who wrote letters at his personal behest and dictation,[2] and who seem not to have registered the briefs in any formal way, but merely to have preserved copies of the briefs (and then, perhaps, only some of them) which they themselves had composed.[3]

The sources for the briefs of Martin V have been fully described by Fink, and I merely list the volumes I have used.

> Arm. 39, vol. 6.
> Arm. 39, vol. 7a.
> Cod. Vat. Chisianus lat. D.VII. 101.
> Cod. Vat. Ottob. lat. 3014.
> Rome, Biblioteca Angelica, cod. 1426.
> Reg. Vat. 356, fols. 36–67.

3. Registers of Provincial Treasurers

(a) *The Patrimony of St. Peter in Tuscia*

These registers have been described by Anzilotti, 'Cenni sulle finanze del Patrimonio', *ASR*, xlii (1919).[4] He lists them on p. 385.

> Archivio Camerale, pt. i, Tesorerie Provinciali, Patrimonio.
> Busta 1.
> Vol. 1 (1420).
> Vol. 1b (1420–1).
> Vol. 2 (1424–5).
> Vol. 3 (1429–30).

---

[1] See, in general, Kaltenbrunner, 'Die Fragmente der ältesten Registra brevium im Vatikanische Archive', *MIöG*, vi (1885); K. A. Fink, 'Die ältesten Breven und Brevenregister', *QF*, xxv (1933/4); idem, 'Die politische Korrespondenz Martins V. nach den Brevenregistern', *QF*, xxvi (1935/6); G. Lang, *Studien zu den Brevenregistern und Brevenkonzepten des XV. Jahrhunderts aus dem Vatikanischen Archiv* (1938).

[2] Cf. *Commissioni*, ii, 227, 'E subito fece (scil. il Papa) chiamare, in mia presenzia, messer Bartolomeo da Montepulciano suo segretario; al quale commisse una lettera, com'io medesimo gli seppi dire; . . . Il detto brieve penso mandarvi in questa . . .'

[3] Possibly copies of secret bulls and briefs were preserved together (Fink, *QF*, xxv, 302), which would explain the appearance of docs. 26 and 27 below, both in Arm. 39 as briefs, and in Reg. Vat. 354 as bulls. Cf. Fink, 'Politische Korrespondenz', no. 348, 'Recepimus binas a te litteras scriptas Dertuse alteras die XVII octobris, in quibus erant copie duorum brevium, alteras vero die XVIII. Quoad priores litteras scias fuisse nobiscum Ferentini tres secretarios, quorum Cincius et Poggius asserunt se illa brevia non scripsisse; Melchior de Scribanis, qui erat tertius et iunior, defunctus est et is forsan illas scripsit. Sed nos non meminimus eidem talia commisisse.'

[4] For the series of which they are a part, see A. Lodolini, *L'Archivio di Stato in Roma e l'Archivio del Regno d'Italia*, 49–50. See also Bååth, 'L'Inventaire de la Chambre', p. 156, 'Item volumina computorum thesaurariorum doaneriorum et depositariorum terrarum ecclesie ligata et non ligata in numero —septuagintaseptem.'

(b) *The March of Ancona*

L. Fumi describes these registers in 'Inventario e Spoglio dei registri della Tesoreria Apostolica della Marca', *Le Marche*, iv (1904).

Arch. Cam., pt. 8, Tesorerie Provinciali, Marca.

Busta 1.
Vol. 1 (1422–4), Fumi, p. 4.
Vol. 2 (1422–3), Fumi, p. 110.
Vol. 3 (1423–4), Fumi, p. 111.

Busta 2.
Vol. 1 (1424–5), Fumi, p. 163.
Vol. 2 (1425–6), Fumi, p. 167.

Busta 3.
Vol. 1 (1427–8, Fumi, p. 282.
Vol. 2 (1428–9), Fumi, p. 284.
Vol. 3 (1429–30), Fumi, p. 292.

Busta 4.
Vol. 1 covers the period 1430–32, and not 1431–2, as said by Fumi, p. 295.

(c) *Perugia*

L. Fumi, *Inventario e Spoglio dei registri della Tesoreria Apostolica di Perugia e Umbria* (1901), describes these registers.

Arch. Cam., pt. i, Tesorerie Provinciali, Umbria.

Busta 1.
Vol. 1a (1424–5), Fumi, p. 3.
Vol. 1b (1424–5), Fumi, p. 18.
Vol. 2 (1425), Fumi, p. 18.
Vol. 3 (1425), Fumi, p. 18.

Busta 2.
Vol. 1 (1425–6), Fumi, p. 20.
Vol. 2a (1425–6), Fumi, p. 21.
Vol. 2b (1425–7), Fumi, p. 22.
Vol. 3 (1425–6), Fumi, p. 22.
Vol. 4 (1424–6), Fumi, p. 23.
Vol. 5 (1426–7), Fumi, p. 26.
Vol. 6 (1426–7), Fumi, p. 30.

Busta 3.
Vol. 1 (1429–30), Fumi, p. 31.
Vol. 2a (1429–31), Fumi, p. 33.
Vol. 2b (1430–31), Fumi, p. 36.
Vol. 3 (1429), Fumi, p. 36.
Vol. 4 (1429), Fumi, p. 38.
Vol. 5 (1430–31), Fumi, p. 39.

(d) *Ascoli*

Arch. Cam., pt. i, Tesorerie Provinciali, Ascoli.

Busta 1.

Vol. 1 (1426–7). The accounts of Astorgio Agnesi, Treasurer of the March of Ancona. Contemporary binding, with leather clasps. On cover, 'B. . . . Computus domini Astorgii episcopi Anconitan''. Title, fol. 4, 'Hic est liber continens omnes summas et pecuniarum quantitates introitum et gabellarum camere civitatis Esculane eiusque comitatus et districtus pervenientes apud reverendum in christo patrem et dominum, dominum Astorgium, dei gratia episcopum Anconitanum et Humanat', pro sanctissimo in christo patre et domino nostro, domino Martino, divina providentia papa quinto, et sancta Romana ecclesia, in provincia Marchie Anconitane et nonnullis aliis partibus, et in dicta civitate Esculi thesaurario generali, per manus diversorum depositariorum camere, de duobus mensibus in duos menses deputatorum per eundem dominum thesaurarium necnon per reverendem patrem et dominum dominum M[attheum] abbatem Sublacensis Esculi gubernatorem etc., secundum morem antiquum et consuetudinem antiquitus observatam in dicta civitate, et secundam formam statutorum eiusdem, necnon omnes et singulas pecuniarum quantitates expositas et exponendas . . . scriptis . . . per me Marinum Ser Antonii Ser Cole de Monte Elparo, publicum apostolica et imperali auctoritate notarium et nunc notarium et officialem prefati domini thesaurarii et camere esculane, ad scribendum introytus et exitus dicte camere per prefatum dominum thesaurarium specialiter deputatum.'

(e) *Campania*

Arch. Cam. pt. i, Tesorerie Provinciali, Campagna.

Busta 1.

Vol. 1. The accounts of Jacopo Gori of Alatri, Treasurer of Campania, for the third year of his office of Treasurer, beginning 25 January 1427.

4. Documents of the Commune of Rome

(a) *Accounts of the Treasurer of Rome*

The system of accounting used by this official is still far from clear.[1] Of the two account books preserved from the pontificate of Martin V, one (IE 381) is written in Italian, and appears to record receipt and expenditure in the way common to registers of the same type and period. Many of the expenses are not listed separately, but are referred to as contained in a comprehensive *rotulus*, which is said to have been signed by the Pope. The other (IE 386) is written in Latin, and lists only expenditure said to have been ordered by the Vice-Chamberlain; it may be in effect a register of the cameral mandates sent to the Treasurer of Rome.[2]

IE 381.

Accounts of Johannes de Astallis, Treasurer of Rome, from 1 January 1423 to 31 December 1424. There is no title. The accounts were approved by a commission of the Apostolic Chamber (fols. 179–180v).

[1] See above, pp. 166–7; and cf. Gottlob, *Aus der Camera apostolica*, 147–9.
  ibid.; see also Malatesta, *Statuti delle gabelle di Roma*, doc. 24, p. 147.

IE 386.
Accounts of the same, from 1426–1430.[1] Contains accounts only of expenditure.
No title.

(b) *Accounts of the Chamberlain of Rome*[2]

Arch. Cam. pt. i, Camera di Roma, B.84, vol. 342.
Title, fol. 1. 'Liber sive cartelarius continens in se omnes et singulas receptiones
et pacamenta facti et positi (sic) ad introitum camere alme urbis penes Petrum
Juliani Sclavi camerarium camere urbis predicte . . . temporum magnificorum
virorum Pauli Lelli Petrucii, Antonii de Valentinis, et Johannis Pauli della Toure,
conservatorum camere alme urbis'. Written in Italian. Deals with the period
1421–1425.

(c) *Accounts of the Commissioners of the Salt and Focage Tax*

These volumes are described by G. Tomassetti, 'Del sale e focatico del Comune
di Roma nel Medio Evo', *ASR*, xx (1897), 341–6.

Arch. Cam. pt. i, Camera di Roma, B.72, vols. 1 and 2.

(d) *Appointments of the Officials of Rome* [3]

Vatican Archives, Fondo Borghese, Serie 4, vol. 60. A sixteenth-century MS.,
headed, fol. 2, 'Extractum ex registro dominorum conservatorum tempore Martini
V summi pontificis'. Fols. 2–110 contain the briefs appointing the *conservatores*
and other officials, from December 1424 to March 1430. Fols. 116–202v contain a
list of Senators, from the thirteenth century to 1580.

5. Roman Archives and Libraries other than the Vatican and the Archivio di Stato

(a) *Biblioteca Angelica* [4]

Cod. 1426.

(b) *Archivio Capitolino*

Archivio di Casa Orsini.[5]
Pergamene, II.A.XIII, nos. 11, 12, 15, 17, 37, 39, 40. I have also consulted a
seventeenth-century abstract of the same documents, II.A.XXXVIII.

---

[1] See above, p. ibid.. Gottlob, *Aus der Camera apostolica*, does not deal with this official.
[2] See above, p. ibid.
[3] See above, p. 164. I have not used the lists of officials in the Archivio di Stato (see *ASR*, xx, 1897,
346–9).
[4] Cf. H. Narducci, *Catalogus codicum manuscriptorum praeter graecos et orientales in Bibliotheca
Angelica olim Coenobii Sancti Augustini de Urbe.*
[5] Cf. De Cupis, 'Regesto degli Orsini e dei Conti Anguillara', *BDA*, 3rd Ser., i (1910).

6. Communal Archives of the Provinces

(a) *Ancona* [1]

> Atti Consigliari.
> Vol. 29 (1419–20).   Spadolini (p. 31) dates it 1417.
> Vol. 30 (1421–2).
> Vol. 31 (1427).
> Vol. 32 (1428).
> Vol. 33 (1430).
> Vol. 34 (1431).   Spadolini dates it 1430.
> Vol. 35 (1432–3).

(b) *Ascoli*

> Archivio storico comunale.
>
> Buste 1, 2, 3, 7, 9.
>
> Pergamene.
> N. fasc. 1, no. 3; ibid., no. 9; R. fasc. 1, no. 8; R. fasc. 3, no. 5.

(c) *Macerata*

I have been unable to find the former Archive of the Legates of the March—if, indeed, it still exists.   In the Archivio Priorale of the Commune [2] I have used :

> Riformanze.
> Vol. 11 (1416–19).
> Vol. 12 (1421–2).
> Vol. 13 (1424–6).
> Vol. 14 (1426–9).
> Vol. 15 (1429–32).
>
> Pergamene.
> Cartaccio Grande, no. 3; Busta B, nos. 7, 45; Cass. VIII°, A.

(d) *Fermo*

I have consulted various original briefs in the Archivio Priorale,[3] notably nos. 1451, 1476, 1646, 1525, 471 (copy); and also the parchments 173, 1244 and 1352.

---

[1] See E. Spadolini, *L'Archivio storico comunale d'Ancona* (Ancona, n.d.); C. Ciavarini, *Croniche Anconitane* (1870), xxix–lix; G. Mazzatinti and G. degli Azzi, *Gli Archivi della Storia d'Italia*, 2nd ser., ii (1911).

[2] L. Zdekauer, 'L'Archivio del comune di Macerata', *ASI*, 5th ser., xix (1897); idem, 'L'Archivio ex-pontificio a Macerata', *Gli Archivi Italiani*, ii (1915), only the first part published; idem, 'Sulle fonti delle Constitutiones Sancte Matris Ecclesie, con alcune osservazioni sull'antico Archivio dei Legati delle Marche', *Rivista italiana per le scienze giuridiche*, xxxi (1901); G. Mazzatinti, *Gli Archivi della storia d'Italia*, iii (1903), 261 f.

[3] G. Mazzatinti, *Gli Archivi della storia d'Italia*, ii (1899), 126–59; F. Filippini and G. Luzzato, 'Archivi Marchigiani', *AMSM*, n.s., vii (1911/12).

(e) *Rimini*

I have consulted the *schede* of Garampi in the Biblioteca Gambalunga, the *Apografi Riminesi*. Most of the relevant documents are versions of Martin V's briefs, and were taken by Garampi from the Vatican Archives.

Apografi Riminesi.
No. 729 (Fink, 'Politische Korrespondenz', no. 448); no. 730 (Fink, no. 463); no. 731 (Fink, no. 414); no. 746 (Fink, nos. 465, 412); no. 747 (Fink, no. 402); no. 748 (Fink, no. 412).

(f) *Spoleto*

The *Riformazioni* in the Archivio Storico del Comune are not numbered or classified, and their state of repair is poor. I have used only the volume 1423/4, as the rest of the volumes for Martin V's pontificate are missing. There is a collection of original parchments, the only ones of interest for this period being a papal brief of 8 December 1424 (no. 353), an original bull (no. 349) of 1418, and a parchment of 1424 (no. 352). No. 360, which is dated 16 January 1420 in the MS. inventory, is in fact an original brief of Eugenius IV, dated 16 January 1432.

APPENDIX OF DOCUMENTS

1 *Louis Aleman, Apostolic Vice-Chamberlain, orders the Apostolic Treasurer to have 500 florins paid from the cameral monies held by Bartolomeo de' Medici to the papal* cubicularius *Oddo (Poccia de Varris), for the use of the Pope and for the maintenance of the Apostolic Palace. Constance, 14 December 1417.*

Reverendo in christo patri domino Henrico dei gratia episcopo Feltren', domini nostri pape thesaurario, Ludovicus etc., salutem etc. Paternitati vestre tenore presentium commictimus et mandamus, quatenus de pecuniis existentibus penes Bartholomeum de Medicis campsorem florentinum, Romanam curiam sequentem, ad cameram apostolicam pertinentibus, detis et tradatis venerabili viro domino Oddoni domini nostri pape cubiculari (*sic*) quingentos florenos auri de camera pro ipsius domini nostri pape et sui palatii apostolici oneribus supportandis et negociis peragendis exponendos et expediendos, quos ad rationem computorum vestrorum allocetis, facientes de dicta summa vobis fieri per dictum dominum Oddonem quietanciam oportunam, quam, una cum presenti, in reddibitione dictorum computorum vestrorum in camera apostolica presentare debeatis. Datum Constantie, sub dicti domini camerarii signeti secreti impressione, die xiiii Decembris, anno a nativitate domini millesimo ccccxvii^{mo}, indictione x^a, pontificatus vero sanctissimi in christo patris et domini nostri domini Martini pape quinti anno primo.

Text. Div. Cam. 4, fols. 218v–219.

Note. This is part of a gathering which should have been bound into the *liber bullectarum* (which is now in the Archivio di Stato, Arch. Cam., pt. i, vol. 824) instead of in this, the *liber diversarum*. The error appears from the heading on fol. 215, 'Inferius annotantur bullete seu mandata tradendi pecunias'.

2 *Louis Aleman, Apostolic Vice-Chamberlain, orders the brothers Manfredi to pay 1,000 florins of the* census *due for their vicariate of Faenza, direct to Angelo della Pergola, a papal mercenary, towards the sum which the Apostolic Chamber owes him for his* condotta. *They are to obtain two receipts from him, and to send one of them to the Chamber. Florence, 12 and 21 February 1420.*

(a)

Ludovicus etc. Magnificis viris Carolo et Guidantonio de Manfredis fratribus ac eorum germanis domicellis Faventin', in civitate territorioque et districtu Faventin' ac nonnullorum aliorum castrorum et villarum ad dominum nostrum et sanctam Romanam ecclesiam pertinentium pro ipsis domino nostro et Romana ecclesia in temporalibus vicariis generalibus, salutem etc. Cum camera apostolica suis propter plurimas necessitates ipsi dietim ingruentes plussolito exhausta pecuniis, nobili viro Angelo de Pergula nonnullarum gentium armigerarum ad stipendia domini nostri et ecclesie prefatorum militantium capitaneo, ex nova conducta dicti capitanei ad stipendia prefata cum ipsa camera firmata, in certa pecuniarum quantitate etiam ratione prestancie faciende teneatur, et licet necessitates apostolice camere plussolito eandem urgeant, tamen satisfactionem dicto Angelo impendendam conspicimus oportunam. Nos de mandato domini nostri pape super hoc nobis facto oraculo vive vocis, in deductionem eorum in quibus vos ratione vicariatus civitatis terri-toriique et districtus Faventin' predictorum dicte camere sub modis et formis in concessione dicti vicariatus specificatis usque in diem presentem tenemini et effica-citer obligamini, mille florenos auri de camera eidem Angelo capitaneo in deductione sui stipendii duximus assignandos et assignamus per presentes, mandantes propterea vobis et cuilibet vestrum, quatenus mille florenos huiusmodi prefato Angelo aut eius legitimo procuratori ad hoc ab eo speciale mandatum habenti, in deductionem stipendii sui predicti tradere et realiter assignare quamtocius non postponatis. Nos enim Angelo et procuratori predictis summam mille florenorum huiusmodi a vobis petendi levandi et recipiendi, ac de receptis nomine dicte camere, et per vos eidem Angelo seu procuratori solutis et assignatis quitandi et liberandi, plenam tenore presentium concedimus facultatem. Facientes de assignatione huiusmodi, cum vos eam facere contiget, duo confici consimilia documenta, quorum uno penes vos retento, reliquum ad dictam cameram transmittere non postponatis. In quorum etc. Datum Florentie die duodecima mensis Februarii, sub anno domini millesimo quadringentesimo vicesimo, indictione tertiadecima, pontificatus etc. anno tertio.

Text. Div. Cam. 6, fol. 22v–23.

Note.—A cancelled letter, with the same text, dated 2 January 1420, is in Div. Cam. 5, fol. 241, marked 'Cancellata de mandato domini. L. Robring.'

(b)

A second letter, dated Florence, 21 February 1420, reproducing the text above, and instructing the brothers Manfredi 'Quo propter vobis tenore presentium mandamus, quatenus Angelo aut eius procuratori predictis, vigore preinsertarum litterarum si cepte fuerint, aut vigore presentium tenore predicto observato, summam superius expressam solvere teneamini . . .'

Text. Div. Cam. 6, fol. 25v.

3 *The Rector of the Patrimony of St. Peter in Tuscia reports to the Apostolic Treasurer that he has imposed a tallage as he was ordered, and informs him of the instalments by which the money is collected in the province. Viterbo, 3 April 1420.*

Copia unius littere scripte per dominum episcopum Apten', rectorem patrimonii, dominis Senensi et Ebroicen'. Reverendi etc. Sicut per alias vobis scripsi, imposui subsidium sicut mihi mandatum est. Et quamvis primus terminus esset in medio mensis Maii proxime futuri, abbreviavi tamen terminum antedictum ipsumque prefixi die primo mensis Maii. Secundus est in medio mensis Augusti et tertius in medio mensis Decembris. Hii etiam sunt termini in hac provincia consueti, et ut solutiones debitis et ordinatis fiant temporibus, omnem mihi possibilem diligenciam, servatis tamen modis quos mihi scripsistis, et operam adhibeo. Datum Viterbii tertio aprilis 1420.

Text. Arm. 34, vol. 4, fol. 148.

4 *Louis Aleman, Apostolic Vice-Chamberlain, orders Jacopo of Bagnorea, Treasurer of the province of the Patrimony of St. Peter in Tuscia, to pay 1,200 florins of the money from the tallage of the province to the mercenary Aloisio de Verme, towards the payment of the latter's salary. He is to obtain a receipt for the payment. Rome, St. Peter's, 30 March 1422.*

Ludovicus etc. Venerabili viro domino Jacopo de Balneoregio in provincia patrimonii beati Petri in Tuscia pro sanctissimo domino nostro papa et Romana ecclesia thesaurario generali, salutem etc. Vobis de mandato sanctissimi in christo patris et domini nostri domini Martini, divina providencia pape quinti, super hoc vive vocis oraculo specialiter nobis facto, presencium tenore committimus et mandamus, quatenus de pecuniis tallearum dudum in dicta provincia impositarum per vos, iam collectis seu quamprimum colligendis, detis et solvatis aut dari et solvi faciatis magnifico viro Aloysio de Verme nonnullarum gentium armigerarum ad stipendia dicti domini nostri pape militantium capitaneo, aut eius procuratori legitimo, florenorum mille ducentos auri de camera in deductione stipendiorum suorum, mandatis et aliis presentibus contrariis non obstantibus quibuscumque. Nos enim summam huiusmodi in vestris computis admittemus, recipientes ab eis de hiis que vigore presencium tradideritis nomine camere apostolice quitancias oportunas. In quorum etc. Datum Rome apud Sanctum Petrum die tricesima mensis martii, sub anno a nativitate domini millesimo quadragintesimo vicesimo-secundo, xvᵃ indictione, pontificatus etc. anno quinto.

Text. Div. Cam. 7, fol. 16.

5 *Benedetto Guidalotti, Apostolic Vice-Chamberlain, instructs Paolo of Sulmona, Treasurer of Perugia and the Duchy of Spoleto, to exact tallage for the year beginning in November 1424, in the same manner as has previously been ordered, and according to a list which is attached to this letter. The money is to be sent to the Apostolic Chamber as soon as collected. Rome, Church of the Holy Apostles, 3 March 1425.*

Benedictus etc. Venerabili viro domino Paulo de Salmona dicte camere clerico, in ducatu Spoletan' ac Perusii pro dicto domino nostro papa et sancta Romana ecclesia thesaurario, salutem etc. Ecce de mandato domini nostri Pape super hoc nobis facto oraculo vive vocis, talleam per vos nomine apostolice camere in infrascriptis civitatibus terris et locis prout inferius per ordinem continentur, pro conservacione et salubri statu civitatum castrorum et terrarum earumdem ac aliorum locorum domino nostro et ecclesie predictis subiectorum, et aliis oneribus multiplicibus supportandis imponendam ordinavimus. Quare vobis de simili mandato super hoc nobis facto, tenore presencium committimus et mandamus, quatenus talleas infrascriptas iuxta tabulam inferius descriptam pro presenti anno de mense Novembris proxime lapso incepto, et sic deinceps in terminis solitis et consuetis exigendas nomine camere predicte, ac easdem in terminis consuetis a reverendis patribus dominis episcopis, necnon venerabilibus et nobilibus viris clericis communitatibus castris civitatibus et locis inferius descriptis et declaratis ac earum personis prout quemlibet concernit usque ad completam solucionem rate quemlibet tangentur, nostro et apostolice camere nomine petatis recuperetis et exigatis. Nos enim vobis talleas ipsas ac restas earumdem exigendi petendi levandi et recipiendi, ac de receptis dumtaxat dantes et solventes liberandi et quittandi, necnon renitentes et contumaces compellendi et constringendi, multandi et puniendi, cavalcatas fieri mandandi, et alia graviora faciendi prout iustum fuerit et vobis videbitur expedire, ac etiam per censuram ecclesiasticam composcendi, invocato ad hoc auxilio brachii secularis, plenam tenore presencium concedimus facultatem. Mandantes omnibus et singulis officialibus inibi deputatis et quos ad hoc duxeritis requirendos, quatenus vobis ad premissa auxilium prestent pariter et favorem. Vos igitur in premissis diligenciam debitam apponatis, quod de vestris operibus valeatis non immerito commendari. Volumus autem quod totum et quidquid vos recipere et habere continget ex premissis, statim ad nos et dictam cameram tutiori celeriorique modo quo poteritis transmittere debeatis. In quorum etc. Datum Rome apud Sanctos Apostolos, die tercia mensis Martii anno domini millesimo quadragintesimo vicesimoquinto, indictione tercia, pontificatus etc. anno octavo.

Tabula vera hec est

Gualdum Capitaneorum octuaginta	florenos lxxx
Bittonium centumquinquaginta	f. cl
Colismancia centum	f. c
Nucerium ducentos	f. cc
Monsfalcus trecentos quinquaginta	f. cccl
Assisium quadringentos	f. cccc
Canarium centumviginti	f. cxx
Spellum ducentos	f. cc
Tudertum mille ducentos	f. Mcc
Episcopus Eugubin' centum octuaginta	f. clxxx

In the margin

Die xxviiii mensis Martii predicti fuerint admitti (*sic*) prefati prelati quatuor cum terra Trivii, et taxatio eorum videlicet :

Episcopus Nucerin' cum clero	florenos lxx
Episcopus Tudertin' cum clero	f. cc
Episcopus Assisin' cum clero	f. c
Episcopus Fulginas cum clero	f. cxx
Trivium cum comitatu	f. cccc

et littera fuit directa domino Paulo de Sulmon'.   L. Robring.

Text.   Div. Cam. 9, fols. 22v–23.

6 *Astorgio, Bishop of Ancona and Treasurer of the March of Ancona, acknowledges the receipt of 190 ducats 15* bolognini *from the commune of Macerata, as part of the tallage due for the year beginning in September 1426.   Recanati, 5 May 1427.*

Mccccxxvii indictione quinta et die v mensis Maii.   Reverende in christo pater et dominus dominus Astorgius episcopus Anconitan' et Humanat', Marchie commissarius et thesaurarius generalis, fuit confessus habuisse et recepisse a comunitate Macerate per manus Petri Johannis de Macerata, in duabus partitis, pro parte tallearum presentis anni incepti in kalendis Septembris Mccccxxvi, ducatos centum nonaginta et bol' quindecim ad rationem xl bol' pro ducato, de quibus idem dominus commissarius et thesaurarius predictum Petrum Johannem presentem et recipientem nomine dicte comunitatis quietavit liberavit et absolvit.   Actum Racaneti in palatio comunis, presentibus egregio viro domino Petro de Nangelis de Viterbio et Aloysio de Cepellis de Laude testibus.

duc' clxxx bo' xv

Item solvit pro capitibus solidorum duc' unum et bol' xxiiii.
Item pro quitantia bol' iii.
Astorgius predictus manu propria.
Mathias de Pileo scripsi.

Text.   Original, paper, 23 × 18 cm., Macerata, Archivio Priorale, Busta B, no. 45.
Seal.   Round wafer, 1·8 cm. diameter, title surrounding shield.
Note.   The signature of the Treasurer of the March is autograph.

7 *The Bishop of Alatri, Treasurer of the March of Ancona has written to the Pope that the ordinary revenues of the March do not suffice for the expenditure.   In reply he is told to collect the tallage of the province in advance of the date on which it is normally due.   Rome, Church of the Holy Apostles, 17 April 1429.*

Venerabili fratri Johanni episcopo Alatrino, in provincia Marchie Anconitane thesaurario nostro, salutem etc.   Cum tu pridie nobis scripseris, quod pro nostris et ecclesie negotiis exequendis in omnibus, suplere et providere non poteris de pecuniis que ad manus tuas ordinarie in provinciis tibi commissis provenerint, sicut res regende et requirent et postulant.   Et propterea nobis supplicaveris ut tibi intimare vellemus, quid pro huiusmodi negotiis exequendis per nos tibi commissis facere debeas, nos, ne propterea que gerenda sunt impedimenta subeant, providere volentes, et sperantes quod peculiares ecclesie filii provinciales et vicarii nostri Marchie Anconitane in hac necessitate, quorum tranquillitatem et pacem omni tempore procuravimus et procurare intendimus, usque ad expositionem aliorum bonorum ecclesie, libenter subvenient in opportunitatibus apostolice camere, volumus et mandamus tibi ut dilectos filios provinciales, qui taleas persolverint, nostro nomine exorteris ac requiras, inducendo eos bonis rationibus ipsos nichilominus paternis monitionibus exortando, ut taleas unius anni, vel duas partes ad minus, quas nobis et dicte camere tenentur persolvere infuturum, videlicet a prima die mensis Septembris proxime futuri ad annum, velint tibi exnunc absque aliqua dilatione temporis solvere et assignare nostro nomine et camere supradicte, et deinde retineant sibi in dicto tempore usque ad debitam satisfactionem.   Et volumus exnunc prout extunc quod eis, absque alicuius alterius expectatione mandati, debitas quitantias facias iuxta morem, nec possint dicto tempore in aliquo gravari vel aliter molestari.   Super quibus omnibus tibi dictas taleas petendi exigendi et omnia alia circha ea opportuna et necessaria faciendi, plenam et liberam tenore presentium concedimus facultatem. Volumus insuper quod quicquid egeris in predictis quamcitius apostolicam cameram certificare procures.   Et per premissa non intendimus quod talie et census quos in terminis consuetis usque ad illud tempus solvere tenentur aliqualiter retardentur. Datum Rome apud Sanctos Apostolos xv kalendas Maii pontificatus nostri anno duodecimo.

Text.   Reg. Vat. 351, fol. 113v.

8 *Oddo (Poccia) de Varris the Apostolic Treasurer, as Deputy in the office of Apostolic Chamberlain, orders Giovanni de Astallis, the Treasurer of the City of Rome, to make certain payments to Johannes Betensoen* (alias *Bettynhusen*), *notary of the Apostolic Chamber, which the latter is to transmit to Master Pietro the castellan of the Ponte Nomentana at Rome, and to Mattarello of Genazzano, the castellan of Ponte Molle, as their salary for November and December 1429.   Rome, Church of the Holy Apostles, 24 December 1429.*

Oddo de Varris, apostolice sedis prothonotarius, domini nostri pape thesaurarius, in camerariatus officio eiusdem domini nostri pape locumtenens, nobili viro Johanni de Astallis, thesaurario camere urbis, salutem in domino.   Vobis presentium tenore committimus et mandamus, quatenus de pecuniis dicte camere Johanni Betensoen notario nostro recipienti nomine magistri Petri castellani pontis Numentan' dicte urbis, pro salario duorum mensium videlicet Novembris et presentis mensis Decembris, florenos octo ad rationem bon' quinquaginta pro quolibet floreno, ac etiam dicto Johanni notario recipienti vice et nomine Mattharelli de Genezano castellani pontis Melvii, pro salario eius et pagarum suarum duorum mensium, videlicet Novembris proxime preteriti et presentis mensis Decembris, florenos trigintaduos ad rationem bon' quinquaginta, solvatis et solvi faciatis. Quos in vestris computis admittemus. Datum Rome apud Sanctos Apostolos, anno domini millesimo ccccxxviiii, indictione viiᵃ, die vigesimoquarto mensis Decembris, sub signetti camerariatus officii supradicti quo utamur impressione, pontificatus sanctissimi in christo patris et domini nostri domini Martini divina providencia pape quinti anno tertiodecimo.

Beneath text to left, in the same hand as the text: 'Ita est. B. Dellante.' *Beneath text to right, in the same hand,* 'S. A. de Sarzana', *followed by the curial comma. Beneath the tip of the seal,* 'Registrata'.

At the head of the document, in a different hand, 'Solvatur'. *In the left hand margin* 'florenos viii. florenos xxxii' *opposite the relevant amounts in the text. In the bottom left corner* 'Petro Juliani'. *Beneath this* 'Johanni Fosco castellano civitatis Nepesin' florenos I sol' II den' octo ad rationem xlvii pro floreno'.

Endorsed on reverse of folio 'Registrata A' *in the form of a monogram, with the A within the R.*

Seal. Red wax signet, 1·8 × 1 cm., applied in the lower centre of the document, below the text. The top part of the document was then folded horizontally over the seal.

Text. Original, paper, 22·3 × 15 cm. Inst. Misc. 3890.

Note. For Johannes Betensoen, or Bettynhusen, see Baix, *La Chambre Apostolique et les 'libri annatarum' de Martin V*, cccxxvii.

9 *Benedetto Guidalotti, the Apostolic Vice-Chamberlain, declares the names of those clerks of the Apostolic Chamber who are held, for the purpose of receiving its emoluments, to be actually exercising their office. Rome, in the Apostolic Treasury, 3 December 1425.*

Mccccxxv, die tercia mensis Decembris, reverendus pater Benedictus de Guidalottis, locumtenens prefatus, sedens pro tribunali ad solitum bancum thesaurarie apostolice, in presentia reverendi in christo patris domini Antonii, dei gratia episcopi Senen', domini nostri pape thesaurarii meique notarii publici et testimonii subscriptorum, de mandato sanctissimi domini nostri pape, super hoc ut asservit vive vocis oraculo sibi facto, declaravit quod sanctissimus dominus noster papa intendit et vult haberi atque reputat et habet pro clericis presentibus et exercentibus officium clericatus dicte camere, reverendum patrem dominum Paulum de Zovinatio,[1] sedis apostolice prothonotarium, licet tunc ibidem personaliter non intraessentem, necnon venerabiles et circumspectos viros dominum Paulum de Sulmona,[2] Bartholomeum Dellante de Pisis [3] et Nicolaum de Mercatello [4] decretorum doctores, ac Nicolaum de Valle [5] et Johannem de Azel [6] decretorum doctores tunc ibidem presentes et consentientes, et insuper eundem dominum Benedictum [7] ac etiam reverendos patres dominos Angelotum dei gratia episcopum Anagnin',[8] licet personaliter non existentem, et dominum dei gratia electum Firman',[9] ibidem tunc presentem, dicte camere clericos, cum illis emolumentis agiis honoribus et oneribus de quibus dominus sanctissimus aut idem dominus Benedictus ex eius parte et mandato alias duxerit

P

declarandum; reliquos vero dicte camere clericos, videlicet venerabiles et circumspectos viros dominos Jacobum de Calvis,[10] Ambrosium de Vicecomitibus [11] decretorum doctorem, Simonem de Novaria,[12] Guillelmum de Latinis de Prato [13] et Panthaleonem de Bredis [14] etiam decretorum doctores, ac Menimum de Senis [15] ad presens in Romana curia personaliter residentes, quibus et eorum cuilibet prefatus dominus locumtenens intentionem domini nostri pape predictam in presentia mei notarii die ultima mensis Novembris proxime preteriti declaravit, omnesque et singulos alias dicte camere clericos a dicta curia absentes intendit haberi atque reputat et habet pro clericis absentibus et non exercentibus officium clericatus predictum, a die prima mensis presentis in antea. Cum reservatione tamen illorum emolumentorum de quibus alias declaravit, ut superius est expressum. Actum Rome in thesauraria apostolica, presentibus dicto domino thesaurario et magistris Ludolfo Robring et Johanne de Gallesio notariis sociis etc.

Text. Div. Cam. 3, fol. 175v.

Note. These clerks of the Chamber appear in the list of clerks given by Baix, *La Chambre Apostolique et les 'libri annatarum' de Martin V*, ccclxviii–cDiii, as follows :

1. Baix, no. i.	9. No. xxv.
2. No. ix.	10. No. xi.
3. No. xii.	11. No. xiv.
4. No. xix.	12. No. ii.
5. No. xxiii.	13. No. x.
6. No. xxvi.	14. No. xxiv.
7. No. xvi.	15. Not in Baix' list.
8. No. xv.	

10 *Louis Aleman, Apostolic Vice-Chamberlain, orders Pantaleone de Bredis, Auditor-General of the court of the Apostolic Chamberlain, to sit twice a week to hear the cases of prisoners held for criminal offences in his gaol. He also orders that a record be kept by the soldanus of the gaol, of the names of the prisoners and the dates of their arrest. Further, that another book be kept to record the crimes with which the prisoners are charged, and a third book with details of the sentences passed. All these records are to be kept by the notaries of the court. The money from condemnations is to be kept in a safe place under the care of the Auditor, and an account of it is to be made monthly. Florence, 20 June 1420.*

Ludovicus etc. Venerabili decretorum doctori domino Panthaleoni de Bredis de Utino, domini nostri pape capellano ac ipsius causarum curie domini camerarii camere apostolice auditori generali, salutem etc. Volentes ex officii nostri debito super iusticia unicuique ministranda, et presertim ut cause eorum qui pro aliquibus criminibus captivantur sine debito terminentur, nec sopite et indecise remaneant, quantum possumus modis expedientibus providere, presentium tenore vobis committimus et mandamus, quatenus de cetero bis in unaquaque septimana, ad reddendum iura omnibus et singulis in Romana curia pro criminibus captivatis ordinarie sedere debeatis, et super causis eorum summarie et expedite procedere iusticia mediante. Quodque ut huiusmodi negocia magis ordinate ac maturius regulentur, deliberavimus et ita volumus super infrascriptis execucioni mandandis per vos oportunum ordinem adhiberi, videlicet quod in domo habitacionis soldani carcerum Romane curie sit liber unus, in quo omnia nomina eorum qui pro aliquibus criminibus capientur, cum eorum cognitionibus et diebus quibus capti fuerint, ordinate scribantur. Item quod alius liber ordinetur in quo omnes informaciones contra delatos per notarios curie per ordinem describantur. Item alius etiam liber in quo omnes condempnaciones per eosdem notarios et citra vestra subscripcione scribantur. Et quod huiusmodi informaciones et condempnaciones per notarios curie predictos in dictis tamenmodo libris et non alibi describantur, quodque pecunie condempnacionum in una capsa vel in loco tuto de quo vobis visum extiterit reponantur, et quod singulis mensibus de huiusmodi pecuniis computa reddantur, ita quod cuncta rite fiant et clare disponantur, nec camera apostolica suis iuribus defraudetur, atque unicuique, sicut optamus, iuris debitum ministretur. In quorum etc. Datum Florentie, die vigesima Junii anno domini millesimo quadragintesimo vigesimo, indictione decimatercia, pontificatus anno tercio.

Text. Div. Cam. 6, fol. 144v.

11 *Louis Aleman, Apostolic Vice-Chamberlain, orders the Vice-Senator of Rome, Nicolò of Anagni, and his officials, to hear the case brought by Mariola Baldi against Nardo dello Liscio, concerning a house in the region of Parione in Rome. The case had formerly been refused a hearing, on the grounds of an exemption which the Vice-Chamberlain had in 1421 granted to the inhabitants of the Leonine city, but which is now declared to have been applicable only to debts contracted before the entry of the Pope into Rome. Rome, St. Peter's, 23 May 1422.*

Ludovicus etc. Magnifico viro domino Nicolao de Anagnia legum doctori, alme urbis vicesenatori, eiusque judicibus et collateralibus aliisque officialibus curie Capitolii dicte urbis, salutem etc. Querelam pro parte Mariole filie et universalis heredis quondam Cristofori Baldi vascellarii mulieris Romane de regione Sancti Eustachii accepimus continentem, que ipsa Mariola ut filia et heres predicta quandam causam contra Nardum dello Liscio, civem Romanum, notarium publicum, de et super quadam domo terrinea et solarata cum iuribus et pertinentiis suis sita in regione Parionis iuxta suos confines, olim ad dictum quondam Cristoforum eius patrem, et successive ac hodie ad ipsam Mariolam tamquam filiam et heredem predictam, ut dicitur, spectante et pertinente plene iure, atque ipsius domus invasione occupacione et illicita detencione per eundem Nardum movere et agitare non potest sub pretextu certi rescripti seu indulti per nos alias de mandato sanctissimi in christo patris et domini nostri domini Martini, divina providencia pape quinti, super eo tunc vive vocis oraculo nobis facto, concessi illis qui tempore adventus ipsius domini nostri pape civitatem Leoninam sive burgum Sancti Petri personaliter habitabant, sub datum Rome apud Sanctum Perum, die vigesimaprima mensis Januarii, annorum millesimi quadragentesimi vicesimiprimi, et pontificatus eiusdem domini nostri pape quarto, supplicari fecit humiliter coram nobis, sibi super premissis de oportuno remedio miserecorditer provideri. Nos igitur, considerantes quod indultum sive concessio huiusmodi, que hic haberi volumus pro sufficienter expressis, solum et dumtaxat quo ad debita usque ad adventum domini nostri pape prefati ad dictam urbem quacumque occasione vel causa contracta specialiter extenduntur, auctoritate camerariatus officii, cuius curam gerimus de presente, ac etiam de mandato sanctissimi domini nostri pape prefati super hoc nobis simili oraculo specialiter nobis facto, vobis et cuilibet vestrum presencium tenore committimus et mandamus, quatenus eandem Mariolam atque suam causam huiusmodi audiatis cognoscatis et sine debito terminetis, usque ad executionem inclusive, partibus ipsis equo libramine iusticiam ministretis, rescripto seu indulto et concessione nostris aliis huiusmodi nequaquam obstantibus. In quorum etc. Datum Rome apud Sanctum Petrum die xxiii mensis maii, xv indictione, pontificatus etc. anno quinto.

Text. Div. Cam. 7, fol. 54v.

12 *Louis Aleman, Apostolic Vice-Chamberlain, orders the Senator of Rome, Bartolomeo Gonzaga, and his officials, to desist from attempting to exercise jurisdiction over the courtiers and followers of the Roman Court. The Vice-Chamberlain has already in the past issued an order to the same effect, which the Senator and his officials have ignored, putting various courtiers in prison and taking bail from them. The liberty of the courtiers and followers of the Roman Court has not formerly been held so lightly, and the Senator is now ordered under pain of excommunication to observe the rule that jurisdiction over these courtiers and followers, both male and female, belongs to the Chamberlain or to the court of the Auditor of the Apostolic Chamber if they are ecclesiastics, and to the court of the Marshal of the Roman Court if they are laymen. All such cases pending in his court are to be suspended immediately, and in future no such processes are to be brought, either civil or criminal. The bail which he has exacted is to be restored within three days to the courtiers or followers concerned, through the Marshal of the Roman Court. Rcme, St. Mary Major, 12 December 1422.*

Ludovicus etc. Magnifico viro domino Bartholomeo de Gonzaga militi Mantuan', alme urbis senatori illustri, necnon dominis conservatoribus camere dicte urbis ac marescallis et ceteris officialibus curie Capitolii urbis prelibate presentibus et futuris, salutem etc. Cum ex ordinacione et disposicione sanctissimi in christo patris et domini nostri domini Martini, divina providencia pape quinti, super hoc factis observari mandatum et statutum existat, ut cortesani quicumque Romanam curiam sequentes utriusque sexus, homines tam clerici quam laici, tamque mares quam mulieres, ab omni iurisdictione vestra et curie vestre predicte Capitoli immunes atque liberi esse debeant et exempti, in eum modum quod clerici et ecclesiastice persone coram nobis seu auditore nostro et curie camere apostolice generali, laicales autem persone tam mares quam femine ex cortesanis ipsis coram domino marescallo ipsius domini nostri pape et dicte Romane curie, in casibus quibuscumque conveniri possint et debeant tantummodo, et non per vos aut aliquem vestrum vel dictam vestram curiam casu quocumque molestari vel vexari. Et licet huiusmodi ordinamentum et statutum dudum per nos de mandato sanctissimi domini nostri pape predicti ad ipsam vestram curiam sit directum, et in ea publicatum atque etiam per magnificum dominum Poncellum de Ursinis marescallum ipsius domini nostri et dicte curie interest iurisdictionem sibi debitam in hiis quo ad laicales personas curialium ipsorum conservare et defendere, vos demum senator et conservatores prout intelleximus requisiti fueritis et ammoniti, ut a quibuscumque iniuriis et molestacionibus prefatis cortesanis per vos seu curiam vestram quomodolibet inferendis abstinere et desistere curaretis. Tamen vos huiusmodi monicionibus et mandatis ac requisitionibus expresse recalcitrantes, nonnullis ex cortesanis ipsis utriusque sexus, prout ex conquestione plurimorum ex cortesanis ipsis nobis innotuit, sepius gravatis et gravastis atque molestastis et molestatis, pignora etiam ab aliquo ex eis indebite auferri faciendo. Quiquidem si veritati subsistunt in nonmodicum prejudicium libertatis curialium et Romanam curiam sequentium, que undique cuiuscumque et quamparve condicionis existimacione servari consuevit, illese vergere noscuntur. De mandato igitur prefati domini nostri pape, etiam auctoritate camerariatus officii ipsius domini nostri, cuius curam gerimus de presenti, attendentes quod juris ordo confunditur si cuiquam sua jurisdictio non servatur, vobis et vestrum singulis presentium tenore precepimus ac sub excommunicationis pena, quam merito formidare debetis, expresse mandantes quatenus cortesanos quoscumque, tam mares quam femellas Romanam curiam sequentes, si clerici sint ad nos et nostram sive auditoris dicte camere, si vero laicales persone sexus utriusque sint, ad curiam marescalli prefati, curias, in causis et casibus quibuscumque, absque iniuria offensa vel molestia aut solutione pretextu capture sive carcerationis quacumque in rebus iam ceptis, visis presentibus cum actis et actitatis quibuscumque remictere debeatis, illosque et alios quoscumque cortesanos predictos, sexus utriusque, super rebus quibusvis contractuum observationibus, et aliis quibuscumque etiam criminalibus, nullatenus de cetero molestetis aut molestari vel inquietare quomodolibet faciatis procuretis vel mandetis. Pignora autem que, prout dicitur, aliquibus ex cortesanis sive personis ipsis occasione quacumque auferri fecistis hactenus, per marescallos ipsos, et pecuniam quamcumque quam pretextu capture vel carcerationis personis eisdem auferri feceritis in futurum, libere et absque more dispendia restitui mandetis et faciatis, que et nos etiam auctoritate predicta, per prefatos marescallos personis prefatis infra trium dierum terminum sub pena arbitrii nostri si renitentes fuerint eis realiter infligenda, restitui volumus et mandamus per presentes. Presentes autem litteras in libris et registris camere dicte urbis ad futuram rei memoriam volumus fideliter annotari. In quorum etc. Datum Rome apud Sanctam Mariam Maiorem sub anno domini Mccccxxii, indictione xv^a, die xii mensis Decembris, pontificatus etc. anno sexto.

Text. Div. Cam. 7, fols. 134–5.

13 *Louis Aleman, the Apostolic Vice-Chamberlain, orders the* podestà *of Viterbo, Maggino de Madiis of Brescia, to hear and decide the suit between the spinsters Paoloccia and Giovanna Cecchini of Viterbo, on the one part, and the brothers Pietro and Angelo Cola, also of Viterbo, on the other. Pietro and Angelo Cola, the latter being a scriptor and abbreviator of apostolic letters, brought their suit in Rome before the Vice-Chamberlain, who committed it to Domenico of San Geminiano, Auditor of the court of the Apostolic Chamber. The Auditor proceeded to give sentence against the sisters on account of their contumacy, but the latter then represented to the Vice-Chamberlain that on account of their poverty they were unable to meet the costs of an action in Rome, and that on account of the statutes of Viterbo, and of certain papal privileges, such an action should not have been brought to Rome. The Vice-Chamberlain, therefore, the case having been returned to him by the Auditor, instructs the* podestà *of Viterbo to hear the case, and gives him the same faculties to decide it which had formerly been given to the Auditor. Rome, St. Peter's, 11 January 1423.*

Ludovicus etc. Spectabili et egregio viro domino Maggino de Madiis de Brixia, militi et legum doctori, potestati Viterbien', salutem etc. Pridem nobis auctoritate camerariatus officii cuius curam gerimus de presenti, ac etiam de mandato sanctissimi in christo patris et domini nostri domini Martini, divina providencia pape quinti, super hoc vive vocis oraculo nobis facto, causam et causas inter dilectos nobis in christo Petrum Cole, et dominum Angelum eius fratrem de Viterbio, litterarum apostolicarum scriptorem et abbreviatorem, ex una, ac Paulociam et Johannem, filias et heredas quondam Ser Dominici Cobucci Cecchini de Viterbio, virgines adultas, de et super nonnullis pecuniarum summis et rebus aliis et eorum occasione partibus ex altera, venerabili et circumspecto viro domino Dominico de Sancto Geminiano, decretorum doctori, domini nostri pape capellano, ipsiusque ac nostro et curie camere apostolice auditori generali, cum potestate plenaria duximus committendas. Cuiusquidam commissionis nostre vigore, idem dominus auditor citacione legitima ad partes decreta emissa executa et ad Romanam curiam reportata, ad importunam instanciam dictorum Petri et domini Angeli, ad aliquos actus citra tamen conclusionem in contumaciam dictarum mulierum ut dicitur processit. Postmodum vero pro parte Paulocie et Johanne predictarum fuimus instantissime requisiti, quantum cum ipse, ut asserunt, orphane et pauperime existant, et contra tenorem statutorum civitatis Viterbien' et indultorum apostolicorum, per prefatos Petrum et dominum Angelum in causam huiusmodi ad Romanam curiam tracte sint, et durissimum sit eis contra prefatos eorum adversarios in dicta Romana curia litigare, ac etiam de consanguinitate dictorum adversariorum suorum existant, causam et causas predictas ad nos advocare, et in dicta civitate Viterbien' committere dignaremur. Nos igitur ipsarum exponencium in hac parte supplicationibus inclinati, auctoritate et mandato predictis, causam et causas huiusmodi, ad nos per eundem dominum Dominicum auditorem remissas, vobis presentium tenore committimus audiendas cognoscendas decidendas et sine debito terminendas, cum omnibus et singulis suis emergentibus incidentibus dependentibus et connexis, commissione eidem domino auditori facta, constitutionibus apostolicis et aliis in contrariis facientibus non obstantibus quibuscumque, partibus ipsis hincinde bonam et expeditam justiciam ministrando. In quorum etc. Datum Rome apud Sanctum Petrum, die undecima mensis Januarii, sub anno a nativitate domini millesimo quadragentisimo vicesimotertio, indictione prima, pontificatus etc. anno sexto.

Text. Div. Cam. 7, fol. 139–139v.

14 *Jacopo Orsini, Count of Tagliacozzo, petitions the Pope that execution may be granted in the Capitoline court of a sentence granted in his favour by Domenico of San Geminiano, the Auditor of the court of the Apostolic Chamber. His petition is prefaced by an earlier petition of Orso Orsini of Monte Rotondo, which gives the earlier history of the case. The two had a lawsuit over the* castrum *of Mentana, which was brought in appeal before Tomasso de Virago, judge of appeals of the Capitoline Court of Rome. By special commission of the Pope the case was withdrawn from de Virago before he reached sentence, and committed to Domenico of San Geminiano, who awarded a definitive sentence and costs against Orso Orsini. But as a result of the petition of the latter (which is here attached), the case was transferred, before the sentence could be executed, to Cunczo de Zuola, Auditor of the Apostolic Palace. By reason of the contumacy of Jacopo Orsini, this new Auditor issued an inhibition against execution of the sentence. Jacopo Orsini now petitions against this inhibition, giving reasons why the collateral judge of the Capitoline Court should be allowed to make execution of the sentence, and asking that he be given powers to inhibit Cunczo de Zuola from meddling further with the case. The Pope grants Jacopo Orsini's petition, and orders that the first and second collateral judges of the City procede with the case, with the advice of the assembled council of judges* (assectamentum), *and do justice, giving them powers to inhibit as is petitioned. (Rome, late 1423 or early 1424.)*

Beatissime pater. Vertente lite et causa inter devotum vestrum magnificum dominum Urso de Ursinis de Monte Rotundo reum conventum ex una, et magnificum dominum Jacobum de Ursinis comitem Talliacotii actorem ex alia partibus, in curia capitolii, in possessorio de et super castro Numentane districtus urbis et eius occasione, et a quodam pretenso gravamine pro parte dicte comitis, ad egregium legum doctorem dominum Thomam de Virago judicem appellationum urbis appellato, et tandem per specialem commissionem, dicta causa appellationis, una cum negotio principali, venerabili viro domino Dominico de Sancto Geminiano auditori camere apostolice commissa, et ab eodem domina Thoma advocata, idem dominus Dominicus taliter qualiter procedens diffinitivam sentenciam contra dictum Ursum pertulit, cum condempnacione fructuum et expensarum, a qua sentencia infra tempus debitum appellato, et sepissime per varios interpellationes requisitione facta, ut supradicta appellatione iudex daretur, ad huc tamen datus non extitit, et per consequens fuit justitia denegata. Cum autem, beatissime pater, solum hic una, et in possessorio lata sit sentencia, et appellationis remedium nemini sit auferendum, supplicatur e sanctitate vestra, quatenus alicui ex auditoribus causarum sacri palatii causam et causas predictas comictere dignemini, audiendas et fine debito terminandas, cum omnibus incidentibus dependentibus et connexis, actento quod idem Ursus contentus est ut ante omnia idem auditor videat si potuerit appellari, quibuscumque in contrarium facientibus non obstantibus.

De mandato domini nostri pape audiat magister Cunczo,[1] et iustitiam faciat.

Beatissime pater. Nuper commissio tenoris suprascripti dicto domino Cunczo presentata et eius vigore, pars domini comitis ad dicendum contra commissionem citata exititit, crediturque quod pars adversa primum terminum servaverit, in contumaciam partis dicti comitis fuitque inhibitio decreta et etiam exequeta, eius quoque vigore inhibitum venerabili viro domino collaterali curie capitolii, coram quo pro parte dicte comitis petitum fuit pronunptiari sententiam predictam fore exequendam, prout de iure creditur fieri debere, actento quod de iure civili a sententia momentanee possessionis appellari non potest, vel si possit, appellatio executionem sententie non suspendit, et ius civile secundum statuta capitolii in foro illo servandum est, ac etiam actento quia secundum statuta capitolii a sententia iudicis appellationum non est licitum appellari, et dictus dominus Dominicus, qui sententiam tulit, fuit datus per sanctitatem vestram, ex eo quod cum causa certe appellationis fuisset, coram iudice appellationum urbis introducta fuit pro parte dicti Ursi, idem iudex allegatus suspectus, et propterea sanctitas vestra voluit quod ut iudex appellationum procederet, servatis statutis urbis, et sic creditur intentionis sanctitatis vestre fuisse, a sententia dicti domini Dominici non potuisse appellari, nisi quatenus a sententia iudicis appellationum secundum statuta urbis appellari potuisset, quia alias per commissionem cause predicte, que, pretextu suspicionis, de iure non debuisset advocari a iudice ordinario, set potius alius associari, magnum preiudicium videretur factum dicto comiti, cum per appellationes causa trahi possit in longum, contra intentem statutorum, et, ut creditur, sanctitatis vestre. Supplicatur itaque sanctitati vestre, quatenus super premissis intentionem sanctitatis vestre declarantes, causam ad sanctitatem vestram advocari, et dicto domino collaterali, coram quo ad omnes actus necessarios processum est, et per advocatos in jure allegatum, et non restat nisi ad pronunptiationem venire, cum ante presentatione inhibitionis,[2] citationem ad audiendam sententiam decrevisset, commictere et mandare dignemini eius officium ordinarium excitando et cohadiuvando, ut si ex actitatis in causa huiusmodi sibi constet, a sententia huiusmodi, si fuisset per iudicem appellationum urbis promulgata, appellari non potuisse, aut etiam alias de iure civili a sententia super possessorio taliter lata appellari non potuisse, sive etiam appellationem non impedire executionem ipsius, ad pronunptiationem suam et totalem executionem sententie predicte procedat perinde, ac si de apostolica commissione et inhibitione predictis non constaret, cum potestate eidem domino Cunczo, et quibuscumque aliis iudicibus forsitan datis vel dandis, inhibendi ne de causa huiusmodi se ulterius intromictant, premissa commissione et deinde sequtis, et aliis commissionibus impetratis vel impetrandis et aliis non obstantibus quibuscumque.

De mandato domini nostri pape audiant primus et secundus collaterales, procedant et inhibeant ut petitur, cum consilio tamen assectamenti, premissis non obstantibus, et iustitiam faciant.

Text. Rome, Archivio Capitolino, Archivio di Casa Orsini; the text is given several times in the acts of the case, II.A.XIII, nos. 11, 12, 15, 17.

Var.R. 1. Cunczo. II.A.XIII, no. 15 has Conzo; the other MSS. have Cunczo. Both spellings of this name appear to have been in use. Conzo in Cerchiari, *Capellani papae et apostolicae sedis*, ii, 47, and so also *The Register of Henry Chichele*, ed. E. F. Jacob, iii, 185, 194. Cunczo in *Calendar of entries in the Papal Registers*, viii, 46, 104; in Finke, *Acta Concilii Constanciensis*, iii, 18 et passim; in Eubel, *Hierarchia Catholica*, i, 376 (Eubel gives 'Conradus' as an alternative). K. A. Fink, *Repertorium Germanicum*, iv, col. 555–6, gives 'Cuntzo'. He came from Zwolle in Holland, and was later Bishop of Olmütz.

2. inhibitionis   all MSS. have   inhibitionem

15 *The commune of Macerata appoints a proctor (whose name is left blank in the MS.) to represent the commune at the Parliament which the Vice-Legate is shortly to hold at Ancona. Macerata, 4 September 1418.*

In dei nomine amen. Anno eiusdem Mccccxviii, indictione xi, tempore sanctissimi in christo patris et domini domini Martini, divina providencia pape quinti, die iiii mensis Septembris, publico et generali consilio ac consilio credentie comunis et populi civitatis Macerate, de sero ut moris est pro mane bannito, et mandato viri nobilis Maxutii domini Santis de Fermo, honorabilis potestatis dicte civitatis Macerate, necnon prudentium virorum Ser Aldovranni Johannis Francisci Firmani Vanutii, Antonii Andree Cicchi, et Francisci Maxii, honorabilium ac magnificorum dominorum priorum dicte civitatis, ad sonum campane vocemque preconis, sono tube premisso, in sala palatii dicti comunis residentie solite dictorum dominorum priorum, sita in dicta civitate in quarterio Sancti Johannis iuxta platea comunis, vias et alia latum, convocato congregato et adunato in uno sufficienti et valido secundam formam statutorum et ordinamentorum dicte civitatis, in ipso consilio supradicti domini potestas et . . .[1] priores cum presentia consensu et voluntate consiliariorum dicti consilii ibi stantium ex una parte, et dictum consilium et consiliarii ipsius cum presentia consensu et voluntate dictorum dominorum potestatis et priorum, ex altera parte, invicem auctoritates non revocando aliquem eorum et dicti comunis nec gesta et facta per eum, sed potius ipsum et ea ratificando confirmando et approbando, omni modo via et forma que magis inclius et efficacius de iure fieri poterit, fecerunt constituerunt creaverunt et ordinaverunt eorum et dicti comunis sindicum procuratorem actorem factorem et nunptium specialem, vel si quo alio nomine melius et validius de iure censeri potest, virum providum . . .[2] absentem tamquam presentem et acceptum, et mandatum in se recipientem ad comparendum, et se nomine comunis et hominum dicte civitatis personaliter presentandum coram reverendissimo domino nostro domino Marino, dey gratia episcopo Maceraten' et Racanaten', ac vicelegato et cetera, in parlamento de proximo celebrando in civitate Ancone, et ipsi domino prestando, si opus erit, fidelitatis debitum sacramentum : ad promictendum obligandum et realiter observandum et adimplendum omnia et singula que pro statu ecclesie sacrosancte matris et domine nostre et dicti domini pape, necnon pro universali pace quieta[3] bono et commodo totius huius provincie Marchie et provincialium ipsius, et maxime ipsius civitatis, in ipso parlamento fuerint declarata obtenpta et reformata, et generaliter ad omnia alia et singula facienda gerenda et exercenda que ipsemet constituentes facere possent si personaliter interessent. Dantes et concedentes dicti constituentes eidem suo sindico et procuratori auctoritatem arbitrium potestatem et baiulam in predictis circa predicta et quodlibet predictorum, quod quam ipsi constituentes habent vel habere possent, promictentes ratum gratum et firmum habere tenere actendere et observare, et in nullo contrafacere vel venire aliqua ratione, vel de iure vel de facto, omnem id et totum quod per dictum eorum syndicum et procuratorem factum gestum et promissum fuerint, et non revocare iure aliquo vel quesito colore, relevantes quem ipsum eorum syndicum et procuratorem ab omni onere satisfactionis, et pro eo in omnem casum causam et eventum legitime fideiubentes. Que omnia et singula dicti constituentes promixerunt michi Paulo notario et cancellario . . .

Text. Macerata, Archivio Priorale, Riformanze, vol. ii, fol. 263v.
Var.R. 1. There is here a gap left in the MS, perhaps to indicate the names of the priors, which have just been given above.
2. The MS. again leaves a gap, for the name of the proctor.
3. quieta MS. quiete

16 *The commune of Macerata appoints two proctors, confirming all that they have already done and promised on behalf of the commune, at the provincial Parliament held at Macerata on 25 March 1425. Macerata, 29 March 1425.*

The two proctors are appointed [1] ad ratificandum omnia et singula que conclusa et facta essent in parlamento provincialium Marchie Anconitane, pro statu sancte matris ecclesie et pastoris eiusdem et provincialium predictorum, et similiter pro pacifico bono et tranquillo statu dicte civitatis Macerate, celebrato die xxv mensis Martii in civitate predicta, de mandato reverendissimi in Christo patris et domini, domini Petri de Columna, abbatis Rosacen', Marchie Anconitane pro sancta Romana ecclesia et sanctissimo domino nostro, domino Martino, divina providencia papa quinto, gubernatoris dignissimi, et ad ratificandum omnes et singulas eorum comparitiones et dicta per eos in dicto parlamento ante productione presentis ynstrumenti, nomine cuiuslibet; et generaliter tunc omnia alia et singula facienda gerenda et exercenda, quod in predictis circa predicta et quolibet predictorum fuerint utilia necessaria et opportuna, et que quilibet veri syndici et procuratores et ipsimet constituentes facere et exercere possent etiam si personaliter interessent. Dantes et concedentes dicti constituentes dictis eorum syndicis et procuratoribus liberum et generalem mandatum cum plena libera et generale administratione, promictentes ratum gratum et firmum habere attendere et observare omnem id et totum quod per dictos eorum syndicos et procuratores factum promissum et procuratum fuerit, et non revocare sub ypoteca et obligatione omnium bonorum dicti comunis presentium et futurum.

Text. Macerata, Archivio Priorale, Riformanze, vol. 13, fol. 149.

Note. 1. The first part of this document, which I have not here reproduced, is more or less the same as in Doc. 15 above.

17 *Domenico Capranica, Governor of Perugia, explains to Malatesta Baglioni the reasons for the arrest of Pier Filippo of Perugia. Montefalco, 10 January 1431.*

Malateste de Perusios. Magnifice vir, amice nostre carissime, salutem. Havemo riceputa vostra lettera soural facto de pierophilippo, il quale come screveti, non senza gravi casone et rasone havemo sostenuto qua, et non senza grandissimo nostro dispiacere, per che la condictione nostra e de fare rincrescimento al mancho che noy possiamo a qualunque persona. Ma noy faremo trare in scripti tutte quelle cose ha dicto de noy, et in vergogna del officio nostro, et siamo contento se manda a consiglio de savio, et che sene faza che vole la raxuni. Et se non fosse per che e partesano del stato vostro, come scriveti, noy haverissimo facta altra rasuni summaria de luy. Et fra le altre cose habe a dire de noy, queste parole : Facimo al pezo che poy (*sic*) luy et le mosche de zenaro, et oltra di questo have a dire : luy ce ha promesso, cosa in su la soa maledetta fede, se fede e, in parte che non ce vole attendere, et molte altre cose. A noy non ce pare haviere facto per fino a mo cosa alchuna per liquale meritassimo che ce fosse dicta villania, ni anche non habiemo manchato la fede nostra, et cosi havemo speranza di fare per lo advenire, et siamo certi che a noy, et ad ongni persona da bene, dispiace che si sia dicto villania, nonlo meritando. Per vostro amore in quello che ce sia possibile laveremo per ricomandato. Ex Montefalcone, xᵃ Januarii 1431.

Text. Div. Cam. 12, fol. 58v.

18 *Domenico Capranica, Governor of Perugia, informs the* podestà *of Perugia that he is holding Pier Filippo of Perugia prisoner, while the charges against him are reduced into writing. (Montefalcone) 10 January 1431.*

Domino Petro Antonio. Egregie doctor, socie noster carissime. Ne nil obedientia prodesse [1] videretur humilibus, si contemptus contumacibus non obesset, cum quedam sunt culpe in quibus culpa est relaxare vindictam ; ea propter Petrum Philippi de Perusio, qui in officio suo multa gravia contra officium nostrum commisit, ut a fidedignis personis sufficientes informationes habuimus, hic captum remanere duximus, et singula que adversus nos commisit in scriptis redigi faciemus, et vobis transmittemus ut omnibus ostendere possitis. Et in hoc ita mature et iustificate procedere intendimus, ut omnia, cum in scriptis redacta fuerint, contentemur consilio sapientis committi, ut fiat secundum quod iustitia persuaserit, et ita referre possitis [2] illis magistris prioribus et omnibus qui de hac materia vobiscum loquerentur.   Datum die xᵃ Januarii 1431.

> *Text.*   Div. Cam. 12, fol. 60.
> *Var.R.*   1. prodesse   MS.   prodesset
> 2. possitis   MS.   potestis

19 *Domenico Capranica, Governor of Perugia, justifies his action against Pier Filippo of Perugia to the priors of Perugia, alleging Pier Filippo's insolence and tyrannical behaviour.   Montefalco, 12 January 1431.*

Prioribus civitatis Perusii.   Magnifici viri amici carissimi, salutem etc.   Receptis litteris vestris super facto Petro Philippi, quemadmodum pridie per ambassiatores vestros intelligere potuistis, intuitu et complacentia magnificentie vestre, quantum in nobis erit in hac et in omni alia re quicquid fieri poterit id fiet libenter et iuxta posse, continuo delinquentes et non delinquentes recommissos habebimus.   Sed putamus sanctissimi domini nostri, sancte Romane ecclesie, et status civitatis vestre honori et commodo cedere, ut delinquentes castigentur, et maxime hi qui cervicem eorum ita erigunt, ut velint sua tyrannide ceteros opprimere, ut recte existimari potest de prefato Petro Philippi, qui annuatim centum homines illi status atque populo arrogantia sua effecit inimicos, qui cum sint predicti status benivoli, propter suam tyrannidem, voluissent celum corrumpere et quod totus terrarum orbis subverteretur, et nobiles et alii maiores civitatis calumpniantur qui nullam penitus culpam commiserunt.   Sed profecto nunquam successit sibi melior dies quam cum ab his qui sanctissimi domini nostri servitores sunt, apud nos recommissus extitit, quod nisi factum fuisset aliam penam substinuisset, necesse est enim cornua peccatorum confringi ut exaltentur cornua iusti, et talem rationem faciemus quod unusquisque poterit merito contentari.   Ex Montefalcone, xxi Januarii.

> *Text.*   Div. Cam. 12, fol. 62v.

20 *Domenico Capranica, Governor of Perugia, orders the* podestà *of Perugia to visit him to discuss the offences committed by Pier Filippo of Perugia.   He intends to have the latter tried publicly, to answer for the manner in which he has defamed the offices of the Governor and the priors.   Montefalcone, 12 January 1431.*

Domino Petro Antonio.   Socie carissime, velut aliis nostris litteris intelligere potuisti, tam accurate et mature procedere in facto Petri Philippi coram omni populo proposuimus, ut nichil propere aut non mature gestum quisquam arguere possit.   Quam ob rem volumus postquam peccatis nostris exigentibus illo venire non possumus, ut crastina die ad nos venias ut litteris et verbo, in tuo redditu qui festinus erit, magnificos priores ceterosque certiores de bene gestis prefati Petri reddere possis, nec eum intendimus ab aliis quam a Perusinis, et legibus et doctoribus condempnari ; quoniam etsi in re nostra omni etiam privata, consilium illius status plurium faceremus, tanto magis in hac, quam si non fallimus, popularem actionem nemo est qui nesciat. Cum ultra que specialissime nostrum officium concernere evidenter apparent, aliqua in verecundiam et iacturam prioratus commiserit, quem sanctissimus dominus noster vult et plusquam vult tueri, venerari, et tamquam pupillam oculi custodiri. Et vere, si non officium illud offendisset, nostram iniuriam, ut nostri moris est,[1] postergassemus; licet posuisset sedem ab aquilone, dicens cum diabolo ero similis altissimo,[2] et postquam displicuit fontis unda purissimi cenosos rivolos bibet. Sentiet inter cardinales et Januarii muscas differentiam cauda leporis maiorem. Informes te diligenter de conditione pestis, si alioquin reverti possemus. Ex Montefalcone, xii Januarii 1431.

In the margin. Dominus ipsemet edidit.
Text. Div. Cam. 12, fol. 59v.
Var.R. 1. iniuriam ut nostri moris est—in another hand, possibly that of Capranica himself, for iacturam cancelled.
    2. licet . . . altissimo—cf. Isaias, xiv. 13–14.

21 *Domenico Capranica, Governor of Perugia, orders the* podestà *of Perugia to try Pier Filippo of Perugia for the charges which have been formulated against him, notwithstanding the clause in the statutes which forbids the* podestà *to try the priors. Montefalco, 16 February 1431.*

Domino potestate Perusii. Magnifice miles amice nostre carissime, salutem. Cum Petrus Philippi de Perusio nonnullos excessus tempore officii sui prioratus commiserit, quod in duodecim capitulos in scriptis redigi fecimus, volumus et ita vobis tenore presentium committimus, ut adversus eum inquiratis secundum illa capitula, et processum formetis, non obstante aliquo statuto civitatis Perusii, et maximo illo, quo cavetur quod potestas capitaneus vel alius officialis qui tempore fuerit, de commissis per priores tempore officii sui cognoscere non possit. Volumus enim quod si tempore officii vestri executio fieri non possit, appareat saltem in actis curie vestre, pro informatione successoris vestri. Super qua re penitus dispensamus et ex nostra certa scientia etc., omnibus in contrariis facientibus derogamus. Ex Montefalcone, xvi Februarii 1431.

Text. Div. Cam. 12, fol. 67.

22 *Giovanni Vitelleschi, Bishop of Macerata and Recanati, and Governor of the March of Ancona, orders the commune of Macerata to send representatives to a Parliament which he is to hold at Recanati. San Severino, 29 November 1432.*

Magnificis amicis nostris carissimis, prioribus et comuni Macerate. J[ohannes], episcopus Maceraten' et Racanaten', gentium armorum ecclesie commisarius ac Marchie etc. gubernator. Magnifici amici nostri carissimi. Pro quibusdam urgentibus provincie necessitatibus, singularum communitatum oratores in uno loco habere deliberavimus. Quare vobis mandamus oratores vestros unum vel duos Racanaten' ad nos mittatis, qui ibidem sint die xii futuri mensis Decembris. Et tale mandatum illis faciatis, quod circa ea que tractabuntur concludenturque, ipsi sine alia relatione possint omnibus consentire. Ex Sancto Severino, xxviiii Novembris Mccccxxxii.

Text. Macerata, Archivio Priorale, Riformanze, vol. 15, fol. 225.

23 *The commune of Ascoli Piceno submits to Pietro Emigli, Governor of the March of Ancona. Mozano, 8 August 1426.*

In dei nomine amen. Infrascripta sunt capitula que comunitas et populus Esculi petit et supplicat humiliter eis concedi et fieri per sanctissimum dominum nostrum Martinum papam quintum, in casu quo eadem civitas redeat immediate ad gremium sancte matris ecclesie.

Inprimis, quod considerato quod cassera et fortillicia Esculi fuerint hactenus causa omnis mali et discipationis dicte civitatis Esculi, ut eadem civitas liberius gubernetur et manuteneatur sub fidelitate perpetua sancte matris ecclesie, dicta cassera et fortillicia penitus et funditus destruantur, et quod nullo unquam tempore reconstruantur, et similiter de castro castri Appongiani.

Remittimus in deliberatione et voluntate sanctissimi domini nostri. P[etrus] gubernator etc.

Secundo, quod in casu predicto, videlicet quod dicta civitas redeat ad gremium sancte matris ecclesie, omnia et singula delicta crimina et excessus actenus commissa et perpetrata et commissi et perpetrati per cives comitatenses et quoscumque districtuales civitatis Esculi vel comunitates dictorum locorum civitatis et comitatus et territorii et districtus remictantur et inteligantur esse remissa, tam cognita quam incognita, et nullo unquam tempore de predictis et quolibet predictorum possit procedi vel cognosci vel quolibet condepnari aut executio fieri per aliquos officiales ecclesie vel quoscumque alios directe vel indirecte.

Concessum ut petitur. P. gubernator etc.

Item quod officium ancianatus et confaleriorum et conciliariorum atque concilii generalis et ordinis et aliorum conciliariorum conserventur in eorum honore et iurisdictione, secundum quod solebat esse temporis felicis recordationis pape Urbani sexti, quo tempore populariter vivebatur et regebatur civitas Esculan'. Et quod dictum officium ancianatus, ultra salaria que solebant habere tempore popularis status, possit expendere de introitibus dictarum gabellarum vigintiquinque ducatos singulis duobus mensibus pro necessitatibus occurentibus in comuni tempore eorum officii.

Concessum ut officium ancianatus reguletur prout erat consuetum tempore ecclesie, scilicet Urbani. Et de xxv florenis ultra consuetum, sanctissimus dominus noster providebit oportune. P. gubernator etc.

Item quod cives comitatenses et inchole et habitantes, tum originarii tum advene, tam christiani quam judey, cum personis et rebus ipsorum sint salvi, et perpetuum salvum conductum habeant, et quod per gentes armigeras vel alias nullatenus molestentur vel agraventur.

Concessum ut petitur. P. gubernator.

Item quod potestati et vicepotestati et medicis et omnibus officialibus dicte civitatis et aliis conductis et maxime magistris scolarum et aliis creditoribus dicti comunis integre solvatur et satisfiat de introitibus dicte communitatis, et maxime de prestantiis et mutuis factis de mandato domini Obizonis et suorum officialium.

Concessum ut petitur. P. gubernator.

Item quod electiones potestatis et officialium appellationis et gabellarum et vialis et aliorum officialium de quibus statuta dicte civitatis locuntur, et etiam medicorum et magistrorum scolarum, spectent et pertineant et fieri possint et debeant per ancianos et concilia dicte civitatis, et quod per camerarios camere recipientes introytus comunis Esculi debeat eis solvi, et sportulas vel salaria de aliquibus commissionibus et cognitionibus recipere possint vel debeant, sub penis in statutis Esculi contentis.

Supplicabimus sanctissimo domino nostro ut civitas habeat intentum. Sed in iste principio volumus ponere officiales fidos. P. gubernator.

Item quod gabelle molendinorum et vini, quod mictitur per portas dicte civitatis, solvantur ordine et modo infrascriptis, videlicet quod pro quolibet centenario grani ad molendinum, solvantur duo soldi tantum, et quolibet salma vini ad portas, solvantur duo alii soldi tantum.

Concessum ut communitas sit in eo statu solvendi gabellas in quo erat tempore acquisitionis dominii per illos de Cararia. P. gubernator.

Item quod alie gabelle exigantur more solido sine aliqua augmentationis, et quod nulla alia gravimina collecte vel munera realia vel personalia imponi possit vel debeant civitati vel comitatu, aut personis vel rebus eorum in genere nec in specie, nec universitatibus vel specialibus personis eorumdem, vel habitantibus vel incholis aut advenis, aut etiam judeis.

Concessum ut non graventur ultra debitum. P. gubernator.

Item humiliter supplicant quod universitates et singulares persone comitatus et districtus dicte civitatis Escule non molestentur ultra tacchas consuetas. Et quod de gracia speciali exgraventur saltem per tres annos de omnibus quantitatibus dictarum taccharum. Et quod homines de Mozano dicti comitatus sint exempti per decem annos, maxime respectu dapnorum receptorum per ipsos.

Concessum ut non molestentur ultra consuetum, et quod homines de Mozano sint exempti per quinque annos. De exemptione vero civitatis remittimus sanctissimo domino nostro. P. gubernator.

Quod omnes captivi capti tempore presentis guerre per gentes ecclesie vel domini Jacobi Caudole, vel alios faventes dicte ecclesie et officiales suos,[1] tam equestres quam pedestres, relassentur sine aliqua solutione vel redemptione, amore dei et pietatis (*sic*) quam sancta mater ecclesia habere debet circha omnes tribulatos, et potissime quia non erant in eorum propria libertate.

Promittimus operari iuxta posse ut relaxentur. P. gubernator.

Item quod statuta et ordinamenta et reformationes civitatis Esculi facta et fienda serventur prout non obstarent predictis capitulis suprascriptis vel infrascribendis, prout reperiuntur in antiquis statutis civitatis Esculi.

Concessum ut statuta serventur, qui non sint contra libertatem ecclesie. P. gubernator.

Item omnes exemptiones et immunitates iuste concesse civibus esculanis vel comitatensibus per comunem civitatis Esculi manuteneantur eis et observentur, prout actenus manutente et observate fuerunt.

Concessum ut petitur. P. gubernator.

Item quod omnia et singula castra communitates et universitates hactenus possessa et possesse per comunem Esculi vel gubernatores eius, que actenus reverse essent ad manus officialium ecclesie Romane et separate a comitatu et districtu Esculi, restituentur sub iurisdictione comunis et populi civitatis Esculi.

Concessum de castris qui sunt de comitatu. P. gubernator.

Item quod omnes emptores vel conductores gabellarum dicte civitatis Esculi possint et debeant dictas gabellas fructare et retinere et exigere pro toto tempore ipsorum conductionis et emptionis, et quod pro dapnis per ipsos receptos occaxione presentis guerre fiat eis debita et iusta exgravatio pro rata, et quod si aliqua ipsorum solvissent aliquas quantitates [pecunie] pro dictis cabellis domino Obizoni vel suis officialibus admictantur eis, ac si solvissent officialibus ecclesie Romane vel domini nostri pape.

Concessum ut teneant, et de solutis Obizoni non molestentur. P. gubernator.

Item quod omnes et singules represalee concesse civibus vel comititativis Esculis habeant robur et observentur prout concesse sunt.

Providebimus quod cives habebunt debitum suum. P. gubernator.

Item quod omnibus et singulis qui actenus fuerunt anciani et qui nunc sunt, quibus non essent integre solutum de ipsorum salariis, solvatur per eum qui recipiet introhitus dicti comunis, prout recipere solebant et debebant.

Concessum de presentibus. P. gubernator.

Item quia occasione presentis guerre Linctius Angeli ebreus Esculi mutuavit comuni Esculi quatraginta ducatos, et pro securitate dicti Linctii, quia aliter mutuare nolebat, certi cives Esculi specialiter se obligaverunt per ynstrumentum depositi dicto Linctio, quod dicti cives conserventur indepnes pro dicta promissione et obligatione, et quod dicto Linctio satisfiat de introytibus comunis Esculi, et quod aliter dicti cives occaxione predicta molestari non debeant.

Providebimus quod Linctius remanebit contentus. P. gubernator.

Item quod expense in festivitate sancti Emidii et sancte Marie de mense Augusti et de mense Septembris fiant de introytibus predictis prout fieri consueverant (sic) tempore popularis status.

Concessum ut petitur. P. gubernator.

Item quod vicepotestas qui adpresens est Esculi et iudex gabellarum Esculi cum eorum officialibus et familia et eorum rebus sint salvi liberi et securi, stando et recedendo pro eorum libito voluntatis, et quod eis satisfiat de introitibus dicti comunis de eorum salario pro tempore quo steterunt et serviverunt usque in presentem diem, per deputandum ad recipiendeum introitum dicte civitatis.

Concessum ut petitur. P. gubernator.

Item quod omnes et singuli vicariatus comitatus et districtus Esculi sint et esse debeant notariorum matriculatorum civitatis Esculi, qui notarii debeant inbussulare et extrahi de bussula de semestre in semestre pro singulo vicariatu.

Concessum ut serventur ordo consueto temporis ecclesie. P. gubernator.

Item quod dicta civitas Esculi et eius comitatus et districtus nullo unquam tempore per sanctissimum dominum nostrum Martinum papam quintum et eius apostolicos successores alienetur vel quolibet tradatur aliquo domino temporali, ad hoc ut ipsa civitas et eius comitatus et districtus valeat perpetuo regi et gubernari sub fidelitate sancte matris ecclesie Romane.

Remittimus sanctissimo domino pape. P. gubernator.

Item quod tubbatores seu tubicines et pifari necessarii et tamorinus in dicta civitate Esculi pro honore officii ancianatus debeant retineri et manuteneri perpetuo, cum salario competente eis dando per deputandum ad recipiendum introytum dicte civitatis et comitatus.

Concessum ut servetur ordo consuetus tempore ecclesie. P. gubernator.

Item quod in portu Esculi deputentur et manuteneantur castellanus et vicarius qui sint cives Esculani, et quod de eis solvatur et satisfiat de salario competenti de dictis introytibus per deputandum ad recipiendum dictos introytus dicte communitatis Esculi modo consueto, et hoc ut mercantie merchatorum civitatis Esculi et quorumcumque illuc applicantium liberius et tutius conserventur et custodiantur.

Concessum ut petitur. P. gubernator.

Anno domini millesimo quadragintesimo vigesimo sexto, indictione quarta, die octavo mensis Augusti, presentata fuerunt suprascripta capitula per oratores comunitatis Esculane reverendo patri domino . . .[2] gubernatori prescripto, in villa Mozani in quam tunc idem dominus . . .[2] moram trahebat. Qui illa modo qui supra patet in singulorum capitulorum subscriptionibus obsignavit. Mandans michi notario infrascripto ut hic me subscribam cum solito mei sigilli appositione.

Ego igitur Odoardus Jacobi Bergognini civis Astensis, publicus imperiali auctoritate notarius, eiusdem reverendi patris domini . . .[2] gubernatori ssecretarius, iussu eiusdem, hic me subscripsi signum quod meum consuetum apposui pro maiori fide testimonio premissorum.

[notary's sign]

Text. 1. Original, parchment, 42 × 54 cm. Ascoli, Archivio storico comunale, Pergamene, N, fasc. 1, no. 3.

2. Ibid., contemporary copy on parchment, N, fasc. 1, no. 9.

Seal. Since removed, but traces remain at the foot of the document.

Var.R. 1. officiales suos MS. officialibus suis

2. A gap is left in the MS. instead of the name of the Governor.

Q

24 *Antonio Casini, Apostolic Treasurer, and Rector-General in Narni, Terni, Orvieto and certain other territories, is commissioned by the Pope to receive these lands on behalf of the Holy See, from Braccio of Montone, in consequence of certain agreements made between Braccio and the Pope. Florence, 22 May 1419.*

Martinus etc., venerabili fratri Anthonio episcopo Senen', thesaurario nostro, ac in Narnien' Urbevetan' et Interamnen' civitatibus et terra Utricoli, ac nonnullis aliis terris et earum fortiliciis castris locis comitatibus territoriis et districtibus pro nobis et Romana ecclesia in temporalibus rectori generali, salutem etc.   Adhibite per te circha magna et ardua Romane ecclesie et eius camere apostolice tibi commissa negocia fidelitas et diligencia laude digne, rationabiliter suggerunt menti nostre ut alia fraternitati tue fiducialiter committamus.   Cum itaque dilectus filius nobilis vir Brachius de Fortebrachiis comes Montoni, Narnien' Urbevetan' et Interamnen' civitates, ac terras Utricoli Miliani [1] Colliscipionis Calvi ac certa alia loca cum arcibus fortiliciis comitatibusque terris locis et villis districtibus iuribus et pertinentiis eorumdem ac cuiuslibet ipsorum, ad nos et Romanam ecclesiam pleno iure spectantibus, nobis et dicte ecclesie infra certum tempus proximo futurum sub certis modis formis et condicionibus tradere et realiter consignare teneatur, ut in certis super hoc initis capitulis plenius continetur ; nos de tue fraternitatis circumspectione, et in hiis et maioribus plene confidentes, eidem fraternitati cives [et] terras Utricoli Miliani [1] Colliscipionis et Calvi, castra villas comitatus loca arces predicta, et alia fortilicia cum eorum territoriis districtibus iuribus et pertinentiis eorumdem, ac arnesiis furnimentis et munimentis et aliis provisionibus in eis existentibus et quolibet predictorum, a prefato Brachio vel alio seu aliis ab eo deputatis seu deputandis nostro et Romane ecclesie nomine recipiendi acceptandi et habendi, et in illis intrandi standi et morandi, ac illa et quodlibet eorumdem regendi et gubernandi iuxta tui rectoratus officii potestatem, et alias prout expediens tibi visum fuerit, ac in eis et eorum quolibet rectores gubernatores castellanos custodes et alias officiales de quibus tibi videbitur, cum salariis stipendiis et provisionibus dicto nomine ponendi instituendi et destituendi quotiens tibi placuerit, fidelitatis et quidlibet aliud juramentum in predictis et quodlibet eorum et aliis de quibus oportuerit recipiendi, dictumque Brachium vel eius deputatum vel deputandum et alias quoslibet de hiis que receperis dumtaxat quittandi liberandi et absolvendi, pactumque de ulterius non petendo faciendi, litterasque et instrumenta quelibet necessaria et oportuna, cum obligationibus renunciationibus [2] et aliis clausulis consuetis et necessariis dandi et concedendi, ceteraque alia omnia et singula in premissis et quolibet ipsorum necessaria et oportuna faciendi gerendi mandandi et exercendi, fierique faciendi et mandandi, ac contradictores quislibet et rebelles per censuram ecclesiasticam et alia juris remedia oportuna compellendi et cohercendi, plenam et liberam concedimus auctoritate apostolica tenore presentium potestatem, ratum et gratum habituri quicquid per fraternitatem tuam actum extiterit in premissis et quolibet eorum, idque faciemus auctore domino usque ad satisfactionem condignam inviolabiliter observari.   Datum Florentie xi kalendas Junii pontificatus nostri anno secundo.

Text.   Reg. Vat. 348, fol. 120.
Var.R.   1. MS. Miliani, but *rectius* Maliani
2. obligationibus renunciationibus   MS.   obligationis renunciationis

25 *Martin V relates the offences of Braccio of Montone, excommunicates him, and places his lands under interdict.   Florence, 8 August 1419.*

Martinus episcopus servus servorum dei, ad perpetuam rei memoriam.   Rex regum et exercituum dominus clementissimus unigenitus dei filius Jhesus Christus, qui sempiternus regnans in celis perpetua mundum ratione gubernat, quamquam sit fortis et patiens ac misericordiarum pater et opifex est tamen judex iustus longaminis et dominus ulciscens, et quo punitionem benignius differt, eo [1] punit acerbius dies suos in detestandis et obstinatis malignantibus perducentes.   Nos itaque superna clementia in specula militantis ecclesie constituti, cui divine sapientie inscrutabilis altitudo dispositione incommutabili precipuum super terras ac illarum potestatum contulit magistratum, actendentes quod nuper facti notorietate referente a [2] dilecto filio magistro Johanne de Scribanis fisci nostri procuratore in generali consistorio per dilectum filium magistrum Augustinum de Lente [3] legum doctorem, eiusdem fisci et consistorii apostolici advocatum, nuntiante ad nostram perducto audientiam,[4] quod iniquitatis alumpnus Braccius de Fortebracciis, domicellus Perusinus, dicte ecclesie vasallus, etiam contra proprium juramentum per ipsum dudum eidem ecclesie prestitum, more tirannico ac predonico, non advertens varios et diversos processus dudum per felicis recordationis Bonifatium viii et Johannem xxii Clementem vi et nonnullos alios Romanos pontifices predecessores nostros, et nos in cena domini, adversus et persequentes sancte Romane ecclesie cardinales, necnon usurpatores invasores detentores et turbatores alme urbis, Marchie Anconitane, ducatus Spoletan', Patrimonii beati Petri in Tussia (*sic*), Romandiole, Campanie et Maritime provinciarum, Bononien' et Urbevetan' civitatum terrarum castrorum villarum et aliorum quorumcumque locorum et iurium Romane ecclesie quomodolibet subiectorum aut alicuius eorum, seu occupantibus detentoribus et turbatoribus dantes auxilium consilium vel favorem, ipsorum quoque filios et nepotes, etiam si huiusmodi invasores persecutores occupatores detentores et turbatores imperiali regali vel pontificali aut alias qualitercumque ecclesiastica vel mundana perfulgerent dignitate, excommunicationis anathematis privationis inhabilitationis prescriptionis et perpetue relegationis aliasque penas et sententias continentes, de fratrum suorum eiusdem Romane ecclesie cardinalium factos et promulgatos quos iidem predecessores vim perpetuarum constitutionum de simili consilio [fol. 1v] habere decreverunt, Perusin' primo et deinde Tudertin' Narnien' Urbevetan' etiam de manibus dilecti filii nostri Jacobi Sancti Eustachii ipsius ecclesie diaconi cardinalis, in partibus illis, ac alma urbe pro tunc apostolice sedis legati et vicarii generalis, in cuius dictione ipse Tudertin' Narnien' et Urbevetan' existebant, ac Interamnen' civitates, Roccham Contratam, Exium cum suis comitatibus et districtibus, terras Arnulphorum et specialis commissionis ad eandem ecclesiam pertinentes usurpaverat, ac vi et de

facto habuerat et receperat. Et insuper talleas in Marchia Anconitana pro defensione provincie alioquin imponi solitas, ab incolis et habitatoribus eiusdem Marchie
per vim et etiam de facto, sine aliqua assignatione saltem legitima, de eis sibi facta,
extorserat, ac hiis non contentus, sed ut insatiabili quadam vorragine almam urbem
invaserat, ipsamque ceperat, excepto castello sancti Angeli, ad quod idem cardinalis,
ipsius Bracchii adventum presentiens, eiusque intentionis non ignarus, cum diversa
cum eo habuisset colloquia, ipsiusque merito sevitiam et potentiam formidans,
cum quibusdam suis familiaribus et servitoribus, necnon [5] pluribus aliis pro sue et
aliarum tutela personarum confugerat, et in quo idem Braccius, predictas et alias
penas et sententias non verens, nec in tantum sacrilegii genus incidere abhorrens,
cardinalem ipsum tunc legatum a die xvi mensis Junii anno domini millesimi
quadragintesimi decimiseptimi usque ad diem xxvi Augusti eiusdem anni obsederat,
ipsumque castrum cum gentibus armigeris balistis trabocchiis machinis ingeniis
aliisque pluribus armorum generibus plures insultus faciendis, durius quo poterat
invadendo, hostiliter impugnaverat barilia piscium putredissimorum et [fol. 2r]
aliarum imunditiarum quas os humanum nominare abhorret plenam intra castrum
ipsum, cum eisdem ingeniis proiciendo, et alias fecerat quicquid poterat pro captione
dicti cardinalis et suorum ac aliorum in dicto castro existentium, et taliter se
gesserat quod nisi dilectus filius nobilis vir Sffortia comes Cotignole, tunc capitaneus
nonnullarum gentium armigerarum in regno Sicilie militantium, nunc vero Romane
ecclesie confalonerius, de Neapoli veniendo dicto cardinali succurrisset, ac ipsi
Braccio in virtute sua obstitisset, cardinalem et castrum huiusmodi cum omnibus in
eodem, ut verisimiliter creditur, cum ad hoc omnes eius traderentur conatus, cepisset.

Et nichilominus, postquam ad hanc civitatem applicueramus, et concordie
tractatus aliquos antea cum eodem habueramus, Assisinat' et Spoletan' civitates
nostras cum pluribus castris et villis ceperat et usurpaverat, ac arcem Spoletan'
obsederat, et multa alia crimina et excessus contra nos et eandem ecclesiam commiserat, licet nobis tunc contra eundem Braccium suosque complices et fautores
propter commissa, que notoria existebant, procedere potuissemus, ac tamen volentes
in premissis ut pius pater mite agere, erga eundem in Mantua et postmodum hic
gratiose per licteras et nostros diversos nunptios, etiam magne auctoritatis et
excellentie viros, requiri patenter et exortari feceramus, ut civitates terras arces
rocchas fortillicia aliaque predicta per ipsum ut prefertur usurpata, et que cum suis
comitatibus districtibus iuribus et pertinentiis in sue anime periculum detinebat
occupata, reddere et restituere vellet nobis, sibi aliqua ad certum tempus in regimine
et gubernatione sub certis pactis et condictionibus dimictere volentibus eandem (sic).
Cum ipse Braccius ad nostram et prefate ecclesie graciam devotionem et obbedientiam
venire velle se asseret, nonnullis prius et variis super hiis hincinde tractatibus habitis,
demum per Rogierum Nicolai civem Perusin' procuratorem et dilectum filium
nobilem virum Conradum de Trinciis domicellum Fulginat', tunc nunptios suos
credentes, eundem Braccium per ipsos tunc premissa conventa et iurata implecturum
[fol. 2v] eisdem procuratori et nunptiis in nostra presencia personaliter constitutis,
presentibus etiam venerabili fratri Jordano episcopo Albanen' et dilectis filiis nostris

Alamano tituli sancti Eusebii presbitero et Raynaldo sancti Viti in Macello diacono dicte ecclesie cardinalibus, et diversis aliis egregiis viris, benivolentiam et plenam exhibuimus audientiam. Et die decimanova mensis Maii proxime preterito, prefatus Rogierus procurator promiserat inter cetera et convenerat quod cum idem Braccius nostrum et dicte ecclesie, ut ipse Rogierus asserebat, pacificum et tranquillum desideraret statum, ipse nobis aut a nobis speciale mandatum habenti, Urbevetan' cum castris et locis comitatus eiusdem, ac Narnien' et Interamnen' civitates, cum earum rocchis fortallitiis comitatibus et districtibus, necnon Calvi Magliani Utricoli et Colliscipionis et nonnulla alia castra et fortallitia cum rocchis districtibus et per- tinentiis eorumdem, nuntio nostro infra unum mensem, rocchas necnon Narnien' infra viginti dies, necnon civitatem Spoletan'etiam sub certis modis et condictionibus, libere et integraliter traderet, ac ipsarum et cuiuslibet earum possessionem realem et corporalem liberam et vacuam expediret, quodque per se vel homines armorum aut alios subditos suos predictas aut alias quascumque civitates terras et subditos nostros et ecclesie predicte non offenderet invaderet aut quovis quesito colore iure ratione vel causa dapnificaret seu dapnificari permicteret, set in omnibus civitatibus terris castris locis aliisque dominiis que etiam suo regimini per concordiam huiusmodi dimicteremus, nobis nostrisque licteris et mandatis ac nostrorum officialium tam in spiritualibus quam temporalibus plenarie obediret, et quamplura alia in capitulo concordie publicoque super hoc confecto instrumento contenta observare et obervari facere promiserunt convenerunt et ab sancta dei evangelia juraverunt iidem Rogierius procurator dicti Braccii et Conradus propriis nominibus. Post hoc venerabilem fratrem Anthonium Senen' [6] episcopum, thesaurarium nostrum, cum potestate sufficienti predictas [fol. 3r] possessiones recipiendi, Bracciumque et alios suo nomine tradentes de ipsis quietandi absolvendi et liberandi, pro prefatis civitatibus castris locis rocchis comitatibus districtibus et pertinentiis eorumdem recipiendis, nuntium et procuratorem nostrum specialiter constitutum ad partes illas destina- veramus, et premissa omnia et alia [in] dictis capitulis contenta, tam per prefatos procuratores et nuntios ipsius Bracchii, quam dilectos filios Marcellum de Stroziis civem Florentinum, Antonium de Baldinotis legum doctores et magistrum Angelum de Reate secretarium et nuntios nostros eidem Braccio notificata et intimata fuissent, ac ipse Braccius per Marcellum Anthonium et Angelum prefatos nomine [7] pape requisitus extitisset, ut iuxta per eius procuratorem et nuntios capitula conventa et promissa jurata, civitates castra loca terras comitatus et districtus cum iuribus et pertinentiis eorumdem prefato nostro thesaurario et nuntio nostro tradere reddere et assignare, ac libere et vacue expedire, ac alia ad quas iuxta tenorem et continentiam dictorum capitulorum tenebatur facere et adimplere vellet.

Cum nos ea que venerabilis frater Ludovicus episcopus Magalonen' noster vicecamerarius in eisdem capitulis promiserat omnino exsequi vellemus, idem tamen Braccius suo more aspidis aures obturans, id efficere minime curaverat neque cura- bat. Quinymo contra nos et dictam ecclesiam ac subditos et adherentes nostros etiam Bracchius prefate concordie foederibus hostilis converterat impetus Montis- flaschonis occupando, ac Viterbien', civitates nostras proposse obsidiendo, arcemque

Spoletan' strictius impugnando, Sffortiam comitem predictum, quamvis ipse per medium Antonii predicti eidem Braccio omnes de ipsum et suos offendendo securitatem daret, secundum quod in pace cum eo esse volebat, suum filium ob id etiam in obsidem tradere offerendo, hostiliter invadendo; gentesque ipsius Sffortie ac alia ad nostra et ipsius ecclesie servitia militantes ac nostros alios subditos capiendo, et ab eis magnas pecuniarum summas extorquendo [fol. 3v] dictisque carceribus mancipando, predicte urbis ac civitatis Tiburtin' territoria etiam hostiliter discurrendo et invadendo, gentes animalia et bona quemcumque capiendo et usurpando, aliasque multiplices invasiones cavalcatas gravissimasque, offensiones tam reales quam personales noctu dieque in Patrimonio et aliis terris districtibus et ditiis ad nos et ipsam ecclesiam pertinentiis, nobis et eidem ecclesie subditisque nostris intulerat et inferre dietim non desinebat, impios viros mittendo assidue, ultra alia civitates terras castra et loca que detinuerat prout et detinebat contra nos et ipsam ecclesiam occupata, alia civitates terras castra et loca usurpare invadere et occupare, multaque alia varia crimina excessus et iniurias contra nos et eandem ecclesiam intulerat et commiserat et commictere non formidabat contra deum et justiciam, penas et sentencias in prefatis dictorum nostrorum predecessorum et nostris processibus contentas damnabiliter incurrendo et damnabilius sustinendo, in cuius autem suorumque complicum et fautorum grave periculum, divineque majestatis offensam, nostrum et prefate ecclesie grande preiudicium et scandalum plurimorum, ex quibus truculentissimis sceleribus [8] quamplurimum hominum strages, agrorum depopulationes, civitatum terrarum locorum ecclesiarum monasteriorum devastaciones, excidia rapine spolia odia incendia et devoluciones, et innumerabilium nostrorum et eidem ecclesie subditorum et adherentium infinita dispendia fuerant sequita, ac dietim provenirent flebiliter maiora nisi salutari succureretur remedio infuturum preter, que augebamur interius, et dolebamus nostris non mediocriter afflictis subditis pie compatiendis.

Et quamvis premissa omnia et singula adeo forent notoria, quod nulla possent tergiversatione celari, nosque absque alia informatione iuste potuissemus animadvertere in Braccium, complices et fautores predictos : attamen ex habundanti et ad maiorem certitudinem premissorum venerabili fratri [fol. 4r] Antonio Portuen' episcopo et dilectis filiis nostris Petro tituli sancti Stephani in Celiomonte [presbytero] et Alphonso sancti Eustachii sancte Romane ecclesie diacono cardinalibus in generali consistorio commisimus oraculo vive vocis, ut se de premissis summarie informarent, et [ea] quod per informationem huiusmodi reperirent nobis referre curarent, qui huiusmodi informatione per eos recepta nobis in consistorio retulerint, se reperisse premissa fuisse et esse vera notoria atque manifesta. Idcircha nos actendentes quod error cui non resistitur approbari videtur, et latum pandit delinquentibus additum, qui perversis eorum conatibus non resistit, ac nolentes [9] sicut nec velle debebamus nos qui alias iniusticias confoveremus iura Romane ecclesie sponse nostre negligere, nec tot et tam notorios excessus sub dissimulacione oculis convenientibus pertransire, versus eos absque gravi offensa Christi et nostre conscientie remorsu amplius tollerare nequiremus, adversus eosdem Braccium complices [et] fautores, de fratrum nostrorum consilio, in virtute altissimi exurgendos duximus iusticia mediante. Quapropter Braccium complices et fautores predictos etiam in consistorio generali, presente fidelium multitudine copiosa, huiusmodi citandi formam excommunicationis [ex certis] causis elegimus, per nostras certi tenoris litteras citavimus, ut die quintadecima a dato ipsarum litterarum computando, si ea die consistorium generalem foret, alioquin prima [die] extunc immediate sequenti, qua per nos consistorium huiusmodi teneri contingeret, hora consistoriali compareant personaliter coram nobis ubicumque tunc cum nostra curia resideremus, visuri et audituri per nos decerni et declarari ipsos Braccium complices et fautores et eorum quemlibet propter premissa fuisse et esse sacrilegos excommunicatos reos criminis lese maiestatis conspiratos etiam contra nos et ecclesiam predictam, eundem etiam Braccium periurum, ac ipsum suosque complices et fautores propter premissa incidisse in penas et sententias supradictas et in alias talia perpetrantes tam a iure quam ab homine inflictas et promulgatas, ipsosque Braccium complices et fautores et quemlibet ipsorum fore privatos et per nos privari quibuscumque vicariatibus dignitatibus dominiis honoribus et gratiis et terris, necnon [fol. 4v] feudis retrofeudis bonis et iuribus que a nobis et dicta Romana et quibuslibet aliis ecclesiis aut personis ecclesiasticis seu Romano imperio et quibusvis aliis quocunque titulo obtinerent, ipsorumque Braccii complicum et servitorum bona omnia et iura fuisse et esse conficata et per nos confiscari; et nichilominus visuri et audituri per nos eis alias penas infligi prout iusticia suaderet aperte, predicentes eisdem quod sive venirent sive non, nos ea die ad declarationem et privationem ac inflictionem huiusmodi et alias prout justum foret procederemus, eorum absentia seu contumacia non obstante. Ceterum voluimus et auctoritate apostolica decrevimus, quod citatio electio assigna- tio et voluntas nostre et alia contenta in huiusmodi nostris litteris perinde valerent et robur obtinerent firmitatis, dictosque Braccium complices et fautores et alios quos contravenirent omnino arctarent, quacumque constitutione contraria non obstante, ac si eis intimata et confirmata personaliter et presencialiter extitissent, et ulterius eisdem Braccio complicibus et fautoribus de opportuno salvoconducto duximus providendo, prout in dictis nostris inde confectis litteris plenius continetur. Quas- quidem litteras ostiis sacri palatii causarum apostolici sive sancte Marie Novelle et maiorum Florentinarum ecclesiarum tribus diebus etiam ex superhabundanti affigi fecimus, ne iidem Braccius complices et fautores quod ad ipsas non pervenissent vel eandem citationem ignorassent, nulla possent excusationem pretendere vel ignorantiam allegare, cum non esset verissimile quod ad eos remaneret incognitum, quod tam patenter omnibus publicabatur.

Adveniente igitur predicta quintadecima die videlicet hodierna, nobisque cum dictis fratribus nostris in consistorio generali existentibus et protribuna sedentibus, predictus procurator per organum prefati advocati predictorum Braccii complicum et fautorum citatorum et non comparentium contumaciam accusavit, et petiit ipsos per nos contumaces reputari ac descrivi, et declarari ipsos Braccium complices et fautores fuisse et esse sacrilegos excommunicatos anathematizatos reosque criminis lese maiestatis, ac conspiratores contra nos et [fol. 5r] eandem ecclesiam, ipsumque

Braccium periurum, ac cum suis complicibus et fautoribus in penas et sentencias in processibus dictorum predecessorum nostrorum atque nostras contentas, et alia propter premissa a iure vel a homine in talia perpetrantes inflicta et quomodolibet promulgata incidisse, et alias penas per nos infligi et contra ipsos procedi, iuxta termini assignationem prout iusticia suaderet, propter quos nos etiam ad maiorem contumacie iudicium, dilectis filiis nostris Carolo sancti Georgii et Lucido sancte Marie in Cosmedin etiam diaconis dicte Romane ecclesie cardinalibus dicto oraculo mandavimus ut ad portas palatii predictas accederent, et ibi per se seu alios publice et alta voce clamarent et clamari facerent, ut si predictus Braccius complices et servitores vel alius seu alii ibidem pro eisdem existerent, dictum palatium intrarent audituri et recepturi quod iure foret in premissis; ac demum dicti cardinales, ad nos redeuntes, per organum ipsius Caroli retulerunt se ad predictas portas accessisse, et ibidem clamasse et clamari fecisse prout mandaveramus, ad [10] quemdam Johannem de Monthone ibidem existentem, dicens se pro dicto Braccio comparere, vel qui (*sic*) ad presentiam nostram veniens asservit et allegavit, tam per suam quam prefati Rogerii organum, dicto Braccio non fuisse securitatem ad presentiam nostram accedendi, ex eo quod a dilectis filiis populo civitatis Florentin' salvumconductum non habuerat, et quod dictus Sfortia et dilectus filius nobilis vir Guidanthonius comes Montisfereti guerram eidem Braccio inferrent, qui a nobis interrogatus si ab ipso Braccio mandatum haberent, illud exhiberent recepturi inde quod iuris foret et racionis, respondit idem Johannes se mandatum in publicam formam non habere, sed per quemdam scriptorem [11] existentem quem asserebat tabellionem publicum de mandato rogatum in publicam formam redigi faceret. Cui et dicto Rogerio diximus quod si saltem [fol. 5v] habebant extensam notam, quod illam legi per eundem assertum tabellionem facerent, aut illam legendam ibidem exiberent, cum ipsum Braccium licet personalis foret citatio, et de talibus delictibus et criminibus ageretur quod quis per procuratorem admicti non deberet. Nichilominus eundem eximia de gracia speciali et benignitate nostra solita auduissemus. Et ita cum dictis fratribus nostris deliberavimus si procuratorem mississet. Ipse autem Johannes modo predicto respondit notam non habere extensam, sed quod illam inibi scribi faceret, quibus dictus prefatus procurator per organum dicti advocati asserens verba predicta calupniosa et ad differenda maliciose prolata, cum dictus Johannes debuisset mandatum in publicam formam produxisse, iterato cum instantia petiit a nobis pronunptiari decerni et declarari ut supra.

Nos igitur attendentes premissa que frivola et frustratoria existunt, cum non appareat quod dictus populus Florentin' salvumconductum ipsi Braccio denegaverat, comesque predictus eidem guerram non faciat, quinpotius ipse Braccius dicto Sfortie, [12] prefatos Braccium complices et fautores minime comparentes, de dictorum fratrorum consilio reputavimus, prout sunt, merito contumaces. Unde nolentes prout nec debentes huiusmodi ipsorum Bracci complicum et fautorum crimina et excessus amplius tollerare, in ipsorum Braccii complicum et fautorum contumacia, de dictorum fratrorum consilio per hanc nostram diffinitivam sentenciam pronunptiamus decernimus et declaramus eosdem Braccium complices et servitores fuisse et esse excommunicatos sacrilegos, ipsumque Braccium periurum, eumque et dictos complices et fautores contra nos et eandem ecclesiam conspiratores ac reos criminis lese maiestatis, ipsosque propterea in penas et sentencias in dictis processibus contentas incidisse, ac eosdem Braccium complices et fautores omnibus dignitatibus vicariatibus dominiis honoribus officiis civitatibus terris locis feudis retrofeudis et bonis aliis et iuribus que a prefata Romana et quibuslibet aliis ecclesiis et ecclesiasticis personis Romanoque imperio ac regibus principibus [fol. 6r] vel aliis obtinuissent vel detinerent fuisse et esse privatos, ipsosque tales nuntiamus, ac ipsa bona mobilia et immobilia iura et iurisdictiones fuisse et esse confiscata, et personas eorumdem Braccii complicum et fautorum pronuntiamus et decernimus detestabiles et infames fuisse et esse, ipsasque exponendas fore, et exponimus a christifidelium capiendas, et nichilominus Perusin' Tudertin' Narnien' Urbeveteri et Interamnen' Esium Assisinat' et Spoletan' civitates, ac castra Magliani Utricoli Colliscipionis ac alia civitates castra villas terras et alia quecumque loca et dominia ad nos et eandem ecclesiam spectantia que ipse Braccius detinet et occupat ecclesiastico supponimus interdicto duraturo quamdiu illa detinebit et occupabit, et quia dignum est tam nephandarum ratione flagitiorum ulterius severitas amplius extendatur . . . [*a series of provisions for the application of the interdict and excommunication follows, more or less in the same terms as Theiner, iii, no. 57, at pp. 109–110*] . . . [fol. 8r] . . . Datum Florentie vi idus Augusti pontificatus nostri anno secundo.

Text. Macerata, Archivio Priorale, Busta B, no. 7.

Var.R. 1. differt, eo MS. desfert et

2. a MS. et

3. de Lente *rectius* de Lante. He was sworn in for this office on 26 January 1418 by Louis Aleman the Vice-Chamberlain, Cod. Vat. lat. 8502, fol. 12.

4. ad nostram perducto audientiam MS. ad nostrum perducto auditum

5. necnon MS. non

6. Senen' MS. Conen'

7. nomine MS. nostri

8. sceleribus MS. sceleratibus

9. nolentes MS. volentes

10. mandaveramus, ad quemdam—there seems to be a missing phrase here.

11. MS. s̄c̄m̄ scriptorem—or, equally well—scrinarium

12. Sfortie MS. Ex fortie

Note. This document is a contemporary copy, consisting of four paper sheets which have been folded to form eight folios, and loosely sewn together. The work of copying the document was shared by four scribes, who each took a sheet, so that scribe A wrote folios 1 and 8, scribe B folios 2 and 7, scribe C folios 3 and 6, and so on. To do this they must have copied exactly the foliation of the document from which the transcript was made. The writer of folios 1 and 8 was master Paolo, the chancellor of the commune of Macerata (cf. doc. 15 above).

26 *Jacopo of Siena is told to hand over the fortress of Spoleto to Jacopo, Bishop of Aquino, and is also told that if anything was paid him by the Apostolic Chamber by way* *of usury on the sum he had lent the Pope, he is absolved for the offence of usury, and may retain the money. Rome, St. Peter's, 12 February 1423.*

Dilecto filio nobili viro Jacobo quondam Marci militi domicello Senen', salutem etc. Commisimus venerabili fratri Jacobo episcopo Aquinat' ut arcem nostram Spoletan', quam pro certis per te nobis pecuniis mutuatis pro tui securitate de nostro beneplacito tenuisti et de presenti tenes, a te recipiat vel de quocunque alio per quem eam sibi feceris assignari, propterea fidelitatem tuam requirimus ut arcem ipsam eidem episcopo tradas et assignes vel tradi et assignari facias indilate. Nos enim pro dicta arce ipsi episcopo assignanda, eam nostro et Romane ecclesie nomine recepturo, te et heredes ac successores tuos predicto nomine quittandi et liberandi auctoritate nostra tenore presentium plenam et liberam concedimus facultatem. Et si quid pro summa pecunie nobis mutuate ultra sortem ratione interesse vel usure per cameram apostolicam fuit solutum, omnibus et singulis qui pro huiusmodi interesse aliquid receperunt liberaliter et gratiose remictimus per presentes tam a reatu, quam a restitucione taliter receptorum, auctoritate nostra absolventes eosdem de gratia speciali. Datum Rome apud sanctum Petrum, ii idus Februarii, pontificatus nostri anno sexto.

Text. 1. Reg. Vat. 354, fol. 185v.
2. Cod. Vat. Ottob. lat. 3014, fol. 49.
3. Arm. 39, vol. 7a, fol. 22v.
4. Arm. 39, vol. 6, fol. 123.
Ptd. Bandini, *La Rocca di Spoleto*, app. xiv. Cf. Fink, 'Politische Korrespondenz', no. 475.

27 *Bindo ae Tholomeis is absolved for his part in the quarrel which he had with the* podestà *and inhabitants of Spoleto. Rome, St. Peter's, 16 February 1423.*

Dilecto filio nobili viro Bindo de Tholomeis domicello Senen', salutem etc. Sedis apostolice benignitas delectatur in conservatione proprie caritatis et dubiarum imputacionum ac etiam certarum remissione culparum. Cum itaque sicut accepimus propter nonnullos actus qui a te dicuntur esse commissi in displacentiam et offensam nostram, et civitatis nostre Spoletan', dum illius arcis custodie prefuisti, precipue in dissencione atque discordia quam habuisti cum dilecto filio nobili viro potestate predicte nostre civitatis de mense Decembris [1] nuper elapsi, te indignationem nostram dubites incurrisse, quamvis asseras omni te culpa carere, et nichilominus ad cautelam humili corde desideres remissionem huiusmodi tibi imputatis per nostram graciam obtinere. [*He is therefore absolved for all acts committed against the* podestà *and inhabitants of Spoleto, and any process brought against him is suspended.*] Datum Rome apud sanctum Petrum, xiv kalendas Martii pontificatus nostri anno vi.

Text. 1. Reg. Vat. 354, fol. 185v.
2. Cod. Vat. Ottob. lat. 3014, fol. 48.
3. Arm. 39, vol. 6, fol. 121v.

Var.R. 1. Decembris—so Reg. Vat. 354. Both other texts have Septembris but Reg. Vat. 354 is the best MS., and in the absence of other evidence I have adopted its reading.

Note. Cf. Fink, 'Politische Korrespondenz', no. 478.

28 *Jacopo of Siena is informed that the money owed him on the security of the fortress of Spoleto will be repaid him through the commune of Siena, and is asked to co-operate in the restoral of the fortress to the Pope's representatives. Rome, St. Peter's, 4 February 1423.*

Dilecto filio nobili viro Jacobo quondam Marci militis domicello Senen'. Gratum valde fuit nobis illud tuum liberale servitium quod fecisti in concessione pecunie, pro qua ad tui securitatem arcis nostre Spoletan' custodiam et tenutam tibi fecimus assignari. Et cum te carum antea tuis virtutibus haberemus, hoc etiam servitio nos et Romanam ecclesiam obligasti, quod, ut nobis omni ex parte sit gratius et honorabilius tibi, velis in restitucione dicte arcis, et receptione pecunie tue sine aliquo damno tuo, cum tua solita liberalitate procedere, et differencias que videntur inesse circa modum rei perficiende referes et postponas, tibique persuadeas nos curam habere indemnitatis et securitatis tue. Et propterea pecuniam tibi debitam deliberavimus transmittere ad manus dilectorum filiorum priorum et capitanei populi et comunis Senen', ut arce nostra illi quem deputavimus assignata, sine mora per eos tibi debita pecunia persolvatur, quibus scribimus ut sua auctoritate provideant, ne ab aliis arrestetur, promittentes quod pro camera apostolica nullum arrestum fiet. Nam super hiis te sensimus dubitare. Preterea super expensis, si que in arce facte sunt per Bindum de Tholomeis, quem eius custodie prefecisti, ad quas rationabiliter teneamur, stabimus determinacioni illius civis, quem priores prefati ad hoc per nostras litteras requisiti duxerint transmittendum ad expensas ipsasi nspiciendas, simul cum magistro Bartholomeo de Pistorio familiari nostro, et illo, quem tuo nomine destinabis verum circa hec omni sine scrupulo concludenda. Utaris ea liberalitate animi quam possimus merito commendare. Datum Rome apud sanctum Petrum, sub anulo piscatoris, iv Februarii anno vi.

Text. 1. Arm. 39, vol. 7a, fol. 23.
2. Arm. 39, vol. 6, fol. 122v.
Ptd. Bandini, *La Rocca di Spoleto*, app. xv. Cf. Fink, 'Politische Korrespondenz', no. 474.

29 *Gabriel Condulmer, papal Legate in the March of Ancona, is ordered to treat the Count of Carrara as an ally of the Holy See, and to allow him to keep those lands which he conquers in war. Rome, St. Peter's, 29 April 1421.*

Dilecto filio Gabrieli tituli sancti Clementis presbytero cardinali, sedis apostolice legato, salutem etc. Cum dilectus filius nobilis vir comes de Carraria nostri et ecclesie Romane devotissimus existat, circumspectionem [tuam] requirimus ac paterne in domino exortamur, tibi harum serie iniungentes, quatenus illis quos dictus comes pro inimicis suis habet et reputat et contra quos guerram facit, ulla ex causa aut quovis quesito colore, consilium aut favorem minime impendis aut impacciastis. Quinimo volumus ut si huiusmodi guerra durante alique terre cuiuscumque jurisdictionis et domini existentes sub potestate prefati comitis devenerint, eundem minime molestans aut offendens eas terras ipsum retinere et gubernare permictas. Datum Rome apud sanctum Petrum, iii kalendas Maii, pontificatus nostri anno quarto.

Text. Reg. Vat. 353, fol. 176v.

LIST OF PRINCIPAL WORKS CONSULTED

I. PRINTED SOURCES

(i) *Collections of Documents*

Baumgarten, P. M.   Untersuchungen und Urkunden über die Camera Collegii Cardinalium für die Zeit von 1295 bis 1437.   1898.

Bzovius, A.   Continuatio Annalium Baronii.   Cologne, 1616–30.

Bullarum Romanum.   Editio Taurinen.   1857–72.

Caetani, G. (ed.).   Regesta Chartarum.   Regesto delle Pergamene dell'Archivio Caetani.   1925–32.

Calendar of entries in the Papal Registers relating to Great Britain and Ireland.   Papal Letters.   vii, viii (1906–9).   Ed. J. A. Twemlow.

Canestrini, G.   Documenti per servire alla storia della milizia italiana dal XIII sec. al XVI.   ASI, 1st ser., xv, 1851.

Capitoli del Comune di Firenze, ed. C. Guasti.   1864–93.

Colucci, G.   Antichità Picene.   Fermo, 1786–96.

Commissioni di Rinaldo degli Albizzi, ed. C. Guasti.   1867–73.

Coppi, A.   Documenti storici del medio evo relativi a Roma ed all'Agro Romano.   Dissertazioni della Pontificia Accademia Romana di Archeologia, 1st ser., xv, 1864.

Costituzioni Egidiane, ed. P. Sella.   1912.

Deutsche Reichstagsakten unter Kaiser Sigmund, ed. D. Kerler.   1878–87.

Fabre, P.   Un registre caméral du Cardinal Albornoz.   Mélanges, vii, 1887.

Fabretti, A.   Le biografie dei capitani venturieri dell'Umbria.   Note e documenti.   1842.

——   Documenti di storia Perugina.   1887–92.

Fantuzzi, M.   Monumenti Ravennati de' secoli di Mezzo.   1801–4.

Federici, V. (ed.).   Statuti della Provincia Romana (Fonti per la Storia d'Italia, 1930).

Fink, K. A.   Die politische Korrespondenz Martins V. nach den Brevenregistern.   QF, xxvi, 1935/6.

Finke, H.   Forschungen und Quellen zur Geschichte des Konstanzer Konzils.   1889.

——   Acta Concilii Constanciensis.   1896–1928.

Fumi, L.   Codice diplomatico della città di Orvieto.   1884.

——   Inventario e Spoglio dei Registri della Tesoreria Apostolica di Perugia e Umbria.   1901.

——   Inventario e Spoglio dei registri della Tesoreria Apostolica della Marca.   Le Marche, iv.   Fano, 1904.

——   Braccio a Roma.   Lettere di Braccio e del card.   Isolani raccolte e pubblicate da luigi fumi nelle nobilissime nozze di Margherita Bracci d'Orvieto con Fabio Sergadi-Biringucci di Siena.   Siena, 1877.

——, and E. Lazzareschi.   Il Carteggio di Paolo Guinigi (*is* vol. iii, pt. 1 *of the* Regesti *of the* R. Archivio di Stato in Lucca).

Göller, E.   Repertorium Germanicum, i.   1916.

——   Die Einnahmen der apostolischen Kammer unter Benedikt XII.   1920.

——   Die Einnahmen der apostolischen Kammer unter Johann XXII.   1910.

Guasti, C. Gli avanzi dell'Archivio di un pratese vescovo di Volterra. ASI, 4th ser., xiii, 1884.

Haller, J. Concilium Basiliense, i, 1896.

Kirsch, J. P. Die Rückkehr der Päpste von Avignon nach Rom. 1898.

Kühne, U. Repertorium Germanicum, iii. 1935.

Levi, G. Nuovi documenti sulla legazione del Cardinale Isolani in Roma. ASR, iii, 1880.

Liber Pontificalis, ed. L. Duchesne. 1892.

Lanciani, R. Il patrimonio della famiglia Colonna al tempo di Martino V. ASR, xx, 1897.

Lünig. Codex Italiae Diplomaticus. iv Frankfort, 1735.

Mabillon. Museum Italicum. Paris, 1687–9.

Malatesta, S. Statuti delle gabelle di Roma. 1885.

Mansi. Sacr. conciliorum nova et amplissima collectio. Venice, 1784.

Marri, G. C. I documenti commerciali del fondo diplomatico mediceo nell'Archivio di Stato di Firenze. 1951.

Martène, E., and Durand, U. Thesaurus novorum anecdotorum. Paris, 1717.

Minieri Riccio, C. Saggio di codice diplomatico, formato sulle antiche scritture dell'Archivio di Stato di Napoli. 1879.

Mohler, L. Die Einnahmen der apostolischen Kammer unter Klemens VI. 1931.

Monzani, C. Di Leonardo Bruni Aretino. ASI, 2nd ser., v, pt. 2, 1857.

Osio, L. Documenti diplomatici tratti degli archivi Milanesi. 1864–72.

Von Ottenthal, E. Die päpstlichen Kanzleiregeln von Johannes XXII. bis Nicolaus V. 1888.

Raynaldus, O. Annales ecclesiastici post Baronum. Lucca, 1747–56.

Re, C. Statuti della città di Roma del secolo XIV. 1883.

R. Archivio di Stato in Lucca. Regesti. iii, pts. 1 and 2. 1925–33.

Romano, G. Contributi alla storia della ricostituzione del Ducato Milanese sotto F. M. Visconti. ASL, 3rd ser., vi, 1896.

Schäfer, K. H. Deutsche Ritter und Edelknechte in Italien während des 14. Jahrhunderts. 1911–41.

—— Die Ausgaben der apostolischen Kammer unter den Päpsten Urban V. und Gregor XI. 1937.

Sella, P. Rationes Decimarum Italiae. Marchia (1950). Umbria (1952).

Tangl, M. Die päpstlichen Kanzleiordnungen von 1200–1500. 1894.

Tellenbach, G. Repertorium Germanicum, ii. 1933.

Theiner, A. Codex diplomaticus temporalis S. Sedis. 1861–2.

—— I due concilii generali di Lione del 1245 e di Costanza del 1414. 1861.

Vincke, J. Schriftstücke zum Pisaner Konzil. 1942.

—— Acta Concilii Pisani. RQ, xlvi, 1938.

Zonghi, A. Repertorio dell'antico archivio comunale di Fano. 1888.

(ii) *Chronicles and other literary sources*

Aliprando, Buonamente. Cronica, in Muratori, Antiquitates Italicae Medii Aevi, v.

Annales Estenses. Muratori, RRIISS, xviii.

Annales Forolivienses. Muratori, RRIISS, xxii, pt. 2.

Billii, A. Historia. Muratori, RRIISS, xix.

Biondo, Flavio. Italia Illustrata (*Italian trans.*). Venice, 1543.

—— Hist. ab inclinatione Romanorum (*or* Decades). Basel, 1569.

Bonincontri, L. Annales. Muratori, RRIISS, xxi.

Bracciolini, Poggio. Historiae de varietate fortunae. Paris, 1723.

Bruni, Leonardo Aretino. Epistolae. Florence, 1741.

——— Rerum suo tempore gestarum commentarius. Muratori, RRIISS, xix, pt. 3.

Buoninsegni, M. Piero. Historia fiorentina. Florence, 1581.

——— Storie della città di Firenze. 1637.

Campano, J. A. Braccii Perusini Vita et Gesta. Muratori, RRIISS, xix, pt. 4.

Cavalcanti. Istorie fiorentine, ed. Di Pino. 1944.

Cobelli, L. Cronache forlivesi, ed. G. Carducci and E. Frati. 1874.

Corpus Chronicorum Bononiensium. Muratori, RRIISS, xviii, pt. 1.

Cronache della città di Fermo, ed. De Minicis. 1870.

Cronache e Statuti della città di Viterbo, ed. Ciampi. 1872.

Cronica volgare di anonimo fiorentino. Muratori, RRIISS, xxvii, pt. 2.

Cronaca Bolognese di Piero di Mattiolo, ed. C. Ricci. 1883.

Chronicon fratris Hieronymi de forlivio. Muratori, RRIISS, xix, pt. 5.

Cronaca Sanese. Muratori, RRIISS, xv, pt. 6.

Cronaca Malatestiana del secolo XV. Muratori, RRIISS, xv, pt. 2.

Cronaca di Ser Guerriero di Gubbio. Muratori, RRIISS, xxi, pt. 4.

Dello Schiavo, Pietro. Diarium. Muratori, RRIISS, xxiv, pt. 5.

Delphini, Gentile. Diarium. Muratori, RRIISS, ed. vet., iii, pt. 2, 841–6.

De Tummulillis, A. Notabilia Temporum, ed. A. Corvisieri, 1890.

Dietrich of Niem. De vita et factis Constantiensibus Johannis Papae XXIII, *in* Von der Hardt, Rerum concilii oecumenici Constanciensis, ii, pt. 15. 1697.

——— De Scismate, ed. G. Erler. 1890.

——— Nemus Unionis. 1609.

Filelfo, F. Epistolae, Speyer, 1506.

Finke, H. Eine Papstchronik des XV. Jahrhunderts. RQ, iv, 1890.

Frati, L. Il 'Diario' di Cambio Cantelmi. ASI, 5th ser., xlviii, 1911.

Giaffri, Saba. Relazione. *In* ASR, v, 1882.

Graziani, Cronaca, ed. Fabretti. ASI, 1st ser., xvi, pt. 1, 1850.

Griffoni, Matteo. Memoriale historicum. Muratori, RRIISS, xviii, pt. 2.

Lazzaro, M. de' Bernabei. Croniche Anconitane, ed. Ciavarini, 1870.

Martinus de Alpartil. Chronica actitatorum temporibus domini Benedicti XIII, ed. Ehrle. 1906.

Minerbetti, *see* Cronica volgare di anonimo fiorentino.

Minuti, A. Vita di Muzio Attendolo Sforza, ed. G. B. Lambertenghi. Miscellanea di storia italiana edita per cura della Regia Deputazione di storia patria, vii, Turin, 1869.

Pedrino, Giovanno di Mº. Cronica, ed. Borghezio and Vattasio, 1929.

Piccolomini, A. S. De Viris Illustribus. *In* Bibliothek des literarischen Vereins in Stuttgart, i, 1843.

Pulka, Petrus de. Ed. F. Firnhaber. Petrus de Pulka, Abgesandter der Wiener Universität am Concilium zu Constanz, AKöG, xv, 1856.

Ristretto di fatti d'Italia e specialmente d'Urbino dal 1404 al 1444, ed. G. Baccini. Zibaldone, i, Florence, 1889.

Salviati, J. Cronica, o memorie. *In* Delizie degli eruditi Toscani, xviii.

Sanudo, M. Vite de' Duchi di Venezia, Muratori, RRIISS, xxii.

Simonetta. Rerum gestarum Francisci Sfortiae commentarii. Muratori, RRIISS, xxi, pt. 2.

Sozomenus. Chronicon. Muratori, RRIISS, xvi (ed. vet.) and xvi, pt. 1 (ed. alt.).

Zampolini, Paruccio. Annali di Spoleto. *In* Documenti storici inediti in sussidio allo studio delle memorie Umbre, ed. A. Sansi, i, 1879.

II. OTHER WORKS

Adami, F. De rebus in civitate Firmana gestis. 1592.

Ady, C. M. The Bentivoglio of Bologna. 1937.

Alfieri, V. L'amministrazione economica dell'antico comune di Perugia. BSU, ii, 1896.

Aloisi, U. Sulla formazione storica del liber constitutionum sancte matris ecclesie. AMSM, n.s., i–v, 1904–8.

Amettler y Vinyas, D. José. Alfonso V de Aragon en Italia y la Crisis Religiosa del Siglo XV. 1903.

Amiani, P. M. Memorie storiche della città di Fano. Fano, 1751.

Anzilotti, A. Cenni sulle finanze del Patrimonio di S. Pietro in Tuscia nel secolo XV. ASR, xlii, 1919.

Avicenna, O. Memorie della città di Cingoli. Iesi, 1644.

Bååth, L. M. L'Inventaire de la Chambre Apostolique de 1440. *In* Miscellanea Archivistica Angelo Mercati. 1952.

Baethgen, F. Quellen und Untersuchungen zur Geschichte der päpstlichen Hof- und Finanzverwaltung unter Bonifaz VIII. QF, xx, 1928/9.

Baix, F. La Chambre Apostolique et les 'libri annatarum' de Martin V. 1947.

—— Notes sur les clercs de la Chambre Apostolique. Bulletin de l'Institut historique belge de Rome, xxvii, 1952.

Baldassini, G. Memorie istoriche dell'antichissima e regia città di Jesi. Iesi, 1765.

Bandini, C. La Rocca di Spoleto. 1934.

Barraclough, G. Public notaries and the Papal Curia. 1934.

Battaglini, F. G. Della vita e de' fatti di Sigismondo Pandolfo Malatesta. (Rimini), 1794.

Bauer, C. Die Epochen der Papstfinanz. Historische Zeitschrift, cxxxviii, 1928.

—— Studi per la storia delle finanze papali. ASR, l, 1927.

Baumgarten, P. M. Oddo Potii de Varris de Genazzano. Historisches Jahrbuch, xxxi, 1910.

—— Von der apostolischen Kanzlei. 1908.

Beloch, K. J. Bevölkerungsgeschichte Italiens. 1937–9.

Benigni, T. San Ginesio illustrata con antiche lapidi, ed annedotti documenti. Fermo, 1795.

Benigni, U. Die Getreide Politik der Päpste. Berlin, n.d.

Berlière, U. Inventaire analytique des Diversa Cameralia des Archives Vaticanes au point de vue des anciens diocèses de Cambrai, Liège, Thérouanne et Tournai. 1906.

Besta, E. Storia di diritto italiano. Fonti, i, pt. 2. 1925.

Bock, F. Einführung in das Registerwesen des Avignonesischen Papsttums. QF, xxxi, 1941.

Bollea, L. C. Per l'edizione delle opere storiche di Lorenzo Bonincontri. Archivio Muratoriano, i, 1910.

Bonoli, P. Istorie della città di Forlì. Forlì, 1661.

Borgia, S. Memorie istoriche della pontificia città di Benevento. Rome, 1763–9.

Borgia, A. Istoria della chiesa, e città di Velletri. Nocera, 1723.

Bosdari, O. Il comune di Bologna alla fine del secolo XIV. AMDR, 4th ser., iv, 1914.

Briganti, F.   Città dominanti e comuni minori nel Medio Evo.   1906.

Brogi, T.   La Marsica antica, mediovale.   1900.

Brosch, M.   Geschichte des Kirchenstaates.   1880–2.

Calisse, C.   Gli usi civici nella provincia di Roma.   1906.

—— Storia di Civitavecchia.   1936.

—— Costituzione del Patrimonio di S. Pietro in Tuscia nel secolo XIV.   ASR, xv, 1892.

Campanani, S.   Tuscania e i suoi monumenti.   ii.   1856.

Cecchi, D.   Il Parlamento nella Marca di Ancona dal 1357 alla fine del secolo XVIII. Unpublished thesis, Biblioteca Comunale di Macerata.

Cerchiari, E.   Capellani papae et apostolicae sedis, auditores causarum sacri palatii apostolici seu sacra Romana Rota.   1921.

Cipolla, C.   Storia delle Signorie italiane.   1881.

Clementini.   Raccolto istorico della fondazione di Rimino.   Rimini, 1617.

Coppi, A.   Memorie Colonnesi.   1855.

Celani, E.   Le pergamene dell'Archivio Sforza-Cesarini.   ASR, xv, 1892.

Compagnoni, P.   Memorie istorico-critiche della chiesa e de' vescovi di Osimo.   Rome, 1782.

Compagnoni, P.   La Reggia Picena.   Macerata, 1661.

Contatore, A.   De Historia Terracinensi.   Rome, 1706.

Contelori, F.   Genealogia Familiae Comitum Romanorum.   1650.

—— Vita Martini V.   Rome, 1641.

Corsignani, P. A.   La Reggia Marsicana.   Naples, 1738.

Cusin, F.   Il confine orientale d'Italia.   1937.

Cutolo, A.   Re Ladislao d'Angiò-Durazzo.   1936.

Da Mosto, A.   Ordinamenti militari delle soldatesche dello Stato Romano dal 1430 al 1470.   QF, v, 1903.

Dasti, L.   Notizie storiche archeologiche di Tarquinia e Corneto.   1878.

De Boüard, A.   Le Régime politique et les institutions de Rome au Moyen Age.   1920.

De Cupis, C.   Regesto degli Orsini e dei Conti di Anguillara.   BDA, 3rd ser., i, 1910.

—— Delle vicende dell'agricoltura e della pastorizia nell'Agro Romano.   1911.

De Luca, Giovanni Battista, Cardinal.   Theatrum veritatis et iustitiae.   Rome, 1669–77.

De Töth, P.   Il beato cardinale Nicolò Albergati e i suoi tempi.   1935.

De Vergottini, G.   Ricerche sulle origini del vicariato apostolico, *in* Studi in onore di E. Besta, 1938.

—— Note per la storia del vicariato apostolico durante il secolo XIV, *in* Studi in onore di C. Calisse, 1940.

—— Il papato e la comitatinanza nello stato papale.   AMDR, n.s., iii, 1953.

Dieterle, K.   Die Stellung Neapels und der grossen italienischen Kommune zum Konstanzer Konzil.   RQ, xxix, 1915.

Dorio, D.   Istoria della famiglia Trinci.   Foligno, 1648.

Durandus, G.   (Speculator) Speculum Juris.   Venice, 1566.

Edler, F.   (Mrs. R. de Roover.)   Glossary of medieval terms of business.   Italian series.   1934.

Egidi, P.   Soriano nel Cimini e l'archivio suo.   ASR, xxvi, 1903.

Eitel, A.   Der Kirchenstaat unter Klemens V.   1907.

Ercole, F.   Dal Comune al Principato.   1929.

Ermini, F.   Gli ordinamenti politici e amministrativi nelle constitutiones Aegidianae.   Turin, 1894.

R

Ermini, G.   Guida bibliografica per lo studio del diritto comune pontificio.   1934.

—— I rettori provinciali dello Stato della Chiesa da Innocenzo III all'Albornoz.   RSDI, iv, 1931.

—— I giudici provinciali della Monarchia pontificia nel medio evo.   Studi Economico-Giuridici publicati per cura della facoltà di Giurisprudenza.   Cagliari, 1931.   Anno 18–19.

—— Caratteri della sovranità temporale dei papi nei secoli XIII e XIV.   ZSSRG, Kanon. Abt., xxxvii, 1938.

—— I parlamenti dello Stato della Chiesa dalle origini al periodo albornoziano.   1930.

—— La libertà comunale nello Stato della Chiesa.   First part in ASR, xlix, 1926 : second part, L'amministrazione della giustizia, published separately, Rome, 1927.

Eubel, K.   Series vicariorum Urbis.   a. 1200–1558.   RQ, viii, 1894.

—— Hierarchia Catholica Medii Aevi.   Editio altera.   i, 1913.

Falco, G.   I comuni della Campagna e della Marittima nel Medio Evo.   ASR, xlii, xlvii–ix. 1919 f.

—— Il comune di Velletri nel Medio Evo.   ASR, xxxvi, 1913.

Fantuzzi, G.   Notizie degli scrittori Bolognesi.   Bologna, 1781.

Faraglia, N. F.   Storia della Regina Giovanna II d'Angiò.   1904.

Fedele, P.   I capitoli di pace fra Re Ladislao e Giovanni XXIII.   ASPN, xxx, 1905.

—— Contributo alla storia economica di Roma, in Raccolta di scritti storici in onore del Prof. G. Romano.   1907.

Ferranti, P.   Memorie storiche della città di Amandola.   1891.

Ficker, J.   Forschungen zur Reichs- und Rechtsgeschichte Italiens.   1868–74.

Fink, K. A.   Martin V. und Aragon.   1938.

—— Martin V. und Bologna.   QF, xxiii, 1931/2.

—— König Sigismund und Aragon.   Deutsches Archiv, ii, 1938.

—— Das Vatikanische Archiv.   1951.

—— Die ältesten Breven und Brevenregister.   QF, xxv, 1933/4.

—— Dominicus Capranica als Legat in Perugia, 1430–1.   RQ, xxxix, 1931.

Fontanini, J.   De antiquitatibus Hortae.   Rome, 1723.

Fournier, P.   Les officialités au Moyen Age.   1880.

Franceschini, G.   Memorie ecclesiastiche di Urbino.   AMSM, 7th ser., v, 1950.

Fromme, L.   Die Wahl des Papstes Martin V.   RQ, x, 1896.

Fumi, L.   Il conte Guidantonio di Montefeltro e Città di Castello.   BSU, vi, 1900.

—— I Colonna contro Roma e Papa Eugenio IV nel 1431.   BSU, i, 1895.

Gentile, G. C.   Sopra gli Smeducci vicarii per Santa Chiesa in Sanseverino dal secolo XIV al XV.   Nozze Servanzi-Valentini.   Macerata, 1841.

Ghirardacci, C.   Della historia di Bologna.   Bologna, 1596.

Giusti, M.   I registri vaticani e le loro provenienze originarie, in Miscellanea Archivistica Angelo Mercati.   1952.

Göller, E.   Der Gerichtshof der päpstlichen Kammer und die Entstehung des Amtes des Procurator fiscalis im kirchlichen Prozessverfahren.   AKKR, xciv, 1914.

—— Die Constitution 'Ratio iuris' Johanns XXII. und die Camera apostolica.   RQ, xvi, 1902.

—— Zur Stellung des päpstl. Kamerars unter Clemens VII. (Gegenpapst).   AKKR, lxxxiii, 1903.

—— Aus der Camera apostolica der Schismapäpste.   RQ, xxxii, 1924.

—— Untersuchungen über das Inventar des Finanzarchivs der Renaissancepäpste (1447–1521).   In Miscellanea Francesco Ehrle, iv.   1924.

Göller, E.   Mitteilungen und Untersuchungen über das päpstliche Register- und Kanzlei-
wesen im 14. Jahrhundert.   QF, vi, 1904.
—— König Sigismunds Kirchenpolitik.   1902.
Gottlob, A.   Aus der Camera apostolica des 15. Jahrhunderts.   1889.
Gregorovius, F.   History of the city of Rome in the Middle Ages.   1900–2.
Grosse-Wietfeld, F.   Justizreform im Kirchenstaat in den ersten Jahren der Restauration,
1814–16.   1932.
Guerrieri, R.   Storia civile ed ecclesiastica del comune di Gualdo Tadino.   1933.
Guiraud, J.   L'Etat Pontifical après le Grand Schisme.   1896.
Hagemann, W.   Fabriano im Kampf zwischen Papsttum und Kaisertum bis 1272.   QF,
xxxi, 1941.
Heere, H.   Die Beziehungen König Sigismunds zu Italien, vom Herbst 1412 bis zu Herbst
1414.   QF, iv, 1901.
Hofmann, W. von.   Forschungen zur Geschichte der kurialen Behörden vom Schisma bis
zur Reformation.   1914.
Hollerbach, J.   Die gregorianische Partei, Sigismund und das Konstanzer Konzil.   RQ,
xxiii–iv, 1909–10.
Jansen, M.   Papst Bonifatius IX. und seine Beziehungen zur deutschen Kirche.   1904.
Jones, P. J.   The vicariate of the Malatesta of Rimini.   EHR, lxvii, 1952.
—— The Malatesta of Rimini.   Unpublished Ph.D. thesis.   1950.   Bodleian Library.
Kaltenbrunner, F.   Die Fragmente der ältesten Registra brevium im Vatikanischen Archive.
MIöG, vi, 1885.
Katterbach, B.   Referendarii utriusque signaturae.   1931.
Kirsch, J. P.   Die Finanzverwaltung des Kardinalkollegiums im XIII. und XIV. Jahr-
hundert.   1895.
Lang, G.   Studien zu den Brevenregistern und Brevenkonzepten des XV. Jahrhunderts
aus dem Vatikanischen Archiv.   1938.
Leonii.   Giovanni XXIII ed il comune di Todi.   ASI, 4th ser., iv, 1879.
Leopardi, M.   Series Rectorum Anconitanae Marchiae.   1824.
Lilii, C.   Dell'Historia di Camerino.   Macerata, 1649–52.
Lodolini, A.   L'Archivio di Stato in Roma e l'Archivio del Regno d'Italia.   1932.
Longhi.   Nicolò Piccinino in Bologna.   AMDR, 3rd ser., xxiv, 1906.
Marongiu, A.   L'Istituto parlamentare in Italia.   1949.
Mazzatinti, G., and others.   Gli Archivi della storia d'Italia.   1899–1915.
Menchetti, A.   Storia di un comune rurale della Marca Anconitana, Montalbodo oggi
Ostra.   1913–37.
Mercati, A.   Una fonte poco noto per la storia di Gregorio XII.   ASR, l, 1927.
Michaeli, M.   Memorie storiche della città di Rieti.   1897–9.
Miltenberger, F.   Das Itinerarium Martins V. von Constanz bis Rom.   MIöG, xv, 1894.
—— Versuch einer Neuordnung der päpstlichen Kammer in den ersten Regierungsjahren
Martin V.   RQ, viii, 1894.
Mitteis, L. von.   Curiale Eidregister.   MIöG, Erbgd. vi, 1901.
Mollat, G.   Contribution à l'histoire de l'administration judiciare de l'Eglise Romaine au
XIVᵉ siècle.   RHE, xxxii, 1936.
—— Contribution à l'histoire du Sacré Collège de Clément V à Eugène IV.   RHE, xlvi–
vii, 1951–2.
—— Les Papes d'Avignon.   1949.
Monaldeschi della Cervara.   Commentarii historici.   Venice, 1584.
Moroni, G.   Dizionario di erudizione storico-ecclesiastica da S. Pietro sino ai nostri giorni.
1840–1861.

Narducci, E.   Catalogus codicum manuscriptorum praeter graec. et orientales in bibliotheca Angelica olim coenobii S. Augustini de Urbe.   1893.

Natale, A.   La felice società dei balestrieri e dei pavesati a Roma e il governo dei banderesi
dal 1358 al 1408.   ASR, lxii, 1939.

Orlandelli.   Note di storia economica sulla signoria dei Bentivoglio.   AMDR, n.s., iii,
1953.

Ottenthal, E. von.   Römische Berichte IV : Bemerkungen über päpstliche Kameralregister des 15. Jahrhunderts.   MIöG, vi, 1885.

—— Die Bullenregister Martin V. und Eugen IV.   MIöG, Ergbd. i, 1885.

Palmieri, A.   Gli antichi vicariati nell'Appenino Bolognese.   AMDR, 3rd ser., xx, 1902.

Pardi, G.   Serie dei supremi magistrati e reggitori di Orvieto.   BSU, i, 1895.

Partner, P. D.   Camera Papae : problems of Papal Finance in the later Middle Ages.
JEccH, iv, 1953.

Pastor, L. von.   Geschichte der Päpste.   8/9 edn.   1926.   *English translation*, History
of the Popes, vol. i, 1923.

Pellegrini, A.   Gubbio sotto i conti e duchi di Urbino.   BSU, xi, 1905.

Pellini, P.   Dell'Historia di Perugia.   Venice, 1664.

Pérouse, G.   Le Cardinal Louis Aleman, Président du Concile de Bâle, et la fin du Grand
Schisme.   1904.

Peruzzi, A.   Storia d'Ancona dalla sua fondazione.   1835.

Petracchi, C.   Vita di M. Iacopo Isolani.   In Miscellanei di Varia Letteratura, i, Lucca,
1762.

Petrini, P. A.   Memorie Prenestine.   Rome, 1795.

Pieri, Piero.   Il Rinascimento e la crisi militare italiana.   1952.

Peto, Luca.   De iudiciaria formula Capitolini fori.   Rome, 1610.

Pinzi, L.   Storia della città di Viterbo.   1887–1913.

Presutti, G.   I Colonna di Riofreddo.   ASR, xxxv, 1912.

Pulignani, D. M. Faloci.   Il vicariato dei Trinci.   BSU, xviii, 1912.

Re, E.   Maestri di Strada.   ASR, xliii, 1920.

—— Il 'Tesoro' di Gregorio XII e la sua divisione.   AMSM, 3rd ser., i, 1916.

Redlich, O.   Die Privaturkunden des Mittelalters.   1911.

Ricotti, E.   Storia delle compagnie di ventura in Italia.   Re-issue of 2nd edn., 1929.

Roia, Remo.   L'amministrazione finanziaria del comune d'Ancona nel secolo XV.   AMSM,
4th ser., i, 1924.

Sägmuller, J. B.   Lehrbuch des katholischen Kirchenrechts.   1904.

Salimei, A.   Senatori e Statuti di Roma nel medio evo.   1935.

Salvioni, G. B.   Sul valore della lira bolognese.   AMDR, 3rd ser., xix, 1901.

Samaran, C., *and* Mollat, G.   La fiscalité pontificale en France au XIV*e* siècle.   1905.

Scalvanti, O.   Considerazioni sul primo libro degli statuti perugini.   BSU, i, 1895.

—— Un opinione di Bartolo sulla libertà perugina.   BSU, ii, 1896.

Scarafoni, C. Scaccia.   L'antico statuto dei 'magistri stratarum'.   ASR, l, 1927.

Schiff, O.   König Sigismunds italienische Politik bis zur Romfahrt.   1909.

Schneider, F. Egon.   Die Römische Rota.   Nach geltendem Recht auf geschichtlichen
Grundlage.   1914.

Schröder, H.   Die Protokollbücher der päpstlichen Kammerkleriker 1329–1347.   Archiv
für Kulturgeschichte, xxvii, 1937.

Sella, P.   Il procedimento civile nella legislazione statutaria italiana.   1927.

—— *and* Laurent, M.-H.   I sigilli dell'Archivio Segreto Vaticano.   1937.

Signorelli, G.   Viterbo nella storia della Chiesa.   1907–38.

Silvestrelli, G.   Città Castelli e Terre della Regione Romana.   1940.

Spadolini, E.   L'Archivio storico comunale d'Ancona.   Ancona, n.d.

Souchon, M.   Die Papstwahlen in der Zeit des Grossen Schismas.   1898–9.

Sugenheim, S.   Geschichte der Entstehung und Ausbildung des Kirchenstaates.   1854.

Tomassetti, G.   Sale e focatico del comune di Roma nel medio evo.   ASR, xx, 1897.

—— and Tomassetti, F.   La Campagna Romana.   1910–26.

Tommasini, O.   Il Registro degli Officiali del Comune di Roma esemplato dallo scriba-senato Marco Guidi.   ARAcLinc, Classe di scienze morali, storiche e filologiche, 4th ser., iii, 1887.

Tonini, L.   Storia civile e sacra Riminese.   1848–88.

Turchi, O.   De Ecclesiae Camerinensis Pontificibus.   Rome, 1762.

Valentini, R.   Lo Stato di Braccio e la guerra aquilana nella politica di Martino V (1421–4).   ASR, lii, 1929.

——   Braccio da Montone e il comune di Orvieto.   BSU, xxv–vi, 1922–3.

Valois, N.   La France et le grand Schisme d'Occident.   1896–1902.

——   La crise religieuse du XVe siècle.   Le pape et le concile.   1909.

Vancini, O.   Bologna della Chiesa.   AMDR, 3rd ser., xxiv–v, 1906–7.

Vehse, O.   Benevent als Territorium des Kirchenstaates bis zum Beginn der Avignonesischen Epoche.   QF, xxiii–iv, 1930/2.

——   Benevent und die Kurie unter Nicolaus IV.   QF, xx, 1928/9.

Vito la Mantia.   Storia della legislazione italiana.   i. Roma e Stato della Chiesa.   1884.

Waley, D. P.   Mediaeval Orvieto.   1952.

——   An Account-Book of the Patrimony of St. Peter in Tuscany, 1304–1306.   JEccH, vi, 1955.

——   Papal Armies in the Thirteenth Century.   EHR, lxxii, 1957.

Zaoli, G.   Libertas Bononie e papa Martino V.   1916.

Zdekauer, L.   L'Archivio ex-pontificio a Macerata.   Gli Archivi italiani, ii, 1915; *only part 1 published*.

——   L'Archivio del comune di Recanati ed il recente suo riordinamento.   Le Marche, v, 1905.

——   Sulle fonti delle Constitutiones Sancte Matris Ecclesie, con alcune osservazioni sull' antico Archivio dei Legati delle Marche.   Rivista italiana per le scienze giuridiche, xxxi, 1901.

INDEX

ABBAZIA de Ponzano, 59 n., 121.
Abbiamonte, Romano de, 60 n.
Achariis, Gratiolus de, 66 n.
Acziapaziis, Nicolò de, Bp. of Tropea, 83 n., 92, 98 n., 182.
Adimari, Alamanno, Cardinal, 54, 237.
affictus, 117, 188–9.
Agazzia, Menimus de Senis, 134 n., 218.
Agnesi, Astorgio, Bp. of Ancona, 82 n., 94, 103 n., 104, 105 n., 110, 207, 215; appointed Deputy in March, 84.
Aistulf, K. of Lombards, 3.
Alatri, Giovanni Bp. of, 104 n., 215–6.
Albergati, Nicolò, Bp. of Bologna, 53, 90; mediates between Pope and Bologna, 50–1; second attempt at mediation, 65; negotiates peace of Ferrara, 89.
Alberic II, *princeps et senator*, 8.
Albertis, Francesco Altobianchi de, 166 n.
Albertoni, Battista Piero Mattei, 75.
Albizzi, Rinaldo degli, 87–8.
—, Ugone degli, 152.
Albornoz, Gil, Cardinal, 14–15, 98, 101, 126, 130, 155, 182, 196.
Aleman, Louis, 56, 71, 127–8, 132, 135 n., 211, 213, 218, 219, 220, 222, 237; Legate in Bologna, 89–90.
Alexander III, Pope, 10–12.
Alexander V, Pope, 22, 31, 161 n., 166.
Alexandris, Antonio Alexandri de, 177 n.
Alfano, Raynaldo, 97, 118; accepts vicariate of Rieti, 59; expelled, 85–6.
Alfonso, K. of Aragon, 38, 42, 68, 69, 70–3, 74, 76, 89.
Alidosi, Lucrezia, 76–7.
—, Ludovico, 65–6, 76, 89, 145, 191; granted vicariate, 48.
Alviano, Ugolino de, 60 n.
Amelia, 3, 30, 28, 37, 49, 60, 63 n., 68 n., 71, 96, 124 n.
Anagni, Bp. of, see Fuschis, Angelotto de.
—, Antonio de, Bp. of Montefiascone, 97 n., 184 n.
—, Jacopo de, 109 n., 144 n.
—, Nicolò de, 219.
Ancona, 4, 6, 32, 34 n., 35, 50, 72, 83, 129, 160, 186; abortive rebellion, 76; *affictus*, 117 n.; appeals, forbidden, 126–7; castle, 107; Jews, 118; government of commune, 179–81; parliament held, 109; salt monopoly, 145.

Ancona, Bp. of, see Agnesi, Astorgio.
Anglona, Domenico de, Bp. of Sutri, 74 n., 100 n.
Anichini, Ricardo, 143–5.
Anjou, Louis of, 21, 23–4, 31 n., 61, 68, 72, 76.
Annibaldi, Giovanni, 197.
—, Mascia, 197.
—, Paluzio, 186.
Antico, 107.
Anzio, 198.
Apiro, 82 n., 83.
Apoggio, Antonuccio de, 98 n.
Appeals, 105; jurisdiction in, 126–8; in Perugia, 174–5; from courts of apostolic vicars, 191. *See curia generalis provincie*.
Appignano, 190 n.
Appognano, 230.
Aquapendente, 9, 123 n.
Aquila, 75–6; battle at, 78–9.
Aquino, Bp. of, see Buccii, Jacopo.
Aragon, Infante of, 38.
Archipreti, Jacopo dei, 33, 72, 82.
Ardea, 72, 198.
Arquata, 83, 97 n.
Ascoli Piceno, 17, 19, 24, 28, 32, 60, 98–9, 111, 124 n., 182, 185, 230–3; Carrara brothers expelled, 83–4; government of commune, 181.
Aspicino, Jacopo de, 122 n.
Assignano, 72.
Assisi, 54, 60, 62, 80, 97, 124 n., 146 n., 214.
Astallis, Giovanni de, 69 n., 166 n., 167 n., 169, 207, 216.
Astura, 198.
Atlow, Robert, 66 n.
Attis, Atto de, 145 n.
—, Francesco Aloisio de, vicar in Sassoferrato, 49.
auditores causarum sacri palatii apostolici, see Rota, apostolic.
Aversa, 69–73.
Azel, Johannes de, 217.

Baglioni, Malatesta, 79, 175 and n., 227–9.
—, Nello, 175 n.
Bagnorea, 31, 68 n., 124 n.
—, Jacopo de, 64 n., 86 n., 142, 213.
Baldinotti, Antonio, 57, 237.
Barbiano, Alberigo da, 21.
Bardi, Ylarione dei, 25 n.
Bartolinis, Roberto de, 127 n.
Bassanello, 195.